# HOLLYWOOD
# ESCAPES

# HOLLYWOOD ESCAPES

## THE MOVIEGOER'S GUIDE TO EXPLORING SOUTHERN CALIFORNIA'S GREAT OUTDOORS

## HARRY MEDVED
## WITH BRUCE AKIYAMA

Maps by Robert B. Lindquist of
Great Pacific Recreation Maps

St. Martin's Griffin 🦁 New York

# For Michele, Shoshana, and Aviva

HOLLYWOOD ESCAPES. Copyright © 2006 by Harry Medved. All rights reserved. Printed in the United States of America. No part of this book may be used or reproduced in any manner whatsoever without written permission except in the case of brief quotations embodied in critical articles or reviews. For information, address St. Martin's Press, 175 Fifth Avenue, New York, N.Y. 10010.

Maps copyright © 2005 by Harry Medved.

Motion picture stills featured in this book are copyright of each film's production entity.

A portion of the proceeds from this book will be donated to the California Film Commission, California State Parks, and the National Park Service.

www.stmartins.com

Design by Nancy Singer Olaguera

Medved, Harry.
    Hollywood Escapes : the Hollywood guide to Southern California's great outdoors / Harry Medved and Bruce Akiyama ; maps by Robert B. Lindquist.—1st St. Martin's Griffen ed.
        p. cm.
    ISBN-13: 978-0-312-30856-8
    ISBN-10: 0-312-30856-6
    1. Motion picture locations—California, Southern—Guidebooks. 2. Television program locations—California, Southern—Guidebooks. 3. Walking—California, Southern—Guidebooks. 4. Hiking—California, Southern—Guidebooks. 5. Outdoor recreation—California, Southern—Guidebooks. 6. California, Southern—Guidebooks. I. Akiyama, Bruce. II. Title.

PN1995.67.C2M43 2006
384'.8097949—dc22

                                                                2005044645

First Edition: July 2006

10  9  8  7  6  5  4  3  2  1

# Contents

# MOVIE DESERTS

# MOVIE MOUNTAINS

# MOVIE LAKES AND RIVERS

# Acknowledgments

This book would have not been possible without the generous assistance from the following individuals, whose recollections, knowledge, and resources are greatly appreciated.

The fact that you are holding this guide is in no small part due to the efforts of **Bruce Akiyama,** whose writing and contributions you will find throughout the book (e.g., *Cautionary Tail Lights*, our list of road thrillers). Bruce and I have been friends since high school, and the two of us grew up in L.A. haunting theater screens from Panorama City to Culver City to the City of Carson. For his help creating, editing, and researching the text, I can't thank him enough.

**BOOK PRODUCTION** Many thanks are due to my supportive agent Jeff Gerecke, my enthusiastic editors at St. Martin's Press, Daniela Rapp, Michael Connor, and Elizabeth Beier, copy editor Catherine Revland, and production editor Mark Steven Long and our publicist, Gregg Sullivan. Gratitude is also owed to research director and photo editor Brian Rooney, whose contributions to this book are invaluable. Special thanks to Tim Dirks, whose impeccable research assistance is greatly appreciated. Thanks also to mapmakers Bob Lindquist and David Peckarsky of Great Pacific Recreation Maps.

**ORIGINAL PHOTOGRAPHS AND ART** Cheryl Himmelstein, Greg Tucker, Daniel Frommer, Ed Lawrence, Mark Frauenfelder, Clara Nelson.

**LOCATION MANAGERS AND SCOUTS** Bob Craft, Jerry Jaffe, Ned Shapiro, Kathy McCurdy, Michael Neale, Mike Burmeister, Janice Polley, Laura Sode-Matteson, Deborah J. Page, Jeff Crandell, Molly Allen, Lori Balton, Russ Fega, Alasdair Boyd, Steve Dayan, Mike Fantasia, John Panzarella, Mark Benton Johnson, Liz Matthews, Robin Citrin, Scott Allen Logan, Jeremy Alter, Kayla Thames-Berge, Scott Trimble, Scott Dewees, Julie Duvic, Richard H. Prince, Jody Hummer, Richard Davis, Larry Ring, Jordana Kronen, and Robert Graf.

**PRODUCTION DESIGNERS** Robert Boyle, Henry Bumstead, Polly Platt, James H. Spencer, Jon Hutman, William Sandell, Alex McDowell, Gene Allen, Harold Michelson, John Vallone, Lawrence Miller, Joe Alves, Jim Bissell, Jeannine Oppewall, and Jackson DeGovia. Many thanks to Edward Hutson, manager of the Twentieth Century Fox Art Department, who provided valuable insight.

**PRODUCERS** Anthony Bregman, Paul Lewis, Terry Sanders, Hawk Koch, Robert Lorenz, Howard G. Kazanjian, C.O. "Doc" Erickson, Robert Evans, Frank P. Rosenberg, William Horberg, Tom Engelman, Rodney Liber, Kenneth Kokin, Richard Crystal, Todd Lewis, and Mark Johnson.

**DIRECTORS** Frank Darabont, D. J. Caruso, Chuck Russell, Paul Mazursky, John Landis, Roger Corman, Arthur Hiller, Robert Harmon, Randal Kleiser, Christopher Coppola, Curtis Harrington, Delbert Mann, Nick Castle, Donald Petrie, Herbert L. Strock, Michael Tolkin, Curtis Hanson, and cinematographer Laszlo Kovacs.

**ACTORS** Bruce Dern, Jesse Vint, Norman Lloyd, William Schallert, Dennis Weaver, Joan Weldon, Paul Koslo, Noel Neill, Carla Laemmle, Andre Philippe, Peter Fonda, Kevin Spacey, Bill Pullman, and Paul Clemens.

**STUNT COORDINATORS** Loren Janes, Mickey Gilbert, and Gilbert Perkins.

**RANGERS, LIFEGUARDS, DOCENTS, AND PARK ADMINIS-TRATORS** Mike Malone (National Park Service) whose Santa Monica Mountains research has been indispensable, Lynette Hernandez (Malibu), Diane Isaacs (Franklin Canyon), Mark Faull (Red Rock), Charlie Callagan (Death Valley), Alice M. Allen (Paramount Ranch), Don Roberts (Joshua Tree), Ray Dashner (Arroyo Seco), Daniel Patterson (Imperial Sand Dunes), Mark Klosterman (Laguna), Mike Watkin (Griffith Park), Tex Ward (Wildwood), Janet Carle (Mono Lake), Jim Harris (Santa Monica Pier), Cliff Kjoss (L.A. County Beaches), and Barbara Croonquist (Angeles National Forest).

**REGIONAL HISTORIANS AND LONGTIME RESIDENTS** Lee Cozad, Mary Barlow and Tom Core (San Bernardino Mtns.), John W. Robinson (San Gabriel Mtns.), Brian Rooney (Santa Monica Mtns.), Ben Costello and Bob Stephenson (Joshua Tree), Doug Bombard, Chuck Liddell, Bill Bushing and Lee Rosenthal (Catalina), Pat Smith, Lavender Vroman, and Paul Bond (Antelope Valley), Joe Hasson (San Fernando Valley), Dave Holland (Alabama Hills), Linda and David Morrow (Palm Springs), Richard Thompson and Bob Moore (East Mojave), Glen Howell (Malibu), Jeff Stai (Lucerne

Dry Lake), Jeffrey Stanton (Venice), Greta Crouper (Guadalupe Dunes), Robert Coe (Wasco), Sheila Meyer, George Meyer, and Lynnda Hart (Idyll-wild), Neil Scott and Alan Busby (Mammoth Lakes), Donald Nicholson (Mt. Wilson), Chris Donovan and Lauren Ash Donoho (Coronado), Melanie Winter (L.A. River), Mary Elles and Jana Seely (Hearst Castle), Randy Young and David Booth (PCH).

**MUSEUM REPRESENTATIVES** Sally McManus (Palm Springs), Edra Moore (Antelope Valley), Jeannine Pedersen (Catalina), Doris Weddell (Weedpatch), Elizabeth Scott-Graham (Dunes Center), and Dinah LeHoven (The Huntington).

**FILM HISTORIANS** Marc Wanamaker, Rudy Behlmer, Tim Dirks, Richard Rowe, Kendall Miller, Tom Weaver, Bill Warren, Forrest J Ackerman, Kevin Brownlow, Dennis McLellan, Donald Spoto, Pat Hanson (AFI), Michael Marshall, Richard Koszarski, Boyd Magers, Tinsley Yarbrough, Mike Schlesinger, Leonard Maltin, Keith Simanton (IMDb), John Bengston, Jerry Schneider, and Greg Williams.

**LIBRARIANS, ARCHIVISTS, AND PROGRAM COORDINA-TORS** Ned Comstock and Randi Hokett (USC), Randy Haberkamp, Sandra Archer, and Leslie Unger (AMPAS), Lillian Michelson (DreamWorks), and Leith Adams (Warner Bros.).

**FILM COMMISSIONERS AND LOCATION INTERMEDIARIES** Lisa Mosher (California Film Commission librarian), Holly Starr (Palos Verdes), Dave Hook (Kern County), Chris Langley (Inyo County), Kresse Armour (Big Bear Lake), Sheri Davis (Inland Empire), Martine White (Santa Barbara), Kathy McCurdy (San Diego), Billy Adams and Alison Martin (Imperial Sand Dunes), Diana Klein (Malibu), Shirley Davy (Catalina), Jason Crawford (Santa Clarita), Pauline East and Barbara La Fata (Antelope Valley), Ray Arthur (Ridgecrest), Fred Jee (Anza Borrego), Ronnie Mellen (Santa Ynez Valley).

**VIDEO, MAP, AND STILL PHOTO RESEARCH** Meg Johnson, Anthony Miller, Sean Schlemmer, Patrick McGilligan and Aimee Groener at Vidiots, Claire and Donovan Brandt at Eddie Brandt's Saturday Matinee, Pete Bateman at Larry Edmunds Bookshop, Eric Caidin of Hollywood Book and Poster Company, California Map & Travel Center, Pamela Stollings, Mo McFadden, Kim McNulty, Wade Williams, and Ronnie Semler.

**MORAL SUPPORT** Michele, Shoshana, and Aviva Medved, David and Yael Medved, Michael and Diane Medved, Jon and Jane Medved, Ben and

Anne Medved, Gary, Leora and Joshua Raikin, David and Raymonde Barishman, Abe and Barbara Barishman, Greg Tucker, Jack Barth, Valerie Yaros, Karie Bible, Meyer and Marni Denn, Michelle Kleinert, Maria Lopez, Steve Honig, John Geirland, Ilyanne Kichaven, Timothy Blake, Chris Kern, Rex Pickett, Michael Levin, Julie Garfield, and the entire Barishman, Hasson, and Boroda families. At Yahoo! Movies: Jim Moloshok, Kurt Bensmiller, Carla Fazio, Greg Dean Schmitz, Joanna Stevens, and staff. At Fandango: Miyuki Kitamura, Art Levitt, Ted Hong, and Rachel Dardinski. My brothers deserve special thanks for their guidance, support, and friendship over the course of this project.

A hearty thank-you is due to all the pioneers who previously authored books on film locations, including Jack Barth, Richard Alleman, Marc Wanamaker, Tony Reeves, Carlo Gaberscek, John Bengston, Jeff Kraft and Aaron Leventhal, Chris Epting, and William A. Gordon.

# For My Family

My father, **DR. DAVID MEDVED**, is responsible for his four boys' penchant for escaping to the great outdoors. He was first exposed to Southern California's geographical diversity in 1954 through San Diego's Heaven-on-Earth Club, whose devotees included Sierra Club leaders who water-skied Mission Bay and skied the snowy Laguna Mountains, often on the same day. My dad's sunny disposition and his zest for exploration thrived in the Golden State. This book is a product of the love for adventure that he instilled in his appreciative sons.

My late loving mother, **RONNIE MEDVED**, always supported my crazy notions, whether it was collaborating with big brother **Michael** on books about bad movies or heading off into the wilderness with brothers **Jon** and **Ben**. I know that her nature-loving, benevolent spirit survives and that she still gets joy from her sons' journeys.

My wife and I are delighted to see that our daughters **SHOSHANA** and **AVIVA MEDVED** have acquired the Medved passion for getting outside. These two beautiful girls wake up each morning with a craving to experience our wonderful world.

**MICHELE BARISHMAN MEDVED** was a newcomer to Los Angeles when we first met. She had recently emigrated from South Africa and had not yet explored California. During our many excursions discovering the state's natural treasures, the seed of this guide was planted. I was lucky to find a caring, patient, wise, and wonderful companion for the road . . . and for life.

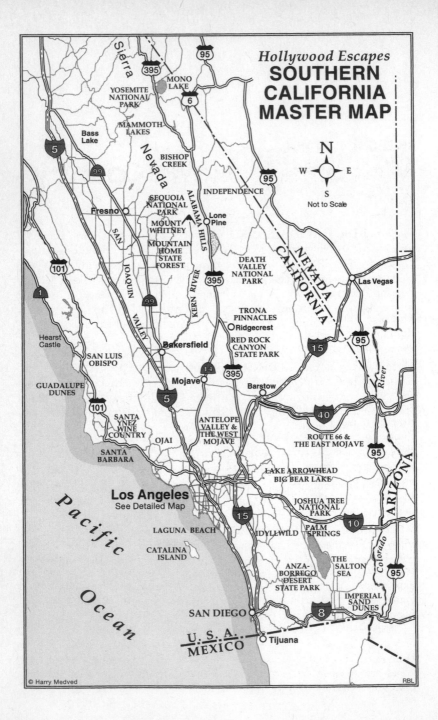

*Hollywood Escapes*
# SOUTHERN CALIFORNIA MASTER MAP

Sierra

95

MONO LAKE

395

6

YOSEMITE NATIONAL PARK

MAMMOTH LAKES

Bass Lake

Nevada

BISHOP CREEK

95

N
W    E
S
Not to Scale

INDEPENDENCE

SEQUOIA NATIONAL PARK

Fresno

ALABAMA HILLS

Lone Pine

MOUNT WHITNEY

MOUNTAIN HOME STATE FOREST

SAN

KERN RIVER

DEATH VALLEY NATIONAL PARK

395

NEVADA
CALIFORNIA

99

JOAQUIN

Las Vegas

1

TRONA PINNACLES

VALLEY

99

Ridgecrest

RED ROCK CANYON STATE PARK

15

95

Hearst Castle

Bakersfield

SAN LUIS OBISPO

Mojave

14

395

Barstow

GUADALUPE DUNES

5

40

101

SANTA YNEZ WINE COUNTRY

OJAI

ANTELOPE VALLEY & THE WEST MOJAVE

ROUTE 66 & THE EAST MOJAVE

95

SANTA BARBARA

ARIZONA

LAKE ARROWHEAD
BIG BEAR LAKE

Pacific

**Los Angeles**
See Detailed Map

JOSHUA TREE NATIONAL PARK

PALM SPRINGS

10

15

LAGUNA BEACH

IDYLLWILD

CATALINA ISLAND

Colorado

ANZA-BORREGO DESERT STATE PARK

THE SALTON SEA

95

River

IMPERIAL SAND DUNES

Ocean

SAN DIEGO

8

U.S.A.
MEXICO

Tijuana

© Harry Medved

RBL

# INTRODUCTION
# Welcome to Movie Country

It's my feet. They keep itchin' for me to go places.

—*John Garfield explaining his wanderlust in*
The Postman Always Rings Twice (1946)

Outdoors enthusiasts and moviemakers have long sought the same kind of destinations: awe-inspiring dream locales within a day's drive from the City of Angels. Both groups crave the variety found in Southern California, with its beautiful countryside, beaches, deserts, dunes, lakes, rivers, caves, mountains, vineyards, and waterfalls.

*Hollywood Escapes* is the first comprehensive guide to spotlight the motion picture industry's love affair with the Southern California landscape, from Anza-Borrego (site of *The Scorpion King*'s "Valley of the Dead" desert) to Zuma Beach (a seaside location for the Frankie Avalon/Annette Funicello *Back to the Beach*). These places not only serve as escapes from the studio backlot, but in many cases they double as "location vacations" for filmmakers and moviegoers alike. This guide is designed to inspire visitors, new residents, industry personnel, and Southern California natives to explore nature's hidden gems in their backyard.

Sometimes the best part of a movie is its scenery. Like the faces of character actors whose names you don't know, many of these places are instantly familiar. As more and more fans seek out these on-screen locations, a new travel trend has emerged. New Zealand and England's tourism industries have experienced significant boosts from the *Lord of the Rings* trilogy and the *Harry Potter* series. And California's Santa Ynez wine country has experienced a boom in tourism thanks to *Sideways*.

And yet, movie travel is nothing new. In the late 1920s, enterprising tour operators charged visitors to stay overnight at a South Seas village built by Hollywood at Catalina's Two Harbors. On March 14, 1934, a *Los Angeles Times* article openly suggested that "studio location folks" know the best places to vacation in Southern California.

"There are location experts who can produce any type of scenery on demand," added *L.A. Times* reporter Harry Carr in his 1935 guidebook, *Los Angeles: City of Dreams*. "The Austrian Alps are in back of the town of Lone Pine. There are Sahara Deserts near Yuma and Guadalupe above Santa Barbara . . . the scenery of California is so varied that almost any country in the world can be duplicated." That same geographical diversity appeals to nonindustry lovers of the outdoors.

As trail master and author John McKinney states, "In California you can hike the world and stay at home." More than ever, Californians are following his message and rediscovering their home state by car, thereby avoiding the hassles associated with plane travel.

To identify previously undisclosed movie landmarks, we've worked closely with the men and women who have made a career of discovering these treasures of cinematic California: location scouts and location managers. If not for the work of these unsung professionals, Southern California's presence on the big screen would be considerably, well, *smaller*. Additionally, on-set anecdotes from production designers, performers, crew, and area residents help bring these places to life.

Purists will note that we've covered more ground than just Southern California but most of the destinations are less then a day's drive from L.A.

## GET YOUR MOTOR RUNNING: HOW TO USE THIS BOOK

This guide's chapters are grouped into four categories: Movie Beaches, Movie Deserts, Movie Mountains, and Movie Lakes & Rivers. Each chapter highlights a recognizable destination, with everything the visitor needs to know.

*Major Roles* highlights the location's key movie appearances.

*Behind the Scenery* explores the destination's history in the real and *reel* world.

*Top Billing* recommends the "Best Bet" activity for those who only have limited time at a given location.

*Where to Walk or Hike* highlights a destination's best paths or trails.

*Where to Stay* offers tips for those who are seeking more than a day trip.

*On the Road* lists points of interest en route to your destination.

*Detour* suggests nearby areas for additional exploration.

*It Came from California* appears when a location is hallowed ground as a movie-monster lair in the history of sci-fi/horror cinema.

As you head out on the highway, we hope you'll enjoy exploring these Southern California destinations as much as we did. If you haven't yet escaped to Hollywood's great outdoors, to paraphrase the words of Al Jolson in *The Jazz Singer*, "You ain't *seen* nothin' yet."

## USING THE DVD ITINERARY TO PLAN YOUR TRIP

So your prospective travel companions can't work up any enthusiasm for driving out to one of your favorite destinations? As we all know, a picture is worth a thousand words, so with the help of DVD technology it's easier than ever to change couch potatoes into willing road mates using this guide's *DVD Itinerary* at the end of each chapter.

If, for example, your misguided, video-game-obsessed youngster can't appreciate the fun factor in journeying to a place called Vasquez Rocks, illustrate your point. Simply refer to this book, pop in the *Flintstones* DVD, access the proper scene selection, and show the sedentary tyke that Vasquez Rocks is where the town of Bedrock was built. Junior will have his rear end in the backseat before you can utter the words "PlayStation."

Or maybe your incurably romantic better half doesn't like the sound of a location named Wildwood. No problem. Spin that DVD of *Wuthering Heights* and before you know it, you two will be canoodling on the very Mountclef Ridge hillside where Laurence Olivier rendezvoused with Merle Oberon.

So use the *DVD Itinerary* sections to get a sneak preview of your road trip—or stay at home and enjoy the scenery on your television screen. It's the next best thing to being there. (Note: Scene numbers are based on the most current U.S. DVD editions available at press time.)

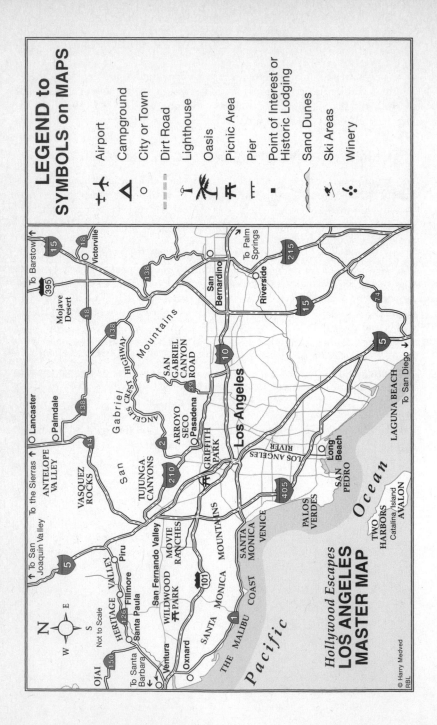

Hollywood Escapes
LOS ANGELES
MASTER MAP

© Harry Medved
RBL

**LEGEND to SYMBOLS on MAPS**

- ✈ Airport
- △ Campground
- ○ City or Town
- ==== Dirt Road
- 🗼 Lighthouse
- ⚘ Oasis
- ⊼ Picnic Area
- ▪ Pier
- ▪ Point of Interest or Historic Lodging
- ∿ Sand Dunes
- ⛷ Ski Areas
- ⁖ Winery

# Things to Know Before You Roll

There's nothing more fun (or romantic) than finally hitting the road to visit that favorite location you've seen on the big screen and now want to experience in person. But even the shortest afternoon outing requires one cheap but necessary provision you can never do without: common sense. Here, then, are some reminders to ensure a satisfying escape to Hollywood's Great Outdoors in Southern California:

1. Make sure your car is in tip-top working order. Water, oil, belts, and tires (including the spare) should be checked. And, of course, keep your gas tank full.

2. Don't forget plenty of drinking water, especially if you're headed for the desert.

3. Travel with a companion. And let others know where you're going and when you plan to return.

4. Bring a cell phone (though reception may be spotty in isolated areas). GPS units are more affordable than ever.

5. Come prepared: you'll be glad you brought your maps, first-aid kit, sunscreen, compass, and toiletries when you need them. Check with the ranger or visitors center to confirm directions.

6. Call ahead for restaurant, hotel, and museum info and hours, as business establishments sometimes close without warning.

7. Be a good citizen: stay on marked trails, and leave the landscape in better shape than when you found it.

8. Heed weather advisories and road closures before you go: avoid hiking in the desert on hot days; avoid hiking in the higher-elevation mountains in winter conditions.

9. Beware of poison oak in mountain areas. Remember the old adage: "Leaves of three, let it be."

10. Bring cash for requisite day passes to the national forests and state parks. Year-long permits are available if you plan to visit the parks frequently.

Sure, this may all seem obvious. But like a memorable movie, a safe road trip is one you can tell your friends about after it's over. Now go climb a mountain, jump in a lake, hit the beach, or take a hike. The highway is OPEN.

# MOVIE BEACHES

There's nothing like the beach early in the morning, so quiet and peaceful and mysterious.

—*Annette Funicello in* Beach Party *(1963), the first of many Malibu-based surf-and-sun pictures*

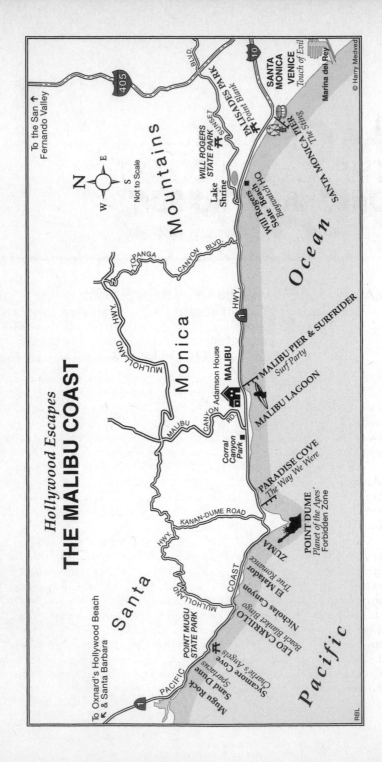

Hollywood Escapes
**THE MALIBU COAST**

© Harry Medved

To the San
Fernando Valley

N
W · · E
S
Not to Scale

Santa

Monica

Mountains

Santa

TOPANGA CANYON BLVD.

MULHOLLAND HWY.

MULHOLLAND HWY.

MALIBU CANYON RD.

KANAN-DUME ROAD

PACIFIC COAST HWY.

MULHOLLAND HWY.

SUNSET BLVD.

405

10

SANTA
MONICA
**VENICE**
*Touch of Evil*

Marina del Rey

Point Dume

PALISADES PARK

WILL ROGERS
STATE PARK
Lake
Shrine

Will Rogers
State Park
Baywatch HQ

SANTA MONICA PIER
*The Sting*

Ocean

1

**MALIBU**
Adamson House

**MALIBU PIER & SURFRIDER**
*Surf Party*

**MALIBU LAGOON**

Corral Canyon
Park

**PARADISE COVE**
*The Way We Were*

**POINT DUME**
*Planet of the Apes*
*Forbidden Zone*

**ZUMA**

El Matador
*True Romance*

**LEO CARRILLO**
Beach Blanket Bingo

Nicholas Canyon

POINT MUGU
STATE PARK

Sycamore Cove
*Charlie's Angels*

Mugu Rock
Sand Dune
*Spartacus*

To Oxnard's Hollywood Beach
& Santa Barbara

1

Pacific

Pacific

RBL

# THE MALIBU COAST
## Drive the Wild Surf

The freeway is faster, but it lacks a certain majesty . . .

—*Peter Fonda, on the Pacific Coast Highway, in* The Limey (1999)

**MAJOR ROLES:** *How to Stuff a Wild Bikini, True Romance, The Notebook*

### BEHIND THE SCENERY

The origins of Malibu's world-famous Pacific Coast Highway (also known as PCH) date back to the late nineteenth century. Frederick Rindge, a wealthy landowner from Massachusetts, and his wife May purchased the sprawling Rancho Malibu in 1891. For several decades, the Rindge clan held on to twenty-four miles of spectacular coastline from Las Flores Canyon to the Ventura County line, claiming "only heaven is more beautiful."

After Rindge died in 1905, his wife followed his wish to protect their vast wilderness from intruders. Dubbed "Queen of the Malibu" by the local press, May Rindge fought against construction of a coastal highway through her property. But California won the battle for coastal access in 1925 and completed the entire road four years later.

To help pay her legal bills, May Rindge leased and eventually sold plots of her Malibu real estate to movie folk like Clara Bow, Ronald Colman, studio chief Jack Warner, and silent screen star Anna Q. Nilsson, who helped form the Malibu Beach Motion Picture Colony in 1926. To this day The Colony still thrives as an exclusive parcel of Hollywood history near Pacific Coast Highway. It has been home to such diverse personalities as Pamela Anderson, Sting, and former Malibu mayor Larry Hagman. One-time Malibu resident Robert Altman even poked fun at The Colony's security gates and armed patrols in his adaptation of Raymond Chandler's *The Long Goodbye:* in several funny scenes Elliott Gould (as Philip Marlowe) deals with a movie-mad Colony gate guard who can't resist imitating Walter Brennan and Barbara Stanwyck.

## THE SAND AND SEA AT A.I.P.

The Malibu Coast is memorably captured on film in the lovably inane Frankie Avalon/Annette Funicello *Beach Party* series produced by American International Pictures (AIP), the most successful independent film company of its time. Although the films are remembered today for their camp value, they also provide a remarkable cinematic record of the Malibu landscape of the early sixties.

In a chase scene in *Pajama Party*, you can see how the Malibu Colony Plaza looked more than forty years ago and how little the area has changed since 1964.

Other films in the series include *Muscle Beach Party, Bikini Beach, Beach Blanket Bingo, How to Stuff a Wild Bikini,* and *The Ghost in the Invisible Bikini.* Similar AIP fun-in-the-sun spin-offs include *Ski Party,* and *Dr. Goldfoot and the Bikini Machine.*

"Tourists still arrive in Malibu expecting to see Frankie and Annette dancing around in the sand," notes beach party film historian Michael Marshall. "The musically romanticized imagery of girls, surfers and cars in these movies defined the coastline, and that 'endless summer' aura remains to this day."

## DRIVING THE MALIBU COAST

*The following Malibu driving tour actually begins on the Santa Monica stretch of Pacific Coast Highway and affords plenty of stopovers where you can soak in the view, stretch your legs, or throw your own beach party (see also MALIBU PIER, PARADISE COVE, ZUMA, and LEO CARRILLO chapters). Set your odometer at zero as you start your trip at the Santa Monica Pier. All mileage counts are approximate distances from the pier or the McClure Tunnel at the western end of the 10 Freeway.*

### BACK ON THE BEACH *(1.3 miles north of the pier)*

This unique kid-friendly café in the sand is based in an old Santa Monica beach location that appears in *Ski Party,* starring Frankie Avalon, Dwayne Hickman, Yvonne Craig, and Dick Miller. To the immediate north is the former 1929 estate built by newspaper magnate William Randolph Hearst for his mistress (and favorite actress) Marion Davies, hostess of legendary Hollywood beach parties. All that remains of the expansive 100-room complex is the guesthouse, site of a proposed public beach facility. A block south of the café is the former home of Peter Lawford, where the Kennedys allegedly rendezvoused with Marilyn Monroe. *445 Pacific Coast Highway; 310-393-8282.*

## PATRICK'S ROADHOUSE *(1.7 miles)*
This eccentric and cozy local favorite is known for its pancakes, waffles, and banana cream pie. Full of nautical memorabilia, Patrick's was a house of ill repute in the 1920s. Today it attracts celebrities like Arnold Schwarzenegger and Maria Shriver, Bruce Willis, and Sean Penn. *106 Entrada Drive; 310-459-4544.*

A short block north of Patrick's is the Santa Monica Canyon intersection of Chautauqua Blvd., W. Channel Road, and Pacific Coast Highway, glimpsed in two different crime dramas shot in 1950: *In a Lonely Place* with Humphrey Bogart and *Quicksand* with Mickey Rooney.

## WILL ROGERS BEACH *(2.8 miles)*
Cowboy, social commentator, and actor Will Rogers once owned this long stretch of sand that was purchased by the state in 1941. In the 1950s, according to sci-fi historian Tom Weaver, the beach was the setting of the eerie clawprints-in-the-sand prologue for *The Creature from the Black Lagoon.* Today it's best remembered as the lifeguard headquarters for TV's *Baywatch.* For the finale of the infamous Ben Affleck/Jennifer Lopez comedy *Gigli,* the original *Baywatch* set was re-created at Will Rogers, with hundreds of hard-bodied extras added for effect. *To find the lifeguard station, enter the parking lot at Temescal Canyon Drive and drive .7 miles south to the lot's end.*

## MALIBU PIER *(11 miles)*
See pages 12–14.

## MALIBU SEAFOOD *(14.5 miles)*
A coast highway tradition since the sixties, the outdoor café at Malibu Seafood (*25653 Pacific Coast Highway; 310-456-3430*) is a great spot for a quick, affordable lunch. From the parking lot here check out the **Corral Canyon Trailhead,** a gateway to a steep three-mile loop trail that affords great views of Point Dume, Paradise Cove, Puerco Canyon, and Corral Beach (aka Dan Blocker Beach) across the highway.

In *Beach Party's* opening number, Frankie and Annette drive their yellow convertible roadster onto the sand at Corral Beach while crooning the title song. Corral can also be seen in *Beach Ball, Bikini Beach, How to Stuff a Wild Bikini,* and *Don't Make Waves* (a 1960s sex farce starring Tony Curtis and Sharon Tate as a surf bunny named Malibu).

From your Corral Canyon Trail vantage point, you can also see the

## THE ORIGINAL CALIFORNIA BEACH GIRL

Pinups of bikini-clad California girls were popular way before the *Baywatch* era. During World War II, one of the most sought-after poster girls (after Betty Grable) was Noel Neill in her classic shot reclining against the coastal rocks. Later to play Lois Lane in the original *Superman* TV series, Neill remembers Will Rogers Beach as a volleyball mecca and 1940s hangout for up-and-coming actors waiting for their big break. "All of our agents would contact us at the beach's pay phone in front of the old bath house," recalls Neill. "When that phone would ring, we all waited with bated breath and burst into applause when someone got a part." Still a beach local after all these years, Neill calls nearby Santa Monica Canyon her home and holds court at Patrick's Roadhouse.

1940s pin-up girl Noel Neill at Will Rogers Beach today.

stretch of highway where William Holden picks up sun-worshipping hitchhikers Rosanna Arquette and Jennifer Edwards in *S.O.B.* (directed by former Malibu resident Blake Edwards).

If you look northwest to Latigo Beach you'll see the former site of the Rindge Home that appears as Zachary Scott's beach house in *Mildred Pierce*. In the same area, Spencer Tracy is pursued by Mickey Rooney, Buddy Hackett, and others in the finale of *It's a Mad, Mad, Mad, Mad World*. The Union 76 gas station at Corral Canyon Road, clearly visible in this 1963 comedy, is still there.

### GEOFFREY'S *(16.7 miles)*

This is the upscale Malibu restaurant seen in *The Player*, where ambitious studio exec Tim Robbins glad-hands star Burt Reynolds, and in *Hollywood Homicide*, where Harrison Ford meets with Martin Landau, Frank Sinatra Jr., and Master P. In real life, you can savor the sunset over a romantic dinner at Geoffrey's. If you want to hit the beach before or after your meal, you'll find a long staircase to Escondido Beach just past the restaurant (look for the COASTAL ACCESS sign). *27400 Pacific Coast Highway; 310-457-1519.*

### PARADISE COVE *(17.7 miles)*

See pages 15–17.

### ZUMA BEACH AND POINT DUME TURNOFF *(19.6 miles)*

See pages 18–22.

### TRANCAS CANYON/BROAD BEACH ROAD *(21.5 miles)*

The corner of Trancas Canyon Road, Broad Beach Road, and Pacific Coast Highway is where Vin Diesel and Paul Walker drag race a Ferrari on their way to Neptune's Net cafe in *The Fast and the Furious (2001)*. Don't follow their lead, as the Malibu police are very efficient at handing out speeding tickets here. Broad Beach is a popular and *very private* celebrity enclave, as seen in Blake Edwards' *10*, with Dudley Moore.

### Top Billing: EL MATADOR STATE BEACH *(23.4 miles)*

Its picturesque, rocky sea stacks protruding from the water make El Matador one of the most photogenic beaches in Los Angeles County. You have to hike

Greg Tucker

El Matador doubles for the Carolina Coast in *The Notebook*.

down a short but steep and winding dirt trail to get to the beach, but it's worth the trek. El Matador doubles for an exotic Mexican beach in the coda of Tony Scott's *True Romance*, as Christian Slater, Patricia Arquette, and their movie son start their new life free of bullets and blood.

El Matador also appears in the Ashton Kutcher/Amanda Peet romantic comedy *A Lot Like Love*, the Mel Gibson–produced *Paparazzi*, and Nick Cassavetes' *The Notebook*, with Rachel McAdams and Ryan Gosling.

## NICHOLAS CANYON COUNTY BEACH (26 miles)

For his wartime comedy-spectacular *1941*, Steven Spielberg picked Nicholas Beach for the seaside residence of the film's panicky civilians Ned Beatty and Lorraine Gary.

According to local lore, Spielberg knew the beach well, as he and *1941* executive producer John Milius, plus other young filmmakers of the 1970s, had hung out at the Nicholas Beach party home shared by actresses Margot Kidder and Jennifer Salt.

## PAUL MAZURSKY: NAKED IN MALIBU

"I love El Matador," says director Paul Mazursky. "It looks like no other beach. And when we shot there, it was relatively inaccessible to most tourists."

Mazursky utilized El Matador for the surreal counterculture epic *Alex in Wonderland*. Donald Sutherland plays a movie director who, in an outrageous dream sequence, imagines hundreds of naked African dancers undulating toward the beaches of Malibu. You can see the African American extras curling around the switchbacks of the Matador Trail, which Mazursky remembers as being a "helluva hike" for the camera crew lugging equipment down to the shore.

As if that weren't enough of a production hurdle, the extras supposedly refused to get naked unless the white crew undressed too. "It was a touchy situation," Mazursky recalls. "Most of the crew members stripped down to their underwear and wouldn't go any further. So in the spirit of fairness, I got *completely* naked. There's a great photograph in some Swedish newspaper showing me sitting on a camera crane in El Matador, where all I'm wearing is a big ol' hat." The film's El Matador escapade was so infamous that it merited a spread in *Playboy* magazine.

Forty-nine of these homes—including the Kidder-Salt beach house—were eventually torn down to make way for public beach facilities, allowing Spielberg to return to the spot to build his *1941* house. The two-story structure, which slides off a cliff in the film's finale, was constructed on the knoll where the Nicholas Beach lifeguard station now stands.

Today surfers call this beach "Zeroes" and flock to its point break waves. It makes an appropriate location for Dennis Franz's and angel Nicolas Cage's bodysurfing scenes in the *Wings of Desire* remake, *City of Angels*. Dozens of beatific extras in long black coats play angels, who every day watch over the sunrise and sunset.

## LEO CARRILLO STATE BEACH (27 miles)
See pages 23–27.

## SYCAMORE COVE BEACH/POINT MUGU STATE PARK (31.8 miles)
The beachside headquarters for Point Mugu State Park has a peaceful, shady picnic area near the shore. A twisted rock formation on the far side of the cove marks the location for the climax of *Charlie's Angels*, in which Cameron Diaz, Drew Barrymore, and Lucy Liu hang from a helicopter. The trio later enjoys cocktails on the beach with Bill Murray. Sycamore Cove is also a good spot for a family outing, as seen in *Junior*, in which Arnold Schwarzenegger, Danny De-Vito, Emma Thompson, and Pamela Reed celebrate their offsprings' birthdays. On the other side of PCH, a restored 1929 Spanish Colonial home is now the **Sycamore Canyon Nature Center** (*open weekends, 10 a.m.–2 p.m.*) adjacent to the 55-site **Sycamore Canyon Campground** (*reservations: 800-444-PARK; hiking info: 818-880-0350*).

## THE GREAT SAND DUNE (32.3 miles)
This distinctive Point Mugu landmark can be glimpsed as a romantic backdrop for Vincente Minnelli's *Goodbye Charlie*, with Debbie Reynolds and Pat Boone, and *Move Over, Darling*, with James Garner and Polly Bergen. In *Spartacus*, John Ireland leads an army of slaves-turned-soldiers down the dune to **Thornhill Broome Beach**, crossing the cleverly concealed Pacific Coast Highway. In 1972, the dune was the site of the climatic confrontation between Yaphet Kotto, Joyce Van Patten, and Andrew Duggan in Larry Cohen's controversial black comedy, *Bone*.

## MUGU ROCK (36.8 miles)
The massive Mugu Rock is briefly glimpsed in *Windtalkers* and the *Chinatown* sequel, *The Two Jakes*. It's from a nearby phone booth that Jack Nicholson

makes a call to informant Tracey Walter. If you circle around Mugu Rock you'll find remains of the old Pacific Coast Highway before it was destroyed by storms. According to an April 16, 1940 Warner Bros. production report, the Point Mugu area plays a Panama jungle inlet in the classic swashbuckler *The Sea Hawk*, starring Errol Flynn. The *American Film Institute Catalog* cites Mugu as appearing in *Citizen Kane* for a quick shot of an automobile caravan heading up the coast to Xanadu.

## DETOUR: OXNARD'S HOLLYWOOD-BY-THE-SEA

Travelers heading from Malibu to Santa Barbara may want to schedule a stopover at the Oxnard Dunes along the way. According to Ventura County historian Richard Senate, the dunes area was a filming site for Rudolph Valentino's *The Sheik*. Claiming ownership of *The Sheik* location is common in movie production lore. Oxnard is one of five areas contending for that honor; the other four are Guadalupe Sand Dunes, Imperial Sand Dunes, El Segundo, and Palm Springs. Senate, however, maintains that this beach was the only one used for the film, as the ice plant in the dunes is a clear giveaway.

Real estate speculators took advantage of the legend and dubbed the sands Hollywood-by-the-Sea, promoting the film industry's connection with the land. Big screen stars bought lots here, with the most exclusive properties named Hollywood Beach and Silver Strand.

Several noted filmmakers have used these beaches since. King Vidor shot the dunes in his Southern soap opera, *Ruby Gentry*, with Charlton Heston and Jennifer Jones. And the D-Day landing in the Paddy Chayefsky–scripted *The Americanization of Emily* took place here, with James Garner and James Coburn landing at Omaha Beach. Director Arthur Hiller admits he almost backed out of his location.

"When I saw this beach, I thought it looked great. But when I heard the name of this location, I balked. I thought, 'I can't shoot D-Day at *Hollywood-by-the Sea!*' But it worked fine, despite its corny name," recalls Hiller.

Today these sands are mostly a residential strand. But tourists may enjoy checking out the clumpy dunes in the accessible area near the Embassy Suites Mandalay Beach Resort. *Call for directions; 805-984-2500; or www.embassymandalay.com.*

## DVD ITINERARY: THE MALIBU COAST

*Bikini Beach*, Corral Beach, Scenes 1 and 3

*The Fast and the Furious*, Trancas Canyon/Broad Beach, Scene 12

*Spartacus* [The Criterion Collection], The Great Sand Dune, Scene 32

*The Notebook*, El Matador State Beach, Scene 5

Michael Marshall Archives

The third of the Malibu-based AIP Beach Party movies

# THE MALIBU PIER
# The Shore Thing

In Huntington and Malibu, they're shooting the pier . . .

—*The Beach Boys' 1962 hit, "Surfin' Safari"*

**MAJOR ROLES:** *Devil in a Blue Dress, 711 Ocean Drive, Surf Party, Beach Ball, Back to the Beach*

### BEHIND THE SCENERY

When the Beach Boys sang about "shooting the pier," they were immortalizing the daredevil surfers who negotiated the structure's pilings. Nowadays, "shooting the pier" might refer to the film and commercial crews frequently found here.

If you're looking for the heartbeat of Malibu, this is it. The Malibu Pier is a prime destination for sports fisherman or outdoors people looking to rent a boat or a kayak to better see the coast.

Harry Medved

The Malibu Pier, seen in many a beach party movie.

The pier has a history as a shady film-noir rendezvous. In *711 Ocean Drive*, gangster Edmond O'Brien does away with a blackmailer by forcing him off the pier's end with his car. Carl Franklin's period crime thriller, *Devil in a Blue Dress*, features a re-creation of the Malibu Pier in a tense scene where detective Denzel Washington is harassed by rednecks until sadistic thug Tom Sizemore scares them off.

The pier has a lighter side on film too. In the 1965 *Beach Ball*, surfer dude Aron Kincaid comically leaps off the pier. And in the 1987 movie *Back to the Beach*, the building at the end of the pier makes cool living quarters for teenager Lori Loughlin (who returned to the pier in the TV series *Summerland*). As *Mr. Jones*, Richard Gere does an eccentric balancing act on the pier railing for his psychiatrist Lena Olin. *Moment by Moment's* unlikely lovers John Travolta and Lily Tomlin and *California Suite's* divorced couple Jane Fonda and Alan Alda share scenic lunches at the pier's one-time Alice's Restaurant.

## WHERE TO EXPLORE

### SURFRIDER BEACH

Just west of the pier is Surfrider Beach, famous for its perfect waves and considered by some to be the birthplace of surfing in Malibu. Also shot here was the 1964 Bobby Vinton vehicle *Surf Party*, with glimpses of the Malibu Pier and the Adamson House. And the 1966 ski-party romp *Wild, Wild Winter* features bikinied singing sensations Jackie and Gayle serenading the surfers from the sand.

As a holy spot in surf history, Surfrider and its recognizable retaining wall inspired the location for John Milius' *Big Wednesday*. Gary Busey recalls Surfrider as the beach where he learned how to surf for the film. But when it came time to actually shoot the movie, Milius admits that Surfrider was too expensive and its crowds too unmanageable, so he re-created the scene farther north on the Santa Barbara coastline.

Check with Heal the Bay (*www.healthebay.org*) before enjoying the waves, as Surfrider sadly ranks as having the most polluted water in Malibu.

### ADAMSON HOUSE and MALIBU LAGOON MUSEUM

Next to Surfrider Beach you'll find the Adamson House, a 1929 Moorish-Spanish Colonial Revival masterpiece designed by Stiles O. Clements, whose firm designed Los Angeles's Wiltern Theater. This former home of Rindge family member Rhoda Adamson is known for its exceptional use of Malibu tile and its spacious lawns. Check out the adjoining **Malibu Lagoon Museum** for its vintage photos of area history. *23200 Pacific Coast Highway; open 11 a.m.–3 p.m. Wednesday–Saturday; www.adamsonhouse.org; 310-456-8432.*

## Top Billing: MALIBU LAGOON STATE BEACH

Up the coast from the Adamson House you can observe the herons, pelicans, terns, godwits, and other odd birds enjoying the Malibu Lagoon, where the waters from Malibu Creek enter the ocean. A short boardwalk takes you through the marsh to a beach with views of the Malibu Pier and, on a clear day, Catalina Island. Just northwest of the lagoon is the Malibu Colony site of Barbra Streisand's and Robert Redford's beach house in *The Way We Were*. *Enter the lagoon parking lot from PCH at Cross Creek Road, just north of the Adamson House. Beach info: 818-880-0350.*

## WHERE TO STAY

### CASA MALIBU

One of the only L.A. County inns located right on the sand, this 1949 bungalow-style hideaway has a central garden courtyard, brick patio, and lots of old world charm. In fact, part of its character is due to its past cast of characters: Lana Turner stayed in the Catalina Suite for a full year in the 1950s, and Rod Steiger was a regular guest in the 1960s. *Best rates are available on weekdays or in the wintertime. 22752 Pacific Coast Highway; 310-456-2219.*

## HOW TO GET TO MALIBU PIER

*On PCH, 11 miles from the Santa Monica Pier.*

### DVD ITINERARY: MALIBU PIER

*Devil in a Blue Dress*, Scene 9

*Back to the Beach*, Scene 3

# MALIBU'S PARADISE COVE
## Eden by the Sea

> When the fog rolls in at Paradise Cove, you'd swear you were anywhere from Northern California to the Eastern seaboard. Any place but Southern California.
>
> —Ned Shapiro, location manager for Indecent Proposal and Apollo 13, both shot partially at Paradise Cove

**MAJOR ROLES:** Beach Blanket Bingo, Pajama Party, Monster-in-Law, House of Sand and Fog

### BEHIND THE SCENERY

A former hideaway for bootleggers and opium smugglers, Paradise Cove is home to a secluded beach, high cliffs, and a restaurant in the sand, and provides the quintessential California beach experience. Paradise Cove's exotic topography and proximity to L.A. has made it a natural location for low-budget filmmakers. A number of beach party musicals were shot here, including *Beach Blanket Bingo, Catalina Caper,* and *Pajama Party,* in which teenager Teri Garr and other bikinied extras dance in front of the high cliffs.

In the 1960s, the cove was a popular setting for action sequences. A motorcycle gang led by Harvey Lembeck is chased by Frankie Avalon, Jody McCrea, and Buster Keaton in *Beach Blanket Bingo,* with Keaton's car flying off a cliff. In *Dr. Goldfoot and the Bikini Machine,* title villain Vincent Price also drives a vehicle off the bluffs. And in *Rebel Rousers,* bikers Jack Nicholson, Bruce Dern, and Harry Dean Stanton terrorize Cameron Mitchell and Diane Ladd along this beach. Recalls Bruce Dern: "When he wasn't shooting, Jack would be out there by himself on the Paradise Cove rocks, hard at work on the script for *The Trip.*"

Paradise Cove also makes a nostalgic setting for Sydney Pollack's *The Way We Were,* according to the film's assistant director Hawk Koch. Cove moments include a romantic shot of Robert Redford and Barbra Streisand sailing, and a later boating sequence in which Redford and Bradford Dillman remi-

*American Pie 2's* lighthouse set was built on this pier.

Harry Medved

nisce about the good old days. A more dramatic cove sequence shot on open water is the splashdown in *Apollo 13*, with Tom Hanks, Kevin Bacon, and Bill Paxton.

The **Paradise Cove Pier** is a rickety, wooden structure built in 1945, often used by filmmakers searching for evocative seaside flavor. In 1952, it was the site of a Nantucket barbecue in the *Cheaper by the Dozen* sequel, *Belles on Their Toes*, with Myrna Loy, Jeanne Crain, and Debra Paget. Robert De Niro takes Ingrid Boulting here for an outing in *The Last Tycoon*, where they meet local salt Seymour Cassel and his pet seal. The pier figures prominently in the opening flashbacks in *Indecent Proposal*, where Woody Harrelson proposes to Demi Moore. They are reunited on the pier in the moody fog-enshrouded finale.

For *American Pie 2*, production designer Richard Toyon re-created a Lake Michigan retreat, complete with beach house, sailboats, Midwestern flora, and a lakeside lighthouse (erected on the pier's edge) where hormonally charged hero Jason Biggs almost gets lucky with Shannon Elizabeth. And in *House of Sand and Fog*, the pier plays a dramatic Northern California locale where Jennifer Connelly and Ron Eldard get to know each other over lunch.

The cove has made countless appearances in TV series, most memorably as the site of James Garner's trailer home/detective agency in *The Rockford Files*. It was also featured in *Baywatch Nights* (with Angie Harmon) and *The O.C.* (the pilot episode).

## WHERE TO EAT

### PARADISE COVE BEACH CAFÉ

This colorful beachside restaurant, with vintage Malibu photos adorning its walls, is one of the best places to show off the coast to out-of-town visitors. Call ahead for reservations or you may have a wait to be seated. Either way, you can head to the comfortable Adirondack chairs in the sand for drinks and appetizers.

This patio area is where military helicopters and a strike team unexpectedly swoop down on the café and Orlando Jones and Eddie Griffin at the close of *Double Take*. In *X-Men*, a creature rises from the sea and morphs into naked bad guy Bruce Davison, much to the shock of Paradise Cove beachgoers (including ex–Marvel Comics mogul Stan Lee as a hot dog vendor).

After dining at the cafe, take a stroll along the surf toward the high cliffs and tide pools seen in *Monster-In-Law*, with Jennifer Lopez and Michael Vartan. Music fans may recognize the cliffs as the perfect SoCal backdrop for the Beach Boys' *Surfin' Safari* album cover. *Beach Café reservations: 310-457-2503.*

## HOW TO GET TO PARADISE COVE

*On PCH, 17.8 miles from the Santa Monica Pier. Look for the tall* PARADISE COVE BEACH CAFÉ *sign and make a left onto the private road. Beachcombers be aware: there is a steep parking fee unless your ticket is validated at the cafe, so plan on eating here.*

## DVD ITINERARY: PARADISE COVE

*Beach Blanket Bingo*, Scene 15

*Pajama Party*, Scene 8

*X-Men*, Scene 19

*House of Sand and Fog*, Scenes 10 and 20

*Monster-in-Law*, Scene 3

# 4

# ZUMA AND POINT DUME
# Into the Forbidden Zone

You might not like what you'll find . . .

—Dr. Zaius (Maurice Evans) to Charlton Heston in the Point
Dume–lensed climax of the original Planet of the Apes

**MAJOR ROLES:** Planet of the Apes (1968), Kiss Me Deadly,
Barton Fink, Charlie's Angels: Full Throttle

## BEHIND THE SCENERY

Despite Dr. Zaius's ominous warning, most beachgoers, film buffs, and moviemakers have always liked what they've found on these shores. Two different regions lie side by side in this popular stretch of Malibu: Zuma, with its endless miles of wide, sandy beach; and Point Dume (also known as Westward Beach), home to high cliffs, wildflower-blanketed headlands, and secret coves. Point Dume wins hands-down as the more cinematic of the two.

If the Point Dume rockscape appears monumentally familiar, it's because it was the backdrop for the climactic shot of the Statue of Liberty rising up from the sand in the original Planet of the Apes. In the Fox Home Entertainment documentary Behind the Planet of the Apes, production designer William Creber recalls: "[The Point Dume location] had rocks with moss on them at the end of the beach which looked kinda like disintegrated bronze . . . we integrated the rocks with the base of the statue, which was a [matte] painting." Thus was born an unforgettable moment in movie history.

Flash forward three years: in the third Apes movie, Escape from the Planet of the Apes, a spaceship lands in the water adjacent to where the Statue of Liberty stood in the original film. This time, however, the arriving visitors (Roddy McDowall, Kim Hunter, and Sal Mineo) are revealed to be time-traveling simians returning from our "future." (The same location appears in Apes parody sequences in Spaceballs and Jay and Silent Bob Strike Back.)

Marc Wanamaker/Bison Archives

*Planet of the Apes'* Linda Harrison, Charlton Heston, Roddy McDowall, and Kim Hunter at Point Dume.

## WHERE TO EXPLORE

### ZUMA BEACH

"This is one of the finest white sand strands in California," says trail master John McKinney, longtime hiking columnist for the *Los Angeles Times*. Zuma is also one of the closest beaches to the San Fernando Valley, as seen in Martha Coolidge's *Valley Girl*. In this Romeo-and-Juliet high school romance, it's here that the title heroine Deborah Foreman first lays her eyes on wrong-side-of-the-hills Nicolas Cage.

Because of its flat, anonymous look (with no distinguishing rocks or coves) Zuma can also play "Any Beach U.S.A." It doubles for a San Diego beach in *Mr. Jones,* where Richard Gere and his shrink Lena Olin pull off the road for a bite after passing by Zuma's landmark FOOD sign. It's the Santa Barbara beach where Christopher Lloyd's spaceship crash lands in the big-screen *My Favorite Martian*. In Vincente Minnelli's film version of *Tea and Sympathy*, Zuma is the New England shore visited by Deborah Kerr and John Kerr.

## POINT DUME COUNTY BEACH
## (AKA WESTWARD BEACH)

The combination of dunes, cliffs, and rocky shore give Point Dume's beach a romantic yet haunting look. In addition to those in *Planet of the Apes*, other haunting cinematic images created in the area include:

*Kiss Me Deadly*    Director Robert Aldrich filmed the wild apocalyptic climax of his 1955 L.A. film noir up the coast from Point Dume. When a Pandora's box of atomic trouble is opened, Ralph Meeker and Maxine Cooper escape a burning beach house and take refuge in the waves.

*What Ever Happened to Baby Jane?*    Aldrich returned to Malibu in 1962 for another chilling climax, featuring the intense performances of Bette Davis and Joan Crawford as, respectively, a psychotic former child star and her tormented invalid sister. In the final scene, Bette dances on the Dume sands for a crowd of startled beachgoers.

*Barton Fink*    New York playwright-turned-screenwriter John Turturro is transfixed by an image on his hotel wall of a California beach girl shielding herself from the sun at Point Dume. In the Coen Brothers' surreal epic, fantasy becomes reality when Turturro actually enters that idyllic scene at the end of the movie. (The Coens returned to Dume for *The Big Lebowski*'s festive nighttime beach party with Ben Gazzara.)

Point Dume has seen its share of big-screen romance, too. Cinema couples who have appeared here include Josh Hartnett and Kate Beckinsale (*Pearl Harbor*), Anne Hathaway and Erik von Detten (*The Princess Diaries*), Linda Purl and Donny Most (*Crazy Mama*), Jayne Mansfield and Tom Ewell (*The Girl Can't Help It*), Diane Lane and Robert Downey Jr. (*Chaplin*), Mike Myers and Heather Graham (*Austin Powers: The Spy Who Shagged Me*), and Frances O'Connor and Brendan Fraser, who are distracted by devilish Elizabeth Hurley (*Bedazzled*).

In the much-hyped beach scene in *Charlie's Angels: Full Throttle*, forty-year-old mother Demi Moore looks great in a black two-piece and goes toe-to-toe with Cameron Diaz (under the watchful eyes of Drew Barrymore and Lucy Liu). Director McG picked the location partially because of its rich film history. "I'm a huge fan of what the Coen Brothers did here," says McG. "I love this beach!"

### Top Billing: POINT DUME NATURAL PRESERVE

The coastal headlands at the top of the Point Dume feature a magnificent whale-watch platform with panoramic views. Bring binoculars to observe the seals on the jutting rocks directly below the point: In the late winter, look for whales migrating to and from Alaska's Bering Sea. You can easily walk to the terrace (see *Following the Apes' Footsteps*, below) or take the Dume Shuttle Service (summer only) from the Westward Beach parking lot. The preserve can be seen in Richard Rush's *The Color of Night*, with Bruce Willis and Scott Bakula, and in *Pumpkin* with Christina Ricci.

# FOLLOWING THE APES' FOOTSTEPS: POINT DUME TO PARADISE COVE

A long ninety-minute one-way trek will take you from Point Dume County Beach, over the headlands, through isolated coves, and all the way to Paradise Cove.

The trail starts near the base of the Dume cliff where the *Apes'* Statue of Liberty was located. Follow the marked trail that leads up the dunes to the headlands. At the top of the headlands, follow the cordoned walkway to the right for the greatest view of the coast. You'll find a spectacular lookout with a viewing platform. Don't stray from the path here, as the cliffs are steep and subject to erosion.

From the lookout, continue on the path and take the steep staircase that leads to the sand below. Head down the coast toward the secluded "Forbidden Zone" cove. Once you hit the beach, just hug the cliffs.

When you finally hit Paradise Cove, you can get food and drink at the Paradise Cove Beach Café. Return to Point Dume the way you came, tide permitting, or go back in style by calling a cab or shuttle from the cafe. *Malibu Taxi: 310-456-0500.*

*CAUTION/HIGH TIDE ADVISORY: To amend what Roddy McDowall's character says at the conclusion of Planet of the Apes, "You can't ride or hike along the shore at high tide." Check with lifeguards before heading out on this lonely stretch of beach.*

## WHERE TO EAT

### THE SUNSET RESTAURANT

This former beach house reportedly hosted such luminaries as Marilyn Monroe and Frank Sinatra. Today it's a hidden café specializing in California cuisine. Request a table by the windows at sunset for a panoramic view. The Sunset is the Malibu restaurant where foster mother Renée Zellweger unwinds with teenager Alison Lohman in *White Oleander*. In *Back to the Beach*, Frankie Avalon and Annette Funicello come here to relive the old days. *1600 Westward Beach Road; closed Mondays; 310-589-1007.*

## HOW TO GET TO ZUMA BEACH AND POINT DUME

*On PCH, the Zuma turnoff is 19.6 miles from the Santa Monica Pier. To reach Point Dume, make a left from PCH onto Westward Beach Road and continue 1.2 miles to its end.*

## DVD ITINERARY: ZUMA BEACH AND POINT DUME

*What Ever Happened to Baby Jane?*, Scenes 33–35

*Planet of the Apes* (1968), Scenes 23, 25–27

*Charlie's Angels: Full Throttle*, Scene 8

Harry Medved

Point Dume, a.k.a. Westward Beach, has hosted a cast of characters from Barton Fink to Austin Powers.

# LEO CARRILLO STATE BEACH
## Babes, Waves, and a Cave

Our story begins in the tropical waters of the Pacific Ocean along whose shores native villages have existed for thousands of years, but where the white man is a newcomer . . .

—*Narration for Roger Corman's first sci-fi production,* Monster from the Ocean Floor *(1954), partially shot at Carrillo*

**MAJOR ROLES:** *Gidget, Beach Blanket Bingo, Grease, Journey to the Center of the Earth, 50 First Dates*

### BEHIND THE SCENERY

Named after the L.A.–born actor and parks commissioner who helped preserve this beach, the fantastic Carrillo shoreline includes headlands, coves, and an underground tunnel. Leo Carrillo was best known for playing the comic sidekick Pancho on the 1950s TV Western series *The Cisco Kid.* In real life, he was a descendant of local landowners dating back to 1769 and an activist dedicated to preserving portions of the original Rancho Malibu Spanish land grant. The property at Sequit Point was named in his honor in 1953.

Six years later, Leo Carrillo State Beach became the birthplace of all beach culture movies (and even received its own screen credit) when it was used in *Gidget,* starring Sandra Dee and Cliff Robertson. James Darren costars as "Moondoggie," whose shack was built near Lifeguard Tower #2. The Carrillo beach scene continued with *Beach Blanket Bingo,* whose title dance number with Frankie Avalon and Annette Funicello was shot here. The 2000 spoof *Psycho Beach Party,* with Lauren Ambrose as a Gidget-like wannabe surfer named Chicklet, is among Carrillo's latest on-screen roles.

Though far beyond his teenage years, Peter Sellers walked barefoot in the Carrillo surf while listening to the words of his guru in *I Love You, Alice B. Toklas,* in which future director Randal Kleiser plays a disciple extra. Kleiser would return to Carrillo for the precredits sequence of his hit musical *Grease,*

*Gidget*'s Sandra Dee, James Darren, and Cliff Robertson hit the
surf at Leo Carrillo.

where John Travolta and Olivia Newton-John enjoy their "summer lovin'"
fling by the crashing waves.

Other stars who have worked at Carrillo include Robert Mitchum and
Jane Greer (*Out of the Past*), James Stewart and Maureen O'Hara (*Mr. Hobbs
Takes a Vacation*), Barbara Eden and Peter Lorre (*Five Weeks in a Balloon*),
Robert Wagner (*Prince Valiant*), Elvis Presley (*Live a Little, Love a Little*),
Nicollette Sheridan (*The Sure Thing*), Patrick Swayze, Keanu Reeves, and Lori
Petty (*Point Break*), Ethan Hawke and Jude Law (*Gattaca*), Ralph Macchio,
Elisabeth Shue, and Pat Morita (*The Karate Kid*), Gene Kelly (*Xanadu*),
Rachael Leigh Cook and Paul Walker (*She's All That*), Britney Spears (*Cross-
roads*), and Vin Diesel (*The Pacifier*).

## WHERE TO EXPLORE

### Top Billing: LEO CARRILLO CAVE

From the beach parking lot, hike along the coastal bluffs until you reach Lifeguard Tower #3, near the rocks where Uma Thurman and Janeane Garofalo
commiserate in *The Truth About Cats & Dogs*. Just east of the tower, take the
short staircase to the beach and make a right in the sand. Tide permitting, you
can scramble over some rocks and find Leo Carrillo Cave. It's at the entrance
of this hidden passageway where Stephen Baldwin, Kevin Spacey, Kevin Pollak, and Gabriel Byrne bury the body of fellow thief Benicio Del Toro in *The
Usual Suspects*.

The use of the cave as a filming location dates back to at least 1935, in George Cukor's *Sylvia Scarlett*, with Cary Grant and Katharine Hepburn as a male impersonator. Almost seventy years later, Adam Sandler and Drew Barrymore share their first kiss here in *50 First Dates*.

Monster-movie fans will recognize the cave as the lair of giant crustaceans in *Attack of the Crab Monsters*, Jon Hall's bug-eyed *Monster from the Surf* (aka *The Beach Girls and the Monster*) and a two-headed creature in *Jack the Giant Killer*. In *Journey to the Center of the Earth*, James Mason, Pat Boone, and Arlene Dahl seek refuge in the cave from prehistoric dimetrodons (played by iguanas outfitted with fins). And witches Fairuza Balk, Neve Campbell, Robin Tunney, and Rachel True venture through the cave en route to a ritual invocation in *The Craft*. *Check with lifeguards for current ocean conditions.*

## IT CAME FROM CALIFORNIA: ROGER CORMAN'S LEO CARRILLO

B movie mogul Roger Corman has always enjoyed filming at Carrillo Beach. "It's a very picturesque beach, where the rocks come right down to the ocean," recalls the filmmaker today. "I shot so many movies here that it became known in the industry as *Corman* Beach." Carrillo appearances in Corman movies include *Attack of the Crab Monsters*, *Viking Women and the Sea Serpent*, and *Monster from the Ocean Floor*.

Corman was also a guiding force behind Peter Bogdanovich's *Voyage to the Planet of Prehistoric Women*. The low-budget *Voyage* stars Mamie Van Doren, a number of local beach girls (as Venusians), and a rubber pterodactyl-

*Leo Carrillo Cave,
a setting for romance,
suspense, and horror.*

Harry Medved

## CARRILLO BEACH: HANKS FOR THE MEMORIES

Tom Hanks paid the beach party genre loving tribute in *That Thing You Do!*, his directorial debut chronicling the adventures of a one-hit-wonder band. One sequence was shot near the same spot where *Gidget* and *Beach Blanket Bingo* were filmed. Hanks plays the shrewd manager who cajoles his group into making an appearance in a beach opus entitled *Weekend at Party Pier*. *That Thing* coproducer Jonathan Demme makes a cameo as the laid-back beach party movie director.

Hanks returned to the Carrillo environs for Robert Zemeckis' *Cast Away*, for a scene in which he scales a seaside cliff, in reality a set constructed in the Carrillo film commissioner's parking lot. Visual effects were added later to make the area look like a deserted tropical island.

Another Hanks came to Leo Carrillo in 2002: Tom's real-life son Colin starred in *Orange County*, in which the Malibu beach stood in for the Laguna Beach area.

god designed by wife Polly Platt. "I hired the Gill Women of Venus," Bogdanovich told Corman's biographer Jim Jerome. "Just a bunch of stoned kids walking around Carrillo Beach dressed like mermaids, with seashells covering their breasts." The location proved to be memorable for Bogdanovich for another reason: while scouting the rocks for producer Corman, he and Platt were knocked into the sea by the unpredictable surf.

## WHERE TO EAT

### NEPTUNE'S NET

You'll find this 1950s biker-and-surfer hangout near the Los Angeles/Ventura County Line. The no-frills seafood shack is the site of the climactic food fight in Curtis Hanson's *Losin' It*, featuring young Tom Cruise, John Stockwell, Jackie Earle Haley, and Rick Rossovich. Neptune's Net also has been a favorite rendezvous for undercover movie lawmen. In *Point Break*, FBI agent Keanu Reeves asks cashier Lori Petty for surfing lessons. And the patio dining area is where cop Paul Walker asks Vin Diesel for a piece of the action in *The Fast and the Furious*. *42505 Pacific Coast Highway; 310-457-3095.*

## WHERE TO STAY

### LEO CARRILLO STATE PARK CAMPGROUND

The state park's **North Beach** area is one of the few places in L.A. County where it's legal to barbecue on the beach. On the opposite side of PCH, **Canyon Campground** has 135 sites for tents or RVs near the mouth of the Arroyo Sequit Canyon. Numerous hiking trails lead into the hills from here. *Campground Reservations: www.reserveamerica.com, 800-444-PARK; Hiking Information: 805-488-1827.*

### HOW TO GET TO LEO CARRILLO STATE BEACH

*On PCH, 27 miles from the Santa Monica Pier. Follow signs to beach parking.*

### DVD ITINERARY: LEO CARRILLO STATE BEACH

*Beach Blanket Bingo*, Scenes 1, 11

*Journey to the Center of the Earth*, Scenes 30–31

*The Karate Kid*, Scenes 3, 18

*Grease*, Scene 1

*The Craft*, Scenes 16–17

# 6

# SANTA MONICA'S PALISADES PARK
# A Walk Through the Palms

Do you know that [from here] you can hear the moment when the sun hits the hills?

—Ben Chaplin to Janeane Garofalo, *watching a Palisades Park sunset in* The Truth About Cats & Dogs *(1996)*

**MAJOR ROLES:** *Point Blank, The Truth About Cats & Dogs*

## BEHIND THE SCENERY

The city of Santa Monica was cofounded in 1874 by John Percival Jones. A Brit who made millions on silver mines, Jones served as U.S. Senator for Nevada and retired to Southern California. His palatial residence, which he dubbed the Miramar (Spanish for "sea view"), stood at the corner of Wilshire Boulevard and Ocean Avenue and has long since become the Fairmont Miramar Hotel. The beautiful bluff-top terrain in front of his former home comprises today's Palisades Park. Jones' family and business partners donated the land to the burgeoning city of Santa Monica, to be preserved forever.

Today Palisades Park is a 1.5-mile stretch of grassy space lined with Canary Island palm trees, a rose garden, and sculptures seen in countless TV series from *7th Heaven* to *Alias* and movies including *Harry and Tonto, Xanadu,* Disney's *The Kid, Cisco Pike, Stuck on You,* and *Friends with Money.* It's the ideal L.A. location for jogging, biking, skating, people watching, or a romantic sunset stroll high above the waves of the Pacific.

## A WALK IN THE PARK

*Although many of the following landmarks are located on the east side of Ocean Avenue, there's no need to cross the street as you can easily see them from Palisades Park. This walking tour follows the route from the park's quieter midsection to its busy terminus at the Santa Monica Pier. Begin at the green arbor between Idaho and Washington Avenues.*

## Top Billing: *THE TRUTH ABOUT CATS & DOGS* ARBOR

Palisades Park's extensive Asian-inspired pergola is a Craftsman-era rest area recognizable to fans of *The Truth About Cats & Dogs*. Under this arbor "pet vet" Janeane Garofalo and dog lover Ben Chaplin watch the sun set over the Santa Monica Mountains. The two are reunited in the park for the film's romantic climax. Nicole Kidman and Will Ferrell also share a sunset moment in this area in the 2005 feature *Bewitched*.

*Walk a block and a half to California Avenue.*

## A *MAD WORLD* VIEW OF THE CALIFORNIA INCLINE

A turquoise forty-foot-tall beacon now towers beside the viewpoint where police chief Spencer Tracy tracks the chase in *It's a Mad, Mad, Mad, Mad World*. Below this observation area slopes the California Incline (a popular throughway leading down to Pacific Coast Highway), where two cab loads of cashcrazy comedians—including Sid Caesar, Edie Adams, Peter Falk, Eddie "Rochester" Anderson, Mickey Rooney, and Buddy Hackett—almost collide while in hot pursuit of the hidden loot.

*Look east and find the tall beige building with the exterior elevator.*

## A *POINT BLANK* VIEW OF THE HUNTLEY HOTEL

In John Boorman's crime classic *Point Blank*, Lee Marvin recruits Angie Dickinson at a Palisades Park viewpoint for a scheme that involves two nearby hotels:

Cheryl Himmelstein

Palisades Park is seen in *Point Blank*, *White Men Can't Jump*, and *Cisco Pike*.

A hair-raising stunt (on the bluffs north of Palisades Park) for a 1916 Keystone Kops comedy.

Marc Wanamaker/Bison Archives

the Huntley and the Miramar. Marvin uses one of the park's telescopes (alas, no longer here) to study mobster John Vernon's penthouse lair at the Huntley Hotel. When Dickinson later arrives at the Huntley, she rides the hotel's glass-exterior elevator to the penthouse as Marvin watches from the Miramar across the street.

Nowadays the Huntley's top floor is home to **Toppers Restaurant**, whose breathtaking views make it a popular dinner-and-drinks spot for locals and tourists alike. *Huntley Hotel: 1111 2nd Street; www.thehuntleyhotel.com; 310-394-5454.*

*Continue one block south to Wilshire Boulevard. Look east for the bungalows among the palms.*

## THE FAIRMONT MIRAMAR HOTEL

This former estate of Santa Monica founder John P. Jones has plenty of connections to Hollywood history. Legend has it that when Swedish sensation Greta Garbo first arrived in Hollywood in 1925, she stayed for four years in the hotel's Palisades wing.

According to director Delbert Mann, the Miramar was also the location of the swimming pool where newlywed husbands console each other in his Cary Grant/Doris Day movie *That Touch of Mink*, although the pool area has been substantially expanded and remodeled.

The garden area in back of the hotel was allegedly the setting for the "ritzy, exclusive Wilshire Boulevard hotel bungalows," which Raymond Chandler renamed Cavendish Court in his screenplay for *The Blue Dahlia*. Alan Ladd stars in the 1946 noir classic as a dedicated navy man who returns from the war to Santa Monica, only to find his drunken and unfaithful wife hosting a wild party in bungalow number 93. In real life, these poolside cottages hosted such luminaries as Jean Harlow and Marilyn Monroe. *101 Wilshire Blvd.; www.fairmont.com; 310-576-7777.*

*Continue one block south to Arizona Avenue.*

## SHANGRI-LA HOTEL

After her successful appearance on TV's *Jeopardy*, Rosie Perez celebrates with Woody Harrelson at this 1939 Streamline Moderne classic in *White Men Can't Jump*. Harrelson later meets up with pal Wesley Snipes at Palisades Park. *1301 Ocean Avenue; www.shangrila-hotel.com; 310-394-2791.*

*A few doors down you'll see a white turn-of-the-century cottage.*

## *BRINGING DOWN THE HOUSE* COTTAGE

For many years developers have tried to bring down this house, a 1905 Victorian home on a block of offices, hotels, and restaurants. Luckily, preservationists have saved it from the wrecking ball. The cottage was seen in the conclusion of *Bringing Down the House* with Steve Martin, Queen Latifah, Jean Smart, and Eugene Levy. *1333 Ocean Avenue.*

*Walk south, past Santa Monica Blvd. Look across the street to the tall aquamarine hotel.*

## THE GEORGIAN HOTEL

This 1931 Art Deco building could be right at home on Miami's South Beach strip. In fact, director Barry Sonnenfeld chose the 84-room hotel as the Florida base for mobster Dennis Farina, who gets popped in the nose by John Travolta in *Get Shorty*. It is also the beach hotel where love-struck lawman Lyle Lovett finds Lisa Kudrow in *The Opposite of Sex*, and it doubles as a Viennese hotel in Carl Reiner's *The Man with Two Brains*, with Steve Martin and Kathleen Turner. *1415 Ocean Avenue; www.georgianhotel.com; 310-395-9945.*

*Continue south to the Santa Monica Pier, the end of your walk.*

## THE LOBSTER RESTAURANT

In Steven Soderbergh's *Ocean's Eleven*, George Clooney and Brad Pitt have a drink at the bar in The Lobster, located at the entrance to the Santa Monica Pier. A remodeled 1923 landmark eatery, The Lobster is known for its great seafood and impressive ocean views at sunset. *1602 Ocean Avenue; 310-458-9294.*

## HOW TO GET TO PALISADES PARK

*The park is located along Ocean Avenue, north of the Santa Monica Pier.*

## DVD ITINERARY: PALISADES PARK

*The Truth About Cats & Dogs*, Scenes 15 and 19

*Bringing Down the House*, Scene 12

*Point Blank*, Scene 12

# SANTA MONICA PIER
# The End of the Road

Carousels everywhere evoke the magic of childhood and the
mystery of the circle that always comes back to itself. For my
film, the Santa Monica Pier merry-go-round was the perfect
embodiment of this mythic entity.

—*Curtis Harrington, director of* Night Tide *(1963)*

**MAJOR ROLES:** *The Sting, Ruthless People, Cellular*

## BEHIND THE SCENERY

It's only fitting that *Forrest Gump's* Tom Hanks finishes one of his self-imposed marathon runs across America here, for L.A. County's only surviving recreational pier is both the symbolic western terminus of Route 66 and the end of the road for movie characters seeking new horizons.

Celebrities flocked here in the 1930s to take a water taxi to one of many offshore gambling casinos moored a few miles off the pier. A certain kind of "pier noir" look emerged in Hollywood crime melodramas (such as *Quicksand, Pitfall,* and *Fallen Angel*), where the pier represented a seedy seaside haunt for desperate characters.

For Joan Crawford's suicide attempt in *Mildred Pierce,* the pier and a café were re-created on Warner Bros. Stage 21, according to the December 15, 1944 production report. (A SANTA MONICA PIER sign was constructed by the property department but never used.) One month later, the same stage was used for the fog-enshrouded Lido Pier (where a Packard is hoisted from the sea) as Raymond Chandler's famed P.I. Philip Marlowe (Humphrey Bogart) investigates a crime in Howard Hawks's *The Big Sleep.*

Throughout Hollywood's Golden Age, the piers in the Santa Monica bay cities area (including nearby Lick Pier and Pacific Ocean Park) were the places to go for music, with regular radio broadcasts featuring bandleaders Lawrence

Welk and Roy Rogers' protégé Spade Cooley. Contemporary efforts to bring music back to the pier include the annual summer-long Twilight Dance Series.

Exteriors of the long-gone pavilions were captured on film in *The Lost Squadron*, *The Glenn Miller Story*, and Sydney Pollack's *They Shoot Horses, Don't They?* (The *Horses* studio set on which Jane Fonda, Michael Sarrazin, Bruce Dern, Bonnie Bedelia, and Red Buttons endure a grueling dance marathon was based on Lick Pier's Aragon Ballroom.)

## PIER HIGHLIGHTS
### Top Billing: THE CAROUSEL

A time capsule from another era, the Santa Monica merry-go-round is one of the last antique carousels still operating in North America. The elegant machine was manufactured in Philadelphia in 1922 and moved to this building from Nashville in the 1940s. Forty-four unique hand-carved horses revolve around the base of an antique Wurlitzer band organ.

A flat-for-rent above the carousel was available throughout the 1960s, allowing filmmakers access to Santa Monica's most eccentric living quarters. In Curtis Harrington's 1963 cult film *Night Tide*, carnival mermaid Linda Lawson is the upstairs tenant who beguiles sailor-on-furlough Dennis Hopper in his first lead role. In *The Sting*, rookie con man Robert Redford finds veteran grifter Paul Newman hiding out with Eileen Brennan, who operates a brothel here. Today the off-limits unit serves as the offices for the staff that rents the building for private parties. Other carousel appearances include *The Net*, *Cellular*, *Crime & Punishment*, *USA*, and *Inside Daisy Clover* with Natalie Wood and Ruth Gordon. *Closed Tuesdays; general info: 310-394-8042; private event info: 310-395-4248.*

### THE FERRIS WHEEL AT PACIFIC PARK

A carnival area on the pier called Pacific Park includes a roller coaster, kiddie rides, and an arcade. For filmmakers the main attraction is the nine-story-high Pacific Wheel. When the wheel is lit brightly it makes an ironically festive backdrop for movie characters in tense situations. The Ferris wheel is a scary meeting spot for cyber-savvy fugitive Sandra Bullock, who rendezvouses with Jeremy Northam here in Irwin Winkler's *The Net*. In Frank Darabont's *The Majestic*, blacklisted screenwriter Jim Carrey drowns his sorrows under the bright lights of the Ferris wheel, then decides to drive up the coast "until the sun comes up or gas runs out." In the climax of *Cellular*, Kim Basinger and Chris Evans play a deadly game of cat-and-mouse with Jason Statham in Pacific Park. And in *Cursed*, pier seer Portia de Rossi foretells the bloody future for Shannon Elizabeth and Mya.

## TODDLIN' TOWN ON THE PACIFIC

Before its renovation, the Santa Monica Pier's 1916 Hippodrome building was in such a sorry state of disrepair that it made the perfect double for Newman's seedy Chicago hideaway in *The Sting*. "It didn't need much work," recalls production designer Henry Bumstead. "The carousel definitely evoked that 1930s period flavor, but it was in sad shape. It was ready-made for a flashy character down on his luck." But how could the Hippodrome exterior pass for Chicago when the Pacific Ocean was clearly in view? Simple. A matte painting of the Windy City's period skyline and an elevated train trestle obscure the Santa Monica coast.

## PIER'S END

At the end of the pier you'll find an interpretive display of Santa Monica Pier history, public bathrooms, a bait-and-tackle shop and the Mariasol restaurant and bar, a cool location for watching the sunset. In the 1986 Zucker Brothers/ Jim Abrahams comedy *Ruthless People*, Judge Reinhold drives a car off the pier in a climactic sequence. An impressive helicopter shot of Santa Monica Bay can be seen at the end of Wim Wenders' second American film, *The End of Violence*, featuring Bill Pullman at Pier's End.

## BELOW THE PIER

Where the waves crash against the pilings lies a traditionally mysterious place for movie seductions or crime scenes. This is allegedly where Burt Lancaster in his Oscar-winning role as *Elmer Gantry* seduces fellow evangelist Jean Simmons below her "Waters of the Jordan Tabernacle" revival tent. It's also where Westside bad girl Kirsten Dunst, collecting garbage as part of her community service, meets up with inner-city nice guy Jay Hernandez in *Crazy/Beautiful*. Chevy Chase in *Fletch* investigates drug traffic at the pier, and encounters millionaire Tim Matheson near the pilings.

Perhaps the most bizarre on-screen visitor to the pier's nether environs is the below-the-sand creature who sucks hapless beachgoers to their doom in the 1981 monster movie *Blood Beach*. Alluding to *Jaws 2*'s effective ad campaign, *Blood Beach* slyly warned, "Just When You Thought It Was Safe to Go Back in the Water—You Can't Get to It!"

Also under the pier you'll find the **Santa Monica Pier Aquarium**, a small interactive education center with touch tanks and exhibits on Santa Monica Bay. It's operated by Heal the Bay, a nonprofit activist group whose "Beach

Bummer Awards" (for California's dirtiest beaches) calls attention to the water quality along the Southern California coast. *310-393-6149.*

## SOUTH OF THE PIER

### ORIGINAL MUSCLE BEACH SITE

The nation's physical fitness boom was "born in Santa Monica," according to the Muscle Beach Alumni Association. Muscleman/historian Harold Zinkin recalls the Muscle Beach site as the regular workout spot for future *Hercules* star Steve Reeves and Hollywood stuntman Russell Saunders. Celebrity bodywatchers Jayne Mansfield and Jane Russell often joined the crowds. Although some gymnastic equipment can be found here, Muscle Beach moved south to the Venice boardwalk in the sixties. In 1965 the Beach Boys' Brian Wilson lip-synched "The Lonely Sea" near old Muscle Beach in the low-budget surf musical *The Girls on the Beach*.

## WHERE TO EAT

### CHEZ JAY

This nautical-themed steak-and-seafood hideaway from the 1950s has attracted such famed clientele as Elizabeth Taylor, Marlon Brando, Nicolas Roeg, Ava Gardner, Frank Sinatra, Vivien Leigh, Angie Dickinson, Warren Beatty, Chris Penn, Viggo Mortensen, Michelle Pfeiffer, and Bronson Pinchot. According to restaurant legend, former Secretary of State Henry Kissinger brought his dates to a private booth in the rear of the restaurant, now called the Kissinger Room. In Curtis Hanson's *Bad Influence*, Rob Lowe and James Spader meet here for a beer. Actor-owner Jay Fiondella claims that Matt Damon and Ben Affleck wrote a first draft of their Oscar-winning screenplay *Good Will Hunting* in Chez Jay's back room. *1657 Ocean Ave.; 310-395-1741.*

## WHERE TO STAY

### SHUTTERS ON THE BEACH HOTEL

This posh hotel is one of L.A.'s most romantic places for a drink. Steven Spielberg hosted a convocation of futurists here for a brainstorming session while prepping *Minority Report*. **Pedals**, the hotel's cafe, appears in *Something's Gotta Give* as the Hamptons restaurant where Keanu Reeves and Diane Keaton have their first date. The hotel's environs can also be glimpsed in *Species*, as Alfred Molina, Ben Kingsley, Forest Whitaker, and Marg Helgenberger search for missing fem-alien Natasha Henstridge on nearby Appian Way. *1 Pico Blvd.; 310-458-0030.*

## CASA DEL MAR

This classic luxury hotel opened in 1926 as a beach club and soon became a favorite haunt for the Hollywood crowd, including director Erich von Stroheim. In the 1980s it became the Pritikin Longevity Center, where stars such as Chris Farley stayed while attempting to shed pounds. For Jonathan Demme's *Swing Shift*, art director Bo Welch helped create a roller rink in front of Casa del Mar where Goldie Hawn and Ed Harris skate by the sea. And in *Be Cool*, bickering Vince Vaughn and The Rock hold up traffic at nearby Ocean Way and Bay Street. Today Casa del Mar is owned by the same folks who run Shutters and has become a fashionable hotel for celebrities like Britney Spears and Justin Timberlake. The wood-paneled lobby is a popular meeting place, with picture windows in the restaurant/bar area facing the ocean. *1910 Ocean Way; 310-581-5533.*

## HOSTELLING INTERNATIONAL, SANTA MONICA

Here's an inexpensive way to stay overnight in a clean and cool environment in Santa Monica. Online reservations are available (*reserve@hilosangeles.org*) for both private and shared dorm rooms with bunk beds. The location can't be beat: it's only a few blocks away from the pier and close to the Third Street Promenade and Palisades Park.

The hostel was built atop **Rapp's Saloon**, Santa Monica's oldest (1875) brick building and the city's early tavern and town hall. In 1911 it was home to Vitagraph Studios, a Santa Monica film-production center that rivaled Hollywood. Because the studio depended on natural light, the Santa Monica fog forced Vitagraph to move east by 1915. *Open to travelers of all ages. Next door is a travel center offering discounted sightseeing tours. 1436 Second Street; 310-393-9913.*

## LOCAL MOVIE CELEBRATION:
## SANTA MONICA "DRIVE-IN" AT THE PIER

Free films are screened Tuesday nights during the summer in the pier's parking lot, west of the carousel. *For ticket info: www.smff.com.*

### HOW TO GET TO THE SANTA MONICA PIER

*The pier is located at the intersection of Ocean and Colorado Avenues. Limited parking is available on the pier; look for metered parking along Ocean Avenue.*

### DVD ITINERARY: SANTA MONICA PIER

*The Sting*, Scenes 3–4

*Ruthless People*, Scenes 11–12

*Cellular*, Scenes 14–15

## VIDIOTS: WHERE TO RENT A MOVIE BY THE BAY

You'll find one of L.A.'s most eclectic video stores across the street from the Santa Monica Civic Auditorium, the 1960s home of The Academy Awards (and location for the legendary bad movie *The Oscar*). With over forty thousand videos and DVDs classified by categories like Beach Party Movies and Disaster Pictures, Vidiots is a cineaste's smorgasbord. A variety of directors' oeuvres are represented, from P. T. Anderson to William Wyler. If you can't find your film here, the knowledgeable staff can suggest alternate venues. Actor Adam Goldberg filmed scenes here for his directorial debut, *I Love Your Work*, starring Giovanni Ribisi and Christina Ricci. *302 Pico Blvd., between 3rd and 4th Streets; www.vidiotsvideo.com; 310-392-8508.*

Production Designer Henry Bumstead recreated 1930s Chicago in Santa Monica for *The Sting*.

Jeffrey Stanton Archives

# 8

# VENICE BEACH AND CANALS
## The Beat Goes On

If you're a UCLA student shacking up with a girlfriend . . . your [Venice] neighbors will not complain about your bongo drums as long as you do not complain about their Saturday night, all-night, open-house, drunk parties.

—*Lawrence Lipton in his 1959 book,* The Holy Barbarians

**MAJOR ROLES:** *Touch of Evil, White Men Can't Jump, Lords of Dogtown, Falling Down*

### BEHIND THE SCENERY

Conceived as a fantasyland re-creation of the Italian city on the water, "Venice of America" was built in 1905 by tobacco baron Abbot Kinney. Draining the local marshes and building a network of canals in their place, Kinney created what is now a thriving community filled with artists' galleries and trendy eateries.

Because of its once-thriving amusement parks, Venice was a popular locale for lively sequences in silent films, including Buster Keaton's *The Cameraman* and "King of Comedy" Mack Sennett's bathing-beauties shorts that introduced future stars Gloria Swanson and Carole Lombard.

Venice gradually deteriorated in the late 1920s, after Kinney's death. Oil was discovered in Venice and wells were installed next to the canals, polluting the water. By the early 1930s, most of the canals were filled in, paved over, and renamed as streets, and only six miles remain. Venice landmarks that have survived over the years include Venice High (Rydell High's entrance in *Grease*) and the old police station (seen in John Carpenter's *Assault on Precinct 13*).

Cheap rents attracted beatniks during the Eisenhower years. As Beat icons like Jack Kerouac, Allen Ginsberg, and Gregory Corso gravitated to Venice in the late 1950s, so did experimental directors in search of a bit of seedy post-neorealism. John Parker's nightmarish *Dementia* (aka *Daughter of*

Roller-skating Jim Bray in the 1970s camp classic *Roller Boogie*.

*Horror*), for example, depicts Venice as a malevolent seaside haunt inhabited by predatory men and desperate women.

"Hollywood writers [are] dropping in to refresh their souls, hoping, perhaps, that some of the creative energy of [Venice's] dedicated artists will somehow rub off a little on them," noted Lawrence Lipton in his 1959 Beat history *The Holy Barbarians*. The same year director Roger Corman memorably lampooned the area's anything-goes art world in his cult classic *A Bucket of Blood*.

After the beatniks came the hippies, as portrayed in the 1969 comedy *I Love You, Alice B. Toklas*. Upper middle class disdain for Venice could be summed up in a line from the film; when asked where her dropout son lives, troubled Beverly Hills mother Jo Van Fleet cries, "Bernie's gone to live with the bums . . . *in Venice!*"

In the early seventies, "Venice was a relatively quiet place," recalls the city's unofficial historian Jeffrey Stanton, author of *Venice of America*. "But in a few years, a new bicycle path, nude sunbathers, new murals, the building renovation boom and the roller skating phenomenon brought tourists back."

Today the community contains a bizarre blend of trendy professionals and eccentric artists, making Venice a true smorgasbord of humanity. It has also been the neighborhood of preference for a select group of actors and maverick moviemakers. John Cusack, Dennis Hopper, Julia Roberts, Tony Bill, and Catherine Hardwicke are among the industry figures who have set up homes or offices nearby this boardwalk city area known for its color, climate, and cutting edge.

## VENICE'S "LITTLE TRAMP"

Venice visitors might be surprised at the sight of the boardwalk's homeless population, but it's nothing new. In 1914 Hollywood immortalized the Venice area when Charlie Chaplin's lovable vagabond character, the Little Tramp, made his first screen appearance in the comedy short *Kid Auto Races at Venice*. Chaplin returned in 1928 to shoot *The Circus* (on the old Venice Pier) as well as to relax in a penthouse suite at the Waldorf Hotel. The neighborhood's Cadillac Hotel, Gingerbread Court, a brick bungalow on Rose Avenue, and even The Chaplin Apartments have all boasted at one point that "Chaplin slept here," but not all of those claims are substantiated.

## THE VENICE BEACH WALKING TOUR

*Longtime residents and visitors all know that the best way to see Venice Beach is on foot. Officially known as Ocean Front Walk, this "boardwalk" along Venice Beach has been used in countless films and TV shows.*

*ADVISORY: Parking fees are exorbitant on summer weekends when the boardwalk is packed with tourists and becomes a noisy urban parade. To avoid the crowds, check out the boardwalk on weekdays.*

*Your starting point for this walking tour of the famed Venice Beach boardwalk is just north of the corner of Rose Avenue and Ocean Front Walk.*

### ON THE WATERFRONT CAFE (205 Ocean Front Walk)

This local watering hole is known for its European beer and cameo appearance in Clint Eastwood's Oscar-winning *Million Dollar Baby*, where aspiring boxer Hilary Swank waits tables. The stretch of the boardwalk between Rose Avenue and Barnard Way is your best bet for finding beach stands where you can rent skates, bikes, or tandem cruisers. It's also where you'll find the minimalist condo (*at 119 Ocean Front Walk*) in which Ashley Judd and cops await Val Kilmer in Michael Mann's *Heat. Cafe info: 310-392-0322.*

### "THE PAUL MAZURSKY CORNER BENCH"
### (Ocean Front Walk and Dudley)

Director John Ford is known for his Monument Valley vistas, and Clint Eastwood has his Bay Area landmarks, but Oscar-nominated writer/director Paul Mazursky can proudly claim this park bench as his personal icon. It was on this corner, directly across from the Cadillac Hotel and the Titanic clothing store, that Mazursky set scenes for three of his works: *I Love You, Alice B. Toklas*, *Harry and Tonto*, and *Down and Out in Beverly Hills*. "There's still a multinational, motley crowd down there," says Mazursky. "It reminds me of Greenwich Village in the 1950s."

In *Toklas*, which Mazursky cowrote with Larry Tucker, this area is where uptight attorney Peter Sellers tries to save his brother-turned-hippie from bad influences, including hash brownies. The bench appeared in Mazursky's *Harry and Tonto*, for which former *Honeymooner* Art Carney won a Best Actor Oscar as a road-tripping senior. It's here in the film's bittersweet finale that the aging Carney considers a future with a flirtatious "cat lady" played by Sally K. Marr (best known as comedian Lenny Bruce's mother). And in *Down and Out in Beverly Hills*, tycoon Richard Dreyfuss spends a day here with homeless houseguest Nick Nolte.

This block on Dudley is also the site of Juliette Lewis' boutique in *Mixed Nuts* (next to the restaurant at 5 Dudley), Ally Sheedy's shop in the cult film *Sugar Town*, the mural where Olivia Newton-John comes to life in *Xanadu*, and the spot where Woody Harrelson first arrives on the boardwalk in *White Men Can't Jump*.

## VENICE SUITES *(417 Ocean Front Walk)*
This 1920s apartment hotel housed the Venice pad for airhead alums Mira Sorvino and Lisa Kudrow in *Romy and Michele's High School Reunion*. *The Champ*, starring Jon Voight and Ricky Schroder, used the bike path by the hotel, as did TV's *Three's Company* with John Ritter. A few doors south are **Figtree's Café** (310-392-4937), a vegetarian-friendly patio restaurant, and Pacific Jewish Center, an Orthodox synagogue that can be glimpsed in *Down and Out in Beverly Hills*. Hotel info: *www.venicesuites.com*; *310-566-5224*

## WALDORF APARTMENTS
### *(Ocean Front Walk at 5 Westminster)*
A white 1914 walk-up with hardwood floors and a classic marquee, this former hotel's guest list once included Clara Bow, Mary Pickford, Roscoe "Fatty" Arbuckle, and Charlie Chaplin.

In the 1980s, the rooftop apartment provided a hip penthouse suite for police detective Sylvester Stallone in *Cobra*, according to location associate Janice Polley. Polley returned to the Waldorf for Nora Ephron's *Mixed Nuts*, casting the apartment building as a creaky old suicide-prevention center manned by Steve Martin, Madeline Kahn, and Rita Wilson. The trio interacts with a rogue's gallery of boardwalk eccentrics played by Adam Sandler, Garry Shandling, Jon Stewart, and Parker Posey.

The Waldorf also serves as home for Timothy Hutton (as real-life spy

Christopher Boyce) in John Schlesinger's *The Falcon and the Snowman*. He and fellow spy Sean Penn later exchange state secrets on the boardwalk fronting the building.

The same stretch of boardwalk was used for the 1965 Venice Beach sequences in *The Doors* with Val Kilmer (as Jim Morrison), Meg Ryan, and Kyle MacLachlan. (Incidentally, the apartment building next door at 14 Westminster, The Morrison, was reportedly named after the singer, for his notorious partying on the building's rooftop.)

Today the Waldorf is an apartment building. Its **Groundwork Coffee Company** (*310-452-2706*), located on the bottom floor, offers gourmet coffee brews and pastries.

## THE SIDEWALK CAFÉ AND BAR (1401 Ocean Front Walk)

The area between Clubhouse and Windward seen in Catherine Hardwicke's hard-hitting drama *thirteen*, is often considered the heart of the Venice boardwalk. The skate circle in front of the Sidewalk Café can be seen in the 1979 camp classic *Roller Boogie* starring Linda Blair, and Hardwicke's *Lords of Dogtown* with Heath Ledger. The proprietors of the crowded café claim that their 1915 building was once an artists' studio and crash pad for Beat legend Jack Kerouac. The Sidewalk specializes in omelettes, waffles, and French toast. *310-399-5547.*

## VENICE BEACH COTEL/ST. MARK'S (Speedway at 25 Windward Ave.)

Just a half-block east of Ocean Front Walk you'll find what's left of *Touch of Evil*'s sleazy south-of-the-border Ritz Hotel (where narcotics officer Charlton Heston leaves his new wife Janet Leigh on their nightmarish honeymoon). It's the 1905 St. Mark's annex building, home of the trendy Venice Cantina, and one of the few structures left in Venice with its original columned archways.

As an in-joke to film buffs, St. Mark's once again plays the seedy Ritz in the opening sequence of the 2001 comedy *Double Take*, according to location manager Molly Allen. In *L.A. Story*, Steve Martin escorts Sarah Jessica Parker to her home here. For those traveling solo, and/or looking to save cash, St. Mark's also houses the Venice Beach Cotel, a no-frills youth hostel with shared bathrooms and limited services. (*www.venicebeachcotel.com*; *310-399-7649*)

A counterculture bazaar was built in front of St. Mark's in the late sixties for *I Love You, Alice B. Toklas*. "We had two hundred extras down there, playing hippies," recalls the film's assistant director Howard Kanzanjian. "When we went to feed them, suddenly a whole bunch of hungry real hippies joined us for the catering break and blended in. We couldn't tell the difference between the extras and the locals, so we ran out of food. Some things on the boardwalk never change."

Today there's a still a lively and diverse scene outside of St. Mark's, with dozens of vendors selling sunglasses, T-shirts, and tchotchkes. On the hostel's west wall is a familiar mural of a Botticelli-inspired Venus on roller skates. Painted by artist Rip Cronk, this mural can be seen in *White Men Can't Jump*, *Point of No Return*, *Venice/Venice*, and *L.A. Story*. The 1983 remake of *Breathless* features this and a dozen other local murals, offering a virtual travelogue of outdoor art in the Venice and Santa Monica areas.

## Top Billing: MUSCLE BEACH *(1817 Ocean Front Walk)*

This popular beachside athletic center, noted for its weightlifting arena and basketball courts, can be been seen in *American History X* (in which Oscar-nominated Edward Norton, as a ruthless skinhead, engages in a tense playoff) and *Molly* (where mentally challenged Elisabeth Shue makes faces at the musclemen, much to the chagrin of brother Aaron Eckhart). Contrary to popular belief, the Venice Beach basketball sequences for *White Men Can't Jump* were not shot here. Due to shooting constraints the courts had to be re-created in a parking lot at the end at Rose Avenue.

## VENICE PIER *(Ocean Front Walk and Washington Blvd.)*

Fisherman caught halibut and rock cod off the Venice Pier when it opened in 1965. *Falling Down*'s nostalgic policeman Robert Duvall recalls its heyday during a tense pier standoff with psychotic defense worker Michael Douglas: "You used to be able to fish right here, now you can't even swim in the water." Nevertheless, this 1,200-foot-long landmark still attracts visitors looking for a scenic daytime stroll. Other brief pier area appearances include *Bounce* with Gwyneth Paltrow and Ben Affleck, *Lovely and Amazing* with Catherine Keener, and *Just Married* with Ashton Kutcher and Brittany Murphy.

## DETOUR: THE VENICE CANALS

In 1966, when Peter Fonda pulled up to the entrance to the Venice Canals in *The Wild Angels*, the neighborhood was much different than it is today. "The place was a dump with dirt walkways, cracked sidewalks, and scummy, slime-infested water," recalls crew member and Venice resident Polly Platt. Since then the canals have been cleaned up and have served as a one-time home for television personalities like *Simpsons* creator Matt Groening and actors Ed O'Neill, Camryn Manheim, and Orson Bean. TV viewers know the canals as home to lifeguard David Hasselhoff on *Baywatch*.

The canals have seen their share of danger, most memorably in Welles' *Touch of Evil*, shot along the Grand Canal (near today's Ballona Lagoon). In Bill Norton's crime drama *Cisco Pike*, Kris Kristofferson (in his starring debut) is first seen walking among the canals. It's on a footbridge that young Johnny Depp and Heather Langenkamp discuss how to thwart Freddy Krueger in *A Nightmare on Elm Street*. Toni Basil shoots at ambulance drivers Bill Cosby and Bruce Davison at Howland Canal before taking her own life in *Mother, Jugs & Speed*. Josh Hartnett and Harrison Ford pursue rapper/actor Kurupt in a low-tech comic foot chase through the canals in *Hollywood Homicide*. In Nic Bettauer's forward-looking feature *Duck* (2005), Philip Baker Hall rescues the title critter from the canal's contaminated waters.

Cars driven by both Sylvester Stallone (*Cobra*) and Roy Scheider (*The Outside Man*) have shot through the air during deadly pursuits on the raised Dell Avenue bridges.

The cult 1978 monster movie *Slithis* tells the story of a reptilian mutation that arises from Venice's backwaters. *Slithis* director Stephen Traxler remembers that "the water was so murky when I lived in Venice in the 1970s that you could easily imagine some creature emerging from the canals."

*HOW TO GET TO THE VENICE CANALS You'll find parking on South Venice Boulevard, east of Pacific Avenue. Look for the sign that reads* VENICE CANALS WALKWAY. *Follow the walkway along the Grand Canal as it curves to the left onto Carroll Canal.*

*Wear proper footwear while exploring the canals, as you'll find duck droppings all around the narrow walkways. Since it's a residential area, you'll find no public services here. Please respect the residents' private property.*

## WHERE TO EAT

### THE ROSE CAFÉ and THE FIREHOUSE

On any given day these eateries feature a mix of locals, tourists, and bodybuilders fresh from their workouts at nearby Gold's Gym. Both cafés appear in movies frequently: the Firehouse can be seen in *Speed*, where cop Keanu Reeves gets a coffee before a bus explodes across the street; the Rose is the first-date restaurant for Donald Sutherland and Marsha Mason in *Max Dugan Returns*. Both have pleasant patio seating areas. *Rose Café: 220 Rose Ave.; 310-399-0711/The Firehouse: 213 Rose Ave.; 310-396-6810.*

### SCHATZI ON MAIN

Arnold Schwarzenegger and wife Maria Shriver co-owned this Venice-adjacent restaurant, where diners can feast on Austrian dishes based on family recipes. Next to the parking lot elevator is a mural depicting Hollywood's Golden Age, with Arnold and Maria humorously incorporated into the scene. In the American remake of *Breathless*, you can see the groundbreaking of the future Schatzi building, with noted art director-turned-director

Harrison Ford, Josh Hartnett, Johnny Depp, Val Kilmer, and Meg Ryan have all filmed scenes at the Venice canals.

*Harry Medved*

Eugene Lourie playing the building's architect. *3110 Main Street; 310-399-4800.*

## OCEAN PARK OMELETTE PARLOR

With its hearty three-egg omelettes and garden patio dining area, this old-style breakfast spot is a favorite among locals and tourists alike. The Main Street environs near the parlor can be seen in *Two of a Kind* (with John Travolta and Olivia Newton-John) and *Big Wednesday* (Bear's inland surf shop neighborhood). *2732 Main Street, Mon.–Fri. 6 a.m.-2:30 p.m. Sat. & Sun. 6 a.m.-4 p.m.; 310-399-7892.*

## ABBOT'S HABIT

Named for Venice pioneer Abbot Kinney, this coffee-and-sandwich shop is a favorite hangout for local bohemians who participate in poetry readings and open-mike performances. Janeane Garofalo and Uma Thurman discuss their diets over lunch here in *The Truth About Cats & Dogs*. *1401 Abbot Kinney Blvd.; 310-399-1171.*

## LOCATION SCOUTING: VENICE ON VIDEO

Orson Welles' *Touch of Evil* was shot in Venice in 1957, when the beach community closely resembled a decaying Mexican border town. It's a bay city time capsule with historic views of Windward Avenue, Market Street, Speedway Avenue, Ocean Front Walk, and the canals.

In the film's classic single-take opening, a ticking time bomb is planted in a parked car near the boardwalk, and the camera cranes upward to show the vehicle as it moves toward Windward Avenue. The camera picks up and then follows Charlton Heston and Janet Leigh as they stroll down the avenue and head north on Ocean Front Walk. They continue to a border checkpoint, when the (off-screen) car suddenly explodes and the shot comes to an abrupt end (near what is now the Sidewalk Café).

Another crime thriller, the French-produced *The Outside Man* (starring Roy Scheider and Ann-Margret) offers a vision of Venice and Santa Monica in the early seventies. The movie shows the Ozymandius-like ruins of the Pacific Ocean Park amusement pier (before it was torn down mid-decade), the Ocean View Apartments, and the Venice canals. And the acclaimed documentary *Dogtown and Z-Boys* offers a fascinating look at Venice and Santa Monica's Main Street in the sixties and seventies in its chronicle of the rise and fall of the area's surfing and skateboarding legends. The film was the basis for *Lords of Dogtown,* in which the Pacific Ocean Park pier was re-created at San Diego's Imperial Beach.

## DETOUR: MARINA DEL REY'S CHACE PARK

Some movie fans may think that **Chace Park** was named after the TV cop show chases that take place here (including big-screen versions of *Starsky and Hutch* with Ben Stiller and Owen Wilson, and *Dragnet* with Tom Hanks and Dan Aykroyd). In fact, it was named after Burton Chace, who in the early 1960s helped turn this former swampland into Marina del Rey, boasting the world's largest man-made small-craft harbor. (The marina appears in many movies, including Mia Farrow's nightmare sequence in *Rosemary's Baby.*) Today Chace Park is a great spot for picnicking, strolling along the waterfront, riding the water shuttle, or catching an outdoor concert in the summertime. *The park is located at 13650 Mindanao Way; 310-305-9595.*

## HOW TO GET TO VENICE

*Take the Santa Monica Freeway (I-10) West to Santa Monica and exit at Lincoln Blvd. Head south on Lincoln. Take a right on Rose Avenue and follow it to its end at the parking lot on Venice Beach.*

## DVD ITINERARY: VENICE BEACH AND CANALS

*Touch of Evil*, Scenes 2, 3, 5, and 16

*White Men Can't Jump*, Scenes 1–3 and 20

*Down and Out in Beverly Hills*, Scene 6

Cheryl Himmelstein

The St. Mark's complex has hosted such on-screen guests as Sarah Jessica Parker and Janet Leigh.

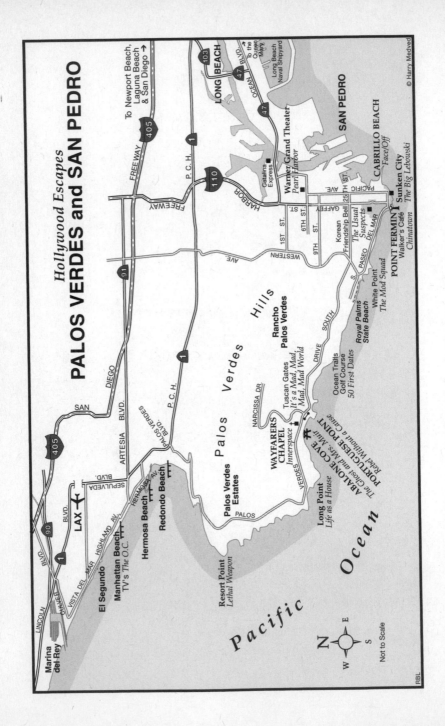

*Hollywood Escapes*
# PALOS VERDES and SAN PEDRO

© Harry Medved

**Marina del Rey**

**El Segundo**

**Manhattan Beach**
*TV's The O.C.*

**Hermosa Beach**

**Redondo Beach**

**LAX**

**Palos Verdes Estates**

*Palos Verdes Hills*

**Rancho Palos Verdes**

Tuscan Gates
*It's a Mad, Mad, Mad, Mad World*

NARCISSA DR.

**WAYFARERS CHAPEL**
*Innerspace*

**ABALONE COVE**
*The Ghost and Mrs. Muir*

**PORTUGUESE POINT**
*Rebel Without a Cause*

**Long Point**
*Life as a House*

**Resort Point**
*Lethal Weapon*

Ocean Trails Golf Course
*50 First Dates*

White Point
*The Mod Squad*

Royal Palms State Beach

DRIVE SOUTH

WESTERN AVE

PASEO DEL MAR

**POINT FERMIN**
Walker's Café
*Chinatown*

**Sunken City**
*The Big Lebowski*

**CABRILLO BEACH**
*Face/Off*

Korean
Friendship Bell

The Usual Suspects

GAFFEY ST.

9TH ST.
6TH ST.
1ST ST.
25TH ST.
PACIFIC AVE.

**SAN PEDRO**

**Warner Grand Theater**
*Pearl Harbor*

Catalina Express

HARBOR FREEWAY

110

**LONG BEACH**

To the
Queen Mary →

Long Beach
Naval Shipyard

OCEAN BLVD.
103
47
47

To Newport Beach,
Laguna Beach
& San Diego →

FREEWAY

405

P.C.H.

1

SAN DIEGO

91

ARTESIA BLVD.

PALOS VERDES BLVD.

SEPULVEDA BLVD.

HERMOSA AV.

HIGHLAND AV.

VISTA DEL MAR

P.C.H.

1

PALOS VERDES DR.

405

90

1

LINCOLN BLVD.

CULVER BLVD.

*Pacific Ocean*

N
W — E
S

Not to Scale

RBL

# 9

# PALOS VERDES
# Screenland of the Pacific

Palos Verdes has a magical sweep about it, with a view of the Pacific that seems to go on forever.

—*Location manager Bob Craft*

**MAJOR ROLES:** *Life as a House, Innerspace, It's a Mad, Mad, Mad, Mad World*

## BEHIND THE SCENERY

The neighboring beach communities of Palos Verdes and San Pedro make up a study in contrasts. While San Pedro is a casual harbor town, Palos Verdes (or "PV" as it's known to locals) is an exclusive Riviera enclave. The majestic bluffs and rocky beaches of the Palos Verdes peninsula make it the perfect double for a Mediterranean or Northern Californian coastline. It can even double for Hawaii; in *50 First Dates* buddies Adam Sandler and Rob Schneider hit the links on PV's "Oahu" (actually Trump National Golf Club, with Catalina clearly visible in the background).

The most accessible and studio-friendly place to capture the coast's rocky look has been Long Point, home of the former Marineland of the Pacific. A seaside oceanarium that opened in 1954 and was once operated by Twentieth Century Fox and producer/director Irwin Allen, Marineland was one of L.A.'s favorite family attractions prior to its closing in 1987.

Though future plans call for development of the premises, Long Point is currently an empty oceanfront lot, a vast landscape upon which production designers have built their sets by the sea. Examples include the *Charlie's Angels* castle infiltrated by Cameron Diaz, Drew Barrymore, and Lucy Liu, and Kevin Kline's cliffside Craftsman dream home in *Life as a House*. Two Disney-produced period pieces constructed sets on the Long Point cliffs: *Pirates of the Caribbean*'s mammoth fortress (from which Keira Knightley falls) and *Hidalgo*'s Wild West show and ocean liner. And though you'd never know it, scenes for *The Rock, Pearl Harbor, Hot Shots!, Spider-Man, Van Helsing,* and *Fun with Dick and Jane* (2005) were shot on the point.

For filmmakers the Palos Verdes bluffs can represent the "rocky" state of their characters' lives or the literal precipice where those same characters find themselves pushed to their limits. "It was the last refuge for these boys," says *Murder by Numbers* producer Richard Crystal of the characters played by Ryan Gosling and Michael Pitt. "Palos Verdes was not only a visually stunning location, but it symbolically represented the two risk-takers who wanted to push the envelope by living on the edge."

To be sure, PV has its share of less edgy locales. In fact, its beaches, though hard to find, are worth the search.

## WHERE TO EXPLORE

### Top Billing: ABALONE COVE SHORELINE PARK

Two classic 1940s Fox films were shot here: in *The Mark of Zorro*, the cove plays the coastal Mexican homeland to which title hero Tyrone Power returns; in *The Ghost and Mrs. Muir*, Rex Harrison haunts Gene Tierney on the Abalone Cove shore.

More recently, the area has been a location favorite for producer/director Irwin Winkler: in *The Net* it's the setting for the Acapulco beach club where computer whiz Sandra Bullock meets seemingly nice guy Jeremy Northam; in *Life as a House*, architect Kevin Kline arises from the waves on the stone-laden shore after jumping into the sea.

*HOW TO GET TO ABALONE COVE SHORELINE PARK Park at the Abalone Cove/Shoreline Park lot off of Palos Verdes Drive South. Take the steep trail down to the shore area. Info: 310-377-1222.*

### PORTUGUESE POINT

There's a habitat at the tip of Portuguese Point that was a favorite inspirational location for early 1900s California impressionist painters, but for film buffs the area is best known as the fictitious Santa Rosita Beach State Park in *It's a Mad, Mad, Mad, Mad World*. It's just north of here that tilting palm trees form a "W" in the film's climax, marking the spot for the sought-after buried cash.

The Portuguese Point area was the site of cinema's most iconic tale of troubled youth. According to the Warner Bros. daily production report of May 17, 1955, the fiery climax to the famous game of "chicken" in Nicholas Ray's *Rebel Without a Cause* was shot here. The memorable footage in which the doomed vehicle plunges off a cliff capped *Rebel's* drag race. (FYI: Though James Dean, Natalie Wood, Dennis Hopper, Corey Allen, and Sal Mineo are key players in the sequence, their scenes were shot at the old Warner Ranch in Calabasas.)

The imposing point has also appeared in *The Creature from the Black La-*

goon (where Richard Carlson and Julie Adams meet up with scientist Antonio Moreno), *Destination Tokyo*, *The Court Jester*, *The Sword and the Sorcerer*, and *Twins* (as Arnold Schwarzenegger's desert island homeland).

*HOW TO GET TO PORTUGUESE POINT There is no parking available at Portuguese Point. Park at the Abalone Cove parking lot (open 10 a.m.–4 p.m. weekends and summers and 12 p.m.–4 p.m. weekdays). It's a half-mile, fifteen-minute walk to the point.*

*Head south along a path paralleling Palos Verdes Drive South. You'll pass Narcissa Road and the 1926 Tuscan gatehouse (seen in Mad World and The Whole Ten Yards). Immediately after the gatehouse, take a right on the dirt road where you'll see a sign for the Abalone Cove Ecological Reserve.*

*Follow the trail uphill and veer to the left toward the point. Be careful of the high cliffs in this area and heed the signs that advise* DO NOT CLIMB ON OR OVER RAILING. DON'T EVEN THINK ABOUT IT!

## WAYFARERS CHAPEL

This is arguably the most scenic seaside church in Southern California. Dedicated in 1951, this glass-and-wood structure by Lloyd Wright offers sensational views of the Pacific Ocean and Catalina Island, with strategically placed benches under the shade of Monterey cypress trees. "It provided that perfect Northern California look," recalls art director James H. Spencer, who chose

Harry Medved

*Rebel's* unforgettable game of "chicken" ended on these rocks.

Wayfarers for the Meg Ryan/Dennis Quaid wedding at the end of director Joe Dante's *Innerspace*. Hollywood celebrities who have exchanged vows in real life here include Beach Boy Brian Wilson, Dennis Hopper, *Bruce Almighty* director Tom Shadyac, and legendary bombshell Jayne Mansfield (to muscleman Mickey Hargitay). *5755 Palos Verdes Drive South; www.wayfarerschapel.org; 310-377-7919, ext. 6.*

## ON THE ROAD: L.A.'S SOUTH BAY, THE REAL "O.C."

TV fans may be surprised to discover that the nighttime soap *The O.C.* is by and large not filmed in Orange County as the title of the show would suggest. For budgetary reasons, the Fox series is mostly shot closer to home in L.A.'s **South Bay** (the Southern portion of Santa Monica Bay), which includes locations like Palos Verdes's Wayfarers Chapel, Trump National Golf Club, Redondo Beach Pier, and the Hermosa Beach boardwalk.

*The O.C.* production designer Tom Fichter says the South Bay is ideal territory for the show's look because "we can find unfamiliar locations, along with dramatic coastlines, beautiful ocean views, and architecture that ranges from expensive Mediterranean-style homes and seaside country clubs to tacky and trendy beachside cafés and surf shops."

The show also shoots in **Manhattan Beach**, a tourist-friendly South Bay town ideal for a quick lunch or leg-stretcher along the pier. Films shot in the region include *Coming Home, Lifeguard, Side Out, The Cannonball Run, Tequila Sunrise, Blow, Jerry Maguire,* and *Starsky & Hutch.*

## RIGGS' "DIGS": THOSE *LETHAL* LOCATIONS

The *Lethal Weapon* movies feature Mel Gibson as loose-cannon L.A. detective Martin Riggs living the single life in his ramshackle trailer by the shore. In step with the series' ever-increasing popularity—and box office receipts—successive installments proved Riggs to be an "upwardly mobile home" kind of cop: first residing at urban Dockweiler Beach near Los Angeles International Airport, Riggs ultimately settles down in Malibu's upscale Paradise Cove.

### *LETHAL WEAPON:* DOCKWEILER STATE BEACH

Riggs' first trailer is parked in a lonely beach lot at the edge of the sand. Cheerful home activities include watching Three Stooges reruns, mourning his late wife, and (unsuccessfully, of course) attempting suicide.

### *LETHAL WEAPON 2:* LONG POINT, PALOS VERDES

Two years later, Riggs moves north and is now the sole resident at the cove below Long Point. He brings home South African diplomat Patsy Kensit for a romantic evening, only to have his trailer destroyed by machine gun–wielding assassins in helicopters. "The cove was isolated enough so that we could discharge as much automatic gunfire at nighttime as we needed to," remembers second assistant director Albert Cho. Palos Verdes also saw action in the original *Lethal Weapon* during the scene in which Tom Atkins is killed by a helicopter-borne sniper. It was filmed at a private mansion at nearby Resort Point in Palos Verdes Estates.

### LETHAL WEAPON 3: LONG BEACH
Art director James H. Spencer chose this site to build a cool new trailer for Riggs and his two dogs. "Since Riggs' trailer had been shot up in the previous picture, we re-created the bullet holes in its shell for continuity," recalls Spencer. "This time around, the Riggs character moved to a different location where he hoped no one would find him so he could do some serious fishing. We found the perfect spot on a tiny isthmus right over the ocean." A scene here in which Riggs and Danny Glover's daughter (Traci Wolfe) discuss her father's whereabouts was ultimately cut from the theatrical releases, but can be seen on DVD.

### LETHAL WEAPON 4: PARADISE COVE, MALIBU
A pregnant Rene Russo gives Riggs' bachelor pad a much needed woman's touch. The Paradise Cove pier and cliffs can be seen in the background as the couple strolls along the shore. Incidentally, Gibson's Malibu trailer rests in the same area where James Garner, his big-screen *Maverick* costar, parked his mobile home-office on TV's *The Rockford Files*.

## HOW TO GET TO PALOS VERDES

*Take the 405 South to the Harbor Freeway (110) South to San Pedro. Take the Gaffey Street off-ramp and turn left on Gaffey to 25th Street. Turn right on 25th (which becomes Palos Verdes Drive South).*

## DVD ITINERARY: PALOS VERDES

# 10

# SAN PEDRO
# Ports of Cool

It's a Mediterranean town that somehow got grafted onto the city of Los Angeles, and the only place you will see a real fishing culture.

—Author-historian and San Pedro native John Geirland

**MAJOR ROLES:** The Usual Suspects, The Big Lebowski, Face/Off, Chinatown

## BEHIND THE SCENERY

Urban San Pedro might not seem like the first choice for an outdoor day trip, but this harbor locale is blessed with stellar beaches, architectural landmarks, and grassy walks that make it a surprisingly cinematic city with a small-town atmosphere.

In the early 1900s San Pedro won a battle with Long Beach and Santa Monica to become the Port of Los Angeles. During Prohibition, Hollywood had two good reasons to come to the area: offshore bootleg booze and shipyard locations for movies like *King Kong* (1933) and *The Captain Hates the Sea*, with the hard-drinking John Gilbert and Victor McLaglen.

One infamous yacht party, hosted by newspaper publisher William Randolph Hearst, departed from San Pedro on November 15, 1924. Guests included Hearst mistress Marion Davies, Charlie Chaplin, and movie mogul Thomas H. Ince. Ince's mysterious death (murder?) in connection with the cruise has been a matter of speculation ever since. The incident was fictionalized in Peter Bogdanovich's *The Cat's Meow*.

San Pedro's U.S. military base Fort MacArthur appears briefly as a military location in features like *Private Benjamin*, *A Few Good Men*, and *Sgt. Bilko*. Ironically, *Pearl Harbor* used former Fort MacArthur land to re-create the headquarters of the Japanese Navy.

The Vincent Thomas Bridge, perhaps the town's most commanding landmark, towers high above the harbor in adrenaline-fueled scenes in films like

William Friedkin's *To Live and Die in L.A.* (the bridge from which cop-on-the-edge William Petersen base-jumps), both versions of *Gone in Sixty Seconds*, and *Charlie's Angels*, in which it is prominently featured in automotive stunt sequences. And for director William Lustig's self-proclaimed "*French Connection* meets *Frankenstein*" action-horror film *Maniac Cop*, San Pedro's harbor area doubles as a New York waterfront for the climactic chase with Bruce Campbell and the title fiend.

## WHERE TO EXPLORE

### KOREAN FRIENDSHIP BELL

A goodwill gift presented by Korea to the United States in 1976, this bronze bell and pagoda-style belfry makes an unusual meeting place for *The Usual Suspects*. Perched on an expansive grassy knoll in **Angels Gate Park,** with a commanding view of the Pacific, it's the peaceful spot where criminals Kevin Spacey, Kevin Pollak, Gabriel Byrne, Benicio Del Toro, and Stephen Baldwin meet with fence Peter Greene. Location associate Chanel Salzer recalls, "It was a beautiful location for a tense confrontation, offset by a stunning, elevated view of the coast." The Angels Gate Park entrance is where Matt Dillon rescues Thandie Newton in Paul Haggis' *Crash*.

*HOW TO GET TO THE KOREAN FRIENDSHIP BELL Adjacent to Fort MacArthur on South Gaffey Street at 37th Street.*

Harry Medved

An unusual meeting place for *The Usual Suspects*.

## Top Billing: POINT FERMIN LIGHTHOUSE

One of the last remaining Victorian lighthouses on the Pacific Coast was built in Point Fermin Park in 1874. In Phil Alden Robinson's 1940s–era romantic comedy *In the Mood*, fifteen-year-old "Woo Woo Kid" Patrick Dempsey enjoys a romantic stroll beside the lighthouse with older flame Beverly D'Angelo. In the black comedy *Freeway*, Reese Witherspoon and Kiefer Sutherland take a nighttime stroll here. Because the lighthouse is located on the *eastern* edge of the Palos Verdes peninsula at L.A.'s southernmost tip, this is one of the few places in L.A. from where you can see the sun *rising* over the ocean.

*HOW TO GET TO POINT FERMIN PARK Take the Harbor Freeway (110) South to Gaffey Street, its last exit. Follow Gaffey south all the way to its end at Point Fermin. Lighthouse info: 310-241-0684.*

## SUNKEN CITY

A block or so past the Point Fermin Lighthouse is unmarked cliffside terrain known to locals and geologists as Sunken City. Slipping remnants of this neighborhood's long-gone houses and streets can be seen along this terra *un-firma*, which continues to slide due to wave action eroding the bluffs.

This landslide area is not recommended for the casual walker, though film crews often stop by. In *Chinatown*, Jack Nicholson discovers that water is inexplicably dumped into the sea at night as he tails Water and Power official Mulwray (Darrell Zwerling). Walker's Café and the Point Fermin Park are also glimpsed in this sequence. And in Jonathan Demme's World War II–era *Swing Shift*, Goldie Hawn spots Christine Lahti at Kurt Russell's home at a trailer park erected at Sunken City.

Perhaps most memorably, Sunken City was the site for the classic eulogy scene in Joel and Ethan Coen's cult comedy *The Big Lebowski*: as Vietnam vet John Goodman casts Steve Buscemi's cremated remains to the wind, an ocean breeze blows the ashes back into Jeff Bridges' face.

## CABRILLO BEACH

Angelenos flock to this harbor-adjacent beach where you can fish off the jetty or barbecue on the picnic grounds. Nearby you'll find the **Cabrillo Marine Aquarium,** where an open-air touch tank allows kids to get a hands-on look at sea life. The aquarium served as a location for the family comedy *Slappy and the Stinkers*, starring B. D. Wong and Bronson Pinchot. *Museum closed Mondays; 3720 Stephen White Drive; 310-548-7562.*

Cabrillo Beach's **Bathhouse** is the site of director John Woo's bullet-riddled (and dove-laden) showdown between Nicolas Cage and John Travolta in *Face/Off*. The 1932 Mediterranean structure has been renovated and includes changing facilities and a ballroom/banquet room. The Bathhouse played the Hawaiian brain-injury clinic in *50 First Dates*, where Drew Barrymore meets with physician Dan Aykroyd.

*The Bathhouse is located at Stephen M. White Drive and 40th Street; Ball-room rentals: 310-548-7554.*

# WHERE TO EAT

## WALKER'S CAFÉ

A favorite among locals, this small roadhouse can claim the honor of being the southernmost restaurant in Los Angeles. Originally built in 1915 as a turn-around station and maintenance stop for L.A.'s streetcars, the structure was re-modeled as a cafe in 1943. Walker's has made appearances in films ever since.

In Bill Condon's *Gods and Monsters*, Walker's Café is the dive bar where gardener Brendan Fraser and waitress Lolita Davidovich debate the merits of old monster movies. At times a real-life watering hole for motorcycle enthusi-asts, Walker's and adjoining Point Fermin Park are well-cast as a biker mecca in the racing picture *Biker Boyz*, starring Laurence Fishburne, Derek Luke, and Kid Rock. FYI: the specialty of the house is the Bessie Burger, a double cheeseburger with fries. *Call for hours. 700 Paseo del Mar; 310-833-3623.*

# WHERE TO STAY

## THE *QUEEN MARY*, LONG BEACH

One of the most unusual places to stay overnight in Southern California, the *Queen Mary* is a titanic transatlantic ocean liner berthed in San Pedro's neigh-boring harbor city of Long Beach. The staterooms have been turned into com-pact hotel rooms, many of which are said to be haunted. (A daily tour is entitled "Ghosts and Legends of the Queen Mary.") *Love Affair* (with Warren Beatty and Annette Bening), *The Natural, Someone to Watch Over Me, Pearl Harbor,* and *The Aviator* have utilized the ship's hotel rooms, lobbies, corridors, ballrooms, restaurant, and Art Deco bar as filming locations. Disaster movie buffs fondly re-member the *Queen* as the ill-fated liner featured in the pre-topsy-turvy sequences of *The Poseidon Adventure* (1972). *The Queen Mary is moored at the south end of the 710 Long Beach Freeway; www.queenmary.com; 562-435-3511.*

## SAN PEDRO YOUTH HOSTEL

These former army barracks offer economical seaview lodging next to the Friendship Bell. *Go to www.lahostels.org/southbay.htm; 310-831-8109.*

# WHERE TO SEE A MOVIE

## WARNER GRAND THEATER

The first sound-equipped theater in L.A.'s South Bay, this 1,500-seat Art Deco movie palace opened in 1931. It was built by B. Marcus Priteca, who later served as the architect of the Hollywood Pantages Theater. Lavishly appointed with glass chandeliers, marble ticket booth, and a colorful neon marquee, this gem is a highlight of the Old San Pedro downtown district.

With its versatile period design, the Warner Grand often shows up in movies, music videos, and commercials. It's the Nevada movie house at the conclusion of *In the Mood*, where a despondent Patrick Dempsey meets theater usher Kim Myers. For the Ike and Tina Turner biopic *What's Love Got to Do with It*, the Warner Grand doubled as Harlem's famed Apollo Theatre, where Angela Bassett and Laurence Fishburne perform "Fool in Love." It's also the small-town bijou where Kate Bosworth and Josh Duhamel go on a date in *Win a Date with Tad Hamilton!*

The Warner Grand and Sixth Street's historic buildings also played a significant role in *Pearl Harbor*, as troubled nurse Kate Beckinsale and flyboy Josh Hartnett walk out on wartime newsreels and head to a diner down the block.

It wasn't by chance that *Chinatown* screenwriter Robert Towne saw his first movie here; his father ran a lingerie store in the 1925 Arcade Building across the street. Now a legitimate theater with live entertainment during the week, the renovated Warner Grand periodically holds revival/special screenings. *478 West 6th Street; www.warnergrand.org; 310-548-7672.*

## HOW TO GET TO SAN PEDRO

*Take the Harbor Freeway (110) South to its end at Gaffey Street. For more info: www.sanpedrochamber.com.*

## DVD ITINERARY: SAN PEDRO

> *The Usual Suspects*, Korean Friendship Bell, Scenes 17–18
>
> *Biker Boyz*, Walker's Café, Scenes 11–12
>
> *Pearl Harbor*, Warner Grand, Scene 14
>
> *The Big Lebowski*, Sunken City, Scene 20

*Chinatown*'s Jack Nicholson and Perry Lopez
on the cliffs of San Pedro.

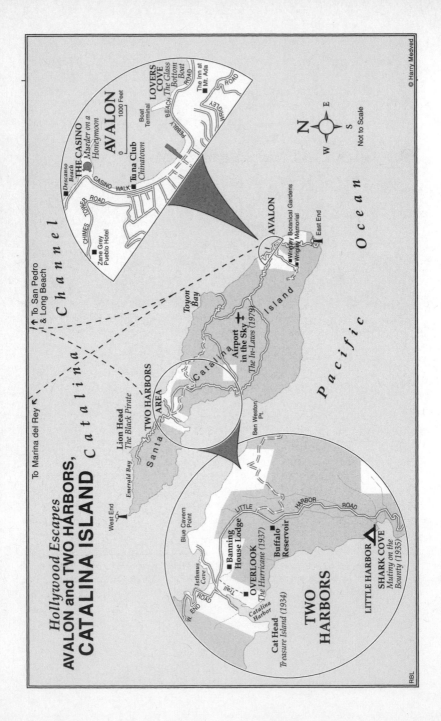

*Hollywood Escapes*
AVALON and TWO HARBORS,
**CATALINA ISLAND** *Catalina*

© Harry Medved

**AVALON**

THE CASINO
*Murder on a Honeymoon*

AVALON

Descanso Beach
Tuna Club
Chinatown
CASINO WALK

CHIMES TOWER ROAD

Zane Grey Pueblo Hotel

0    1000 Feet

LOVERS COVE
BEACH *The Glass Bottom Boat*
PEBBLY BEACH ROAD
The Inn at Mt. Ada
WRIGLEY ROAD

N
W        E
S
Not to Scale

*Channel*

To San Pedro & Long Beach

To Marina del Rey

*Toyon Bay*

AVALON
Wrigley Botanical Gardens
Wrigley Memorial
East End

*Santa Catalina Island*

Airport in the Sky
*The In-Laws (1979)*

Lion Head
*The Black Pirate*

TWO HARBORS AREA

West End

Emerald Bay

Ben Weston Pt.

*Pacific Ocean*

Blue Cavern Point

Banning House Lodge

OVERLOOK
*The Hurricane (1937)*

LITTLE HARBOR ROAD

Buffalo Reservoir

Isthmus Cove

Cat Head
*Treasure Island (1934)*

Catalina Harbor

W. END ROAD

Trail

**TWO HARBORS**

LITTLE HARBOR
SHARK COVE
*Mutiny on the Bounty (1935)*

RBL

# 11

# AVALON, CATALINA
# Casino Royale

> This is the best, and maybe the only place left where you can move to the rhythms of the Southern California of the 1930s.

> —*Charles Moore, from his book* Los Angeles: The City Observed

**MAJOR ROLES:** *The Glass Bottom Boat, The In-Laws* (1979)

## BEHIND THE SCENERY

The Celtic name *Avalon* means "Island of Apples" and springs from Alfred Lord Tennyson's Arthurian legends. According to the stories, Avalon is the island paradise where King Arthur's knights went to heal their wounds. On the island of Catalina, twenty-three miles off the L.A. coast, Avalon is where the kings of Hollywood took a break from production battles, often while the cameras kept rolling on the other side of the island at Two Harbors.

First settled and explored by sheepherders and smugglers in the 1820s, the island was taken over by the Union Army during the Civil War, when soldiers surveyed the land and set up an outpost. Ownership changed hands several times until 1919, when it was sold to Chicago chewing gum magnate William Wrigley Jr. He soon built a mansion with sweeping views for his family.

As part of his plans to lure tourists, Wrigley purchased two steamers for transportation, expanded the island's golf course, held swimming competitions, and constructed The Casino, an Art Deco–Moorish entertainment complex.

"If I can get people to chew my gum, I can get them to come to Catalina," Wrigley told a newspaper reporter. The island became "the Club Med of its time," says local historian Dr. Bill Bushing. "This was back in the day when tourists could not simply hop on a plane for Hawaii, the Caribbean, or Cabo. Because Catalina was the nearest island by boat, all of Hollywood came to play at Avalon." Indeed, the future *Jazz Singer* star Al Jolson (along with Vincent Rose and Buddy de Sylva) wrote the 1920 song "Avalon," an ode to this fabled destination.

Catalina also became the preferred location for underwater photography. For Jaws, the shark's P.O.V. of first victim Susan Backlinie was shot in these waters. "For diving shots, we've got the clearest water in the county. Catalina is a natural film set for shooting underwater habitats," claims Bushing.

## WHERE TO WALK IN AVALON

*While exploring the island by foot or on a bike, you may store your belongings in the lockers at the* **Boat Terminal** *(known to locals as "The Mole"). For guided movie tour info, contact liddel@catalinas.net.*

### Top Billing: THE VIA CASINO WALK
*From the terminal, follow the curve of the bay past the cafés, shops, and Green Pier all the way to the taxi stand. A brick walkway takes you past an arch marked "Via Casino."*

### The Tuna Club
En route to the Casino, you'll pass this 1916 white clapboard building that marks the birthplace of modern big-game sports-fishing in America. Although the landmark is not open to the public, you can get a good look at the exterior of this elite gathering place whose members once included Laurel and Hardy, Cecil B. DeMille, Zane Grey, and Howard Hughes. Film buffs will recall The Tuna Club from a quick but key scene in *Chinatown*: as private eye Jack Nicholson arrives on Catalina Island, he walks past the landmark (called The Albacore Club in the film) to a waiting car. In the background you can clearly see the Casino.

*Proceed to the gleaming white landmark building.*

### The Casino
The Casino never housed a gambling den, as one might expect. The word *casino* actually means "gathering place" or "place of entertainment," which Wrigley's center certainly was. Three years after it opened, the Casino was glimpsed in speedboat footage in the MGM Catalina comedy *Fast Life*. The Casino building is actually comprised of three separate destinations: the Avalon Terrace Ballroom, Avalon Theater, and Catalina Island Museum. The ballroom and theater can be viewed on the one-hour Casino tour, which includes a short film on Catalina history. *Casino tour info: 800-626-1496.*

The circular dance floor in the **Avalon Terrace Ballroom** was once the world's largest. It was once the scene of the crime in *Murder on a Honeymoon*, a 1935 RKO mystery starring James Gleason and Edna May Oliver. But what really put the ballroom on the map were its live radio broadcasts of music from the big bands of Tommy Dorsey, Kay Kyser, and Benny Goodman.

It's a magical experience to see a movie at the **Avalon Theater** (*310-820-8822*), one of Southern California's best-preserved movie palaces still operating as a cinema. Art Deco murals depict an undersea kingdom in the foyer and a fantasy jungle on the auditorium walls. Both were created by Grauman's Chinese Theater artist John Gabriel Beckman in 1929. The lobby still sports its original wood paneling, and lounging sofas. If you're lucky, the theater's organist will play an overture before the lights go down for the main feature. In fact, each June the 1,100-seat Avalon hosts a silent film festival at which you'll be assured of hearing the magical pipe organ.

The opulent Avalon Theater was one of the first designed specifically for sound movies, as evidenced by a vintage sign by the theater's noisy generator that reads DO NOT OPERATE WHILE TALKIES ARE PLAYING. Directors John Ford and Cecil B. DeMille reportedly watched their dailies here while shooting on location. In the mid-sixties, the Avalon Theater hosted premieres of *The Glass Bottom Boat* with Doris Day and Arthur Godfrey, and the Catalina-lensed *Morituri*, starring Yul Brynner, Marlon Brando, and Wally Cox.

Separate from the tour, the **Catalina Island Museum** (*310-510-2414*) features stills from movies shot on the island.

*From the Casino, continue down the coast till you get to Descanso beach.*

### Descanso Beach Club

There's not much of a sandy shore at Avalon, so this public club and cantina is your best bet for sunning, picnicking, or a drink on the beach (though Des-

Harry Medved

The Casino building includes a classic ballroom, movie palace, and museum.

canso may charge you a nominal fee for entry to its sands). The exclusive Hotel St. Catherine, a Hollywood favorite, was once nestled in the tree-lined canyon nearby. The hotel is long gone, however, and the canyon is now open to everyone. Trivia note: A mile away (by boat) is Gallagher's Beach, where Buster Keaton is attacked by cannibals in *The Navigator*.

## WRIGLEY MEMORIAL AND BOTANICAL GARDENS

*This vigorous three-mile round-trip along paved roads is a hiker's best option. An alternative to this long uphill walk: rent a golf cart from Island Rentals: 310-510-1456.*

From the Avalon taxi stand, take Metropole Avenue toward Avalon Canyon. You can stock up on picnic supplies at the grocery store if necessary. Also on Metropole you'll spot the Atwater Building, one-time haunt of seventeen-year-old Catalina resident Norma Jeane Dougherty, wife of a merchant marine stationed on the island during World War II. Norma Jeane would soon find fame under her new name, Marilyn Monroe.

Make a left on Beacon and a right on Sumner. At the five-way intersection, take the middle path, Avalon Canyon Road. The soccer field behind the fire station was the former spring-training area of the Chicago Cubs baseball team, who used the Avalon area for their West Coast spring training camp from 1921 to 1951. Another Wrigley Field favorite traveled west with the Cubs in 1937: radio announcer Ronald Reagan. When not delivering his color commentary on the island, the aspiring actor embarked to the mainland in search of leading roles at the studios. The rest, as they say, is presidential history.

Keep going to the top of the Canyon and you'll find the **Botanical Gardens**, a desert paradise of cactus and succulents planted by Wrigley's widow, Ada. The hillside **Wrigley Memorial**, decorated with beautiful Catalina tile, provides a scenic view of the surrounding mountains and Avalon Canyon. *Garden info: 310-510-2897.*

## WHERE TO STAY

## ZANE GREY PUEBLO HOTEL

Originally the island home of *The Vanishing American* novelist Zane Grey, this 1926 Hopi Indian–inspired landmark is now a cliffside inn overlooking the Casino. It's a fifteen-minute uphill walk from most of the tourist spots to this peaceful getaway. The rooms are decorated with Southwest motifs, and many provide wonderful ocean vistas. Naturally, a collection of Zane Grey novels is available to guests. The Chimes Tower down the street from the hotel sounds a friendly tune hourly. *199 Chimes Tower Road; 800-3-PUEBLO (in CA); 310-510-0966.*

Catalina Island Museum

Paulette Goddard and
Charlie Chaplin play on
Catalina.

## THE INN ON MT. ADA

This luxurious six-bedroom bed-and-breakfast inn is a special spot for a honeymoon or an anniversary getaway, and offers the best view in Avalon. When it was the home of William and Ada Wrigley, its distinguished guests included Rosemary Clooney, and Presidents Woodrow Wilson and Calvin Coolidge. In the 1932 Warner Bros. comedy *You Said a Mouthful*, Ginger Rogers and Joe E. Brown admire the scenery from the inn's veranda. Even if you're not a guest at the hotel you can hike or bike to a picture-postcard viewpoint nearby. *398 Wrigley Terrace Road, www.catalina.com/mtada; 310-510-2030.*

## WHERE TO EAT

## CATALINA COUNTRY CLUB RESTAURANT

This was the former clubhouse of the Chicago Cubs, when radio announcer Ronald Reagan was their official voice. Lunch and dinner specialties include calamari, rack of lamb, and filet mignon. The pub is decorated with classic photos of visiting Hollywood elite like Betty Grable, Mickey Rooney, and Johnny Weissmuller. *1 Country Club Drive; 310-510-7404.*

## AIRPORT-IN-THE-SKY'S BUFFALO SPRINGS STATION

At a 1,602-foot elevation, this circa 1946 airport is the literal high point for many island bus tours. In *The In-Laws*, starring Alan Arkin and Peter Falk, it doubles as a tiny Latin American airport where Arkin dodges bullets by "running serpentine." The airport's Buffalo Springs Station is open for breakfast and lunch and is known for its buffalo burgers and summertime evening barbecues. Hollywood visitors have included Angelina Jolie, Harrison Ford, and Tom Cruise. *On Airport Road; 310-510-2196.*

## HOW TO GET TO AVALON

*There are three companies that will take you to Avalon by boat. FROM SAN PEDRO, LONG BEACH, AND DANA POINT: Catalina Express (www.catalinaexpress.com; 800-481-3470). FROM MARINA DEL REY: Catalina-Marina del Rey Flyer (catalinaferries.com; 888-663-3779). FROM NEWPORT BEACH: Catalina Flyer (www.catalinainfo.com; 949-673-5245). If you embark from San Pedro, you'll get good vantage points of the beautifully landscaped Spanish-style U.S. Coast Guard complex (where Tom Cruise and Demi Moore lunch with Jack Nicholson in* A Few Good Men*).*

## DVD ITINERARY: AVALON, CATALINA

Chinatown, the Casino and the Tuna Club, Scene 7

*The In-Laws* (1979), Airport-in-the-Sky, Scene 16

*The Glass Bottom Boat*, Avalon Bay, Scenes 1 and 11

# 12

# TWO HARBORS, CATALINA
# Hollywood on the Pacific

Movie people came here to film their South Seas adventures . . .
and returned for private adventures of their own.

—Jeannine Pedersen, Catalina Island Museum

**MAJOR ROLES:** *Island of Lost Souls, Mutiny on the Bounty
(1935), MacArthur*

## BEHIND THE SCENERY

While Avalon has long been a favorite tourist and shopping destination, the preferred alternative for outdoor adventurers and working filmmakers is this sleepy outpost at Isthmus Cove. Two Harbors has a rustic charm you can't find anywhere else in Los Angeles County, and it has been the location for dozens of classic seafaring movies from Hollywood's Golden Age. So much filming took place at Two Harbors that in the early 1930s it was nicknamed "The Isthmus Movie Colony."

According to island legend, the first big movie stars to settle in Catalina were a herd of bison, brought over by Paramount Pictures in 1924 for the filming of a Zane Grey Western. Unable to recapture all of the animals after shooting wrapped, the crew literally left the costars out to pasture.

The buffalo scions ended up in the climax of Stanley Kramer's 1972 eco-pacifist epic *Bless the Beasts and Children*, shot at the island's Upper Corral. Hardcore environmentalists debated the removal of the animals, claiming the non-native fauna damaged the landscape. In 2004, a hundred of the herd were transported to a South Dakota Indian reservation.

The Catalina Channel has been the traditional close-to-L.A. refuge for celebrity boaters. Most famously, director John Ford's schooner *Araner* was moored at Isthmus Cove, where his frequent guests included his *Quiet Man* stars John Wayne and Maureen O'Hara. Wayne moored his own boat in the same waters every winter, according to Catalina Express CEO Doug Bombard.

Charlie Chaplin's yacht *The Panacea* was often docked east of Two Harbors at White's Landing in the 1940s, says Chaplin's colleague, actor-producer Norman Lloyd. "One fine day, a bum in a rowboat approached Chaplin's yacht," recalls Lloyd. "Appearing to be down on his luck, this grizzled fellow rows up alongside. He lifts up a basket of shrimp he caught and says, 'Mr. Chaplin, I want you to have this. I'm a great admirer of yours.' The hobo turned out to be Humphrey Bogart, whose boat *The Santana* was anchored nearby."

Unfortunately, Hollywood's visits to these waters have sometimes resulted in celebrity scandals. In 1942, Errol Flynn was charged with statutory rape off Catalina's shores. In 1981, Natalie Wood tragically drowned near the isthmus after apparently slipping off the deck of her boat, the *Splendor*.

## WHERE TO WALK IN TWO HARBORS

### ISTHMUS COVE PIER

Isthmus Cove is the main port of entry for Two Harbors, providing a sultry locale with its colorful pier. Gloria Swanson sashays down this pier in the 1928 silent *Sadie Thompson*, as does Joan Crawford in the 1932 *Sadie* remake, *Rain*. The Isthmus area also appears as a banana republic rendezvous for a gang of criminals in the 1952 film noir *Kansas City Confidential*.

In fantasy films, Two Harbors often plays a mysterious tropical port town. The pier is where Leila Hyams searches for her missing husband in *Island of Lost Souls*, starring Charles Laughton as Dr. Moreau. The pier is also where Robert Armstrong and Helen Mack arrive in "Dakang" in the *King Kong* sequel *Son of Kong*. Beaches and coves around the isthmus play Never-Never Land in the 1924 version of *Peter Pan*, while Little Gibraltar Point (halfway between Two Harbors and Avalon) serves as a fishing village for George Pal's *Atlantis, The Lost Continent*.

### TWO HARBORS DIVE AND RECREATION CENTER

Two Harbors is perhaps best known for the 1935 MGM adaptation of *Mutiny on the Bounty*, starring Clark Gable and Charles Laughton. The Tahitian hideaway, which long-time residents called "Christian's Hut," was located at the foot of the pier, close to the Two Harbors Dive Center. Bicycles, kayaks, scuba and snorkeling rentals, and guided tours are available.

The late *Bounty* stuntman Gilbert Perkins recalled working here for two months alongside some six hundred cast and crew members, "hanging on a yacht arm, out in the middle of the Catalina Channel yelling, 'Land Ho, Sir!'"

*Bounty* director Frank Lloyd, dismayed by Two Harbors' overcast weather, wanted to move the shoot to the controlled conditions of the studio. But MGM studio chief Irving Thalberg, as Perkins recalled, ordered the director to "stay put in Catalina Channel if it takes you six months." MGM also shot extensively in Tahiti and at San Miguel Island, north of Catalina. Sadly,

William Wrigley ordered his engineer Mr. Orval Liddell to tear down the old sets in the 1950s. Liddell later told his family "that was one of the worst things I was ever asked to do."

Fashioned out of eucalyptus trees at Isthmus Harbor for *Rain*, **The Round House** is the one set still standing. It is now employee housing. *Two Harbors Dive Center rental and tour info: 310-510-4272.*

## BLUE CAVERN POINT AND PERDITION CAVE

"For sight-seeing adventure, and just the thrill of diving, Blue Cavern is not to be missed," say *Diving and Snorkeling Guide* authors Dale and Kim Sheckler. "There is color everywhere you turn." This mystical destination on the eastern edge of Isthmus Cove is best explored with a guide or navigated by experienced kayakers or cave-divers.

In the 1955 MGM musical *Jupiter's Darling*, Hannibal's soldiers (including stuntman Loren Janes) take a perilous dive off Blue Cavern Point in pursuit of Esther Williams. They swim through the caves in an attempt to capture her, but they're no match for the female swimming star.

To the east is the Rock Quarry, a spooky cavernous setting for Dr. Moreau's landing in *Island of Lost Souls*. On the hillside to the west is the location of the 1935 MGM romantic comedy *I Live My Life*, starring Joan Crawford as a flighty socialite on a Grecian holiday.

Almost half a century later, Blue Cavern Point was witness to a Hollywood tragedy. It was here in 1981 that Natalie Wood's body was found floating offshore after she was reported missing at Isthmus Cove.

## LION HEAD AND EMERALD BAY

From Isthmus Cove, the West End Trail takes you to this cinematic pirate's paradise marked by a majestic leonine rock formation. The famed swashbuckler Douglas Fairbanks leads a rescue fleet of long galleys here in the early silent Technicolor adventure *The Black Pirate*. He and his men also row west past Little Geiger toward the Boy Scout camp at Emerald Bay. And, according to Catalina Express CEO Doug Bombard, this area was a principal shooting location for the MGM classic *Treasure Island*, starring Jackie Cooper and Wallace Beery.

### Top Billing: CATALINA HARBOR OVERLOOK

Catalina Harbor is the back (or windward) side of Isthmus Cove, hidden behind the commercial boat landing area. This is Catalina at its narrowest, only a quarter-mile strip of land separating the two harbors. The trek to the Catalina Harbor Overlook makes for a scenic afternoon outing.

From Isthmus Cove, walk to the Catalina Harbor marina where you'll pass a war-torn stretch of movie beachfront. The harbor marina is where the venerable *U.S.S. Constitution* invaded the shores of Tripoli in *Old Ironsides*. Across the harbor is Well's Beach, where Gregory Peck in *MacArthur* bids farewell to the Philippines. It's also where Kirk Douglas, Robert Walker Jr., and Nick Adams star in the 1963 Korean War suspense-drama *The Hook*. Near the jetty are the underwater graves of past movie vessels, including the *Ning Po*, an eighteenth-century Chinese junk that appeared in *Old Ironsides* and was sunk here in the 1930s.

After exploring the marina, head uphill to the end of the Catalina Harbor Overlook trail, where a strategically placed bench offers spectacular vistas. In John Ford's 1937 disaster picture *The Hurricane*, this spot is where native boy Jon Hall gets brutally whipped by villain John Carradine. Hall jumps to his freedom from this cliff and later washes ashore at nearby Shark Harbor.

This overlook also offers great views of the distinctive rocky landmark **Catalina Head,** which appears in such films as Harold Lloyd's *The Kid Brother* (1927), *Treasure Island* (1934), and *Wake of the Red Witch*, an East Indies adventure starring John Wayne and Gig Young.

## WHERE TO EAT

### HARBOR REEF RESTAURANT

According to locals, the palm trees shading this laid-back café were planted for the 1935 movie version of *Mutiny on the Bounty*. The back patio bar serves a famous drink called buffalo milk, a decadent concoction of vodka, crème de cacao, crème de banana, kahlua, milk, whipped cream, and nutmeg. This is also the location of Natalie Wood's last meal, as dramatized in Peter Bogdanovich's Australia-lensed TV movie, *The Mystery of Natalie Wood*. 310-510-4215.

## WHERE TO STAY

### BANNING HOUSE LODGE

Two Harbors' only inn was built in 1910 by the Banning Brothers as their hillside residence. It's now a quaint 11-room hotel with impressive views overlooking both Isthmus Cove and Catalina Harbor. Avoid the steep walk from the boat dock to the hillside and arrange to have the lodge's shuttle pick you up. The former poker den on the top floor has the best views. FYI: No TV or phone service is available at the lodge. *www.visittwoharbors.com; 310-510-4228.*

## DETOUR:
## LITTLE HARBOR'S HIDDEN TREASURE

A strenuous and hilly seven-mile bike ride from the Isthmus takes you to the spectacular hideaway known as Little Harbor. This is your best bet for seeing buffalo, since their paddocks and reservoirs parallel the dirt road that leads to this destination.

Little Harbor is the cove where pirates James Mason, Harry Dean Stanton, and Rip Torn terrorize Bull Island settlers in the little-seen 1962 drama *Hero's Island*. It also appears as the coast of Cornwall in the Nathan Juran fantasy *Jack the Giant Killer* and as Jada Pinkett's getaway in *Set It Off*.

There is a sandy beach and a semiprimitive campground with limited facilities at Little Harbor. A surfer's mecca called **Shark Harbor** is farther up the road, but don't be concerned about ocean predators: the beach got its name from the shark fin–shaped rock above the cove. Shark Harbor is also the Tahitian location where Clark Gable bids farewell to his *Bounty* comrades.

Catalina native and historian Mike "Chip" Upton (who worked on some of the films shot in the harbor) can take you on a memorable guided auto adventure through the island's interior to Little Harbor. Kayaking and lunch are available: *www.catalinakayaks.com. Call 310-510-2229 for reservations.*

*HOW TO GET TO LITTLE HARBOR For an alternately demanding and exhilarating ride to Little Harbor, rent a bike from Two Harbors Dive and Recreation Center. Others may prefer to take the pricey bus from Two Harbors during the summertime. Schedules vary, so plan ahead by calling 310-510-2800.*

Harry Medved

**So Cal's most exotic coastline can be
found near Little Harbor.**

## HOW TO GET TO TWO HARBORS

*Catalina Express offers service from San Pedro; see page 66 for ferry info.*

## DVD ITINERARY: TWO HARBORS

*Mutiny on the Bounty* (1935), Shark Harbor, Scene 27

*MacArthur*, Well's Beach, Catalina Harbor, Scene 3

*The Black Pirate*, Lion Head, Scene 16

*Set It Off*, Little Harbor, Scenes 25–26

# 13

# LAGUNA BEACH
# A Sea Star Is Born

Let's swim out there, way, way out. Until we're so tired that we'll just barely be able to get back.

> —*Lana Turner to John Garfield in* The Postman Always
> Rings Twice, *partially shot in Laguna*

**MAJOR ROLES:** *Captain Blood, Now, Voyager, Beaches*

### BEHIND THE SCENERY

An entertainment columnist in the 1950s once wrote, "Film fans around the world remember the location where James Mason leaves Judy Garland in *A Star Is Born*, walks into the setting sun, and drowns himself in the waters of Malibu."

He was half right: the film's setting was the Malibu Colony but the actual location was Laguna Beach, according to the film's production designer Gene

Harry Medved

Treasure Island Beach, named after the Jackie Cooper/Wallace Beery pirate classic shot here in 1934.

Allen. Laguna had previously doubled for Malibu in *The Postman Always Rings Twice* (1946).

Before the movies discovered the Laguna shore, it was the realm of other visual artists: the American Impressionist *plein air* painters. California chronicler Harry Carr described Laguna in the 1920s as "our nearest approach to a Greenwich village . . . largely the permanent residents are happy-go-lucky artists and writers who do not know where their next meal lies." Tourists flocked here to see the bohemians and eccentrics, much like visitors are drawn to Venice Beach today.

Thus the artists helped attract the movie stars. In 1927, "America's Sweetheart" Mary Pickford and Douglas Fairbanks hosted a Pacific Coast Highway ribbon-cutting ceremony in Laguna. Other stars who visited or maintained homes here include Fredric March and Victor Mature.

Laguna's first summer festival of the arts was held shortly after L.A.'s 1932 Olympics, to bring tourists south. One of the highlights was Lolita Perine's "Living Pictures," in which the vaudevillian dressed local residents in costume and seated them behind a frame, thereby creating living, breathing works of art. This exhibit was a hit and later evolved into the Pageant of the Masters, a popular attraction that even today brings crowds to the Laguna Bowl. (Laguna local Bette Davis once posed here as "The Eternal Muse.")

Over the years Laguna's bohemian nature has faded away, as some of the ritziest Southern California resort hotels are located on the area's spectacularly cinematic coastline. The bumper-to-bumper weekend traffic on Pacific Coast Highway, a current problem, may also fade away with the new commuter tram that takes visitors from a central parking lot to Laguna's most popular beaches.

## WHERE TO EXPLORE

*Many of Laguna's beaches are hard to find. For directions call the Visitors Bureau at 949-497-9229 or check out www.lagunabeachinfo.com.*

### HEISLER PARK BEACHES

Heisler is a cliffside park from which you can access several hidden beaches, including **Rockpile Beach**, seen in the Malibu sequences of *A Star Is Born* (1954). Local landmark Bird Rock is visible as James Mason bids farewell to Hollywood for the last time.

### THOUSAND STEPS BEACH

Thousand Steps Beach is a picturesque rocky cove that actually takes little more than two hundred steps to reach. For movie fans it's as close as you can get to the rocky terrain of private **Shell Cove at Three Arch Bay**. This is the scene of the climactic duel between Errol Flynn and Basil Rathbone in *Cap-*

Marc Wanamaker/Bison Archives

Basil Rathbone
and Errol Flynn
prepare for
man-to-man combat
at Laguna's Three
Arch Bay.

*tain Blood* (see box). In the sixties, Timothy Leary and pals allegedly dropped LSD by the waves of Thousand Steps Beach . . . and under those circumstances, two hundred steps might very well seem like one thousand.

## TREASURE ISLAND BEACH
Located below the Montage resort, this exotic cove was named after the 1934 version of *Treasure Island* that was shot here. The beach's **Goff Island** shows up briefly as Devil's Island, the infamous location where Dreyfus (Joseph Schildkraut) is quarantined in *The Life of Emile Zola*. The keyhole arch and rocky cliffs on the beach are also on view in the Maria Montez camp classic *Cobra Woman*, as Jon Hall and Sabu arrive on Cobra Island.

## DETOURS: BEACHES NORTH OF LAGUNA

## CRYSTAL COVE STATE PARK
Before it was turned into a state park, Crystal Cove was home to an array of 1940s beach bungalows, several of which remain on the sands and may be available to rent in the future. One of these appeared in the Garry Marshall tearjerker *Beaches* as the seaside cottage where Bette Midler visits terminally ill, lifelong friend Barbara Hershey to the tune of "Wind Beneath My Wings." Crystal Cove's hills are glimpsed as Guantanamo Bay in Rob Reiner's *A Few Good Men*. *8741 Pacific Coast Highway, at Los Trancos; 949-494-3539.*

## LITTLE CORONA DEL MAR BEACH, NEWPORT BEACH
This exotic little cove is graced with tide pools, palm trees, porous rocks, and small inlets that made Little Corona Del Mar a perfect faraway setting for the 1943 Technicolor extravaganza *White Savage*, starring Maria Montez, Jon

## A "BLOOD"-Y COSTUME DRAMA

According to Warner Bros. production records of September 30, 1935, executive Hal Wallis was not pleased with *Captain Blood* director Michael Curtiz' flamboyant choice of wardrobe for Errol Flynn. "I want the man to look like a pirate, not a mollycoddle," he wrote to the director in one of his blistering, politically incorrect memos. "You have him standing up here dealing with a lot of hard-boiled characters, and you've got him dressed up like a goddamned faggot . . . Let him look a little swash-buckling, for Christ sakes," fumed Wallis.

Nearly seventy years later, Johnny Depp encountered similar studio concerns over his flamboyant makeup, wigs, and costumes when he played Captain Jack Sparrow in *Pirates of the Caribbean: The Curse of the Black Pearl.*

Hall, Turhan Bey, and Sabu. *At the intersection of Ocean Boulevard and Poppy Avenue. No on-site facilities, but there is free street parking.*

## NEWPORT BEACH'S BALBOA ISLAND AND PENINSULA

One of the few places in Southern California where you can take a ferry to an island, this peninsula's past celebrity residents include Shirley Temple, George Burns, and Gracie Allen. The 1905 Balboa Pavilion, which includes the **Harborside Restaurant** (949-673-4633), can be glimpsed in two classic Buster Keaton comedies, *College* and *The Cameraman.* Other parts of the harbor appear in Keaton's silent short *The Boat,* Michael Curtiz's film noir *The Breaking Point,* and Disney's *The Boatniks.* The remodeled Balboa Bay Club (949-645-5000) honors the club's former governor John Wayne with a lounge called "Duke's Place." The surfing spot known as "The Wedge" (where young Kurt Russell surfs in Disney's *Superdad*), and the sands adjacent to the Balboa and Newport Piers are favorite peninsula beaches.

## WHERE TO EAT

### LAS BRISAS

If you plan on dining at this Heisler Park-adjacent Mexican seafood restaurant, be sure to request an outdoor table. According to a Warner Bros. daily production report (April 8, 1942), this is the South American restaurant where Bette

Davis intrigues fellow tourist Paul Henreid in *Now, Voyager*. *361 Cliff Drive at Pacific Coast Highway; 949-497-5434.*

## THE STAND

A no-frills vegan takeout stand, this is a hangout for the last survivors of Laguna's bohemian crowd. The café, across the road from Thalia Beach, serves up great veggie burgers and veggie burritos. *238 Thalia Avenue; open 7 a.m.–7 p.m.; 949-494-8101.*

## WHERE TO STAY

### HOTEL LAGUNA

The first hotel in Laguna was also its first substantial business building. The white stucco and red-tiled Spanish colonial structure was built in 1930 with sixty-five guest rooms, many with views of the hotel's private beach. Bogart and Bacall are rumored to have been frequent guests. *425 South Coast Highway; www.hotellaguna.com; 949-494-1151.*

### MONTAGE RESORT

In the California travelogue-comedy *The Long, Long, Trailer*, Desi Arnaz and Lucille Ball end up living in a colorful trailer park fantasyland partially shot at Treasure Island Trailer Park, where the luxurious Montage Resort stands today. The resort has preserved 130 palms, including what the hotel calls the "Lucy and Desi Trees" near its Studio Restaurant. *30801 S. Coast Highway; www.montagelagunabeach.com; 949-715-6000.*

## HOW TO GET TO LAGUNA

*Take the 405 approximately 50 miles south of L.A. to Highway 133/Laguna Canyon. Go 8.3 miles to the ocean.*

## DVD ITINERARY: LAGUNA BEACH

*Beaches*, Crystal Cove State Park, Scenes 8–9

*Now, Voyager*, Las Brisas and Heisler Park, Scenes 10–11

*A Star Is Born: Special Edition* (1954), Heisler Park's Rockpile Beach, Scenes 50–51

# 14

# LA JOLLA
# Jewel of the Coast

With craggy bluffs, hidden caves, and crystal waters, La Jolla was the ideal choice for Southern California's first natural location for a dramatic film.

—*San Diego film historian Gregory L. Williams*

**MAJOR ROLES:** *The Stunt Man, Top Gun*

## BEHIND THE SCENERY

Pronounced *La HOY-a* (which tourist brochures claim is Spanish for "the Jewel"), this San Diego North County town earns a special footnote in California film history: the cliffside retreat allegedly provided the state's first outdoor location for a dramatic film. It was in 1907 that a Chicago film company reportedly used White Lady Cave for the outdoor scenes in *The Count of Monte Cristo*.

La Jolla soon became a frequent substitute for exotic locales in silent titles like *Tides of Passion* (1925). In later years, Hollywood came to North County for its military base, Camp Pendleton, seen in war movies such as *Guadalcanal Diary*, *The Sands of Iwo Jima*, *Heartbreak Ridge*, and *Top Gun* (where the volleyball sequence was filmed).

## WHERE TO EXPLORE

### THE COVES
### *Top Billing:* CHILDREN'S POOL (CASA BEACH)
This popular little beach is protected by a crescent-shaped breakwater/sea wall built in 1931. As a result, harbor seals currently enjoy the sand and sun in a safe haven. In the 1962 Wonderful World of Disney movie *Sammy, The Way Out Seal*, Billy Mumy and his brother misguidedly take home a local seal that they find nearby at one of La Jolla's coves.

Richard Rush's *The Stunt Man* features the environs in a few key scenes: Children's Pool is a World War I European battlefield with dozens of slaugh-

Greg Tucker

Children's Pool
is featured
prominently in
*The Stunt Man* with
Peter O'Toole.

tered extras; fugitive Steve Railsback rescues seemingly helpless Barbara Hershey from drowning in the cove; later, director Peter O'Toole and Railsback have a crucial discussion on a crane-suspended platform that swings them high above the beach over to the Hotel del Coronado (in reality, the Del is located about half an hour away from Children's Pool).

And in Nick Castle's *Mr. Wrong*, Ellen DeGeneres and title mismatch Bill Pullman take a late-night walk along the Children's Pool sea wall.

*HOW TO GET TO CHILDREN'S POOL South of La Jolla Cove at Coast Boulevard and Jenner Street.*

## THE CAVES
### THE CAVE STORE/SUNNY JIM CAVE

Enter the tunnel here and its "staircase" of 145 steps carved into the sea rock will take you from street level down to Sunny Jim Cave at the ocean's edge. The tunnel, begun in 1902, took laborers two years to complete using picks and shovels.

*The Wizard of Oz* author and Coronado resident L. Frank Baum supposedly named the cave "Sunny Jim" because of the rocks' silhouetted resemblance to a breakfast cereal mascot of the time. According to the cave store, "movie studios used the cave for many settings." CAUTION: *This cave is not for the claustrophobic, and the stairs are steep. www.cavestore.com; 1325 Cave Street; 858-459-0746.*

### SEA CAVE KAYAK TOURS

The seven sea caves of La Jolla are part of an underwater sea preserve that is hard to reach for most visitors, so the best way to see them is via guided kayak tours. Highlights include the kelp forest, dolphins, and seals. La Jolla Kayak can take you to the White Lady Cave, purported location of the historic silent version of *The Count of Monte Cristo. No experience necessary. www.lajollakayak.com; 858-459-1114.*

## THE PINES
### TORREY PINES STATE RESERVE

You'll find a surprising combination of rocky tide pools, crumbling sandstone, and cliff-hugging, gnarled pine trees nestled within this small coastal gem. Torrey Pines are the rarest pine trees in America; here their numbers extend right down to the sea. The best ways to see the reserve's natural magic are via hiking paths like Guy Fleming Trail. The Nicolas Roeg mystery *Cold Heaven* features troubled Theresa Russell scrambling among the preserve cliffs.

South of the reserve and north of Torrey Pines City Beach you will find the **Torrey Pines Gliderport** (where daredevil fliers leap off the sandstone cliffs). Chris Farley did just that in Christopher Guest's comedy *Almost Heroes*. *Torrey Pines Reserve info: www.torreypines.org; 858-755-2063.*

## THE PONIES
### DEL MAR RACETRACK

Del Mar has been popular with Hollywood ever since Bing Crosby and Pat O'Brien opened the racetrack back in 1937. Jimmy Durante, Clark Gable, Al Jolson, Ava Gardner, and W. C. Fields became track regulars. Mickey Rooney, another habitue, came here in 1938 to film *Stablemates* with Wallace Beery. Crosby shot *Sing You Sinners* here with Fred MacMurray and Donald O'Connor. Decades later, director Stephen Frears nicely captured Del Mar's sun-drenched 1940s feel in *The Grifters*, though he filmed the "La Jolla Downs" sequences at an Arizona racetrack. *858-792-4252.*

## WHERE TO EAT

### BROCKTON VILLA RESTAURANT

A beautiful 1894 cottage overlooking La Jolla Cove and the Pacific, the Brockton Villa offers traditional fare at moderate prices. Open for breakfast, lunch, and dinner. Arrive early to get a veranda table with an ocean view. *1235 Coast Boulevard; 858-454-7393.*

## WHERE TO STAY

### LA VALENCIA HOTEL

Because of its rosy hue, this 1926 Spanish-Mediterranean luxury hotel overlooking La Jolla Cove is known affectionately to locals as "The Pink Lady." With its tropical terraced patio for al fresco dining and drinks, La Valencia claims such famous visitors as Chaplin, Garbo, and Groucho. It was preferred lodging for actors working at the nearby La Jolla Playhouse, cofounded by the town's native son Gregory Peck. According to the *San Diego Union-Tribune* critic Welton Jones, "Off-duty film folk loved heading South to La Valencia . . . widely known as a trysting nook for sexual adventures." *1132 Prospect Street; 858-454-0771.*

## LA JOLLA COVE SUITES AND SHELL BEACH MOTEL

These two moderately priced lodging facilities, owned by the same company, offer the closest accommodations to the coves. *1155 Coast Boulevard; www.lajollacove.com; 858-459-2621.*

## ON THE ROAD:
## THE DOUBLE-BARRELED *NAKED GUN* REACTORS

As visitors drive to San Diego from Los Angeles on Interstate 5, they'll see a power plant that resembles a giant pair of breasts. For local surfers, these two landmarks—part of the **San Onofre Nuclear Generating Station**—help identify a great surfing beach known as "The Trestles." For moviegoers, the dual-domed station serves as a quick Southern California sight gag in *The Naked Gun*. Staring out the car window at the station's two half-spheres, Leslie Nielsen (as Sgt. Frank Drebin) reminisces about his ex-wife to partner George Kennedy and muses, "Everywhere I look, something reminds me of her . . ."

## ON THE ROAD:
## OCEANSIDE'S CALIFORNIA WELCOME CENTER

This is a worthwhile stop for maps and information on the way to La Jolla and San Diego. Film buff Mike Francis, the center's director of tourism, can point you to Oceanside's movie landmarks, which include *Bring It On's* Florida-set amphitheater (where Kirsten Dunst and fellow cheerleaders perform next to the Oceanside pier), the San Luis Rey Mission (from the late 1950s Disney TV show *Zorro*, with Guy Williams) and the Victorian *Top Gun* house where motorcycle-riding Tom Cruise visits Kelly McGillis (at the corner of Seagaze and Pacific, site of a proposed seaside resort). *928 N. Coast Highway; open 9 a.m.–5 p.m. daily; 760-721-1101.*

## HOW TO GET TO LA JOLLA

*From L.A., take I-5 South toward San Diego. Take the La Jolla Village Drive West exit and turn right. Turn left on Torrey Pines Road and right on Prospect. Follow the signs to La Jolla Village.*

## DVD ITINERARY: LA JOLLA

*Bring It On*, Oceanside, Scenes 18–19

*Top Gun*, Oceanside, Scene 15

*The Stunt Man*, Children's Pool, Scenes 5–8

← To Laguna Beach & L.A.

Orange Co.
San Diego Co.

San Onofre

Oceanside
*Bring It On*

Mission San Luis Rey
Disney's *Zorro* (TV)

76

*Pacific*

DEL MAR
Racetrack

TORREY PINES
STAT E RESERVE
*Almost Heroes*

La Jolla Caves:
Birthplace of Location
Filming in So. Cal.?
(1907)

LA JOLLA COVE
CHILDREN'S POOL
*The Stunt Man*

LA
JOLLA

5

Pacific Beach
Crystal Pier

Ocean Beach
*Almost Famous*

Sea
World

Mission Bay
*Freaky Friday (1976)*

SAN
DIEGO

Sunset Cliffs

To Anza-Borrego &
Imperial Sand Dunes →

8

The Embarcadero

*San Diego Bay*

BALBOA PARK
*Citizen Kane's Xanadu*

■ San Diego Zoo
■ Old Globe Theater
■ Spreckels Organ Pavilion

Star of India

Point Loma
Tidepools ■

CABRILLO NATIONAL
MONUMENT

Lighthouse
*Antwone Fisher*

CORONADO
ISLAND

Kansas City
BBQ
*Top Gun*

GASLAMP
QUARTER

5

HOTEL DEL CORONADO
*Some Like It Hot, The Stunt Man*

75

Coronado
Bridge

*Ocean*

Silver Strand State Beach
*MacArthur*

75

U. S. A.
MEXICO

Tijuana

© Harry Medved
RBL

Rosarito ■ Fox Baja Studios

1-D

*Hollywood Escapes*
**SAN DIEGO
BEACHES**

N
W · E
S

Not to Scale

# 15

# SAN DIEGO
## City by the Sea

I heard the best of the best were going to be back here.

—*Kelly McGillis to Tom Cruise, at San Diego's Kansas City Barbecue in* Top Gun *(1986)*

**MAJOR ROLES:** *Top Gun, Traffic, Almost Famous*

### BEHIND THE SCENERY

From the early days, San Diego's hospitable climate attracted not only tourists and settlers but eventually moviemakers seeking fresh locations. Since 1907, hundreds of movies have been filmed in San Diego.

The city first gained international prominence in the 1910s with the Panama-California Exposition, a world's fair that celebrated the completion of the Panama Canal. This expo helped create a fervor for Spanish Colonial Revival architecture, which was showcased in San Diego's Balboa Park. These unique buildings and the city's proximity to Mexico made San Diego appealing to Hollywood.

Mission Bay was also a scenic attraction for the movies. It appears as a backdrop for the Douglas Sirk flight saga *The Tarnished Angels*, with Rock Hudson and Dorothy Malone; *The Big Mouth* starring Jerry Lewis; and the original *Freaky Friday*, which features a waterskiing climax in the bay, with Jodie Foster and Barbara Harris. In *Tentacles*, an Italian *Jaws* rip-off, John Huston, Bo Hopkins, and Sea World's team of heroic killer whales team up to destroy killer octopi lurking off Solana Beach. In *Traffic*, Don Cheadle and Luis Guzman surveil unsuspecting Catherine Zeta-Jones at Mission Bay's Bonita Cove Playground.

John DeBello's 1978 camp classic *Attack of the Killer Tomatoes* was filmed all over San Diego and was nominated as "The Worst Vegetable Movie Ever Made" in *The Golden Turkey Awards*. This low-budget feature and its sequels provided early roles for future star George Clooney, politicians Gary Condit and Steve Peace, and Soundgarden/Pearl Jam drummer Matt Cameron (who can be heard singing the first *Tomatoes* movie's theme song, "Puberty Love," at Qualcomm Stadium).

## WHERE TO EXPLORE

### Top Billing: BALBOA PARK

Like New York's Central Park, San Diego's Balboa Park is the verdant heart of the city. Its thousand acres incorporate natural beauty, lush tropical terracing, and a variety of museums housed in Spanish Colonial architecture. The park is huge, so bring your walking shoes and be prepared to spend the better part of the day on its grounds.

Balboa Park makes an appearance as part of Charles Foster Kane's private Florida estate *Xanadu* in Orson Welles' *Citizen Kane*. Seen in the film's "News on the March" footage, shots of the park's florid structures, statuary, and lily ponds were used to create the eccentric millionaire's palatial hideaway.

In the 1939 disaster picture *The Rains Came*, starring Tyrone Power and Myrna Loy, Balboa Park buildings play ornate Indian palaces ultimately destroyed by flood waters.

With its florid churrigueresque design, the **California Tower** and its plaza were the site of many banana republic gatherings in such films as *The Dictator* (starring Wallace Reid), *The Americano* (with Douglas Fairbanks), and *The Magnificent Fraud* (with Akim Tamiroff and Lloyd Nolan).

Perhaps Balboa Park's most romantic spot is the garden in the 1915 **Botanical Building.** Containing over two thousand permanent tropical plants, it's one of the world's largest wood lath structures. This is where Catherine Zeta-Jones meets with hitman Frankie Flowers (played by Clifton Collins Jr.) to plot the death of her husband's enemy in *Traffic*.

Other park highlights include the **San Diego Historical Society, Spreckels Organ Pavillion**, and the **San Diego Zoo**. The park's ecclectic Latin/Italian restaurant, **Prado** (619-557-9441), serves lunch and dinner. Outdoor patio seating is available.

Spending an evening at the **Old Globe Theatre** is a perfect way to end your day at Balboa Park. Home to one of the nation's top five regional drama companies, the faithful replica of England's famed outdoor theater broke ground in 1935 and opened with fifty-minute versions of Shakespeare's works. It soon became a favorite destination for Hollywood actors to preview new plays. Actors who strode the boards at the Old Globe include Peter Ustinov, Jeff Daniels, John Goodman, David Ogden Stiers, Jerry Lewis, Kathy Najimy, and Swoosie Kurtz. *Box Office: 619-239-2255.*

*HOW TO GET TO BALBOA PARK Take I-5 South to the Pershing Dr. off-ramp. Follow the signs to "Zoo/Museums." General park info: www.balboapark.org; 619-239-0512.*

### THE EMBARCADERO

This is the perfect place to stretch your legs. The path goes all the way from Shelter Island to the Embarcadero Marina Park North, a favorite picnic spot

San Diego's Balboa Park plays *Citizen Kane*'s Xanadu.

behind Seaport Village. This is where Derek Luke and Joy Bryant stroll in Denzel Washington's *Antwone Fisher*. Tom Cruise's nighttime waterfront motorcycle ride in *Top Gun* also takes place on the Embarcadero (driving from Harbor Drive and Laurel Street past the *Star of India* sailing ship).

## GASLAMP QUARTER

The Gaslamp Quarter is San Diego's nightlife center, covering several blocks of renovated nineteenth-century buildings. On any given night its movie theaters, restaurant patios, and jazz clubs are packed with visitors. Decades before its rebirth, however, a different kind of nightlife ruled this area. To get an idea of how low the district had sunk by the late 1970s, see Paul Schrader's *Hardcore*. Since L.A.'s skid row and Hollywood Boulevard weren't sleazy enough for him, Schrader chose the Gaslamp Quarter for his tale of George C. Scott's descent into the dark side of adult entertainment. *www.gaslamp.org*.

## WHERE TO EAT

## KANSAS CITY BARBECUE

Known to tourists as "The Top Gun Café," this honky-tonk café and bar is the all-American diner where Tom Cruise, Kelly McGillis, Meg Ryan, and Anthony Edwards belt out a rendition of Jerry Lee Lewis' "Great Balls of Fire." The rickety piano and jukebox are still there.

The eatery specializes in hearty fare like ribs, chicken, and beef sandwiches dripping with barbecue sauce. Its walls are festooned with lots of *Top Gun*, U.S. Navy, and San Diego Police Department memorabilia, as well as keepsakes from Kansas-area colleges. *610 West Market Street at Harbor Drive; 619-231-9680.*

## SUN CAFÉ

This family-owned diner is located in a vintage building in the Gaslamp Quarter. On its menu you'll find selections like hot cakes, chicken-fried steak, and Chinese food. Sun's main claim to cinematic fame stems from an early scene in Cameron Crowe's autobiographical comedy *Almost Famous*. It's here that aspiring writer Patrick Fugit gets an assignment from rock critic and *Creem* magazine editor Lester Bangs, played by Philip Seymour Hoffman. *Cash only; 421 Market Street between Fourth and Fifth Streets; Open 7:00 a.m.–2:30 p.m., closed Thursday; 619-239-9950.*

## WHERE TO STAY

### BALBOA PARK INN

Located within walking distance of Balboa Park, this quiet 1915 bed-and-breakfast is a favorite of actors coming to town to perform at the Old Globe Theatre. *3402 Park Blvd.; 800-938-8181.*

### HORTON GRAND HOTEL

An 1886 Victorian landmark in the heart of the Gaslamp Quarter, the Horton was home to Wyatt Earp, who stayed here for most of the seven years he lived in San Diego. Other past guests include George Raft, Lou Costello, and Babe Ruth. *311 Island Avenue; 619-544-1886.*

## A BORDER CROSSING DETOUR: FOX STUDIOS BAJA, ROSARITO

Okay, so this destination is not a famous location in Southern California's great outdoors. It is, however, a famous Baja, California movie location. Like its sister Mexican city of Tijuana, Rosarito is a classic old-time movie star getaway. The seaside beach town was noted as a quickie wedding destination in the 1966 camp classic *The Oscar*, with Stephen Boyd and Elke Sommer.

Thirty years later, Fox and James Cameron built a forty-acre studio near Rosarito for the filming of *Titanic*. According to Fox Baja, 95 percent of Cameron's epic was filmed here. Tourists flock to see exhibits of seven *Titanic* sets, including the first-class corridor, staterooms, the fireplace in Rose's cabin, and the Palm Court Café. The studio complex includes a small theme park called Foxploration and the *Master and Commander* ship, which fans can climb aboard. Other films with sequences shot at Fox Baja include *The Deep Blue Sea, Pearl Harbor,* and the James Bond adventure *Tomorrow Never Dies.*

When stars like *Titanic*'s Kate Winslet come to work and play in Baja, they often stay at Tecate's luxurious **Rancho La Puerta**, reputed to be North America's first fitness resort destination. "Whenever actors needed to get into shape for their roles, the studios sent them to us," says eighty-three-year-old founder Deborah Szekely. Indeed, the inland mountain retreat has hosted an impressive roll call of Hollywood players, including Burt Lancaster, Charlton Heston, Kim Novak, Gillian Anderson, Alicia Silverstone, and Barbra Streisand. *www.rancholapuerta.com; 800-443-7565.*

*HOW TO GET TO FOX BAJA 45 minutes south of San Diego; from the U.S., www.foxbaja.com; 866-369-2252 for specific hours.*

## PRE-TRIP READING

*Filming San Diego: Hollywood's Backlot, 1898–2002* by Gregory L. Williams is a thorough overview of movies shot in the area, with rare photographs from the collection of the San Diego Historical Society. *To order, e-mail gannj@hotmail.com.*

## HOW TO GET TO SAN DIEGO

*Take the I-5 South and follow the signs to San Diego. To avoid the highway traffic, consider the convenient option of taking the toll roads (www.thetollroads.com) or the train (www.amtrak.com); call 1-800-AMTRAK.*

## DVD INITNERARY: SAN DIEGO

*Top Gun: Special Collector's Edition,* Kansas City Barbecue, Scenes 10 and 16

*Almost Famous,* The Sun Café, Scene 3

*Citizen Kane,* Balboa Park, Scene 2

# 16

# CORONADO ISLAND
## *Some Like It Hot*-el

> If there were such a thing as a masterpiece of location, the Hotel del Coronado as it is used in *The Stunt Man* would be it.

—The late New Yorker *magazine film critic Pauline Kael*

**MAJOR ROLES:** *Some Like It Hot, The Stunt Man*

### BEHIND THE SCENERY

Coronado calls itself the "Crown City," taking its cue from the royal name of its Spanish-explorer namesake. Not a true island, Coronado is physically connected to San Diego by a strip of land called the Silver Strand and the Coronado Bridge.

This beach city's jewel is the Hotel del Coronado, a glorious Victorian resort from the 1880s that's reminiscent of the locale in the Christopher Reeve/Jane Seymour time-travel movie *Somewhere in Time*. Although the movie was shot at another grand hotel from the same era (on Michigan's Mackinac Island), the screenplay was based on Richard Matheson's *Bid Time Return*, a novel set entirely at The Del.

The 1899 Rand-McNally guide *Where To Go In California* claimed that "The Hotel del Coronado is the largest resort hotel in the world . . . this fairyland represents a perpetual advertisement for California." That quote proved to be prophetic as over the years the hotel attracted thousands of guests. "It's like you've gone back one hundred years. I just love the atmosphere of the place," author Ray Bradbury told *Westways Magazine*.

*USA Today* travel editor Laura Bly says The Del has achieved icon status due to Marilyn Monroe's romp along its beach in the 1959 classic *Some Like It Hot*. Monroe and her then-husband, playwright Arthur Miller, stayed in their own private Hotel Del bungalow.

A cult favorite filmed extensively at the Hotel Del is Richard Rush's existential *The Stunt Man*, starring Peter O'Toole, Steve Railsback, and Barbara Hershey. Many people in real life have remarked that the Del looks just like a

Hotel del Coronado

---

Monroe entrances the crowd
at the Hotel Del.

movie set, and that's exactly how director Rush used it: the hotel is the prime shooting location for the film being directed by the monomaniacal auteur played by O'Toole. A false red roof turret was created and destroyed for the World War I action scenes.

The resort has been a meeting place for many on-screen couples, including Rudolph Valentino and Vera Sisson in *The Married Virgin*, Warren Beatty and Goldie Hawn in *$ (Dollars)*, Susan Sarandon and James Coburn and Shirley MacLaine and Stephen Collins in *Loving Couples*.

One skeleton in the Coronado cinematic closet is the horror film *Wicked, Wicked*. In this 1973 curio filmed extensively at The Del, a serial killer terrorizes the resort's guests in split-screen "Duo-Vision."

## WHERE TO EXPLORE

### CORONADO BEACH

1.5 miles long and 300 yards wide, Coronado Beach is a great place for strolling, biking, swimming, and wave boarding. In *Some Like It Hot*, this is where millionaire poseur Tony Curtis deliberately trips Marilyn Monroe while she chases a volleyball. Nearby Silver Strand Beach, just south of Coronado Beach, is the landing area where Gregory Peck makes his triumphant return in *MacArthur*.

## GUEST APPEARANCES

Since opening its doors, the Hotel Del has attracted a virtual who's who of American history. Inventor Thomas Edison stayed here, as have ten U.S. presidents. Literary guests include Henry James and *The Wizard of Oz* author L. Frank Baum, who made Coronado his winter home while working on three Oz volumes. Liberace was discovered while playing piano at the Del, and Lucille Ball and Desi Arnaz honed their comedy routine here during a lengthy stay in the 1950s, according to hotel historian Christine Donovan.

Famed Hotel Del visitors from the silver screen include James Cagney, James Stewart, Ginger Rogers, Bette Davis, Gary Cooper, Lana Turner, Clark Gable, Rita Hayworth, Joan Crawford, Walt Disney, Groucho and Harpo Marx, Cary Grant, Katharine Hepburn, Kirk Douglas, Spencer Tracy, Doris Day, Kevin Costner, Annette Bening, Jodie Foster, Jack Nicholson, Diane Keaton, Madonna, Brad Pitt, Bruce Willis, Whoopi Goldberg, Sharon Stone, Michelle Pfeiffer, Harvey Keitel, and Barbra Streisand.

## WHERE TO EAT

### HOTEL DEL CORONADO RESTAURANTS

The hotel's most elegant eatery is **Prince of Wales Restaurant,** which takes its name from The Del's famous guest of 1920. The future King Edward VIII abdicated his throne for "the woman he loved," Mrs. Wallis Simpson. Hotel legend has it that this famed couple may have met here at a celebration for the prince held in the resort's **Crown Room** dining area.

A less highbrow occasion takes place in the hotel's adjacent **Sheerwater Restaurant** in the comedy *K-9:* detective Jim Belushi lunches with his iced tea–sipping police dog and argues with an arrogant maitre d'. And *My Blue Heaven*'s Rick Moranis and Joan Cusack dance the merengue on the hotel's **Sun Deck Bar and Grill.** *619-522-8490.*

### CORONADO BOAT HOUSE 1887

Known as "the diminutive Del," this restaurant was the hotel's original Victorian boathouse, although it is no longer affiliated with The Del. You can dine on macadamia halibut and other specialties while overlooking Glorietta Bay, seen in the memorable conclusion of *Some Like It Hot*. This is where Marilyn Monroe jumps into a skiff with Tony Curtis and Jack Lemmon and aging playboy Joe E. Brown. Upon learning that prospective fiancée Lemmon is a man, Brown then utters the film's immortal last line, "Well, nobody's perfect!" *Open for dinner only, reservations are recommended; 1701 Strand Way; 619-435-0155.*

## WHERE TO STAY

### HOTEL DEL CORONADO

From the moment you arrive at the Hotel Del's porch—where the rocking chair–bound Florida millionaires inspect newcomers in *Some Like It Hot*—you'll feel like you've entered another era. The hotel is like a living museum, from its ornate cage elevator to its spectacularly landscaped grounds. Special perk: guests enjoy free in-room showings of movies shot at The Del. *1500 Orange Avenue; www.hoteldel.com; 619-435-6611 or 800-HOTEL-DEL.*

### EL CORDOVA HOTEL

One block away from the Hotel Del is this budget-conscious alternative, originally built as a home for one of The Del's original owners in 1902 and converted into hotel apartments in 1930. *1351 Orange Avenue; www.elcordovahotel.com; 800-229-2032.*

## LOCATION BLOOPER: SOME LIKE IT HOT

In *Some Like It Hot*, Tony Curtis and Marilyn Monroe are supposed to be flirting in front of the flat Florida coastline, but across the ocean and rising up behind Monroe and Curtis is an improbably high promontory: none other than Point Loma on the other side of San Diego Bay!

## DETOUR: POINT LOMA

Separated by a twenty-five-minute car trip, Coronado Island and Point Loma face each other on opposite sides of San Diego Bay. One could easily spend a day exploring these two dramatic locales.

The old Spanish lighthouse at the end of Point Loma is now part of **Cabrillo National Monument** (619-557-5450). This is where Errol Flynn and Ralph Bellamy attempt to rescue pilot Fred MacMurray after he crashes his plane in *Dive Bomber*. In *Antwone Fisher*, it's a suitably quiet spot where Derek Luke and Joy Bryant share secrets and admire the view of San Diego Bay. According to location manager Molly Allen, director "Denzel Washington felt this was the perfect spot for a moment of honesty and a romantic rendezvous for a navy man."

Adventurers will want to take the road west of the Point Loma light-house down to the tidepools, where they can explore the marine life among the rocks. Also located below the lighthouse is the off-limits Coast Guard Station. Behind these fences are 1920s bungalows where pilot Tom Cruise visits the home of commanding officer Tom Skerritt in *Top Gun*.

## HOW TO GET TO CORONADO ISLAND

*Take I-5 South through the city of San Diego. Head west on the Coronado Bridge (Highway 75) to the island. Make a left on Orange Avenue. The Hotel Del is 1.5 miles on the right.*

Hotel del Coronado Archives

*The Stuntman* leaps from the Hotel Del's signature turret.

## DVD ITINERARY: CORONADO ISLAND

*Some Like It Hot*, Hotel Del, Scenes 8–9

*The Stunt Man*, Hotel Del, Scenes 9, 11–13

*Antwone Fisher*, Cabrillo National Monument, Scene 18

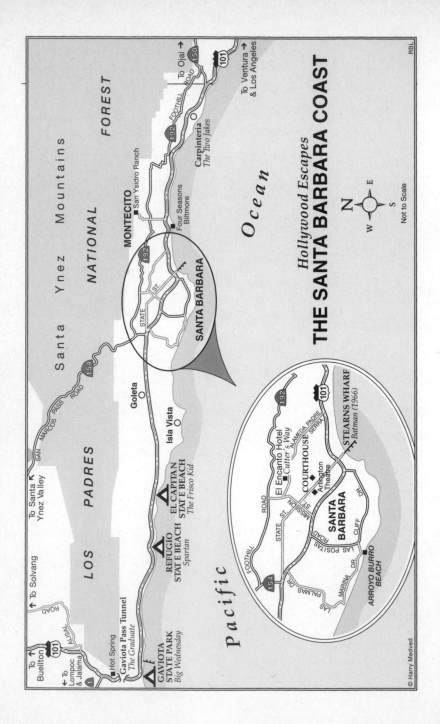

*Hollywood Escapes*

# THE SANTA BARBARA COAST

N

Not to Scale

*Pacific*

*Ocean*

GAVIOTA
STATE PARK
*Big Wednesday*

Gaviota Pass Tunnel
*The Graduate*

Hot Spring

To Buellton

To Lompoc
& Jalama

To Solvang

To Santa
Ynez Valley

ALISAL ROAD

SAN MARCOS PASS ROAD

LOS     PADRES

REFUGIO
STATE BEACH
*Spartan*

EL CAPITAN
STATE BEACH
*The Frisco Kid*

Isla Vista

Goleta

Santa    Ynez    Mountains

NATIONAL     FOREST

SANTA BARBARA

STATE ST.

STATE

MONTECITO

Four Seasons
Biltmore

San Ysidro Ranch

Carpinteria
*The Two Lakes*

FOOTHILL ROAD

To Ojai

To Ventura →
& Los Angeles

RBL

STEARNS WHARF
*Batman (1966)*

El Encanto Hotel
*Cutter's Way*

COURTHOUSE

Arlington
Theatre

SANTA
BARBARA

ARROYO BURRO
BEACH

FOOTHILL ROAD

STATE ST.

MISSION ST.

ALAMEDA PADRE SERRA

LAS POSITAS ROAD

LAS PALMAS DR.

MARINA DR.

CLIFF DR.

© Harry Medved

# 17

# SANTA BARBARA
# The Spanish Colonial Riviera

Omigod, it's so beautiful . . . there's millions of stars there!

—*Sarah Jessica Parker, commenting on Santa Barbara to Steve Martin in* L.A. Story *(1991)*

**MAJOR ROLES:** *Cutter's Way, Big Wednesday, My Favorite Martian, Batman* (1966)

## BEHIND THE SCENERY

Santa Barbara gave Hollywood a run for its money in the 1910s, when the town's branch of American Film Manufacturing Company (nicknamed "Flying A") became a regional production center. According to historian Stephen Lawton, Santa Barbara's stock company at the time included actresses Mary Miles Minter and Constance and Joan Bennett, and directors Victor Fleming, Frank Borzage, and Alan Dwan. Eventually, Hollywood offered better opportunities, and the Santa Barbara studio was bankrupt by 1920.

Unable to resist the beautiful two-hour drive to Santa Barbara, stars didn't stay away from the area for long. In fact, many players invested in local real estate: Charlie Chaplin and Roscoe "Fatty" Arbuckle helped build the Montecito Inn. Today, celebrities like John Travolta, Brad Pitt, Oprah Winfrey, Rob Lowe, Paul Walker, and Jeff Bridges are Santa Barbara locals.

Bridges in fact starred in perhaps the best Santa Barbara-based movie, Ivan Passer's thriller *Cutter's Way*, costarring John Heard and Lisa Eichhorn. Set in and around Santa Barbara during the town's annual Spanish Days festivities, the film showcases such locales as the downtown/State Street area and the El Encanto Hotel.

These days, the Santa Barbara County Film Commission is promoting the town's Spanish Colonial Revival buildings, private mansions (seen in remakes of *Scarface* and *Bedazzled*), and proximity to the wilderness.

## WHERE TO EXPLORE

### Top Billing: SANTA BARBARA COUNTY COURTHOUSE

This picturesque 1928 Spanish-Moorish landmark makes an eye-catching appearance in the Andy Garcia/Alan Arkin comedy *Steal Big, Steal Little*, directed by Santa Barbara local Andrew Davis. The courthouse's main entrance appears in the 1935 MGM short *La Fiesta de Santa Barbara*, which features Judy Garland in an early film appearance. A visit to the courthouse must include a trip to the top of the clock tower, which offers a 360-degree view of the waterfront and mountains. Call ahead for hours as the clock tower often closes early. *805-962-6464*.

### REFUGIO STATE BEACH

One of the most scenic beaches in all of California, Refugio is a peaceful retreat from fall to spring (but beware of the summertime crowds). A stately row of Washingtonia palm trees adds a tropical look to the picturesque coastline, which is often used by commercial directors as a Hawaiian or Mexican seaside locale. Down the coast, David Mamet's thriller *Spartan* filmed suspense sequences with Val Kilmer and Derek Luke at a beach house doubling for a Massachusetts bungalow. *Campground reservations: www.reserveamerica.com; park info: 805-899-1400*.

### EL CAPITAN STATE BEACH

This rocky stretch of coast is where Gene Wilder and Harrison Ford are ambushed by bad guy William Smith and his gang in the 1970s Western-comedy *The Frisco Kid*. El Capitan is a great place to relax, complete with campground, bike paths, and hidden coves. *Campground reservations: www.reserveamerica.com; park info: 805-968-1033*.

### GAVIOTA STATE PARK

In John Milius' *Big Wednesday*, Gaviota State Park's pier is home to the fabled Malibu workshop of surfboard maker "Bear" (Sam Melville). In *Sideways*, Paul Giamatti and Thomas Haden Church reflect on life's failures under Gaviota's railroad trestle. The largest of the three Santa Barbara state beaches, Gaviota is popular with fisherman, surfers, and hikers. Its campground includes picnic tables, fire grills, forty-two sites for tents and RVs. *Campground reservations: www.reserveamerica.com; park info: 805-968-1033*.

### GAVIOTA HOT SPRING

Perhaps more accurately called a *warm* spring, this semisecluded pool can be discovered by taking a one-mile uphill hike off the 101 Highway. To get there, head north from Santa Barbara on Highway 101. As the road leaves the coast, you'll pass through the **Gaviota Pass Tunnel**, built in 1952. (This is the tunnel seen at the beginning of *Sideways'* wine trip and at the climax of *The Graduate*, as Dustin Hoffman races to put a stop to Katharine Ross's Santa Barbara wedding.) Once you're through the tunnel, take the Highway 1 off-ramp. Make a right turn at the stop sign and head down the road that parallels the freeway. You'll find the trailhead to the spring at the end of road.

## DETOUR: JALAMA—*BIG WEDNESDAY* COAST

Because it's only accessible via a long, narrow, and winding road, Jalama is one of California's great hidden coastlines beloved by surfers. For *Big Wednesday's* beach scenes, dozens of local nonprofessional extras cast as surf fans were bused here from Santa Barbara's State Street. The film was also shot at Cojo Bay, near Point Conception, several miles down the coast from Jalama and today only accessible by foot.

To get to Jalama via the scenic (and more cinematic) route, take Highway 101 to the Santa Rosa Road exit (near Highway 246). Head West on Santa Rosa Road, a bucolic country lane featured in a *Sideways* road montage. You'll be passing by Sanford Winery, where Paul Giamatti teaches Thomas Haden Church about the art of sipping wine.

At the intersection of Santa Rosa Road and Highway 1, take a right for a quick stop at Lompoc (pronounced *Lom-POKE*), the hick town setting for the 1940 W. C. Fields comedy *The Bank Dick*. (The town in Fields' movie

Santa Barbara County Film Commission

The observation deck at the courthouse offers great views of the city.

was mostly re-created on the Universal backlot.) Today Lompoc's main attractions are its colorful murals, spring bloom, and artisinal wines, plus its Ocean Lanes bowling alley and Friday Farmer's Market, both seen in *Sideways*. Just outside of town is the La Purisima Mission, which appears in Gary Ross's *Seabiscuit* as the location of the Tijuana wedding of Jeff Bridges and Elizabeth Banks.

From Lompoc, head south on Highway 1 to Jalama Road (look carefully for the turnoff on your right). Follow Jalama Road over the rolling hills. Along the way you'll pass under the canopy of oaks that provides the perfect rural backdrop for Keanu Reeves' and Aitana Sanchez-Gijon's unscheduled bus stop in *A Walk in the Clouds*. The road ends at windswept Jalama Beach, site of a popular summer campground and Jalama Beach Store, known for its "world famous" burgers. *Campground info: 805-736-6316.*

## WHERE TO EAT

### MOBY DICK

A popular tourist hangout that offers both fresh fish and impressive sunsets, this Stearns Wharf tradition is open for breakfast, lunch, and dinner. Moby Dick has a memorable cameo in the 1966 *Batman* feature as Adam West desperately tries to dispose of a lethal explosive on Stearns Wharf. *805-965-0549.*

For dessert, walk down the wharf to **Great Pacific Ice Cream Company** (*805-962-0108*). In the Disney big-screen version of *My Favorite Martian*, Jeff Daniels finds Christopher Lloyd (as his elusive "Uncle Martin") gorging himself here. Take in the view at the outdoor tables overlooking the water.

### SOJOURNER CAFÉ

This cozy health-food restaurant has been a Santa Barbara institution and a favorite of health-conscious locals since 1978. *134 East Canon Perdido; 805-965-7922.*

## WHERE TO STAY

### SAN YSIDRO RANCH, MONTECITO

In the 1930s, this horse ranch was co-owned by *Lost Horizon* star Ronald Colman, whose Hollywood friends were frequent guests. Because of its privacy the ranch has been an elite spot for celebrity weddings and honeymoons, including: Laurence Olivier and Vivien Leigh; JFK and Jacqueline Bouvier; Julia Roberts and Danny Moder; and Gwyneth Paltrow and Chris Martin.

Nestled in the foothills of the Santa Barbara back country, the ranch remains a top choice for many Hollywood moguls in search of a getaway. In fact, John Huston came here to polish the *African Queen* script. In addition to the ranch's deluxe accommodations, its **Stonehouse Restaurant** is a four-star romantic dining spot. The nearby foothills can be seen in John Franken-heimer's *Seconds*, as the site of the nude grape stomp. *900 San Ysidro Lane; www.sanysidroranch.com; 800-368-6788.*

## EL ENCANTO HOTEL
A Spanish Colonial retreat built in 1915, and a onetime home for actress Hedy Lamarr, this hillside hotel may be hard to find for first-time travelers, so make sure you call ahead for directions. The El Encanto has eighty-four suites, cottages, and villas, with beautiful grounds for strolling. The piano bar is a popular nightspot with a view of the sparkling city lights below. Noir buffs may recall the El Encanto (and its classic neon sign) as the hotel where Jeff Bridges has a tryst with Nina Van Pallandt in *Cutter's Way*. The classic Riviera movie theater is across the street. *1900 Lasuen Rd.; 805-687-5000.*

## FOUR SEASONS BILTMORE
This 1927 hideaway is the classic Santa Barbara resort on the shore. In 1955, the hotel's Cottage 5 was the location of the real-life, image-spinning wedding of Rock Hudson and his agent's secretary. Jennifer Lopez and Ben Affleck also planned to tie the knot at this resort. One of the hotel's assets is its location on Butterfly Beach, a narrow strip of sand and one of the few west-facing beaches in Santa Barbara. *1260 Channel Drive; 805-969-2261 or 888-424-5866.*

## EL CAPITAN CANYON CABINS
Located in a former campground across the highway from El Capitan State Beach, this pricey collection of pre-fab cedar cottages and tent cabins includes its own general store and café. During the summer, the canyon hosts a live concert series with bluegrass, jazz, or blues. If you're looking for privacy, ask for a cabin at the top of the canyon. *Reservations: www.elcapitancanyon.com; 805-685-3887.*

## THE ORIGINAL MOTEL 6
Dating from 1962, the nation's first Motel 6 can be found on Corona del Mar and Cabrillo, one block from the beach. Other budget accommodations are nearby. *805-564-1392.*

## WHERE TO SEE A MOVIE
## THE ARLINGTON THEATER
Architecture aficionados as well as film fans will marvel at this classic 1926 two-thousand-seat movie palace and performing arts venue with a Mission

Revival exterior, premiere walkway, and atmospheric interior. As you enter the theater, you feel as if you've stepped into the courtyard of a Spanish villa. When the lights go down, tiny lights embedded in the ceiling give the illusion of stars twinkling above. *1317 State Street; 805-963-4408.*

## LOCAL MOVIE CELEBRATION
### THE SANTA BARBARA FILM FESTIVAL

Every winter the Santa Barbara International Film Festival features big studio premieres, documentary screenings, UCSB student films, craft seminars, and special celebrity salutes. The festival gets a decent turnout from industry players and maintains a laid-back atmosphere. Past tributes include the twenty-fifth anniversary screening of the Santa Barbara-lensed *Big Wednesday* and a salute to the silent film work of the town's historic Flying A Studios. *www.sb-filmfestival.org; 805-963-0023.*

## ON THE ROAD: VENTURA AND CARPINTERIA

Those looking to stretch their legs en route to Santa Barbara may want to exit Highway 101 and check out these two coastal towns in Ventura County.

Downtown **Ventura** was the home of *Perry Mason* creator Erle Stanley Gardner, who tried cases at the 1911 courthouse (now Ventura City Hall). The courthouse interior was used for a trial sequence in the *Chinatown* sequel *The Two Jakes*, with Jack Nicholson, Harvey Keitel, Meg Tilly, and Madeleine Stowe. But downtown Ventura's biggest moment on film is the hostage situation gone bad in *Swordfish*, featuring John Travolta, Hugh Jackman, and a caravan of Humvees smashing through the downtown store windows.

For the casual visitor, Ventura's Main Street is a good place to shop for antiques and browse the used bookstores. The nearby Bella Maggiore Inn *(805-652-0277)* and Pierpont Inn *(805-653-6144)* offer stylish accommodations for those who wish to stay overnight. Ventura features several scenic beaches, including Harbor Cove Beach at the end of Spinnaker Drive. It's here in the Ventura Harbor where Leonardo DiCaprio (as Howard Hughes) lands his plane on a seaside movie set to visit Cate Blanchett (as Katharine Hepburn) in Martin Scorsese's *The Aviator.*

Closer to Santa Barbara, the town of **Carpinteria** is home to Southern California's safest beach in terms of water quality, shallow shore depth, and low crime rate. Carpinteria's main drag is known for its antiquing opportunities and the town's popular Thursday night Farmer's Market.

For those interested in ocean wildlife, the **Carpinteria Bluffs Nature Preserve** can be found at the end of Bailard Avenue *(www.carpinteriabluffs.org).* The preserve's coastal walk leads to a seal rookery (active only in the winter and spring) and a privately owned pier. This area can be seen in *The Two Jakes* when Jack Nicholson meets with oil magnate Richard Farnsworth.

## HOW TO GET TO SANTA BARBARA

*Take the 101 North, past Ventura to Santa Barbara. Take the State Street off-ramp. To avoid weekend traffic, consider taking the train (www.amtrak.com).*

## DVD ITINERARY: SANTA BARBARA

*Big Wednesday*, Gaviota Pier, Scenes 4, 10, and 24

*Cutter's Way*, State Street, Scenes 1 and 5

*Batman* (1966), Stearns Wharf, Scenes 18–20

*Sideways*, Gaviota State Park, Scene 24

Scott Dewees

*Big Wednesday* was partially shot along the lonely Jalama coast.

↑ To San Francisco

To Big Sur
& Monterey

▪ Piedras Blancas

**HEARST CASTLE**
*Spartacus*

*Hearst
State Beach
Commando*

**San Simeon**

**Cambria**
*Arachnophobia*

**Cayucos**
(MGM Town)

Morro Rock ▪ **Morro Bay**

Morro Rock

**Cholame**
James Dean
Memorial Junction

**Paso Robles**
*Jackson County Jail*

**Templeton**

**Atascadero**

Paso Robles
Wine Country

To the San
Joaquin Valley

**MONTANA DE ORO
STAT E PARK**
*Pete's Dragon*

LOS OSOS ROAD

SEE CANYON ROAD

**SAN LUIS OBISPO**
*Murder by Numbers*

*Hollywood Escapes*
# SAN LUIS OBISPO
# COUNTY and
# GUADALUPE
# DUNES

**Avila Beach**
Sycamore Mineral Springs

**PISMO BEACH**
*Poetic Justice*

**Arroyo Grande**

*Oceano Dunes State
Vehicular Rec. Area
Strange Cargo*

**OSO FLACO
LAKE**

**Nipomo**

N
W · E
S

Not to Scale

Dunes Center
Far Western Tavern
**Guadalupe**

**Santa Maria**

MAIN ST.

BETTERAVIA RD.

**GUADALUPE DUNES**
*The Ten Commandments (1923)*

Point Sal

Santa Maria Airport
*The Rocketeer*

Santa Maria River

© Harry Medved
RBL

To Santa Ynez Wine Country,
↓ Santa Barbara & Los Angeles

*Pacific*

*Ocean*

# 18

# GUADALUPE DUNES
# 1,001 Arabian Sites

If 1,000 years from now archaeologists happen to dig beneath the Guadalupe Dunes, I hope they will not rush into print with the amazing news that Egyptian civilization . . . extended all the way to the Pacific Coast.

—*The master showman on his buried* Ten Commandments *set in* The Autobiography of Cecil B. DeMille *(1959)*

**MAJOR ROLES:** *Hidalgo, The Ten Commandments (1923)*

## BEHIND THE SCENERY

Some thirty years before Charlton Heston parted the Red Sea in color and stereophonic sound, ancient Egypt was depicted in Cecil B. DeMille's 1923 silent version of *The Ten Commandments* at Central California's Guadalupe Dunes. DeMille's epic would be one of several films for which these giant sand formations would double for the Middle East.

Guadalupe is part of a vast dunes complex that extends along the coast for eighteen miles from Vandenberg Air Force Base to Pismo Beach. This hidden paradise by the sea attracted a number of turn-of-the-century bohemian intellectuals (i.e., early hippies). Calling themselves "the Dunites," these painters, sculptors, and writers made their home in driftwood shacks, and according to local historian Norm Hammond, they practiced astrology, Hinduism, and nudism.

Just outside of the dunes lies the town of **Guadalupe,** one of Central California's oldest settlements, which flourished as a Japanese American farming community throughout the 1920s and 1930s. Today agriculture remains the dominant industry in Guadalupe, though Hollywood makes an occasional return.

One of the industry's first sojourns into the area, DeMille's *The Ten Commandments,* may have been the most expensive picture made up to that time, the *Titanic* of its day. Half of its $1.5 million budget went to the construction of some of the largest exterior sets ever built for a silent film.

Every local townsperson, farmer, and cowboy within the Guadalupe area was put to work on *Commandments*. Camp DeMille, based along the Santa Maria River, consisted of a small army of 2,500 Hollywood craftspeople, locals, and their livestock, including 400 painters, 1,200 electricians and gardeners, and 200 camels. The producers even provided a kosher kitchen for the 224 Orthodox Jewish extras hired to give the project authenticity.

When the production wrapped, DeMille hired a local Guadalupe farmer and crew to bury the City of Rameses set (about two city blocks in length and 120 feet high) under the dunes. Over a dozen five-ton sphinxes were hidden. Some called it typical Hollywood paranoia, ensuring that future moviemakers could never reuse the set. Others said that DeMille simply ran out of money and didn't have the cash to lug all the props back to Los Angeles. Known today as "The Lost City of DeMille," the dismantled *Ten Commandments* set still exists beneath these dunes, a genuine relic of outdoor movie history.

In the early 1980s, Hollywood preservationists, Guadalupe boosters, and archaeologists got together to see if any remains of the set could be found under the sand. To their surprise, the materials they uncovered appeared to be in good condition. The bronze medallions, large sphinx remnants, wooden hieroglyphics, leather chariot strips, and broken pottery pieces they've found so far can be seen at Guadalupe's Dunes Visitor Center.

Additional Guadalupe Dunes credits include:

*The Sheik* (1921) Legend has it that Rudolph Valentino's iconic desert chieftain rode these sands.

*The Thief of Bagdad* (1924) Mustachioed adventurer Douglas Fairbanks Sr. races his loyal steed along the majestic dunes as he rushes to save the princess from the Mongols.

*Morocco* This 1930 film introduced Marlene Dietrich to American audiences as a desert temptress who follows Foreign Legionnaire Gary Cooper into the dunes. Star-struck local youth George Aratani, future founder of Kenwood stereos and Mikasa tableware, herded sheep for the production and fondly remembers the German bombshell. "Her make up was applied to make her look roughed-up by the desert," recalls Aratani in Naomi Hirahara's biography *An American Son*, "but that could not conceal her beauty."

*G.I. Jane* Überwoman Demi Moore sets off on a military mission with Navy SEAL masterchief Viggo Mortensen. Guadalupe Beach doubles for the Libyan coast.

*Hidalgo* Viggo Mortensen returns to the Guadalupe Dunes for the seaside finish line sequence of this transglobal horserace adventure.

## WHERE TO EXPLORE

## THE DUNES CENTER

Located in a 1910 Craftsman home, the center features an exhibit on the making of *The Ten Commandments* and offers science workshops, guided bird

Sets from the 1923 version of *The Ten Commandments* are
buried under the Guadalupe Dunes.

walks, and hikes. *1055 Guadalupe Street; www.dunescenter.org; 805-343-2455.*

## RANCHO GUADALUPE DUNES PRESERVE

Call ahead to make sure the shifting sands haven't closed down the road to
the dunes preserve at secluded Guadalupe Beach. You can take a wonderful
two-mile walk simply by strolling down the beach and circling back through
the low dunes. If you're ambitious, take a strenuous six-mile round-trip hike
through the higher dunes to five-hundred-foot-high Mussel Rock, the tallest
coastal dune in the state. You'll be rewarded with a sensational view of Paradise Beach below. But remember: hiking in the shifting sand is a lot harder
than walking on hard-packed terrain. *www.cclm.org; 805-343-2354.*

## OSO FLACO LAKE

North of the Guadalupe Dunes lies this peaceful marsh with access to the
dunes and Pacific Ocean. A one-mile boardwalk trail loops around this bird-

watchers' paradise. *Three miles north of the town of Guadalupe, and 3 miles west on Oso Flaco Lake Road; info: 805-343-2455.*

## WHERE TO EAT

### THE FAR WESTERN TAVERN

Guadalupe is best known for its authentic Mexican bakeries, but if you're looking for a hearty sit-down meal, this is the place. Opened in 1913, the Tavern may look like an aging hotel on the outside, but during lunch hours this cowboy hangout is packed with seasoned locals. Jack Lemmon and Walter Matthau visit Far Western's bar in *The Odd Couple II*. *899 Guadalupe Street, near 9th Street; 805-343-2211.*

## WHERE TO STAY

### SANTA MARIA INN

Built in 1917, the Santa Maria has been remodeled substantially since its opening but still offers the most comfortable lodging near the dunes. The Inn has a memorabilia-laden gallery devoted to celebrity guests from Rudolph Valentino to Demi Moore. Dana Andrews stayed here while filming *The Best Years of Our Lives* at the nearby Santa Maria Airport. (Disney's fantasy-action picture *The Rocketeer* also shot its opening sequences in the airport region.) *801 S. Broadway; 805-928-7777.*

## HOW TO GET TO THE GUADALUPE DUNES

*The dunes are approximately 3.5 hours from L.A. The easiest route: Take 101 North to Santa Maria's Main Street exit. Head west on Main Street for approximately 12 miles, passing through downtown Santa Maria and past Guadalupe Boulevard to the preserve's gates.*

### DVD ITINERARY: GUADALUPE DUNES

G.I. Jane, Scenes 21–22

Hidalgo, Scenes 16–17

# 19

# SAN LUIS OBISPO COUNTY
## Hearst in Show

> We offer the best of Northern and Southern California terrain, yet our lifestyle is a little less hectic and folks seem to like it that way.
>
> —*San Luis Obispo County's film commissioner*
> *Baxter Boyington*

**MAJOR ROLES:** *Pete's Dragon, Murder by Numbers, Arachnophobia, Commando*

### BEHIND THE SCENERY

As a crossroads hamlet, San Luis Obispo was the site of the world's first motel (a term coined by "Mo-tel Inn" architect Arthur Heineman in 1925 as a combination of the words "motor" and "hotel"), where a motorist could park his car—and carcass—and stay in inexpensive lodgings. To this day car culture, especially antique car culture, is important to this inland town and its surrounding beach communities.

Although San Luis Obispo is positioned halfway between Los Angeles and San Francisco, filmmakers come here to shoot closer-to-home doubles for Middle America, New England, or even Northern California. And Hollywood heavyweights journey here for rest and relaxation or retirement. (Directors John Sturges and King Vidor spent their last years in SLO County.)

### WHERE TO EXPLORE

#### PISMO BEACH

Pismo has been the butt of many a cinematic joke, from Chuck Jones' classic cartoon "Ali Baba Bunny" (in which Bugs Bunny emerges from his hole after much digging in Baghdad while looking for the way to Pismo Beach) to W. C. Fields' *The Bank Dick* (in which Fields replaces a drunken movie director named "A. Pismo Clam"). The mollusks here were a major attraction many decades ago when the town was promoted as "The Clam Capital of the World" and tourists could just pick 'em off the beach. Back in 1911, hunters were limited to two hundred clams per person. Later, the shelled bounty reached near-extinction (due to greedy humans and sea otters) and strict guidelines were enforced. Now the limit is ten clams a day and you'll need a salt-water fishing license to gather them, lest you face steep fines.

But there's certainly more to Pismo than its shellfish. The town is colder and older than most Southern California coastal towns, brimming with lots of 1950s cottages, inexpensive fish-and-chips and clam chowder hangouts, and a 1,200-foot pier that stretches out to sea.

Just south of town you'll find a unique experience at the **Oceano Dunes,** one of the only places in California where (due to the firmly packed sand) you can actually drive your car onto the beach. Sally Kellerman does just this as she tails James Caan along the surf in the 1973 cult comedy *Slither.* For a fee you may enter this stretch of sand at Grand Avenue in Grover Beach or Pier Avenue in the town of Oceano (*Oceano Dunes Vehicular Recreation Area: 805-473-7220*). Or you can ditch your wheels and ride a horse on the beach by calling **Oceano Stables** (*805-489-8100*).

The dunes proper have appeared on film a few times. Frank Borzage's 1940 *Strange Cargo* shows Devil's Island escapees Clark Gable, Albert Dekker, and Joan Crawford discovering the ocean after a long trek through the wilderness. John Singleton's *Poetic Justice* features Janet Jackson and Tupac Shakur getting to know each other at the Pismo shore.

*HOW TO GET TO PISMO Take the Price St. exit off Highway 101.*

## PASO ROBLES WINE COUNTRY

There are more than sixty-five wineries in this hilly region situated near the antique-filled town of **Paso Robles,** a location for the climactic parade in the crime thriller *Jackson County Jail,* starring Yvette Mimieux and Tommy Lee Jones. The town also has a place in Hollywood history as the 1954 honeymoon site for Joe DiMaggio and Marilyn Monroe. Many of the area's wineries are nestled in the hillsides near scenic Highway 46, including the region's oldest, the 1882 **York Mountain Winery** (*805-238-3925*).

*HOW TO GET TO PASO ROBLES WINE COUNTRY Take Highway 101 North past San Luis Obispo to the Highway 46 West exit. Follow the highway to the wineries.*

## HEARST CASTLE, SAN SIMEON

William Randolph Hearst's private 110,000-square-foot estate, filled with art treasures from around the world, took 28 years to build and served as the inspiration for the fictional Xanadu in Orson Welles' *Citizen Kane.* For many years it was the newspaper tycoon-turned-movie producer's primary residence from where Hearst and his mistress, actress Marion Davies, entertained the Hollywood elite. Preproduction rehearsals for Davies' films took place at the castle, according to director Raoul Walsh's memoirs. Upcoming movies were screened for celebrity guests such as Charlie Chaplin, Greta Garbo, Errol Flynn, David Niven, Harpo Marx, and Cary Grant.

The only major film shot on location at Hearst Castle was *Spartacus*, for a scene in which Laurence Olivier arrives home at his villa and walks by the **Neptune Pool.** In 1957, six years after Hearst's death, the Hearst Corporation deeded the castle to the State of California. In the ensuing years it has become one of California's most financially lucrative tourist stops. Prior to becoming state governor, Arnold Schwarzenegger shot scenes from *Commando* at adjacent **William R. Hearst State Beach,** a spectacular destination for a picnic lunch. *On Highway 1, north of Cambria; www.hearstcastle.com; tour reservations are strongly recommended: 800-444-4445.*

## POINT PIEDRAS BLANCAS
A boardwalk trail will take you to a vista point overlooking the sand where hundreds of elephant seals flock from December to March. (Contrary to creature feature lore, *The Monster of Piedras Blancas* was not filmed at this area's light station, but rather at the Point Conception lighthouse, far south of here.) *Four miles north of Hearst Castle; www.elephantseal.org; 805-924-1628.*

## WHERE TO HIKE
## MONTAÑA DE ORO STATE PARK
With its eight thousand acres of rugged cliffs, sandy beaches, and coastal plains, this is a hiker's paradise reminiscent of coastal Maine. In fact, at the park's southern end, Disney Studios built a New England lighthouse for the animated/live-action musical *Pete's Dragon*, starring Helen Reddy and Mickey Rooney. After production wrapped, the lighthouse was shipped to Disney World, according to *San Luis Obispo New Times'* Jeff McMahon.

*HOW TO GET TO MONTAÑA DE ORO STATE PARK From Highway 101, take the Los Osos exit. Drive 12 miles west on Los Osos Valley Road to the State Park entrance. Park info: 805-528-0513.*

## WHERE TO EAT
## MISSION GRILL, SAN LUIS OBISPO
This restaurant is situated on the beautifully landscaped Mission Plaza, with a few of its tables facing San Luis Creek. Sunday brunch specialties include French toast and eggs Benedict. The Mission Plaza is where Michael Pitt

Harry Medved

Sycamore Springs has attracted such diverse Hollywood guests as W. C. Fields and Sandra Bullock.

meets with both Sandra Bullock and Ryan Gosling in *Murder by Numbers*. *1023 Chorro Street; 805-547-5544.*

## WHERE TO STAY

### Top Billing: SYCAMORE MINERAL SPRINGS

A hot springs resort since the 1880s, the Sycamore Mineral Springs became the place to take the cure for arthritis and other ailments. According to the management, W. C. Fields enjoyed many a soak here on his way to Hearst Castle. Today it's a romantic retreat, with its cottage and creekside suites offering the most private accommodations. Nearby attractions include busy **Avila Beach** (seen in the 1979 beach comedy/drama *California Dreaming*, starring Glynnis O'Connor, Tanya Roberts, and Dennis Christopher) and the spectacularly lonely **See Canyon**, a must for country road cyclists. *1215 Avila Beach Drive; www.sycamoresprings.com; 800-234-5831.*

### MADONNA INN

If you're looking for flash, then this pink, campy, and outrageously decorated 1958 fantasy hotel in San Luis Obispo is just for you. The Madonna was immortalized in the bizarre international anthology film *Aria,* in which Buck Henry and Beverly D'Angelo have a fling in the fictional Neanderthal Room. *100 Madonna Road, right next to Highway 101; 800-543-9666.*

## CAMBRIA PINES LODGE

This lodge is your best bet if your destination is Hearst Castle, only 8 miles away. The Cambria Pines Lodge has 150 comfortable rooms surrounded by Monterey Pines. Fright film buffs will recognize the touristy town of Cambria from Frank Marshall's *Arachnophobia,* starring Jeff Daniels, John Goodman, and hundreds of eight-legged co-stars. *2905 Burton Drive; 805-927-4200.*

## DETOUR: JAMES DEAN'S HIGHWAY 46

On September 30, 1955, 24-year-old James Dean died tragically when his Porsche Spyder crashed on this stretch of Highway 46, not too far from the route's celebrated and scenic wine country.

One week away from the opening of *Rebel Without a Cause,* Dean had just wrapped shooting *Giant* and was heading to an auto race in Salinas. His head-on collision with Cal Poly S.L.O. student Donald Turnupseed (not "Turnup-speed" as often misreported) took place at twilight, in the rural area of Cholame. **The James Dean Memorial Junction,** a monument placed there by fans, commemorates the actor. Every year on Dean's death date, antique car buffs meet in Hollywood and caravan to the location, gathering on September 30th at 5:30 p.m.

Cholame's **Jack Ranch Café** is located beside the monument and sells kitschy James Dean memorabilia. The coffee shop and its staff were fictionalized in the 2001 drama *Almost Salinas,* starring John Mahoney, Virginia Madsen, and Lindsay Crouse. And in a not-so-tasteful choice of film locations, director and star H. B. Halicki shot *The Junkman* (his follow-up to the original *Gone in 60 Seconds*) at this site, breaking a then-Guinness World Record for "the most vehicles smashed up in a single movie."

*HOW TO GET TO THE JAMES DEAN MEMORIAL JUNCTION Take Highway 46 to its intersection with Highway 41, between Paso Robles and Kettleman City.*

## ON THE ROAD: CAYUCOS: AN MGM BEACH TOWN

Affectionately dubbed "Movietown U.S.A." by film critic and historian Leonard Maltin, Cayucos is a charming beach town located on the way to Hearst Castle. During the late 1920s, Hearst had a deal with MGM to distribute pictures starring his favorite actress Marion Davies and often invited her Hollywood cohorts to his castle.

Streets on the southern end of town were named after MGM production execs Louis B. Mayer, Irving Thalberg, Eddie Mannix, and Harry Rapf, and actors Lon Chaney, Norma Shearer, John Gilbert, Renee Adoree, Bill Cody, William Haines, and Davies. As Maltin writes in his *Movie Crazy* newsletter, "It's just plain fun to turn off California Highway 1 at [Lon] Chaney Avenue and explore this quaint seaside community."

The town's recently restored 1876 Cass House, Remember When antique mall, and Cayucos Pier can be seen in 1959's *The Monster of Piedras Blancas*. Historical photographs of Cayucos can be seen at **Hoppe's Garden Bistro** (*78 Ocean Avenue; 805-995-1006*), a California Continental restaurant housed in a restored 1876 redwood building.

*HOW TO GET TO CAYUCOS Take Highway 1 North 20 miles from San Luis Obispo.*

## HOW TO GET TO SAN LUIS OBISPO

*From L.A., take Highway 101 North for approximately 198 miles (roughly 3.5 hours from L.A.).*

## DVD ITINERARY: SAN LUIS OBISPO COUNTY

*Murder by Numbers*, Mission Plaza/San Luis Creek, Scenes 9, 10

*Pete's Dragon*, Montaña de Oro State Park, Scenes 5, 15–16

*Spartacus [The Criterion Collection]*, Hearst Castle, Scene 14

*Arachnophobia*, Cambria and Santa Rosa Creek Road, Scene 3

# MOVIE DESERTS

In the desert . . . you hear a lot of things. See a lot of things, too: the sun and the sky and the heat. All that sand out there with the rivers and the lakes that aren't real at all . . .

*—Character actor Joe Sawyer as a telephone*
   *lineman in 1953's* It Came from Outer Space

# 20

# VASQUEZ ROCKS
# Land of a Thousand Places

An incredible fortune of stones, yet I would trade them all for a hand phaser or a good solid club.

—William Shatner, as Star Trek's *Captain James T. Kirk*, at Vasquez Rocks

**MAJOR ROLES:** *Blazing Saddles, The Flintstones, Jay and Silent Bob Strike Back, Alpha Dog*

## BEHIND THE SCENERY

Vasquez Rocks, according to *The Los Angeles Times*, make up "the most commercially photographed boulders on the planet." Since this county park is in "the Zone" (the Hollywood unions' thirty-mile radius from the Center of L.A., within which no penalties are assessed), filmmakers are able to get that otherworldly look without paying extra out-of-town union expenses for cast and crew.

The tilted 150-foot-high outcroppings are instantly recognizable from the highway as a Western setting (*Apache, Holes*), a prehistoric valley (*One Million B.C., The Flintstones*), a modern-day Arizona wilderness (*Grind, Joe Dirt*), the Middle East (*A Thousand and One Nights, For The Boys*), Tibet (*Werewolf of London*), an alien planet (*Amazon Women on the Moon*), site of a ritual sacrifice (*The Rapture*), a violent crime scene (*Alpha Dog*), and even a mad scientist's domain (Dr. Evil's lair, seen briefly in *Austin Powers: International Man of Mystery*).

Hundreds of hours of episodic television have been shot at Vasquez Rocks, from *The Wild, Wild West* and *Bonanza* to *Roswell, The X-Files*, and *24*. Classic examples of 1960s sci-fi TV were also filmed here: *The Outer Limits* episode "The Zanti Misfits" features Bruce Dern menaced by arachnoid extraterrestrials crawling among the boulders; and several *Star Trek* episodes including "Arena," in which William Shatner eludes his alien adversary, the Gorn, as it hunts him through the escarpments.

Because of the region's many cliffs and crevices, Vasquez Rocks made a perfect mid-nineteenth-century hiding place for their namesake, legendary Mexican bandit and Robin Hood–like folk hero Tuburcio Vasquez. Today visitors will likewise enjoy finding places to explore in this fantastic cinematic landscape. *Los Angeles Times* reporter John Glionna points out that park visitors of all ages say the weird rocks evoke various images, including "whales surfacing from the ocean depths, a sinking ship . . . or a set of bad teeth. *Very bad teeth.*"

Notable film appearances include:

*The Flintstones*   The modern Stone Age family community of Bedrock was constructed here for the 1994 feature. Added to the landscape were the bright orange homes of Fred Flintstone (John Goodman) and Barney Rubble (Rick Moranis), built out of sculpted foam under the supervision of production designer William Sandell.

*Short Circuit*   The military tries to destroy runaway robot "Number Five" (voiced by Tim Blaney) at this hideout, much to the chagrin of human friends Ally Sheedy and Steve Guttenberg.

*Blazing Saddles*   Villain Hedley Lamarr (Harvey Korman) rallies his diverse bad-guy minions at the rocks. Among them are ornery cowboys, Mexican banditos, tough bikers, Nazi storm troopers, and befuddled Klansmen, whom Korman sends off with the salutation, "Now go do that voo-doo that you-do so well!"

*Hearts of the West*   In this affectionate look at the movies' silent era, Jeff Bridges stumbles upon the filming of a low-budget oater here, and meets movie men Andy Griffith, Alan Arkin, and Ron Liebman.

*Army of Darkness*   "The Wiseman" (Ian Abercrombie) points Bruce Campbell to a Vasquez Rocks road that leads to the cemetery where the smart-alec hero will find the dangerous tome known as *The Necronomicon. "Klaatu-barada-nikto!"*

*Bill & Ted's Bogus Journey*   Keanu Reeves and Alex Winter get thrown off the rocks by their evil twins. They later outfox The Grim Reaper by giving him a good, old-fashioned "melvin."

*Jay and Silent Bob Strike Back*   In a memorably raunchy scene, lawmen Will Ferrell and Judd Nelson track Kevin Smith, Jason Mewes, and an orangutan to the movie's Arena Diner, placed in the shadow of the rocks.

## WHERE TO EAT

### SWEETWATER FARMS

Located in the Agua Dulce shopping center close to the park, this upscale market stocks fresh sandwiches, bakery goods, and gourmet coffee. *33301 Agua Dulce Canyon Road; 661-268-0700.*

Marc Wanamaker/Bison Archives

The rocks provide a dramatic backdrop for oaters like
*Law and Order* (1936).

## LE CHÊNE
Situated on a lonely stretch of desert road near Vasquez Rocks, Le Chêne is a surprisingly elegant French restaurant. This river rock structure appeared in Steven Spielberg's acclaimed 1971 TV movie *Duel*, as a rest stop where Dennis Weaver takes refuge from a relentless pursuit by a monstrous semi. *Open for dinner only. Reservations recommended. 12625 Sierra Highway; 661-251-4315.*

## HALFWAY HOUSE CAFÉ
Considered "half way" between L.A. and Palmdale, this circa 1931 cowboy bar and café was built on the Sierra Highway when it was the main route to the Sierra Nevada Mountains. Films that have used the café include director Joe Dante's "It's a Good Life" segment of *Twilight Zone: The Movie*, Albert Brooks's *Lost in America* (where Brooks finds Julie Hagerty with a crazy trucker), David Mamet's *Spartan* (scene of a staged shoot-out with Val Kilmer), and a pair of director Joe Pytka's memorable Pepsi commercials starring supermodel/mom Cindy Crawford, shot ten years apart.

The café also appears in two Clint Eastwood films: in *Heartbreak Ridge*, Mario Van Peebles steals Clint's bus ticket and leaves him at the café without a ride. And in *Space Cowboys*, Tommy Lee Jones races past Clint on the Sierra

Highway and meets him here to join fellow astronauts Donald Sutherland and James Garner for a celebratory brew. *15564 Sierra Highway, Canyon Country; 661-251-0102.*

## HOW TO GET TO TO VASQUEZ ROCKS

*From I-5 take Highway 14 to the Agua Dulce Canyon Road turnoff. Follow the signs to Vasquez Rocks County Park, 2.5 miles north of the freeway. Park info: 661-268-0840.*

## DVD ITINERARY: VASQUEZ ROCKS

*Blazing Saddles*, Scenes 16–17, 20

*Bill & Ted's Bogus Journey*, Scenes 4–5

*Werewolf of London*, Scenes 2–3

*The Flintstones*, Scenes 3–4

Daniel Frommer

This roadside haunt's on-screen visitors include Clint Eastwood, Val Kilmer and Tommy Lee Jones.

Keith Jennings, Jr.

The tilted Vasquez Rocks are the result
of earthquakes and erosion.

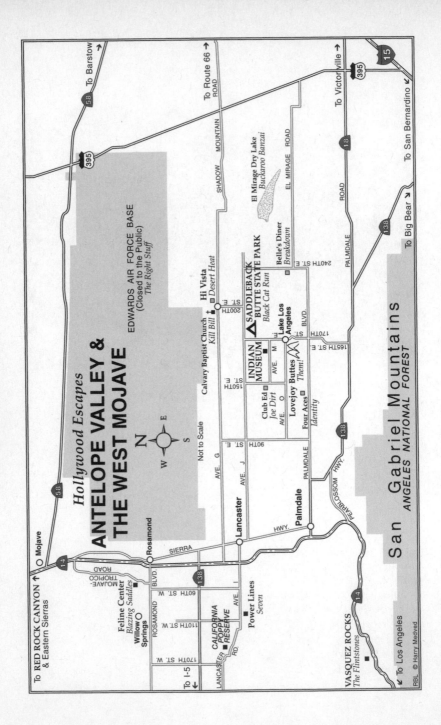

*Hollywood Escapes*

# ANTELOPE VALLEY &
# THE WEST MOJAVE

EDWARDS AIR FORCE BASE
(Closed to the Public)
*The Right Stuff*

To Barstow ↑

To Route 66 →
ROAD

To Victorville ↑

To San Bernardino ↘

To Big Bear ↗

SHADOW   MOUNTAIN

El Mirage Dry Lake
*Buckaroo Banzai*

EL MIRAGE   ROAD

Hi Vista
■ *Desert Heat*

Calvary Baptist Church
*Kill Bill* †

200TH   ST.   E.

Belle's Diner
*Breakdown*

240TH ST. E.

▲ SADDLEBACK
BUTTE STATE PARK
*Black Cat Run*

Lake Los
Angeles

170TH ST. E.

PALMDALE   ROAD

INDIAN
MUSEUM

AVE.   M

Lovejoy Buttes
*Them!*

165TH ST. E.

Club Ed
*Joe Dirt*

AVE.   O

Four Aces
*Identity*

150TH   ST.   E.

AVE.   G

Not to Scale

N

AVE.   J

90TH   ST.   E.

PALMDALE

BLVD.

San Gabriel Mountains
*ANGELES NATIONAL FOREST*

To Red Rock Canyon ↑
& Eastern Sierras

Mojave ○

To Mojave
Rosamond

Lancaster

Palmdale

SIERRA

HWY.

PEARBLOSSOM   HWY.

Feline Center
*Blazing Saddles*

Willow ○
Springs

MOJAVE-
TROPICO
ROAD

ROSAMOND   BLVD.

60TH ST. W.

110TH ST. W.

170TH ST. W.

LANCASTER   RD.

CALIFORNIA
POPPY
RESERVE

AVE.   D

Power Lines
*Seven*

VASQUEZ ROCKS
*The Flintstones*

To I-5 ↓

To Los Angeles ↙

RBL  © Harry Medved

# 21

# ANTELOPE VALLEY & THE WEST MOJAVE
## Wildflowers, Wild Lands

Antelope Valley had a bleak alien look. If giant ants were anywhere they'd probably be out here.

*—Character actor William Schallert, who appeared in the monster insect classic* Them! *(1954)*

**MAJOR ROLES:** *Kill Bill, Mackenna's Gold, Seven, Them!*

### BEHIND THE SCENERY

Antelope Valley is located within the northern boundary of L.A. County, offering Hollywood its closest-to-home desert roads. Pronghorn antelope roamed this valley as late as the early 1900s until farmers and ranchers cleared them out to make way for alfalfa and other crops. Ironically, a number of those farmers were later cleared out with the introduction of the Antelope Valley Freeway (Highway 14). The small-town character of Palmdale and Lancaster (once known as the high school town of Judy Garland) changed forever when a late 1960s housing boom expanded along the highway corridor.

Despite rampant urbanization, the Antelope Valley still retains pockets of wilderness and unique architectural landmarks that have attracted Hollywood. Among them are the Swiss Chalet–themed Indian Museum (see box), and Shea's Castle Ranch, a 1924 Irish/Medieval hilltop fortress that was once a home to Roy Rogers. It was also the main location for director Al Adamson's notoriously anemic *Blood of Dracula's Castle* in 1967. Bloodsuckers returned more recently for a memorable episode of TV's *Buffy the Vampire Slayer.*

The best way for visitors to experience the true nature of the Antelope Valley is to venture beyond the highway sprawl and the commuter traffic and explore the land's twisted buttes, springtime poppies, and Joshua Trees.

# WHERE TO EXPLORE

## THE ROUTE TO THE ANTELOPE VALLEY CALIFORNIA POPPY RESERVE

Although it has not been used as a location for feature films, this haven for California's state flower is certainly cinematic, especially if you time your visit to the peak springtime displays from mid-March to April. Check first with the Reserve (661-724-1180) or the Wildflower Hotline (818-768-3533), for which actor Joe Spano records regular updates of the best Southern California blooming areas. Take the Avenue I exit in Lancaster and turn left, heading west toward the reserve entrance.

The road from the Antelope Valley Freeway to the reserve is dotted with poppies (in season) and memorable film locations. At the intersection of Avenue I and 60th Street West there is a former prison that serves as the jailbreak location in Steven Soderbergh's *Out of Sight*, during which George Clooney and Ving Rhames kidnap U.S. Marshal Jennifer Lopez.

The towering power lines on Avenue I, between 95th and 110th Streets West may look familiar. This is where serial killer Kevin Spacey has a package containing an unforgettable surprise delivered to detectives Brad Pitt and Morgan Freeman in David Fincher's *Seven*. "Those tall power lines were psychologically imposing and made for a challenging shoot," recalls *Seven* first assistant director Michael Allen Kahn. "We couldn't get cell or walkie-talkie coverage and for a while we felt cut off from the world. But they provided an appropriately ominous Fincher-like feel for the film's shocking conclusion."

The intersection of Avenue I and 110th Street West is also a location for the opening of Mark Illsley's 1999 comedy *Happy, Texas*, where convicts Steve Zahn and Jeremy Northam escape from custody.

Continue on Avenue I as it jogs right, then left as it becomes Lancaster Road and follow the signs to the reserve.

## THE BUTTES OF LAKE LOS ANGELES

Though the water in Lake Los Angeles is long gone, this dusty high-desert enclave (eleven miles east of Palmdale), remains and borders a prime filming location full of rocky buttes and Joshua trees. Lake Los Angeles is one of the few towns in Southern California where many of the residential streets are named after Westerns reportedly shot in the neighborhood, including the movies *Mackenna's Gold*, *Jubilee Trail*, *Chuka*, *Wells Fargo*, and TV's *Rawhide* and *High Chaparral*. According to the *Los Angeles Herald Examiner* in 1967, the Lake L.A. area was "used consistently by at least 25 television series."

Lake L.A.'s biggest star is **Lovejoy Buttes**, a collection of rocky protuberances that rises above the encroaching development. Homes border all sides of the buttes, except for the western edge between 145th Street East and 165th Street East (near Avenue Q), which provides the best access.

## CALVARY BAPTIST CHURCH:
## HOLLYWOOD GETS RELIGION

Across the street from the Hi-Vista Diner sits an authentic house of worship often attended by filmmakers, though for less than spiritual reasons. The Calvary Baptist Church serves as the exterior of the El Paso chapel where Lucy Liu, Vivica A. Fox, Daryl Hannah, Michael Madsen, and David Carradine unwisely make Uma Thurman a blood-spattered bride in Quentin Tarantino's *Kill Bill* saga. In director Ulu Grosbard's *True Confessions,* the church plays the desert sanctuary where L.A. detective Robert Duvall visits terminally ill sibling and disgraced monsignor Robert De Niro. More recently, *Crossroads,* Britney Spears' feature debut, used the location as a Southwestern Native American souvenir stand. Productions aren't welcome every day, however: services are held on occasional Sundays.

Harry Medved

Calvary Baptist Church is the *Kill Bill* chapel.

The Lovejoy Buttes is where Gregory Peck and Omar Sharif are attacked by the cavalry in *Mackenna's Gold*. Lovejoy also stands in for Joshua Tree National Park in a recreation of cult rocker Gram Parson's infamous funeral pyre (see page 160) in the independent comedy *Grand Theft Parsons*, starring Johnny Knoxville and Christina Applegate.

There's not much "love" or "joy" to be found in two other famous film sequences shot here, as they involved deadly insects threatening humans. James Whitmore torches the oversized ants' nests here in the 1954 sci-fi/horror classic *Them!*, while Edmund Gwenn and Joan Weldon look on. Costar Weldon recalls, "The buttes had a surreal atmosphere, day or night, and made the perfect lair for those hideous-looking giant ants."

More recently, Lovejoy was used for a suspenseful sequence in Chuck Russell's *The Scorpion King*. Desert warrior The Rock and horse thief Grant Heslov find themselves buried up to their necks in sand, while facing a computer-generated swarm of deadly fire ants.

Hikers looking for easy public access to the buttes are advised to head to the **Saddleback Butte State Park** or the nearby **Alpine Butte Wildlife Sanctuary** on Avenue O, between 130th Street East and Longview Street.

## THE FOUR FAUX ROADSIDE STOPS

Antelope Valley is perhaps the only place where you can find four lonely and rundown roadside establishments that exist only as movie sets in the middle of nowhere. All four complexes are off-limits to the public, but feel free to look at the exteriors.

**Club Ed** is a 1950s diner/motel complex (*150th Street East, between Avenues O and K*) built for the 1991 Lara Flynn Boyle/Dennis Hopper thriller *Eye of the Storm*. Later, it was named for its first caretaker, who jokingly answered his phone with the greeting "Club Ed." Big-screen comedies that have filmed here include *Nothing to Lose*, *Double Take*, and *Joe Dirt*. And it plays the Khaki Palms Motel in Rob Zombie's *The Devil's Rejects*.

**Four Aces** (*145th Street East and Avenue Q*) features a landmark sign that falsely promises "Gas Food Lodging." Films shot here include the killer-thrillers *Identity*, *Black Cat Run*, and Rob Zombie's *House of 1000 Corpses* (in which it plays "Captain Spaulding's Museum of Monsters and Madmen" run by Sid Haig). For *Brother*, his first film made in America, Japanese actor/director Takeshi Kitano chose the Four Aces for the bullet-ridden climax.

**Hi-Vista Diner** (*200th Street East and Avenue G*) This middle-of-nowhere greasy spoon was used in the Jean-Claude Van Damme film *Desert Heat*, with Pat Morita and Jaime Pressly. Neil LaBute's *Nurse Betty*, with Morgan Freeman and Chris Rock, was also shot here.

**Belle's Diner** (*240th Street East, between Avenues O and P*) Unlike its more colorful cousins, Belle's is an easy-to-miss farmhouse set back from the road. It's best remembered as the diner where Kurt Russell desperately searches for wife Kathleen Quinlan in the thriller *Breakdown*. "Belle's is popular for its desolate feel and its lone Joshua tree," says West Coast Film Locations' Pat Smith, who manages the location. The diner also plays a desert jailhouse where Melanie Griffith is held in *Crazy in Alabama*, directed by her husband Antonio Banderas.

## WHERE TO STAY

### SADDLEBACK BUTTE STATE PARK

This volcanic wilderness encompasses a secluded fifteen-unit campground and two-mile hiking trail that takes you to a breathtaking view at the top of the 3,700-foot-high butte. The approach to Saddleback Butte figures prominently in a climactic scene in D. J. Caruso's *Black Cat Run*, starring Patrick Muldoon. In the Ashton Kutcher/Amanda Peet comedy *A Lot Like Love* is an appropriately middle-of-nowhere campsite. *Seventeen miles east of Lancaster on Avenue J East. Campground info: 661-942-0662.*

### THE DESERT INN AND THE SIERRA HIGHWAY

Antelope Valley is so close to L.A., there's no need for the casual tourist to stay overnight. But film crews (including Quentin Tarantino's *Kill Bill* team) have usually stayed at the Desert Inn, located on Lancaster's main drag, the Sierra Highway. Remodeled several times since it was built in 1946, this basic motel offers two pools, two restaurants and bar, a fitness center, and rooms with kitchenettes.

Actress Joan Weldon, the alluring scientist in the 1954 movie *Them!*, recalls one of her character actor costars sleepwalking into her room at the

## A DIRECTOR'S APPRECIATION

*Filmmaker D. J. Caruso recalls preparing the contemporary film noir The Salton Sea in the Antelope Valley:*

"Prior to shooting, I had a wonderful experience driving through the West Mojave in a Corvette flying with the top down. I got caught in a sudden and strong snowstorm and it was surreal seeing the snowflakes stick to the Joshua Trees. The early morning sun and midday burn—finished off by the warm, glowing horizon that bounces off the landscape—is a filmmaker's dream."

Desert Inn during their ten-day Palmdale shoot. "Back in the 1950s, the rooms had no locks on the doors," she recalls. "He finally left when I cried, 'Go back to your room!' and jammed a chair against the door. The next day my fellow actor had no memory of what had happened. There must have been

## TOP BILLING: ANTELOPE VALLEY INDIAN MUSEUM STATE HISTORIC PARK

This quirky architectural curiosity and picnic spot is a worthy half-day trip from Los Angeles. Nestled among the rocks like a phantom hideout, it's a little-known desert outpost on the National Register of Historic Places.

Hollywood huckster and craftsman Howard Arden Edwards built his museum home in 1928, literally conforming the structure to the land: its walls and staircases were built around the terrain's pre-existing boulders, and its roof and furniture were hewn from Joshua tree timber. Although the exterior resembles a Swiss Chalet in its design, Edwards called his retreat *Yato Kya*, claiming the name was Indian for "Ranch of the Sun."

With nearby Piute Butte as his backdrop, Edwards staged Indian pageants for tourists visiting his "Theatre of the Standing Rocks.". According to museum curator Edra L. Moore, future *Music Man* Robert Preston appeared in one of these productions in the 1930s.

Land owner Grace Oliver bought the property in 1940 as a personal hideway and rented the surrounding buttes as a location for B Westerns. As late as 1972, the property was a location for the Western sequel, *The Magnificent Seven Ride!*, with Lee Van Cleef.

In 1975 the museum doubled as an Indian trading post in Jonathan Demme's *Crazy Mama*, where the family of fun-loving fugitives is aided by Native American caretaker Will Sampson (in his movie debut).

Probably the best cinematic showcase for the building is the 1973 Charles Bronson action-thriller *The Stone Killer*. In director Michael Winner's pre–*Death Wish* teaming with Bronson, the museum plays "The Old Western Indian House," actually an organized crime lair and the site of a shootout between the mobsters and cops Bronson, Ralph Waite, Norman Fell, and a young John Ritter. Paul Koslo, an actor in the movie who later moved to the Antelope Valley, says that the location exerted a "pal-

something about that desert air." Thankfully, all of the Desert Inn's rooms now have locks. *44219 N. Sierra Highway; 661-942-8401.*

The Desert Inn is not the only lodging available on Lancaster's main drag. "When a filmmaker needs to evoke the creepy, middle-of-nowhere at-

pable energy that added to our own tension and excitement. When I first discovered the museum, it was as if I had seen a desert mirage and had entered another dimension. It's a really unusual place!"

The eccentric structure, Indian collection, and beautiful surroundings became California State Park property in 1979. Today, Piute Butte is off-limits to the public, but the nature trail at the Indian Museum makes an ideal winter-spring walk, offering a short self-guided tour of the desert flora. Picnic tables in front of the museum afford a great view of the valley floor below and the snow-capped San Gabriel Mountains in the distance.

*HOW TO GET TO THE ANTELOPE VALLEY INDIAN MUSEUM Take I-5 North to Highway 14 (Antelope Valley Freeway), heading northeast toward Lancaster. Exit at Lancaster's Avenue K, making a right-hand turn. Head east 20 miles to 150th Street East. Make a right turn on 150th East (passing the Club Ed diner set) and head south 2 miles. Make a left turn on Avenue M. The museum is one mile ahead.*

*Open Saturday–Sunday 11 a.m.–4 p.m. or during the week by appointment; closed summer months; info: www.avim.av.org and 661-946-3055.*

Strange rock formations surrounding the museum appear in *The Magnificent Seven Ride!*

Harry Medved

mosphere of a roadhouse from which guests may never return," says *Antelope Valley Press* reporter Lavender Vroman, "this stretch of crumbling, vintage motels along the Sierra Highway is made to order." These ramshackle 1950s motels between Avenues M and J include the Sands (*Along for the Ride*), the BonAire (*Joy Ride*), and the Tropic (*The Salton Sea*).

## DETOUR: EL MIRAGE DRY LAKE BED: THE FLAT EARTH SOCIETY

This hardpan lakebed lies in a flat playa with a densely packed, smooth surface. Hikers seeking solitude beware: though it may be quiet here Monday through Friday, El Mirage's main basin is a favorite spot for off-highway vehicle recreation on weekends. El Mirage played Mexico's Sonoran Desert in *Close Encounters of the Third Kind*, the test site in *The Adventures of Buckaroo Banzai*, a desert drag strip for *Herbie: Fully Loaded* and the lakebed where the bad guys capture Mel Gibson and Danny Glover in *Lethal Weapon*. A dusty roadside café called **Murphy's** (760-388-1023) quenches off-roaders' thirsts and has appeared in Martha Coolidge's *Angie* and Antonio Banderas' *Crazy in Alabama*.

*HOW TO GET TO EL MIRAGE DRY LAKE The most popular access to El Mirage is from the town of Adelanto, reachable via Highway 395. From Adelanto take Crippen Avenue west and turn north on Mountain View Road.*

## HOW TO GET TO ANTELOPE VALLEY

*Take I-5 North to Highway 14 (Antelope Valley Freeway).*

## DVD ITINERARY: ANTELOPE VALLEY & THE WEST MOJAVE

*Them!*, Lovejoy Buttes, Scene 14

*The Scorpion King*, Lovejoy Buttes, Scene 6

*The Magnificent Seven Ride!*, Piute Butte, Scenes 13 and 15

# 22

# RED ROCK CANYON
## Jurassic Parkland

*Why, those rocks look positively menacing!*

—*Actress Carol Hughes as heroine Dale Arden in*
*Flash Gordon Conquers the Universe (1940)*

**MAJOR ROLES:** *Westworld, The Big Country,*
*4 for Texas, Holes*

### BEHIND THE SCENERY

Most travelers en route to the Sierras on Highway 14 never expect to see this alien landscape so close to Los Angeles. But with its colorful layers of white, pink, red, and brown sandstone eroded by the wind and rain, Red Rock is a site well worth stopping for.

Michael Crichton, one of America's most popular storytellers, might agree, as three of his big-screen adaptations were shot at Red Rock:

*The Andromeda Strain*   The military discovers the flesh-stripped bones of an Air Force jet pilot whose plane has mysteriously crashed in a Utah desert.

Ray Arthur/Ridge Crest Film Commission

The Red Rock
scenery is easily
accessible from
Highway 14.

Director Robert Wise makes effective use of Red Rock's Hagen Canyon in Crichton's tale of an unstoppable extraterrestrial microorganism set loose on earth.

*Westworld*   Malevolent cyber-gunslinger Yul Brynner pursues defenseless visitor Richard Benjamin through Red Rock's desolate Scenic Cliffs in writer/director Crichton's sci-fi thriller about an interactive (and deadly) amusement park.

*Jurassic Park*   In Steven Spielberg's premier saurian spectacular, Red Rock's Iron Canyon stands in for the Montana Badlands, where paleontologists Sam Neill and Laura Dern lead a fossil dig.

"Production companies have been coming to Red Rock for its unique geological diversity since the mid-1920s," says film historian Richard J. Schmidt. But like filmmakers then and now, hikers should be prepared: there are no gas stations, motels, or restaurants in the park. As if to emphasize the point, the dangerous nature of the area is reflected in trail names such as Last Chance Canyon and Nightmare Gulch.

## WHERE TO HIKE

*Like all desert locales, Red Rock is best hiked in the fall, winter, and springtime. Pick up a map and check on trail conditions at the small* **Red Rock Visitors Center**, *accessible via a clearly marked turnoff from Highway 14. For all destinations outside of Hagen Canyon, get detailed directions here as most Red Rock Trails are hard to find. Guided hikes are sometimes available.*

### Top Billing: HAGEN CANYON NATURAL PRESERVE
A one-mile loop trail through the badlands takes you past locations from films as diverse as *The Mummy* (1932), William Wyler's *The Big Country*, Anthony Mann's *Man of the West*, the Marx Brothers' *Go West*, and *The Egyptian* (featuring cliff-dwelling lions pouncing from Hagen's rocks onto Victor Mature's chariot). You'll also see a pillar dubbed by historian Schmidt as "Reagan Rock," for this is where lawman Ronald Reagan gets shot by his outlaw brother Russell Johnson in the 1953 Western *Law and Order*. Hagen Canyon is also where *Holes'* juvenile escapees Shia LaBoeuf and Khleo Thomas climb a rock formation called "God's Thumb." *Trailhead is west of Highway 14, just before Ricardo Campground on Abbott Drive.*

### RED CLIFFS NATURAL PRESERVE
Although the Red Cliffs are clearly visible from the highway (they're on the right as you approach the Visitors Center from Mojave), the short path called Red Cliffs Trail will take you to an even better view of these awesome three hundred-foot-high sandstone escarpments. Along this trail you'll find loca-

tions for *Ali Baba and the Forty Thieves* and the 1936 version of *Three Godfathers*. This area can also be glimpsed in *The Petrified Forest* as a group of travelers approach notorious fugitive Duke Mantee (Humphrey Bogart in his star-making performance).

Consult with the Visitors Center before heading to Iron Canyon Road, east of Highway 14. The trailhead sign is located at the east end of the parking lot.

### SCENIC CLIFFS TRAIL

Hikers will enjoy this spectacular two-mile round-trip trail that winds among locations for *Jurassic Park*, *Waterhole #3* (starring James Coburn), *Westworld*, and the Mars-landing conspiracy thriller *Capricorn One*. One of the best showcases of this area is the action-packed opening of Robert Aldrich's 1963 comedy-Western *4 For Texas*. It's along this terrain that bad guy Charles Bronson and gang pursue a stagecoach driven by Frank Sinatra and Dean Martin. *Note: The area is closed during the February to June birds-of-prey nesting season at the Scenic Cliffs wildlife sanctuary. Once again, consult with the Visitors Center before attempting this hike.*

## WHERE TO STAY

### RICARDO CAMPGROUND

Although Red Rock is glimpsed in Desi and Lucy's *The Long, Long Trailer*, this campground is unrelated to the Ricardos, their TV namesakes. It actually memorializes Richard (Ricardo) Hagen, son of the Red Rock caretaker who provided locations during Hollywood's golden age.

Films shot in the area include *Bulletproof* (in which cop Damon Wayans' unruly prisoner Adam Sandler desperately needs a place to relieve himself) and Howard Hughes' *The Outlaw* (starring his protégée and 1940s sex symbol, Jane Russell).

As a place to stargaze, Ricardo Campground can't be beat. For those who need a roof over their heads, however, reasonable motels are available in Mojave and Ridgecrest, half an hour away.

## WHERE TO GET SUPPLIES

### JAWBONE CANYON STORE AND DELI

Seven miles south of Red Rock Canyon you'll find this convenient minimart/deli and gas station located near the dirt bike mecca of Jawbone Canyon, scene of a climactic chase and shoot-out in William Wyler's *The Big Country* and an impromptu plane landing in *Bulletproof*. This will most likely be your last chance for sandwiches and cold drinks, so stock up accordingly. *32629 Highway 14; 760-373-2773.*

## IT CAME FROM CALIFORNIA: RED ROCK CANYON

Ever since *The Mummy* (1932) was disinterred at an Egyptian excavation site in Red Rock Canyon, this state park has seen its share of creature features. The high cliffs and deep crevices make perfect hiding places for lurking monsters and aliens waiting to pounce on unsuspecting victims.

"The rocks can be awe-inspiring, foreboding and sinister-looking at the same time," says Red Rock Ranger Mark Faull. "Some people say our Gothic-like spires resemble a lost planet." Indeed, Red Rock has been a favorite outer-space location for sci-fi serials including rocketeer Commando Cody's *Radar Men from the Moon,* Buster Crabbe's *Buck Rogers,* and *Flash Gordon Conquers the Universe,* and TV series such as *Lost in Space.* Fifties B pictures shot at Red Rock include *Rocketship X-M* (in which cavemanlike Martians ambush astronaut Lloyd Bridges and crew with foam rubber boulders), and *Missile to the Moon,* whose crew encounters Gumby-like Rock Men among the canyon's escarpments.

Bigger budget sci-fi movies arrived in 1970 with *Beneath the Planet of the Apes,* in which the subterranean mutants' telepathic vision of crucified apes frightens the simian army. A demonic black sedan tears out of the Red Rock desert in *The Car* and later pursues sheriff James Brolin through the terrain in the film's fiery climax. In a less malevolent encounter, Native American Will Sampson and family man Craig T. Nelson communicate with local spirits here in *Poltergeist II.* And according to Kern County film commission liaison Dave Hook, the climactic capture of the brain bug of *Starship Troopers* was shot here in Red Rock.

## HOW TO GET TO RED ROCK CANYON

*Take I-5 North to Highway 14 and to the town of Mojave. Continue on Highway 14 for 25 miles until you reach the state park. Info: 661-942-0662.*

## PRE-TRIP READING

A *Field Guide to Motion Picture Locations at Red Rock Canyon* by Richard J. Schmidt. A masterful piece of detective work, this in-depth guide covers every film-related cliff and crag in the state park. *Canyon Two Publications, P.O. Box 763, Montrose, CA 91021.*

## DVD ITINERARY: RED ROCK CANYON

*Holes*, Scene 19

*4 for Texas*, Scenes 1–4

*Jurassic Park*, Scene 2

*Westworld*, Scenes 18, 23–24

# 23

# TRONA PINNACLES
## Planet of the 'Scapes

> The [film's] major compensation is repped by the stunning locations . . . notably the incredible Trona Pinnacles in California's high desert.
>
> —Variety's film critic Todd McCarthy, reviewing
> Tim Burton's Planet of the Apes

**MAJOR ROLES:** Planet of the Apes (2001), Star Trek V: The Final Frontier

### BEHIND THE SCENERY

Weird spires, steeples, and domes that were once underwater rise out of a dry desert lake at the 4.5-mile collection of Trona Pinnacles, an isolated alien landscape justly designated a National Natural Landmark in 1968. Originally dubbed "Cathedral City" by early explorers, this freakish territory near Death Valley contains some 500 tufa towers comprised of fossilized soda and brine ascending up to 140 feet.

"This is moon country," points out local historian Roberta Starry in her local guidebook. "It's like traveling to another planet, without the need for a space suit, with the highway only seven miles away." In fact, if you're a science-fiction fan visiting the pinnacles for the first time, you'll get an eerie sense of cinematic déjà vu. That's because the monolithic spires have made a variety of appearances on film and TV (including the first season of Lost in Space).

Features include:

Star Trek V: The Final Frontier   The shadowy pinnacles play a mysterious planet where William Shatner, Leonard Nimoy, and crew search for God. Instead they find an ominous holographic deity nesting in the formations.

Mom and Dad Save the World   Hoping to escape an alien world and return to the San Fernando Valley, Dad Jeffrey Jones crash-lands at the pinnacles and encounters a tribe of feather-wearing primitives (among them supermodel/actress and future entrepreneur Kathy Ireland).

*The Brave*  Johnny Depp's rarely seen 1997 directorial debut features Depp and movie wife Elpidia Carrillo hiking to the crest of the pinnacles and making love at sunset.

## WHERE TO HIKE

Amble over to the first pinnacles on the landmark's north side and you will find the location for the *Apes'* Calima set. To reach this group of pinnacles, stay on the main dirt road and cross the railroad tracks. After the landmark sign, take the middle road of the fork to the highest eastern hill. Hike up to the top of the cliffs where William Shatner communicated with a phantom god in *Star Trek V*.

*For hiking and camping info, call the Ridgecrest Resource Area Office at 760-384-5400.*

## WHERE TO STAY

### RIDGECREST MOTELS

Ridgecrest's large motel complexes, Carriage Inn (760-446-7910) and Heritage Inn Suites (800-843-0693), are where the *Apes* crew stayed along the main drag of China Lake Blvd. Other alternatives include chain motels like Motel 6, Days Inn, or the Comfort Inn.

### DETOUR: RANDSBURG—A LIVING GHOST TOWN

For a touch of desert madness, head to the "living" ghost town of Randsburg. The **Randsburg General Store** is an eccentric roadside gem dating back to 1896. Complete with an old-fashioned pharmacy and marble-countered soda fountain, the store offers homemade fudge and traditional diner fare. Service may be less than prompt, but as the circa 1940s sign says over the counter, WE DON'T GIVE A DAMN HOW THEY DO IT IN LOS ANGELES. The town appears as a desert dump in Russ Meyer's 1965 exploitation classic *Faster, Pussycat! Kill! Kill!* and Johnny Depp's *The Brave*. The General Store stars in Troma (no relation to Trona) Pictures' and director Dan Hoskins' *Chopper Chicks in Zombie Town*, with Billy Bob Thornton (in one of his first leading roles) as the redneck husband of an all-girl motorcycle gang member. Randsburg is also the setting of another sisterhood-in-the-desert flick: *Nevada*, starring Amy Brenneman, Dee Wallace Stone and Kathy Najimy. *Randsburg General Store: 760-374-2418.*

*HOW TO GET TO RANDSBURG Take I-5 North to Highway 14 and to the town of Mojave. Continue on Highway 14 for 20 miles NE of Mojave. Shortly after the Jawbone Canyon Store veer right onto the Redrock-Randsburg Road. Continue for 16 miles and veer right again to Randsburg.*

## LOCATION SCOUTING: *PLANET OF THE APES* (2001)

"When I first saw Trona, it looked like a wrecked spaceship *ought* to be right there, almost pushing these rocks up out of the ground like a force-of-nature happening," *Planet of the Apes* production designer Rick Heinrichs told *IDG* magazine. "There's a part of the pinnacles that had a semi-circle of rocky outcroppings coming up . . . we made it look as if the earth had swallowed [the ship] to some degree and made it feel like part of the environment."

The Trona Pinnacles became the site for the climactic apes vs. human battle at the holy city of Calima, the crash site of the film's simian-laden craft. The spiky remains of the spaceship, jutting up from the pinnacle, were reportedly intended to be a subliminal homage to the Statue of Liberty finale from the original *Planet of the Apes*.

Harry Medved

These surreal towers are composed of brine and soda.

Ray Arthur/Ridgecrest Film Commission

Randsburg has hosted such on-screen residents as Johnny Depp, Amy Brenneman, and Billy Bob Thornton.

## HOW TO GET TO THE TRONA PINNACLES

*Take I-5 North to Highway 14 and to the town of Mojave. Continue on 14 and take the Highway 178 turnoff to the town of Ridgecrest. From Ridgecrest continue on Highway 178 east for 17 miles until you see a sign for the Bureau of Land Management dirt road (RM143) on the right. Go south on this road for 5 miles till you arrive at the spires. Be advised the gravelly washboard road should be driven very slowly. For more info, contact the Ridgecrest Area Convention and Visitors Bureau at www.visitdeserts.com or 800-847-4830.*

## DVD: ITINERARY: TRONA PINNACLES

*Planet of the Apes* (2001), Scenes 28–29, 34

*Star Trek V: The Final Frontier*, Scene 11

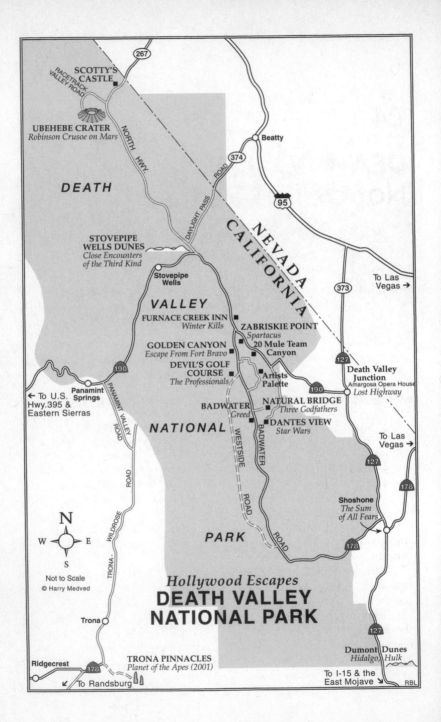

**267**

**SCOTTY'S CASTLE**

RACETRACK VALLEY ROAD

**UBEHEBE CRATER**
*Robinson Crusoe on Mars*

Beatty

**374**

*DEATH*

NORTH HWY.

DAYLIGHT PASS ROAD

**95**

NEVADA
CALIFORNIA

**STOVEPIPE WELLS DUNES**
*Close Encounters of the Third Kind*

Stovepipe Wells

*VALLEY*

**FURNACE CREEK INN**
*Winter Kills*

**ZABRISKIE POINT**
*Spartacus*
**20 Mule Team Canyon**

**373**

To Las Vegas →

**GOLDEN CANYON**
*Escape From Fort Bravo*

**DEVIL'S GOLF COURSE**
*The Professionals*

**190**

Artists Palette

**127**

**Death Valley Junction**
*Amargosa Opera House*
*Lost Highway*

← To U.S. Hwy.395 & Eastern Sierras

Panamint Springs

PANAMINT VALLEY ROAD

**190**

**BADWATER**
*Greed*

**NATURAL BRIDGE**
*Three Godfathers*

**DANTES VIEW**
*Star Wars*

To Las Vegas →

**127**

*NATIONAL*

WESTSIDE ROAD

BADWATER ROAD

**178**

Shoshone
*The Sum of All Fears*

TRONA - WILDROSE ROAD

*PARK*

ROAD

**178**

N
W E
S

Not to Scale
© Harry Medved

*Hollywood Escapes*
# DEATH VALLEY NATIONAL PARK

Trona

**127**

**TRONA PINNACLES**
*Planet of the Apes (2001)*

Ridgecrest

**178**

↙ To Randsburg

**Dumont Dunes**
*Hidalgo, Hulk*

To I-15 & the East Mojave ↘

RBL

# 24

# DEATH VALLEY
# Not of This Earth

What a desolate place *this* is!

—*C3PO to R2D2 in* Star Wars Episode IV: A New Hope *(1977)*

**MAJOR ROLES:** *The Professionals, Robinson Crusoe on Mars, Three Godfathers, Zabriskie Point*

### BEHIND THE SCENERY

Death Valley may not sound like the most enticing location to the typical national park visitor. Indeed, the park's extremes can be daunting to the uninitiated, as the barren terrain is home to:

1. North America's lowest point, near Badwater, at 282 feet below sea level.

2. Record-breaking summer heat, reaching up to 134 degrees Fahrenheit.

3. Vast, uninhabited distances between destinations.

No doubt, Death Valley *is* desolate. But that's also part of its surreal attraction. It's a middle-of-nowhere fantasy landscape filled with multicolored canyons, twisted rocks, and breathtaking vistas.

Although many prospectors searched for gold in Death Valley, these environs are best known for another valuable resource discovered in 1873: borax, the chemical used in laundry detergent, gas additives, and fire retardant.

To transport this precious white powder from the desert floor and onto the nearest railroad cars some 165 miles away, Death Valley pioneers used teams of twenty mules that could pull several tons of borax (plus supplies) on each trek. These journeys were immortalized on both the big and small screen: in MGM's 1940 Western *20 Mule Team* (starring Wallace Beery, Leo Carrillo, and Anne Baxter) and on *Death Valley Days* (the 1950s TV anthology series hosted by Ronald Reagan).

On film and in real life, the theme of "mavericks pitted against the pitiless desert" epitomized the quintessential Death Valley story line. When martinet director Erich von Stroheim shot his silent classic *Greed* here in 1923, fights broke out due to the 128-degree summertime heat. No wonder iced towels were needed to cool off the cast as well as the cameras.

One Death Valley production is known more for its love-in than its infighting: Michelangelo Antonioni's *Zabriskie Point*. Cowritten by playwright Sam Shepard, the film is named after the park's stunning-view location. It's here that the director had dozens of hippie couples make out, much to the consternation of park rangers. "The terrain had a spooky kind of beauty," Antonioni told *Holiday* magazine. "One felt simultaneously protected and isolated, awestruck at its grandeur yet apprehensive about what lay around the next mound of sand."

Like other barren regions in Southern California, Death Valley has played alien landscapes in numerous sci-fi spectacles, most notably *Robinson Crusoe on Mars*, *Rocketship X-M*, and *Star Wars Episode IV: A New Hope*.

## WHERE TO EXPLORE

### THE SAND DUNES AT STOVEPIPE WELLS

Also known as Death Valley Dunes and Mesquite Dunes (named for the rugged plant often seen growing in the sand), this area is often viewed in scenes of desperation and endless isolation. Ironically, in real life the dunes are chosen by filmmakers for their easy access to overnight accommodations and services, including the Stovepipe Wells Motel and cafeteria right across the road. Cinematic stragglers in these sands include Gibson Gowland (*Greed*), Gregory Peck and Richard Widmark (*Yellow Sky*), Stewart Granger and Deborah Kerr (*King Solomon's Mines*), Bette Davis and James Cagney (*The Bride Came C.O.D.*), John Wayne (*Three Godfathers*), Matt Damon and Casey Affleck (*Gerry*) and R2D2 (*Star Wars*). In the Collector's Edition DVD of *Close Encounters of the Third Kind*, Bob Balaban and his team discover a derelict tanker inexplicably buried in Stovepipe's dunes.

### ZABRISKIE POINT

Zabriskie Point, named after the engineer who made his fortune in borax mining, offer sensational views of the yellow mudstone hills in the ancient lake bed below. In *Spartacus*, this area is where Peter Ustinov takes home slave Kirk Douglas from the Libyan mines. Zabriskie Point makes a wild location for a fantasy sequence in the 1970 film of the same name, in which dozens of couples make love in the badlands directly below. Zabriskie's tall sandstone pinnacle, **Manly Beacon**, is clearly identifiable in 1949's *Three Godfathers, The Law and Jake Wade, Robinson Crusoe on Mars, Rocket Ship X-M,* and Gus Van Sant's 2003 art film, *Gerry.* In the Marlon Brando–directed Western *One-Eyed Jacks,* Karl Malden and Brando part ways at Manly Beacon during an ambush. (Incidentally, Death Valley was one of Brando's favorite places, and his ashes have been scattered in the park.)

## DANTES VIEW

Named for its *Inferno*-like vista, the endless badlands viewable from this 5,475-foot overlook are seen in a brief helicopter shot in *The Greatest Story Ever Told* as Jesus journeys through the wilderness. The same badlands serve as the terrain of Mos Eisley in the original *Star Wars.*

## GOLDEN CANYON

This is one of the many colorful canyons you can see from the overlook at Zabriskie Point. Golden Canyon is perhaps the most scenic, as it includes the monumental **Red Cathedral**, seen as a dead end for the cavalry in the John Sturges Western *Escape from Fort Bravo* (with William Holden) and as the site of an ambush in *20 Mule Team* (with Wallace Beery and Leo Carrillo). Just south of the Golden Canyon trail is **Gower Gulch**, which appears in one of the many desert trek sequences in *Three Godfathers.*

Zabriskie Point plays the Red Planet in *Robinson Crusoe on Mars.*

## DEVIL'S GOLF COURSE

The salt of Devil's Golf Course has crystallized into jagged, alien shapes, and no matter where you step you'll trod upon these strange formations. In Richard Brooks' *The Professionals*, Lee Marvin, Burt Lancaster, Robert Ryan, Woody Strode, and Claudia Cardinale rest their horses here. Actor Paul Mantee remembers crossing the area as an astronaut in *Robinson Crusoe on Mars*. "I'll never forget that weird *crunch-crunch-crunch* sound under my feet," recalls Mantee.

## BADWATER

This eerie pool of salty water is a popular tourist destination due to its proximity to the lowest point in North America. About a mile south of here, the **Badwater Basin Salt Flats** are where the area's large, polygonal sheets of salt are most accessible. The cracked-earth terrain has been seen in many films including *Greed*, *Yellow Sky*, *Winter Kills*, and *Gerry*.

## NATURAL BRIDGE

This narrow slot canyon with a sandstone bridge is reminiscent of Utah's Natural Bridges National Monument. Its Western film appearances include *Three Godfathers* (where John Wayne and the baby almost expire), *Escape from Fort Bravo* (the site of an Indian ambush) and the bizarre cult independent film *Six-String Samurai* (where the titular hero joins up with a young admirer).

## WHERE TO STAY AND EAT

### FURNACE CREEK INN

The only luxury resort in Death Valley, this hotel is often the lodging of choice for the casts filming in the area. The inn features a fine-dining restaurant and outdoor bar that affords a spectacular view of the dessicated Death Valley wilderness. Past guests include Matt Damon, Casey Affleck, Kurt Russell, Goldie Hawn, and Diane Keaton. Anthony Quinn frequently held family reunions here. In the political thriller *Winter Kills*, the inn plays the desert compound for businessman John Huston and visiting son Jeff Bridges. 760-786-2362.

### FURNACE CREEK RANCH

Not to be confused with the Furnace Creek Inn, the ranch is a less expensive alternative, with basic motel rooms, a cafeteria, and general store on the premises. Some visitors choose to stay at the ranch and have dinner and cocktails at the inn. *760-786-2345.*

## DETOUR: SCOTTY'S CASTLE AND UBEHEBE CRATER

Though Scotty's Castle and Ubehebe Crater are a full hour away from the Furnace Creek and Stovepipe Wells areas, they're worth the trip. Chicago millionaire Albert Johnson befriended Wild West Show huckster Walter E. Scott (nicknamed "Death Valley Scotty"), who not only convinced Johnson to build a Spanish Colonial mansion in the middle of nowhere, but assured him it would become the new Hollywood hangout. Bette Davis stayed at the Castle during the filming of *The Bride Came C.O.D.*, according to historian Colleen Bath, and John Barrymore was a frequent guest. *Scotty's Castle tour info: 760-786-2395.*

A half-hour drive from Scotty's Castle will take you to the 770-feet-deep and half-mile-wide Ubehebe Crater, a key landmark on the Martian landscape in the cult sci-fi movie *Robinson Crusoe on Mars*. Because of its creepy appearnce, the film's crew referred to this volcanic abyss as "The Heebee Jeebee Crater," according to star Paul Mantee. Dress warmly as the winds kick up here.

## DETOUR: AMARGOSA OPERA HOUSE

The memorably bizarre Amargosa Opera House, hotel, and gas station are all part of a complex of buildings that make up the town of Death Valley Junction, population eighteen.

Aging ballerina and opera house owner Marta Becket (born 1924) moved to Death Valley in the 1960s and has been dancing at the Amargosa ever since. A former chorus-line dancer from Broadway productions like *Wonderful Town*, Marta prefers to be her own boss and puts on a performance each week, even if no one shows up to see it. Marta claims she has had many adoring fans from Hollywood make the journey to see her, including Marlon Brando, Martin Sheen, Red Skelton, and Ray Bradbury. *Amargosa*, a documentary about her eccentric life, premiered at the Sundance Film Festival and Marta will be glad to sell you a DVD or VHS copy of the movie.

The complex has been used as a filming location for *The Hitcher* (see box) and David Lynch's *Lost Highway*, in which Bill Pullman encounters strange goings-on (and pasty-faced weirdo Robert Blake) in Room 7. *Hotel season is October–May. www.amargosaoperahouse.com; 760-852-4441.*

## ON THE ROAD: THE SANDS OF HIGHWAY 127

Los Angeles travelers en route to Death Valley may take Highway 15 through the town of Baker and may opt to continue north on Highway 127 for an ad-

## *STAR WARS* NATIONAL PARK

In addition to the main desert location of Tunisia in North Africa, numerous spots in Death Valley were used for pick-up shots of the planet of Tatooine in *Star Wars Episode IV: A New Hope*. In the last few decades, *Star Wars* fans have been making pilgrimages to Death Valley to pinpoint these hallowed sites with the help of park rangers. They include:

**Artists Palette** This multicolored canyon that is accessible by car is known to *Star Wars* fans as "Artoo's Arroyo," named for the sequence in which the lovable droid wanders in the desert.

**Desolation Canyon** Also known to fans as "Bantha Canyon" for the film's elephant-size creatures who roam here, this site is where Tusken raiders make their appearance.

**Dantes View** This elevated view of the valley provides the backdrop for the Mos Eisley spaceport, as surveyed by Luke, Obi-Wan Kenobi, and the droids.

**The Sand Dunes at Stovepipe Wells** With Death Valley Buttes in the background, R2D2 separates from C3PO and heads over a dune toward the Grapevine Mountains.

**West Side Road** Fans say this dirt road near the Badwater area is the terrain Luke Skywalker streaks across in his landspeeder.

**Twenty Mule Team Canyon** This dirt road appears briefly in *Return of the Jedi* as a location en route to Jabba the Hutt's palace.

Other classic *Star Wars* trilogy sites in the state include Northern California's **Jedediah Smith Redwoods State Park** (the site of the speeder chase through the forest in *Return of the Jedi*) and the Arizona border-adjacent **Imperial Sand Dunes** (the *Jedi* site of Jabba's barge and the sandpit monster's lair; see page 185).

ditional desert movie tour. Lonely **Silurian Dry Lake** is the scene of the Mexico-set climax of Robert Altman's *Dr. T and the Women*. From there, continue north to the Dumont Road turnoff for the **Dumont Dunes,** a popular off-road recreation area that appeared in both *Hidalgo* and *Hulk*. And the sands of **Shoshone** stand in for Israel in Phil Alden Robinson's big-screen adaptation of *The Sum of All Fears*. From Shoshone follow the signs to Badwater and into Death Valley.

## THRILLER ON THE ROAD: *THE HITCHER* DESERT TOUR

While you're driving through the California desert, you may feel a sense of tranquility and adventure. The vastness of the desert is soothing to some, haunting to others. This is what attracted director Robert Harmon to the area for *The Hitcher,* his memorably twisted 1986 cult favorite starring Rutger Hauer and C. Thomas Howell. "I think the California desert is beautiful," Harmon says. "I'm intrigued by horrible things happening in beautiful places."

*The Hitcher* was shot on the highways, largely in sequence. "The process worked well for this kind of road picture," said production manager and coproducer Paul Lewis. "It helped intensify the experience. Usually when you're shooting in L.A., the cast and crew go home at night. For *The Hitcher,* we were one team traveling, staying and working together on the road. We felt like we were living the movie."

This Method-like technique provided for maximum tension with the actors and filmmakers. However, only the strongest of heart will want to retrace the production's route, which spans three major desert locations: Death Valley, Route 66 in the East Mojave, and the Imperial Sand Dunes.

*CAUTION: This demanding journey is not recommended as a day trip, and should not be attempted in hot summer temperatures.*

**Death Valley Junction** makes an appropriately eerie starting point. The town's dusty gas station is where tormentor Rutger Hauer confronts victim C. Thomas Howell, throwing down a gauntletlike set of car keys that formally begins their deadly game of cat and mouse. This forgotten town is the site of the eccentric Amargosa Opera House and its 1923 hotel.

Head south on Highway 127 to Interstate 15 South, toward Barstow. Go east on Interstate 40 to **Daggett.** This is the site of the film's Longhorn Café set. It's here that Howell meets waitress Jennifer Jason Leigh, who unwittingly serves him a surprise lunch special in the infamous french-fried finger sequence.

When you hit the town of Ludlow, take the Route 66 turnoff to Amboy. You'll know you've arrived when you see the tall 1950s-style sign for **Roy's Café,** where Howell pulls a gun on Hauer in a futile attempt to eradicate him.

Continue on Route 66 to Interstate 40 and head toward Arizona. At Needles (on the California-Arizona border), head south on Route 95 until you reach Blythe. Cross under the 10 Interstate and take Highway 78 to the town of **Glamis,** self-proclaimed "Sand Toy Capitol [sic] of the World." The **Glamis General Store and Café** served as the truck-stop location for the film's Outpost Café, where Hauer abducts Jennifer Jason Leigh and masterminds her grisly fate. Some fifteen years earlier, another kind of highway horror descended upon the area in the forgotten shocker *Werewolves on Wheels.* Not by coincidence, that film's locations were also scouted by future *Hitcher* co-producer Paul Lewis.

Glamis is also the gateway for the **Imperial Sand Dunes Recreation Area,** where Howell and Hauer stage their final confrontation. As seen in the film's finale, twilight time is the best hour to see these sun-swept dunes in the shadow of the Chocolate Mountains.

To get back to Los Angeles, take Highway 78 to Brawley and 86 to El Centro, where you'll finally end up on Interstate 8, the main artery heading west to San Diego. From San Diego take Interstate 5 North.

And remember: *Never pick up hitchhikers.*

## HOW TO GET TO DEATH VALLEY

*Take I-5 North to Highway 14, then take the 14 to the town of Mojave. Stay on the 14 as it turns into Highway 395. Take 395 to 178 East and follow the signs to Death Valley. Travel time is approximately 6 hours from L.A. Info: www.nps.gov/deva; 760-786-3200.*

## DVD ITINERARY: DEATH VALLEY

*The Professionals*, Devil's Golf Course, Scene 23

*Close Encounters of the Third Kind: The Collector's Edition*, Sand Dunes at Stovepipe Wells, Scene 7

*Star Wars—Episode IV: A New Hope*, Dantes View, Scene 19

Inland Empire Film Commission

The Dumont Dunes, stomping grounds for Ang Lee's *Hulk*.

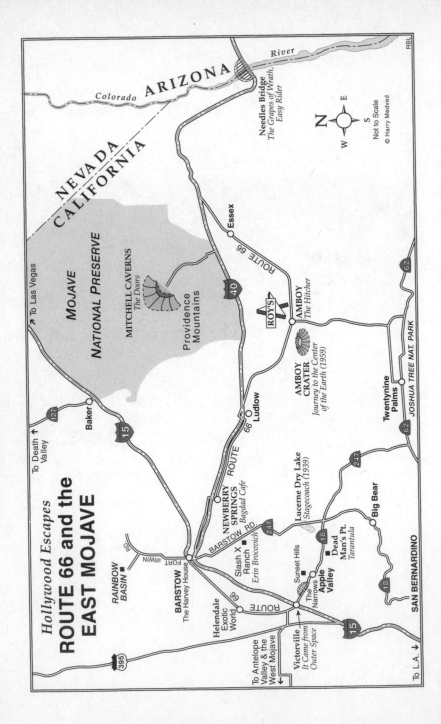

*Hollywood Escapes*
# ROUTE 66 and the
# EAST MOJAVE

Colorado River

ARIZONA

NEVADA

CALIFORNIA

Needles Bridge
*The Grapes of Wrath,*
*Easy Rider*

N
E
S
W
Not to Scale
© Harry Medved

RBL

To Las Vegas

Essex

MOJAVE

NATIONAL PRESERVE

MITCHELL CAVERNS
*The Doors*

Providence
Mountains

ROUTE 66

40

AMBOY
*The Hitcher*

ROY'S

AMBOY CRATER
*Journey to the Center*
*of the Earth (1959)*

62

To Death ↑
Valley

127

Baker

15

66 Ludlow

ROUTE 66

Twentynine
Palms

62

JOSHUA TREE NAT. PARK

Lucerne Dry Lake
*Stagecoach (1939)*

247

NEWBERRY
SPRINGS
*Bagdad Cafe*

BARSTOW RD.

Big Bear

247

18

RAINBOW
BASIN

FORT IRWIN RD

Slash X
Ranch
*Erin Brocovich*

Sunset Hills

Dead
Man's Pt.
*Tarantula*

BARSTOW
The Harvey House

Helendale
Exotic World

99

ROUTE 66

The
Narrows

Apple
Valley

18

SAN BERNARDINO

To Antelope
Valley & the
West Mojave →

Victorville
*It Came from*
*Outer Space*

15

395

To L.A. ↓

# 25

# ROUTE 66 & THE EAST MOJAVE
## Getting Your Kicks

Won't you get hip to this timely tip:
When you make that California trip?
Get your kicks on Route 66.

—*Nat King Cole, singing Bobby Troup's 1946 hit song*

**MAJOR ROLES:** *The Hills Have Eyes* (1977), *Bagdad Café,*
*The Doors, Mr. & Mrs. Smith* (2005)

### BEHIND THE SCENERY

As the first paved road connecting the East with the West in 1938, Route 66 wound its way from Chicago to Santa Monica and found its way into the literature of John Steinbeck, who called it "the Mother Road" in his classic novel *The Grapes of Wrath*. Steinbeck chronicled the Depression-era farmers who made their pilgrimages on Route 66, leaving the Dust Bowls of Oklahoma and Arkansas and struggling across the rugged East Mojave for a new life in California.

One midwesterner who made a timely trip West in the 1930s was an aspiring singer and actor named Leonard Franklin Slye, who later changed his name to Roy Rogers. On his way to Hollywood, the future King of the Cowboys made a fateful stop in the high-desert Route 66 towns of Victorville and Apple Valley. "He loved the area and ended up filming over forty B Westerns there," recalls Bob Moore, author of *The Complete Guidebook and Atlas to Route 66.*

Victorville, now a sprawling high-desert town, was considered the "boonies" for Hollywood during the Golden Age when the industry ventured out to the East Mojave to shoot movies or simply to get away from it all. In the spring of 1940, convalescing screenwriter Herman J. Mankiewicz reportedly stayed for eleven weeks to work on his *Citizen Kane* screenplay at Victorville's (now private) Kemper-Campbell Ranch. This retreat also attracted Greta Garbo, Greer Garson, and Harpo and Groucho Marx.

Alas, with the introduction of faster interstate highways in the 1960s, Route 66 became the road less taken. Even George Maharis and Martin Milner's classic Corvette in the TV series *route 66* hardly ever hit these eccentric desert outposts, according to road scholar Moore. As tourism dropped off in the 1970s, businesses closed, the secluded star ranches shut their doors, and nearly all Route 66 segments were replaced by four-lane highways (a saga retold in Pixar's *Cars*).

Today the classic roadside stops, like the Bagdad Café or Roy's Café, are far and few between in California, so filmmakers and tourists often return to recapture a sense of nostalgia and mystery. "It's as if David Lynch and Ansel Adams got together and designed a roadway, very surreal, stark, and still," says James Hibberd, reporter for *Television Week* and frequent desert traveler.

## THE ROUTE 66 DRIVING TOUR:
## VICTORVILLE TO NEEDLES

*From L.A., take the I-10 East to San Bernardino. Take I-15 North to the D Street exit in Victorville. Follow the signs to Historic Route 66.*

### OLD TOWN VICTORVILLE

This old main street area of Victorville is often cast as a small town in Texas, and it certainly has that parched look. Old Town Victorville is the site of chases in the Robert Blake motorcycle cop picture *Electra Glide in Blue* and Ron Howard's first film as a director, *Grand Theft Auto*. It's also home to the Green Spot Motel, once owned by *Perils of Nyoka* star Kay Aldridge. The Green Spot was known as "a Hollywood hangout where stars like John Wayne and Ward Bond did their heavy drinking and stuntman Yakima Canutt was rumored to have taken on locals in a barroom brawl," according to town historian Richard Thompson.

Just northeast of Old Town Victorville is **Peggy Sue's '50s Diner** (760-951-5001). The RV-traveling family of Harvey Keitel, Juliette Lewis, and Ernest Liu have a meal in Peggy Sue's corner booth before a fateful rendezvous with Quentin Tarantino and George Clooney in Robert Rodriguez's *From Dusk Till Dawn*.

*From L.A., take the I-10 East to San Bernardino. Take I-15 North to the D Street exit in Victorville. Follow the signs to Historic Route 66.*

### EXOTIC WORLD BURLESQUE MUSEUM, HELENDALE

Exotic World gets a footnote in show biz geography as an off-the-beaten-path shrine to the oft-forgotten history of burlesque. It has been the subject of several documentaries and is run by septuagenerian stripper and former Dust Bowler Dixie Evans (billed as "The Marilyn Monroe of Burlesque"). Her Exotic World Hall of Fame includes tributes to Sally Rand, Lili St. Cyr, Betty Page, Tempest Storm, Blaze Starr (subject of Ron Shelton's *Blaze*, with Paul Newman and Lolita Davidovich), and Chesty Morgan, star of the 1974 cult classic *Deadly Weapons* (in which a vengeful widow tracks down and smothers her husband's killers with her lethal seventy-three-inch bust). *Reservations required. www.exoticworldusa.org; 760-243-5261.*

## THE HISTORIC HARVEY HOUSE, BARSTOW

Barstow's must-see tourist highlight is the 1911 Harvey House, a beautifully restored train depot and museum complex. Fred Harvey was the legendary railroad host who helped build accommodations across the West. His famed restaurants were immortalized in the MGM musical *The Harvey Girls*, starring Judy Garland and Angela Lansbury. Today the Harvey House is home to the Western America Railroad Museum and the lively and informative Route 66 Mother Road Museum. *Open Friday–Sunday. 681 N. First Ave.; www.route66museum.org; 760-255-1890.*

HOW TO GET TO THE HISTORIC HARVEY HOUSE *From Route 66, head north on First Avenue. Cross the bridge over the railroad tracks, and the complex will be on your right.*

## RAINBOW BASIN NATIONAL NATURAL LANDMARK

Just eight miles north of Barstow is this gem of a park that gets its name from the multicolored canyons full of limestone green, copper yellow, and rust-colored rocks shaped like mushrooms, cauliflower, and artichokes. The three-mile **Rainbow Basin Scenic Drive** is a county-maintained one-way dirt road that loops around the park, with plenty of opportunities to pull over and hike. The basin's **Owl Canyon Campground** has few facilities, so make sure you bring your own water and take advantage of services in Barstow.

On your way to Rainbow Basin, you'll pass by filming locations for Milos Forman's 1979 movie *Hair*, partially shot at the nearby Ft. Irwin military base. It's on Irwin Road where Beverly D'Angelo seduces military man Richard Bright, steals his car and uniform.

A few miles east of here is the mining camp recreation, **Calico Ghost Town**, and **Calico Dry Lake** (site of the vampires' saloon set in *From Dusk Till Dawn*). Farther east you'll find the Bureau of Land Management area on Mule Canyon Road that was the location of Michael Madsen's trailer visited by vengeful Uma Thurman and one-eyed Daryl Hannah in Quentin Tarantino's *Kill Bill, Vol. 2*.

## BAGDAD CAFÉ, NEWBERRY SPRINGS

Formerly known as the Sidewinder Café, this middle-of-nowhere watering hole was renamed after the cult success of *Bagdad Café*, the quirky 1987

German-American movie shot here. European tourists still flock to this simple eatery to get a sense of "real" Americana. The shuttered motel and trailer next door was where Marianne Sägebrecht and Jack Palance lived, both in *Bagdad*'s story line and during principal photography. *46548 National Trails Highway; 760-257-3101.*

## AMBOY CRATER NATIONAL NATURAL LANDMARK

From seemingly out of nowhere rises this distinctive six thousand-year-old volcanic formation scaled by James Mason in the 1959 version of *Journey to the Center of the Earth*. A steep, rocky hike around the west side of the crater will take you to a breach where lava once burst through the fragile cone. From the breach you can walk *into* the cone's center and then up to the top of the crater's opposite side for a panoramic view. The landscape nearby appears in the New Mexico prologue in *The Doors*.

*HOW TO GET TO AMBOY CRATER Amboy Crater is 2.5 miles west of the town of Amboy. A short dirt road leads to a parking area less than a mile from the crater base. CAUTION: This short dirt road is extremely rugged and is recommended only for four-wheel-drive or high-clearance vehicles. If you don't want to damage your car, simply park on the paved road and walk the extra mile on the rocky dirt road.*

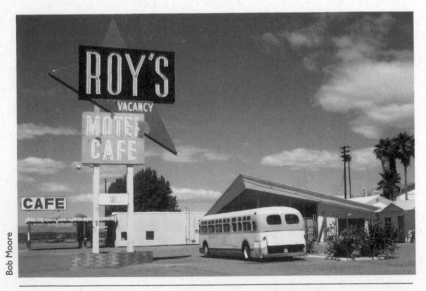

Bob Moore

Movie menaces Rutger Hauer and Brad Pitt
have gone a little crazy here.

## ROY'S CAFÉ, AMBOY

There's not much to Amboy, a destitute desert town that is often in search of an owner. Amboy's Roy's Cafe is a recognizable location for music videos, commercials, and films like *The Hitcher* and Dominic Sena's *Kalifornia* (where serial killer Brad Pitt unleashes his psychopathic ways on Juliette Lewis, Michelle Forbes, and David Duchovny). Since Roy's has often been a demonic setting in the movies, it's not surprising that its address is an extra-devilish 6666 *National Trails Highway. Check with the Route 66 Museum at 760-255-1890 to see if Roy's is open.*

## NEEDLES BRIDGE

This graceful arched bridge at the California-Arizona border dates back to 1915 and plays a special part in the Fonda family's movie history:

Optimistic Okie Henry Fonda and family cross this bridge in an overpacked truck in the 1940 film *The Grapes of Wrath* as they *arrive* in California to seek a better life.

Thirty years later, drug-dealing characters Peter Fonda and Dennis Hopper cross this bridge on motorcycles in *Easy Rider* as they *depart* California to "find America."

The Needles Bridge also offers a view of the Colorado River below, where *Grapes'* Fonda and the Joad family go swimming.

## DETOUR: HAPPY TRAILS TO UFOS— APPLE VALLEY AREA LANDMARKS

*Less famous and almost as colorful as Route 66, Highways 18 and 247 are historic East Mojave arteries that take desert travelers through the Apple and Lucerne Valleys.*

*Highway 18 was named "Happy Trails" after the cowboy song that longtime resident Roy Rogers made famous. Although Highway 18 is jammed with commercial services near Victorville, it eventually becomes the open road. Beyond its intersection with Highway 247 (aka Barstow Road) the Happy Trails Highway follows the tracks of Western icons like Tom Mix and John Wayne.*

## THE NARROWS

From Route 66 in Victorville, follow Highway 18 East as it heads through the rocks of the Narrows, a craggy hilltop that separates Victorville from its neighbor Apple Valley. Crossing the Narrows is the classic steel 1920s Rainbow Bridge. The opening aerial shot of *It Came from Outer Space* shows the Narrows rocks just before the camera swoops over Old Town Victorville (playing the quiet town of Sand Rock, Arizona). You can also see the Narrows in the climactic car chase in Ron Howard's *Grand Theft Auto*.

HOW TO GET TO THE NARROWS *The best way to see the Narrows is by taking the Stoddard Wells Road exit at the intersection of Stoddard and Mineral Road. Here you'll get a good view of the bridge and the rocks above.*

## Top Billing: MITCHELL CAVERNS— OPENING *THE DOORS*

You'll find the only natural limestone caverns in the California State Park System in the 4,300-feet-high Providence Mountains of the Eastern Mojave Desert. The ninety-minute-long guided tour of the caverns includes a "bottomless" pit and strangely shaped stalagmite/stalactite formations that resemble white spaghetti, organ pipes, and wedding gowns.

One of the caverns' sacred Indian spots, **Tecopa Cave** can be seen in Oliver Stone's *The Doors* during the psychedelic trip sequence in which Val Kilmer (as Jim Morrison) has a premonition of his death. To add color to the scene in which Kilmer communes with a shaman, freelance artists painted phony Indian pictographs on the limestone after assuring the State Park the colors were removable. After shooting wrapped, rangers, environmentalists, Native Americans, and crew members were horrified to find that the "artwork" had scarred the cave walls. On his DVD commentary, however, director Stone contends that the damage was temporary.

Other *Doors* "trip" locations in the East Mojave National Preserve are the **Kelso Dunes** and **The Hole-in-the-Wall Rings Trail,** a unique path that requires hikers to use iron rings to descend a rock wall.

*HOW TO GET TO MITCHELL CAVERNS The caves are located in the Mojave National Preserve. From Victorville, take the I-15 North to the I-40 East and take the Essex Road off-ramp, heading northwest. Follow the signs to Providence Mountains State Recreation Area, then follow the signs to Mitchell Caverns. Reservations required. Best times to visit: October to April. There is only one tour per day, so arrive early. 760-928-2586.*

## DEAD MAN'S POINT

"This jumble of rocks was a favorite location for silent-movie Westerns where Tom Mix would ride his horse down to the valley below," says local historian Richard Thompson. It's also the site where news crews report on the "meteor" landing in director Jack Arnold's *It Came from Outer Space*, according to Universal daily production reports from 1953. Cowritten by science fiction legend Ray Bradbury, the film was the seminal fantasy that reportedly inspired Steven Spielberg to write *Close Encounters of the Third Kind* (which coincidentally shot its opening sequence not too far away, on the other side of Interstate 15 at El Mirage Dry Lake).

Arnold returned to shoot the Victorville-Apple Valley area for the 1955 science-gone-amuck creature feature *Tarantula*. It's atop distinctive Dead Man's Point where John Agar and Mara Corday first encounter the hundred-foot-tall arachnid, which shortly thereafter crawls down the Apple Valley highways (and is ultimately exterminated by a squad of jet pilots led by a young Clint Eastwood!).

*HOW TO GET TO DEAD MAN'S POINT Take Highway 18 to Bear Valley Road. You'll find Dead Man's Point to the east of this intersection.*

## LUCERNE DRY LAKE

At the crossroads of the high desert and fifteen miles southeast of Apple Valley lies this popular off-road, camping, and amateur rocket-launching site. The many classic films shot on this flat earth include Frank Capra's 1937 *Lost Horizon* (as the refueling stop) and John Ford's 1939 classic *Stagecoach*. Yakima Canutt performed one of the all-time great stunts here when he doubled for both *Stagecoach*'s John Wayne (jumping from horse to horse) and an Apache raider (dragged under the coach) during the climactic chase.

Incidentally, thirteen years before *Stagecoach*, Ford re-created the action-packed 1889 Oklahoma Land Rush on this same lakebed in his silent *3 Bad Men*.

It's unclear whether Ford knew that his stagecoach attack sequence was shot only a few miles away from the 1867 site of the last Indian skirmish in Southern California. Side-by-side historical markers at **Chimney Rock** identify the spot and offer two differing views of history. One speaks of Indian "hostilities," recalling that the "Indians looted and burned several cabins"; the other commemorates how the "Indians' traditional food-gathering areas [are] lost to white encroachment."

A few miles east of Lucerne is the Johnson Valley off-road area, site of an explosive desert action sequence in *Mr. & Mrs. Smith* with Brad Pitt and Angelina Jolie trying to do each other in.

*HOW TO GET TO LUCERNE DRY LAKE Follow Highway 18 east to its intersection with Highway 247 (Barstow Road). Make a left on 247 and in a few minutes you'll see the most often filmed section of the lake on your left.*

## BARSTOW ROAD/HIGHWAY 247

A few miles north of Lucerne Dry Lake, this desolate stretch of Highway 247 also serves as a popular filming location.

As you leave Lucerne Valley, the road ascending to Goat Mountain Pass is the site of a tense sequence in the Jonathan Mostow thriller *Breakdown*. Searching for missing wife Kathleen Quinlan, Kurt Russell confronts and searches the semi of suspicious trucker J. T. Walsh.

The rocky terrain along nearby Lucerne Valley Bypass is the site of the vacationing family's fateful car trouble in Wes Craven's classic 1977 tale of cannibal horror, *The Hills Have Eyes*. In the film's DVD featurette, Craven says that he chose this area because "I was looking for something primordial. Sort of 'beginning-of-time-ish' . . . you could drive for miles and miles and not see anything. It's really a hauntingly beautiful place." Adds *Hills* star Robert Houston, "They found a really creepy place to shoot . . . with prehistoric rocks which tumble up to the sky. I think the location was one of the stars of the film." Learn from the mistakes of these movie characters: keep your guard up, your car tuned, and your gas gauge on "full."

If you looking for a quick roadside meal, stop at **Slash X Ranch Café.** This is the bar in *Erin Brockovich* where Julia Roberts meets key paper-shredding witness Tracey Walter. *760-252-1197.*

## HOW TO GET TO ROUTE 66

*Take the 10 East to I-15 North. Look for the "Historic Route 66" turnoff at Victorville.*

## DVD ITINERARY: ROUTE 66 AND THE EAST MOJAVE

*It Came from Outer Space*, The Narrows, Old Town Victorville, Scene 1

*The Doors*, Hole-in-the-Wall Trail and Mitchell Caverns, Scene 10

*Stagecoach*, Lucerne Dry Lake, Scenes 17–19

*Mr. & Mrs. Smith*, Johnson Valley, Scene 9

Bob Moore

Route 66's lonely back roads have inspired movies as diverse as *The Hitcher* and Pixar's *Cars*.

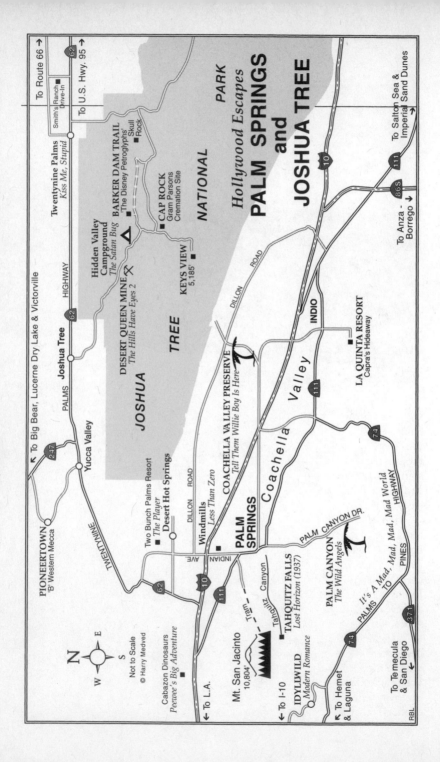

Hollywood Escapes
# PALM SPRINGS and JOSHUA TREE

**Twentynine Palms**
*Kiss Me, Stupid*

To Route 66 →

62 → To U.S. Hwy. 95 →

Smith's Ranch Drive-In

← To Big Bear, Lucerne Dry Lake & Victorville

**PIONEERTOWN**
'B' Western Mecca

Joshua Tree

2-47

Yucca Valley

TWENTYNINE

PALMS

62

HIGHWAY

**JOSHUA TREE NATIONAL PARK**

**Hidden Valley Campground**
*The Satan Bug*

**DESERT QUEEN MINE**
*The Hills Have Eyes 2*

**BARKER DAM TRAIL**
*The Disney Petroglyphs*

Skull Rock

**CAP ROCK**
Gram Parsons Cremation Site

**KEYS VIEW**
5,185'

**Two Bunch Palms Resort**
*The Player*

**Desert Hot Springs**

**Windmills**
*Less Than Zero*

DILLON ROAD

DILLON ROAD

**COACHELLA VALLEY PRESERVE**
*Tell Them Willie Boy Is Here*

**PALM SPRINGS**

INDIAN AVE.

62

10

111

Coachella Valley

**INDIO**

111

7-4

**LA QUINTA RESORT**
Capra's Hideaway

10

111

86S

To Anza - Borrego →

To Salton Sea & Imperial Sand Dunes

**PALM CANYON DR.**

**PALM CANYON**
*The Wild Angels*

*It's A Mad, Mad, Mad, Mad World*

HIGHWAY

PALMS TO PINES

7-4

3-71

To Temecula & San Diego →

To Hemet & Laguna →

**IDYLLWILD**
*Modern Romance*

← To I-10

**Mt. San Jacinto**
10,804'

Tahquitz Canyon

Tram

**TAHQUITZ FALLS**
*Lost Horizon (1937)*

62

111

10

← To L.A.

**Cabazon Dinosaurs**
*Peewee's Big Adventure*

Not to Scale
© Harry Medved

N
W E
S

# 26

# JOSHUA TREE NATIONAL PARK
## Rocks and Roles

There's a profound stillness to this wilderness that is deafening.

—*Director Christopher Coppola*

**MAJOR ROLES:** *Tell Them Willie Boy Is Here, The Satan Bug, Twentynine Palms*

### BEHIND THE SCENERY

Early Mormon emigrants called this basin's tall, thorny shrubs "Joshua trees," imagining that their outstretched branches resembled supplicating arms of the biblical prophet. Frontier explorer John C. Fremont thought they were less inspiring and called them "the most repulsive trees in the vegetable kingdom." In fact, it is said that some motorists would set fire to the limbs and use the trees as beacons to light the road.

Hollywood celebrities had considerably more appreciation for the land and its strange rocks. As nearby Palm Springs grew, stars considered this area equally desirable and moved to the towns of Yucca Valley, Joshua Tree, and Twentynine Palms. Part-time residents and notable visitors have included Esther Williams, Red Skelton, Louis Armstrong, Warren Oates, songwriter Jimmy Van Heusen ("High Hopes"), Eric Burdon, Rat Packers Frank Sinatra and Dean Martin, and Bono, here for U2's *The Joshua Tree* album cover photo shoot. Joshua Tree is also well known as a mecca for rock-climbing enthusiasts.

The environs are often used as an unforgiving land reflecting the characters' desperate motives. Unsettling films shot here include John Sturges' 1965 germ warfare thriller *The Satan Bug* and his little-seen 1953 film noir *Jeopardy*, starring Barbara Stanwyck and Ralph Meeker; Wes Craven's *The Hills Have Eyes Part 2*; the grisly terror tale *Route 666*, with Lou Diamond Phillips; and Bruno Dumont's explicit French exploration of sexual obsession, *Twentynine Palms*.

On a lighter note, the Yucca Valley area was one of many locations for Stanley Kramer's 1963 comedy *It's a Mad, Mad, Mad, Mad World*. It's along the Twentynine Palms Highway that money-hungry Ethel Merman, Milton Berle, and Terry Thomas bicker over a set of car keys and decline an offer of roadside assistance from motorist Jack Benny (in a cameo drive-by).

Billy Wilder shot his underrated 1964 comedy *Kiss Me, Stupid* in Twentynine Palms, in which it plays the desert pitstop "Climax, Nevada." Kim Novak, Ray Walston, and Felicia Farr play the residents of this middle-of-nowhere town that gets a surprise visit from Las Vegas sensation "Dino," played by Dean Martin himself. For Joseph L. Mankiewicz's prison break comedy/drama *There Was a Crooked Man*, a makeshift territorial prison (from which Kirk Douglas tries to escape) was built in the Cottonwood Valley area, according to Joshua Tree film historian Ben Costello.

## WHERE TO EXPLORE

*For directions to the following landmarks, stop by the Visitors Center at the park's east entrance.*

## SKULL ROCK

If you use your imagination, this landmark at Jumbo Rocks Campground resembles the head of actor Michael Berryman, the demented cannibal in Wes Craven's horror classic *The Hills Have Eyes*. It appears the *rocks* have eyes too, as Skull Rock and its twisted-sister formations are pitted with sunken, orbital cavities. Director Robert Harmon's thirty-four-minute thriller *China Lake*, his 1983 precursor to *The Hitcher*, features star Charles Napier as a predatory motorcycle cop prowling this eerie location's environs. You can't miss the sandstone Skull Rock formation from the road.

### Top Billing: KEY'S VIEW

This is the ideal spot in the National Park for watching the sunset. A short path from the road leads to a 360-degree summit view of the Salton Sea, Mexico, and the snow-capped mountains of San Gorgonio and San Jacinto. This road was built by desert loner Bill Keys, who was successfully defended by *Perry Mason* author and lawyer Erle Stanley Gardner in a notorious murder trial of the 1940s.

## CAP ROCK

Country-rock pioneer Gram Parsons, onetime member of the Byrds, told his road manager he wanted to be cremated near Cap Rock, a strange boulder topped with a lidlike stone formation. This is where Parsons and the Rolling

Stones' Keith Richards reportedly got stoned and waited for UFOs. When the rocker died suddenly in the town of Joshua Tree in 1973, his manager honored Parsons' wishes with a funeral pyre here. Although Parsons' ashes are supposedly buried in New Orleans, fans still flock to Cap Rock to remember him.

## BARKER DAM NATURE TRAIL
This one-mile loop trail leads to a seasonal pond, a grove of giant Joshua Trees and a rock bearing the infamous "Disney Pictographs." These were once genuine Indian rock etchings, or *petroglyphs*, which were touched up with paint for a Disney nature documentary to make them more visible on film (unfortunately turning the petroglyphs into Hollywood *pictographs*).

## WHERE TO EAT
## CROSSROADS CAFÉ AND TAVERN
The perfect spot to grab a quick bite before or after visiting the park, the Crossroads offers a menu of healthy soups, salads, and sandwiches. *61715 Twentynine Palms Highway; closed Wednesdays; 760-366-5414.*

Harry Medved

Rock legend Gram Parsons was cremated by his road manager
at Cap Rock.

## DETOUR: PIONEERTOWN

Pioneertown is an off-the-beaten-path novelty stop and Western town built in 1946 by industry investors including cowboy villain Dick Curtis, character actor Russell Hayden, Gene Autry, Roy Rogers, gossip columnist Louella Parsons, and comedian Bud Abbott. In the early 1950s, Autry, Rogers, and "Cisco Kid" star Duncan Renaldo shot many of their B Westerns and TV episodes here. Director John Sturges shot two films near Pioneertown: *Jeopardy* and *The Capture*, starring Teresa Wright. Ultra low-budget fright films shot here include *The Howling: New Moon Rising* and *Legend of the Chupacabra*. There are current plans to renovate the town, with a Western Film Festival in the works. Current attractions include the 1947 bowling alley *(760-365-3615)* and Pappy & Harriet's Pioneertown Palace *(760-365-5956)*.

*HOW TO GET TO PIONEERTOWN From Highway 62 in Yucca Valley, take the Pioneertown Road turnoff. Follow the winding road for approximately 20 minutes to the town. www.pioneertown.com.*

## JOSHUA TREE BEATNIK CAFÉ

This bohemian coffeehouse features independent movie screenings, live music, and Internet access. *61597 Twentynine Palms Highway; 760-366-2090.*

## WHERE TO STAY

### 29 PALMS INN

Located just outside the National Park, this collection of twenty bungalows (some dating back to 1928) has a popular cantina on the premises. According to the owners, Dean Martin caroused here while shooting *Kiss Me, Stupid* and James Cagney frequented the Admiral's Suite in the late 1970s. *73950 Inn Avenue; www.29palmsinn.com; 760-367-3505.*

### JOSHUA TREE INN

Built in 1950, this ten-room hacienda is where twenty-six-year-old rock icon Gram Parsons overdosed in Room 8, on September 19, 1973. *61259 Twentynine Palms Highway; www.jtinn.com; 760-366-1188.*

## RIMROCK RANCH CABINS

About forty minutes away from the National Park lies this tranquil alternative to more conventional accommodations in Joshua Tree and Twentynine Palms. According to Rimrock owner Jim Austin, the ranch is not far from where fugitive Robert Blake meets his fate at the hands of sheriff Robert Redford in Abraham Polonsky's *Tell Them Willie Boy Is Here*. *www.rimrockranchcabins.com*; *760-228-1297*.

## HIDDEN VALLEY CAMPGROUND

This spooky locale is the setting for a fight in the sci-fi thriller *The Satan Bug*, starring George Maharis, Anne Francis, and future TV regulars Ed Asner (*Lou Grant*) and Frank Sutton (*Gomer Pyle's* Sgt. Carter) as the villains. Rangers believe the scene was shot near Campground 11. About two miles down the road is the **Desert Queen Ranch,** the abandoned homestead seen in *The Hills Have Eyes Part 2*. It can only be seen via a National Park Service guided tour of the area. *Campground info: 760-367-5500; Ranch tour info: 760-367-5555.*

## WHERE TO SEE A MOVIE AMONG THE JOSHUA TREES
## SMITH'S RANCH DRIVE-IN

One of the last drive-in theaters in Southern California, Smith's is also unquestionably the most exotic of the bunch. This is where Lynda Carter (TV's *Wonder Woman*) watches a movie while the projectionist is attacked by a monster in director Christopher Coppola's *Bloodhead*. *4584 Adobe Road; 760-367-7713.*

## HOW TO GET TO JOSHUA TREE NATIONAL PARK

*Take the 10 East to Highway 62. Head northeast on 62 past the towns Yucca Valley and Joshua Tree. Follow the signs to the National Park.*

## DVD ITINERARY: JOSHUA TREE NATIONAL PARK

*The Hills Have Eyes Part 2*, Desert Queen Ranch, Scenes 5–6

*It's a Mad, Mad, Mad, Mad World*, Yucca Valley, Scene 12

# 27

# PALM SPRINGS
# The Sun and the Stars

Do places like this really exist?

Only in the movies.

—*Greta Scacchi to Tim Robbins, at the magical Two Bunch Palms
Resort in* The Player *(1992)*

**MAJOR ROLES:** *Lost Horizon (1937), Palm Springs Weekend, Less
Than Zero*

## BEHIND THE SCENERY

According to Southern California chronicler Harry Carr, Palm Springs was
nothing but "a waste desert land" when a San Francisco attorney brought his
tuberculosis-afflicted son to these Native American mineral springs in the
1880s. The boy's health improved and word soon spread throughout California. The construction of the springs' first hotel was begun in 1886. Its guests
would include naturalist John Muir and author Robert Louis Stevenson.

By the 1920s Hollywood discovered the springs and flocked here for exotic
silent film locations, often in the Indian canyons. Actors came for the shoots
then stayed for the real estate. Before long, so many movie people moved to the
northern part of town (close to the weekend homes of studio bosses like Darryl
F. Zanuck) that this area became known as the "Movie Colony."

The film industry's attraction to Palm Springs continued to grow during
the 1963 filming of *Palm Springs Weekend* at the Riviera resort and Congress
Inn. Rat Packers Frank Sinatra, Dean Martin, and Sammy Davis Jr. as well as
Elvis Presley and Liberace bought homes in town.

By the late 1980s, Palm Springs developed a reputation as a haven for se-
nior citizens and rowdy spring break college crowds. According to Palm
Springs historian Arthur Lyons, "Disco died, the thong bikini was outlawed by
Mayor Sonny Bono and the glamorous sheen of Palm Springs acquired a thick
layer of tarnish." But the 1990s saw positive change in the area. Continues
Lyons, "Architectural fans, decorators, and revivalists began to rediscover the

unique 'retro' 1950s core still left in Palm Springs and . . . moneyed New York and Hollywood types began to return to the city."

Hollywood still heads to the springs to shoot everything from independent films like *Alpha Dog* to studio fare like 2001's *Oceans Eleven* (where George Clooney and gang gather at Elliott Gould's private hideaway).

## WHERE TO EXPLORE

### THE INDIAN CANYONS

Several hiking trails just outside of Palm Springs can be found in the historic Indian Canyons. They are monitored by the Agua Caliente Band of Cahuilla Indians, which charges a nominal entry fee. Two biblical camp classics shot brief scenes here: *The Silver Chalice* (with Paul Newman and Virginia Mayo) and *The Big Fisherman* (with Howard Keel and Susan Kohner). The oasis can also be seen in Michael Curtiz's 1935 swashbuckler *Captain Blood,* where Olivia de Havilland slaps Errol Flynn for stealing a kiss. **Murray Canyon** and **Andreas Canyon** are good places to escape the crowds. So is **Tahquitz Canyon**, site of the waterfall in *Lost Horizon* (see *In Search of Shangri-La,* pages 173–174).

The most frequently filmed of the Indian Canyons is **Palm Canyon**, with its fifteen miles of California fan palms lining the rocky passage. A paved footpath takes visitors from an Indian Trading Post/souvenir shop to the streambed below, a perfect picnic spot. This is Dorothy Lamour's island paradise where Ray Milland's plane crashes in the 1938 sarong saga *Her Jungle Love.* As if there weren't enough palm trees in Palm Canyon, "truck-loads of [made-in-Hollywood] palms were imported into the canyon," reported a bemused *Palm Springs Life* magazine at the time.

Palm Canyon is the site of a beer-guzzling bongo party and rumble in Roger Corman's 1966 biker extravaganza *The Wild Angels*, with Peter Fonda,

Palm Springs Historical Society

Spencer Tracy relaxes with John Wayne and wife at the long-gone Desert Inn.

Palm Springs Historical Society

Princess Grace Kelly, Prince
Rainier, and royal family depart
for Mt. San Jacinto.

Nancy Sinatra, Michael J. Pollard, Bruce Dern, and Diane Ladd. According to
crew member and future producer Polly Platt, some of the real Hell's Angels
cast in the film got into trouble, with one intoxicated biker chick attempting
suicide in the canyon. Thankfully, tension in Palm Canyon was limited to the
on-screen action in John Sturges' doomsday thriller *The Satan Bug*. This is
where George Maharis and Anne Francis locate the flasks containing a killer
virus that the villains have hidden in the creek's rocky shallows.

*HOW TO GET TO THE INDIAN CANYONS The Indian Canyons are
generally open 8 a.m.–5 p.m. Call for directions. www.indiancanyons.com; 760-
325-3400; Canyon Jeep Tours: 760-320-4600.*

## Top Billing: PALM SPRINGS AERIAL TRAMWAY

It's the ultimate California experience: you ascend six thousand feet from the
sands of the desert to the snow-capped crags of the San Jacinto Mountains in
ten minutes. At the tram's terminus is a restaurant with a view and a gift shop.
Serious hikers will enjoy the demanding five-mile trail to the top of Mt. San
Jacinto. Snow-tube and cross-country ski rentals are available in season.

In *Kotch*, Jack Lemmon's feature directorial debut, senior citizen Walter
Matthau treats twentysomething waitress Deborah Winters to a tram ride up
the mountain. In the Matt Helm adventure *The Wrecking Crew*, Dean Martin
and Sharon Tate fight with Nancy Kwan at the tram station. Two 1970s TV
disaster movies, *Hanging by a Thread* and *Skyway to Terror*, were also shot here.
And the Golden Turkey classic *Eegah!*, in which a lovesick caveman prowls
Palm Springs in search of a teenage mate, was partially filmed in the nearby

canyons. *Dress warmly and wear comfortable walking shoes. www.pstramway.com; 760-325-1391 or 888-515-TRAM.*

## WHERE TO EAT

### TWISTED FISH COMPANY ALASKAN GRILL
Have a craving for great halibut burgers in a desert town? Then this inexpensive fish restaurant is for you. Sit at their sidewalk patio and survey the Palm Springs clientele in the same spot where *City of Industry's* Timothy Hutton and Harvey Keitel case a jewelry store across the street (in reality the redressed 1941 Welwood Murray Memorial Library). *105 South Palm Canyon Drive; 760-320-9000.*

### RICCIO'S
Conveniently located near the airport, Riccio's offers Northern Italian food with a little bit of history: Frank Sinatra and his Rat Pack hung out in Booth 6. The modern **Palm Springs Airport** down the street, which location manager Jerry Jaffe calls "the coolest airport location in Southern California," appears in both *Bounce* (with Gwyneth Paltrow and Ben Affleck) and the film noir *After Dark, My Sweet* (with Jason Patric, Rachel Ward, and Bruce Dern). *2155 N. Palm Canyon Drive; 760-325-2364.*

## WHERE TO STAY

### KORAKIA PENSIONE
Due to its Moroccan design and popularity among fashion photographers, this 1924 hideaway may be one of the coolest places to stay in the springs. Guests are treated to nightly screenings of classic films in the courtyard. Korakia's designer certainly had an eye for fantasy: bedrooms look like chambers from a sheik's chic getaway. In fact, legend has it that Rudolph Valentino and Natacha Rambova trysted here. Across the street is a second Korakia property, the **Mediterranean Villa**. Its previous owner, character actor J. Carrol Naish, starred in a few desert-based films before making this area his home. *257 South Patencio Road; www.korakia.com; 760-864-6411.*

### CALIENTE TROPICS
This genuine Palm Springs relic from 1964 is complete with Polynesian furnishings and poolside tiki gods and torches, as seen in *City of Industry* and Nick Cassavetes' *Alpha Dog*, with Justin Timberlake. This motel has been extensively renovated and prides itself on being pet-friendly: dogs receive Easter Island head-shaped biscuits upon arrival. *411 East Palm Canyon Drive; 866-HOT-9595.*

## CELEBRITY LODGINGS

"From the late 1930s through the early 1960s," writes Janelle Brown in *The New York Times*, "you couldn't spill a martini [in Palm Springs] without getting a celebrity wet." Many of the stars' former homes are available today as luxury vacation rentals through several companies, including Time and Place Homes (*www.timeandplace.com*) and McLean Rentals (*www.ps4rent.com*). These firms claim you can stay overnight in the former getaways of Elvis, Liberace, Sinatra, and Barry Manilow. You can even rent the futuristic John Lautner-designed *Diamonds Are Forever* house (where Sean Connery as James Bond battles a deadly duo of Amazons). Be prepared for sticker shock, as the price tag for a three-night minimum can be as high as eight thousand dollars.

Another Palm Springs budget motel is the **Royal Sun Inn,** where Christina Ricci wreaks havoc in Don Roos' *The Opposite of Sex*. Easily identified by its classic arch facade, the Royal Sun is close to the heart of Palm Springs' main drag. *1700 S. Palm Canyon Drive; 760-327-1564.*

### BALLANTINES HOTEL
Marilyn Monroe supposedly stayed in the poolside "Pretty in Pink" Suite (Room 103), and the innkeepers have decorated her room with numerous Monroe mementos. Other rooms honor Audrey Hepburn, James Dean, and Courtney Love. *1420 N. Indian Canyon Dr.; 760-320-1178.*

## LOCAL MOVIE CELEBRATIONS
### PALM SPRINGS FILM NOIR FESTIVAL
Palm Springs and its environs have long been a setting for big-screen tales of crime and murder, including *The Damned Don't Cry, 711 Ocean Drive*, and *Mulholland Falls*. This annual celebration boasts a list of past guests that includes Robert Culp, Ann Savage, Eleanor Parker, Jane Russell, Rhonda Fleming, and Mickey Spillane. Under the direction of author/noir historian Arthur Lyons, the festival is held around late spring following January's popular **Palm Springs International Film Festival** (www.psfilmfest.org). *Noir Fest info: www.palmspringsfilmnoir.com.*

## EAST OF PALM SPRINGS: LA QUINTA AND COACHELLA VALLEY PRESERVE

It's a forty-five minute drive from downtown Palm Springs to the town of La Quinta, which has been built around the famed 1926 **La Quinta Resort and Club**. According to *Pictorial California* magazine in 1933, the extra distance was part of the resort's appeal: "Those who desire the utter silence of the wide, open spaces are trekking a few miles farther on into the sagebrush country to sojourn at this caravansary tucked away from the main road."

With cypress trees lining the entrance, spectacular grounds framed by jagged, awe-inspiring mountains, and a gleaming white plaza graced with shimmering pools, it's no coincidence that the hacienda-style La Quinta Resort looks like "Shangri-La" from Frank Capra's movie version of *Lost Horizon*. In real life, Capra (and his collaborator Robert Riskin) wrote the outline for the screenplay here. In fact, Capra worked on almost all of their treatments in La Quinta's Room 136; the room became their good luck charm after they plotted *It Happened One Night* here and the subsequent screenplay earned them an Academy Award. Some of Capra's furniture (including his original desk and typewriter) remains in the room. A memorial bench and plaque outside the villa honor the director and his wife Lucille.

When she "vanted to be alone," Greta Garbo rented a house nearby, which is now La Quinta's La Casa conference center. Dorothy Arzner, one of early Hollywood's most notable female directors, owned what is now the resort's Arzner Villa. Other La Quinta guests over the years included Marlene Dietrich, Ginger Rogers, Joan Crawford, Bette Davis, Errol Flynn, Charles Boyer, Sally Field, and Arnold Schwarzenegger. *49-499 Eisenhower Drive; www.laquintaresort.com; 800-598-3828.*

Unaffiliated with the La Quinta resort, the **La Quinta Cliff House** is a ranch house restaurant built into a craggy hillside. It was used in *City of Industry* for a scene in which left-for-dead thief Harvey Keitel steals a car. During the daytime, the picture windows afford great views of the Santa Rosa Mountains. At night, diners can enjoy drinks and appetizers by the terrace fire pit and man-made waterfall. *78250 Highway 111; 760-360-5991.*

Twenty minutes north of La Quinta, the twenty-thousand-acre **Coachella Valley Preserve** is sheltered by the shade-giving trees that give the preserve's Thousand Palms Oasis its name. The .75 mile-long McCallum Grove trail takes you to a pond swimming with endangered desert pupfish. According to desert historian Choral Pepper, this is the quiet, meditative spot Mia Farrow frequented during her marriage to Palm Springs icon Frank Sinatra.

In 1969 the oasis played the shady hideout for accused murderer-on-the-run Robert Blake in the fact-based *Tell Them Willie Boy Is Here*, the tale of a Palm Springs–area manhunt also starring Robert Redford and Katharine Ross. Just outside of the preserve is scenic **Dillon Road**, beloved by commercial di-

# "GABLE AND LOMBARD HONEYMOONED HERE, HERE, HERE, AND HERE . . ."

No question about it: "The King of Hollywood" Clark Gable and screwball comedy star Carole Lombard had one passionate love affair. Hollywood's favorite couple apparently enjoyed an active, location-hopping, extended honeymoon, too. In this West Coast variation on the historical real estate cliché "George Washington slept here," the site of the legendary couple's postnuptial idyll has been claimed by each of the following establishments:

## THE HISTORIC WILLOWS INN, Palm Springs
This secluded 1927 Mediterranean villa hosted Gable and Lombard in the library room. The suite features a coffered high ceiling, beautiful tiles, antiques, and private garden patio. Other fabled guests over the years include Albert Einstein and Marion Davies. *412 W. Tahquitz Canyon; www.thewillowspalmsprings.com; 760-320-0771.*

## INGLESIDE INN, Palm Springs
Three blocks away from the Willows is another exclusive establishment that has its own Gable/Lombard honeymoon suite. Dating back to 1915, this getaway also claims that "Garbo slept here." Its restaurant and piano bar, **Melvyn's**, is known by regulars such as actor Willie Garson as "a good place to see millionaires looking for their next wives, and divorcees looking for their next millionaires." *200 W. Ramon Road; www.inglesideinn.com; 760-325-0046.*

## GOLD MOUNTAIN MANOR, Big Bear Lake
This homey 1928 bed-and-breakfast includes a Clark Gable Room complete with a potbelly Franklin stove. Owners say the stove was moved here from the Hollywood couple's private honeymoon cabin nearby. The legend claims the amorous couple stocked their room full of wood, lit a fire in the old Franklin stove . . . and never left the room. *1117 Anita Avenue; www.goldmountainmanor.com; 909-585-6997.*

**THE OATMAN HOTEL, Oatman, Arizona**

Gable and Lombard eloped in 1939 and got married in the Route 66 town of Kingman, Arizona, four hundred miles away from Hollywood. Although Kingman is often misidentified as the couple's honeymoon destination, they actually spent their *wedding night* at this modest 1902 miner's lodge in the nearby town of Oatman. Locals say Room 15, "The Gable and Lombard Honeymoon Suite," is haunted by their ghosts. *Note: Rooms are no longer available at this restaurant/bar/museum complex. 1818 Main Street; 928-768-4408.*

rectors. This route also serves as the location in *It's a Mad, Mad, Mad, Mad World* where Phil Silvers meets Jonathan Winters.

*HOW TO GET TO COACHELLA VALLEY PRESERVE Take I-10 approximately 10 miles east of Palm Springs to the Ramon Road exit. Take Ramon Road east to Thousand Palms Canyon Drive and turn north. Drive 2 miles to the preserve entrance.*

## NORTH OF PALM SPRINGS: DESERT HOT SPRINGS

Fifteen minutes north of Palm Springs, the town of Desert Hot Springs is best known for boutique resorts offering naturally hot mineral water. "It started out as a blue collar version of Palm Springs in the 1950s," says Sagewater Spa co-owner Rhoni Epstein. These aging resorts can be seen on film in Robert Altman's 1977 desert dream *3 Women*, starring Shelley Duvall, Sissy Spacek, and Janice Rule. Although much of the town seems frozen in time, a few newly renovated spas and motels—including the John Lautner-designed Desert Hot Springs Motel on the former ranch of MGM moviemaker Lucien Hubbard (*www.lautnermotel.com*), and the truly unique Beat Hotel (*www.dhsbeathotel.com*)—are bringing new blood to the area.

## TWO BUNCH PALMS

This is the granddaddy of the local spas. Some say it was "Big Al's Fortress West" in the 1920s, but it's not clear if legendary gangster Al Capone really used it as a hideaway. Robert Altman returned to Desert Hot Springs to shoot portions of *The Player* at Two Bunch Palms; this is the secluded hideaway where Tim Robbins takes lady friend Greta Scacchi for a romantic candlelit dinner and relaxing mud bath. *www.twobunchpalms.com; 800-472-4334.*

## SAGEWATER SPA

A favorite hangout for Peter Lawford in the 1950s, this six-room retreat offers poolside Internet access. *12689 Eliseo Road; www.sagewaterspa.com; 760-251-1668.*

## HOPE SPRINGS MOTEL RESORT

This former nudist colony is where stars from the Palm Springs Racquet Club would go to work on their "complete" tan, according to spa management. *68075 Club Circle Drive; www.hopespringsresort.com; 760-329-4003.*

## ON THE ROAD: CABAZON'S DINOSAUR DUO

Memorably featured in *Pee-wee's Big Adventure*, Cabazon's famous sculptures of an apatosaurus and Tyrannosaurus Rex are worth an up-close inspection. Indeed, as a Burger King now obstructs your view of the giants from the highway, to get a good look stop at the Wheel Inn truck stop (where trucker "Large Marge" drops off Pee-wee) or visit the gift shop inside the apatosaurus (*Dino info: www.cabazondinosaurs.com; 951-922-8700*). If you've got an urge to snack, nearby **Hadley's** market (888-854-5655) is a great place for dried fruit and date shakes.

Cabazon Dinosaurs from
*Pee-wee's Big Adventure.*

Harry Medved

# IN SEARCH OF SHANGRI-LA

Gentlemen, I give you a toast. . . . Here's my hope that
we all find our Shangri-La.

—*Lord Gainsford, played by Hugh Buckler, in*
Lost Horizon

Ever since James Hilton dreamed up the utopian Himalayan hideaway
for his 1933 novel *Lost Horizon,* the name *Shangri-La* has become syn-
onymous with a "distant and secluded hideaway, usually of great
beauty and peacefulness."

To capture this Tibetan paradise on film, Capra and company built
Shangri-La on the Columbia Pictures backlot for his 1937 adaptation.
According to production records and published interviews, other ex-
teriors include Lake Sherwood, Malibu Creek State Park, Lucerne Dry
Lake, and Ojai Valley in a quick cutaway. "By using some of Southern
California's garden spots to evoke paradise," wrote film historian Sam
Frank in the *Los Angeles Herald Examiner,* "Capra also showed the
world why, in part, thousands of people migrated there in the 1920s
and thirties."

The most scenic sequence in the whole movie, however, was shot
a few blocks from downtown Palm Springs at **Tahquitz Falls.** It's at
the base of this plume that horseman Ronald Colman lovingly waves
to Jane Wyatt, atop her white horse on the cliffs above. Getting that
horse up to the sixty-foot-high location was an ordeal. First, the studio built a special rig-and-pulley system. The animal then had to be
hoisted to the top of the falls. Hidden from public view, the scars
where the rig was fastened to the Tahquitz Falls rock face still remain.

*The Making of Lost Horizon* author Kendall Miller points out that
of all the locations used on the movie, "Tahquitz Falls is the one natural destination that to this day offers a sense of how beautiful Shangri-
La could be . . ."

The Tahquitz Canyon visitor center offers a ranger-escorted tour
of the canyon and screens a short film about how the oasis got its
name. (Tahquitz was an ancient shaman who kidnapped young Indian
maidens bathing in the creek beneath the falls.) The presentation also
includes the short Tahquitz Falls sequence from *Lost Horizon.*

*HOW TO GET TO TAHQUITZ FALLS Because Tahquitz Falls can be closed on short notice, check with the Agua Caliente Band of Cahuilla Indians regarding access periods and entrance fees. 500 W. Mesquite, west of Palm Canyon Drive; www.tahquitzcanyon.com; 760-416-7044.*

Kendall Miller Archives

*Lost Horizon*'s Ronald Colman experiences Shangri-La with Jane Wyatt at Tahquitz Falls.

As you leave Cabazon, you'll pass by power-generating windmills, site of the final scene in *Less Than Zero* (with Robery Downey, Jr., as a doomed addict) and the opening action sequence in *Mission: Impossible III*. As you approach Palm Springs, you'll see Mt. San Jacinto rising out of the desert. This is the view enjoyed by *American Gigolo*'s Richard Gere as he drives to a client while Blondie's "Call Me" pulses on the soundtrack.

## LOCATION BLOOPER: *THE WRECKING CREW*

*The Wrecking Crew*'s Dean Martin and Sharon Tate (in one of her last film roles) battle with Nancy Kwan and other villains on a Luxemburg gondola car . . . but the Alpine cable cars look suspiciously like they're part of the Palm Springs Aerial Tramway. The giveaway? The supposed European tram station is beautifully landscaped with spiny ocotillo cactus shrubs—found only in the Southwestern United States and Mexico.

## HOW TO GET TO PALM SPRINGS

*Take the 10 East to Highway 111. Palm Springs is approximately 100 miles (2.5–3 hours) from L.A.*

## DVD ITINERARY: PALM SPRINGS

*Lost Horizon* (1937), Tahquitz Falls, Scene 11

*The Player*, Two Bunch Palms, Scene 20

*Pee-wee's Big Adventure*, Cabazon Dinosaurs, Scenes 13–15

Don Porter, Joanne Dru, Otto Kruger, and Edmond O'Brien meet in Palm Springs in the 1950 film noir *711 Ocean Drive*.

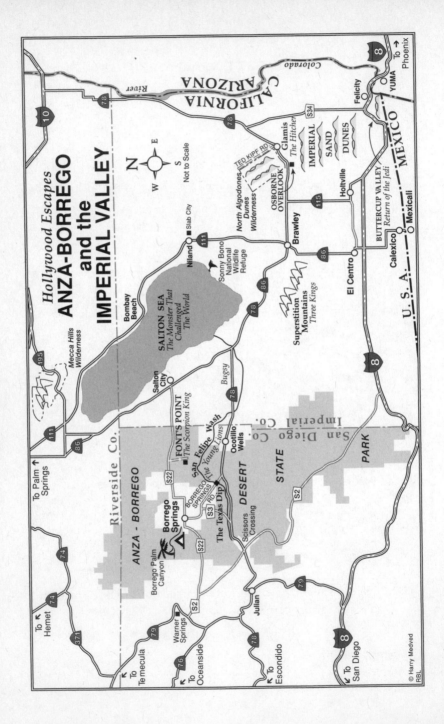

Hollywood Escapes
**ANZA-BORREGO**
**and the**
**IMPERIAL VALLEY**

N
W — E
S
Not to Scale

CALIFORNIA
ARIZONA

Colorado River

To → Phoenix

YUMA

Felicity

MEXICO

Mexicali

Calexico

U.S.A.

El Centro

Brawley

Holtville

Imperial

IMPERIAL SAND DUNES

BUTTERCUP VALLEY
*Return of the Jedi*

Glamis
*The Hitcher*

OSBORNE OVERLOOK

TED KIPF RD.

North Algodones Dunes Wilderness

Sonny Bono National Wildlife Refuge

Niland
Slab City

SALTON SEA
*The Monster That Challenged The World*

Bombay Beach

Mecca Hills Wilderness

To Palm Springs

Salton City

Superstition Mountains
*Three Kings*

Bugsy

FONT'S POINT
*The Scorpion King*

San Felipe Wash

BORREGO SPRINGS

Borrego Springs

*The Young Lions*

Ocotillo Wells

The Texas Dip

Scissors Crossing

ANZA - BORREGO

Borrego Palm Canyon

Riverside Co.

San Diego Co.

Imperial Co.

DESERT STATE PARK

To Hemet

To Temecula

Warner Springs

Julian

To Oceanside

To Escondido

To San Diego

© Harry Medved
RBL

# 28

# ANZA-BORREGO
# Mountains of the Moon

Is this not the most spectacular site you've ever seen? I tell you,
it's breathtaking!

> —*Warren Beatty, as* Bugsy, *on a road outside of*
> *Anza-Borrego*

**MAJOR ROLES:** *Bugsy, The Scorpion King, The Desert Rats*

### BEHIND THE SCENERY

Two hours east of San Diego sprawls one of the largest state parks in the nation and one of the least known in California. With six hundred thousand acres of undeveloped land, five hundred miles of unpaved roads and an endless valley floor sheltered by nine-thousand-foot-high peaks, Anza-Borrego Desert State Park is one of the most remote places in Southern California.

The name Anza-Borrego pays tribute to explorer Juan Bautista de Anza, who led Mexico's overland expedition to San Francisco in 1776, and to the bighorn *borregos* (Spanish for "sheep") that still roam the region's Santa Rosa Mountains.

The state park surrounds a retirement community called Borrego Springs, which has the hushed serenity of Palm Springs of the early 1920s. Over the years a number of actors settled in town, including Bing Crosby, Burgess Meredith, James Arness, and TV character actor Gale Gordon. As Supervising Ranger Fred Jee says, "Anza-Borrego offers a variety of looks that filmmakers can use as foreign countries or alien terrain. We have fresh backdrops that have not been overused."

### WHERE TO EXPLORE
### Top Billing: BORREGO PALM CANYON

As Ann Marie Brown writes in her book *Easy Hiking in Southern California,* the trek to Borrego Palm Canyon is "a three-mile round trip but feels like a trip from the desert to the tropics." The destination feels like a movie set with its palm-grove oasis and two waterfalls. Director Henry Hathaway's 1951 production of *The Desert Fox*, starring James Mason as World War II German field marshal Erwin Rommel, was shot at nearby Borrego Mountain.

## FONT'S POINT

From Borrego Springs, it's a forty-five-minute drive to this ideal sunset viewing area. A fifty-yard walk will take you to a spectacularly colorful vista overlooking the Borrego Badlands, which locals call their "own mini-version of the Grand Canyon." From here you can see the Salton Sea, the San Ysidro Mountains, and the Santa Rosa Mountains. Adventurous hikers may want to go farther and descend into the canyon below the viewpoint.

Font's Point appeared in the Tom Hanks–produced HBO miniseries *From the Earth to the Moon* as the site where geologist David Clennon teaches astronauts about the moon's surface. In Chuck Russell's *The Scorpion King*, The Rock and Kelly Hu ride a camel toward the "Valley of the Dead" below Font's Point. "It was a sheer drop," remembers Russell on the film's DVD commentary track. "Anza-Borrego just happens to be one of my favorite locations. It's remarkable; it looks like the mountains of the moon out there."

## "THE TEXAS DIP"

In Barry Levinson's gangster biopic *Bugsy*, Warren Beatty, Annette Bening, and Harvey Keitel cruise along this mile-wide dip on the paved Borrego Springs Road. It's during this drive that Beatty gets the inspiration to build a casino in the middle of the desert. (The false-front Flamingo hotel set was built six miles away at Ocotillo Wells, standing in for early Las Vegas.) The Dip is also showcased to good effect in *Scorpion Spring* with Alfred Molina and Matthew McConaughey. And *Damnation Alley*, a postapocalyptic sci-fi thriller in which Jan-Michael Vincent encounters giant scorpions, filmed in the nearby Borrego Sink area.

Three miles past the Texas Dip, four-wheel drivers and desert hikers can follow the dirt road to **San Felipe Wash.** This barren area was used by Twentieth Century Fox for explosive battle sequences in *The Desert Fox*, its 1953 follow-up *The Desert Rats* (starring Richard Burton, James Mason, and Robert Newton), and *The Young Lions* (starring Marlon Brando and Maximilian Schell).

## WHERE TO EAT AND STAY

## LA CASA DEL ZORRO

This high-end 1937 hideaway with nineteen casitas has been owned by the Copley newspaper-publishing family since the early 1960s. The resort offers a spa, tennis club, a formal dining room, and a casual restaurant. According to

California State Parks

Font's Point appears in *The Scorpion King* and HBO's
*From the Earth to the Moon.*

Fox daily call sheets, the crew of *The Desert Fox* stayed here. *3845 Yaqui Pass Road; www.lacasadelzorro.com; 760-767-5323 or 800-824-1884.*

## THE PALMS AT INDIAN HEAD

The first major lodging facility in Borrego Springs was built in the late 1940s to accommodate Hollywood guests such as Marilyn Monroe, Charles Laughton, Andy Devine, Raymond Burr, and Lon Chaney Jr. The twelve-room property still retains a postmodern look, surrounded by an Olympic-sized pool and dozens of palm trees. Before renovation, the Palms was a nudist retreat and a juvenile detention center. The hotel's Krazy Coyote Saloon and Grill offers gourmet pizza and pasta. *2220 Hoberg Road; www.thepalmsatindianhead.com; 800-519-2624.*

## BORREGO PALM CANYON CAMPGROUND

Although you may pitch your tent anywhere in Anza-Borrego Desert State Park wilderness, this 120-site campground located 2.5 miles west of the town of Borrego Springs is a popular alternative for those who prefer a developed camping area with on-site water and restroom facilities. *Campground reservations: www.reserveamerica.com; 800-444-7275.*

## HOW TO GET TO ANZA-BORREGO STATE PARK

*Take the 10 East to San Bernadino County, then head south on the I-15. Follow the 15 to Temecula then head southeast on Highway 79 to Warner Springs. Proceed east on S2 East and east again on S22. Follow the signs to Borrego Springs. Park info: www.anzaborregostatepark.org; 760-767-5311.*

## DVD ITINERARY: ANZA-BORREGO DESERT STATE PARK

*The Scorpion King,* Scene 10

*The Desert Rats,* Scenes 9 and 21

*Bugsy,* Scenes 12 and 13

Beatty and Bening filming *Bugsy,* with director
Barry Levinson and producer Mark Johnson.

**29**

# THE SALTON SEA
# Dangerous When Wet

A strange phenomenon in which nature has placed four
hundred square miles of salt water in the middle of the arid
desert...

—*Opening narration in* The Monster That
Challenged the World *(1957)*

**MAJOR ROLES:** *The Salton Sea, The Monster that Challenged
the World, The Island*

## BEHIND THE SCENERY

Formed by an irrigation mishap along the Colorado River in the early 1900s, this once-burgeoning desert paradise was billed as the "Palm Springs Ocean" in its heyday. Thousands flocked to its waters for boating and waterskiing, Rock Hudson and a young Sonny Bono among them. Frank Sinatra, Dean Martin, and Jerry Lewis once entertained at a swank yacht club at the Salton Sea town of North Shore.

Times have changed. Although it surpasses Lake Tahoe as California's largest body of inland water and equals Israel's Dead Sea in its salinity, nowadays the Salton Sea is anything but a holiday resort. Choked with dead fish and powerful, strange odors, it's a mysterious landscape on the drive from Palm Springs to the Imperial Sand Dunes.

The water at Salton Sea is 25 percent saltier than the Pacific Ocean due to runoff from the Colorado River. Waterfowl flock to its environs and can be observed each winter at "The Sonny Bono Salton Sea National Wildlife Refuge," named after the entertainer/congressman who campaigned to clean up the lake.

These environs were for many years a choice location for war epics, including Billy Wilder's *Five Graves to Cairo*, *Wake Island*, and *Tobruk*. And monster-movie buffs will remember the lake as the birthplace of the menacing mollusks in the fifties sci-fi thriller *The Monster That Challenged the World*.

## DIRECTOR D. J. CARUSO'S *SALTON SEA* MEMORIES

"I had flown over The Salton Sea many times and always wondered, *What the hell is that down there, and why is it called a sea?* After reading the first draft of Tony Gayton's screenplay *The Salton Sea,* I hopped into my car and made an impromptu trip out there. Upon arriving, I was overcome by the vastness of this body of water.

"It was indeed visually striking, and I was moved by its haunted beauty. The images at the Salton Sea alone could have made a two-hour picture. I knew this place was the perfect companion to the soul of Val Kilmer's character. What once was beautiful and full of hope, now was lost and searching for a way to survive."

Over forty years later, Val Kilmer and Chandra West would run afoul of monsters of the human kind (cold-blooded meth traffickers) in the contemporary noir *The Salton Sea.* An earlier noir, Nathan Juran's *Highway Dragnet* (cowritten and coproduced by Roger Corman) concludes with Richard Conte knee-deep in Salton Sea's briny waters chasing Joan Bennett. And in 2005, Michael Bay's *The Island* (starring Ewan MacGregor and Scarlett Johansson) filmed at North Shore's decaying yacht club.

Other Salton Sea vicinity films include *The Wild Angels* and *The Professionals*, partially shot in the local town of Mecca and the **Mecca Hills Wilderness**, respectively. The 2002 thriller *29 Palms*, starring Chris O'Donnell, Rachael Leigh Cook, and Michael Rapaport, was also filmed on the west side of the lake near the community of Salton City. And David O. Russell's *Three Kings* filmed its climactic border crossing with George Clooney, Ice Cube, and Mark Wahlberg in the nearby **Superstition Mountains** (a location for *Sahara* with Humphrey Bogart).

The Salton Sea town of **Niland** features a roadside general store and diner that appears as the site for Gary Oldman's dead-end existence in the Peter Medak–directed crime thriller *Romeo Is Bleeding.* Just down the road are decaying buildings and a colorful roadside attraction known as **Salvation Mountain at Slab City**. Comprised of a series of small plaster hills covered with flowers and painted messages like JESUS, I'M A SINNER!, Salvation Mountain appears to be a leftover movie set, but in fact this is the home of a real-life desert denizen named Leonard Knight, whose work here has been named "a national shrine" by the Folk Art Society of America.

*CAUTION: Thrill-seeking road trippers who want to investigate the Salton Sea are strongly advised to do so during daylight hours and to stay on the main highway.*

Marc Wanamaker/Bison Archives

The Salton Sea's rising waters impede Joan Bennett's flight from Richard Conte in *Highway Dragnet*.

## HOW TO GET TO THE SALTON SEA

*Take the I-10 East to the town of Indio, then take 86S Expressway south to 66th Avenue East. Turn left on 66th Avenue, go half a mile to Highway 111 and turn right. Drive eleven miles to the visitors center in the town of North Shore. Salton Sea State Recreation Area: www.parks.ca.gov; 760-393-3052.*

## DVD ITINERARY: SALTON SEA

*The Monster That Challenged the World*, Scene 1

*The Salton Sea*, Scene 7

# IMPERIAL SAND DUNES
## The Mideast Out West

Where do you think we are?

This must be the place where they empty out all the old hourglasses . . .

—*Bing Crosby to Bob Hope amid the Imperial Sand Dunes in* The Road to Morocco *(1942)*

**MAJOR ROLES:** *Beau Geste (1939),* The Lost Patrol, Return of the Jedi, The Flight of the Phoenix *(1965),* Jarhead

### BEHIND THE SCENERY

In 1911, a local author named Harold Bell Wright put the Imperial Valley on the cultural map with his popular novel, *The Winning of Barbara Worth.* Part Western melodrama and part disaster tale, it told the story of a plucky heroine who played a prominent role in the taming of the Colorado River. The story also detailed the covered wagon migration across the dunes, the transformation of a "sun-blistered wasteland" into the fertile valley, and the river calamity that created the Salton Sea.

Director Henry King (*The Gunfighter*) brought the story to the big screen in 1926 with a stellar cast including Ronald Colman, Vilma Banky and, in his first major role, a young Gary Cooper as an Imperial Valley cowboy. This Western saga became such a crucial piece of local lore that when a new hotel was built near the author's home in Holtville ("Carrot Capital of the World"), the resort was dubbed "the Barbara Worth."

The Valley's Imperial Sand Dunes (aka Algodones Dunes) saw lots of action in World War II when General George S. Patton trained his troops here. Hollywood also saw the dunes as a fitting battleground. War movies shot here include *Sahara* (with Humphrey Bogart), John Ford's *The Lost Patrol* (with Victor McLaglin), *Tobruk* (with Rock Hudson and George Peppard), and Sam Mendes' *Jarhead* (with Jake Gyllenhaal).

## IMPERIAL FORCES: *RETURN OF THE JEDI*

Buttercup plays the Tatooine home of the sand-pit-dwelling monster known as the Sarlacc, which almost consumes stalwarts Mark Hamill, Harrison Ford, and Billy Dee Williams. Hovering overhead is Jabba the Hutt's sail barge which was, according to the producers, the largest outdoor set ever built for a movie in California up to that time.

"We needed a very large area for our Sarlacc monster and we found it right in our own backyard," recalls producer Howard Kazanjian. "It took us eleven months of prep and three weeks to film the scene. The Imperial Dunes were the perfect match for a sand trap on another planet. Our only problem was that the wind blew sand into our pit at night, so each morning a special crew had to scoop out the sand and restore it to the top platform via a huge conveyor belt."

*Tobruk* director Arthur Hiller felt he'd found the perfect location. "When I first arrived at the Imperial Sand Dunes," he recalls, "I thought, 'My God, this looks *exactly* like the Sahara Desert!' But then I stopped myself, thinking, 'How would I know what the Sahara looked like? I've never been there!' I then realized that my image of the Sahara was completely based on what I had seen from movies shot at the Imperial Sand Dunes."

Civilians have flocked to the sands in the decades since the off-road vehicle craze took off. On Thanksgiving weekends as many as 240,000 visitors swarm the fragile area. Fortunately, a portion of the terrain north of the dune buggy area, the North Algodones Dunes Wilderness, has been protected since 1995.

## WHERE TO EXPLORE

### OSBORNE OVERLOOK

This scenic turnout provides incredible vistas of the dunes to the north, dwarfed by the rugged Chocolate Mountains. From here, your best bet for seeing the desert is to head north toward the wilderness area. The nearby lonely stretch of highway serves as a haunting climactic backdrop for director Robert Harmon's cult suspense thriller, *The Hitcher*. (See *The Hitcher* Desert Tour sidebar, pages 145–146). *On Highway 78, east of Brawley on the way to Glamis.*

## NORTH ALGODONES DUNES WILDLIFE VIEWING AREA

The twenty-six-thousand-acre North Algodones Wilderness area is a choice destination for explorers who want to escape the engine roar of the desert town of Glamis. It's also a good place to see three-hundred-foot-high dunes in their natural state. There are no official hiking trails here, but you'll find plenty of scenic viewpoints. The Center for Biological Diversity, a natural history organization, hosts guided hikes in the winter. *Two miles north of Glamis along Ted Kipf Road; Hiking info: www.biologicaldiversity.org; 760-337-4400.*

### Top Billing: BUTTERCUP VALLEY

Situated just off Highway 8, the accessible Buttercup Dunes are the most frequently filmed because they include a wide valley where sets can be built and aircraft can land. There are no established hiking trails here, but the San Diego chapter of the Sierra Club leads cross-country sand skiing expeditions in the area.

Exploring Buttercup Valley will likely bring back memories of the films shot here, which include:

*Son of the Sheik*   In his last film, Rudolph Valentino (playing a dual role as father and son) romances Vilma Banky on these sands.

*Beau Geste*   Both the 1926 Ronald Colman and the 1939 Gary Cooper versions of this Foreign Legion adventure were filmed here.

*The Garden of Allah*   This campy 1936 Technicolor extravaganza was produced by David O. Selznick, with stars Marlene Dietrich and Charles Boyer as tormented lovers in the Algerian Desert.

*The Flight of the Phoenix*   Robert Aldrich's gritty 1965 tale of courage stars James Stewart, Richard Attenborough, Ernest Borgnine, and Peter Finch among the survivors of a Sahara Desert plane crash.

Marlene Dietrich luxuriates in the splendor of the desert in *The Garden of Allah*.

Marc Wanamaker/Bison Archives

## CALIFORNIA VS. ARIZONA: WHOSE SAND IS IT ANYWAY?

Because the sand dunes are near the border of California and Arizona, an ongoing rivalry exists between the two states' film commissions. Each state, as it happens, vies to lure movie people to its side. Though Yuma, Arizona, traditionally claimed the nearest facilities and larger airport, the dunes are physically located in California . . . and the Golden State is doing its part to increase its hospitality toward filmmakers.

Production Manager Robert L. Brown (*Return of the Jedi, Space-balls*) says, "We used to set up our crews on the Arizona side of the Yuma Dunes because there were more amenities closer to the location." Barbara Worth Resort owner Billy Adams protests, "It bugs me every time I hear someone refer to the Imperial Sand Dunes as the *Yuma* Dunes. They're a hidden treasure belonging to the Golden State."

*Patriot Games*    Harrison Ford as CIA specialist Jack Ryan tracks the terrorist activities of an IRA splinter group (headed by Sean Bean, Patrick Bergin, and Polly Walker) to this location, a North African training camp.

*Stargate*    Scientist James Spader and military man Kurt Russell discover an alternate universe here, on the other side of the Stargate. "It was the hottest place on earth," recalls director Roland Emmerich on the film's DVD commentary. "It was really murderous. We had several people all of a sudden pass out because they were dehydrated."

*The Scorpion King*    The Rock and Kelly Hu take on ancient evil in this sand-swept action-adventure. "Thanks to our state's incredible diversity," says proud Californian location manager Michael Neale, "we were easily able to recreate an ancient world in California."

### WHERE TO STAY

### BARBARA WORTH RESORT

A secluded and friendly 104-room hotel with conference facilities and an 18-hole golf course, the Barbara Worth was named after the heroine of the aforementioned novel and film. The 1950s dining room is decorated with posters of movies shot in the area. *2050 Country Club Drive; www.bwresort.com; 760-356-2806.*

Marc Wanamaker/Bison Archives

These dunes (seen here in 1939's *Beau Geste*) have appeared in
*Return of the Jedi* and *Jarhead*.

## HOW TO GET TO THE IMPERIAL SAND DUNES

*Take the 10 East to Highway 86 South. Take 86 to the town of Brawley. From
Brawley, head east on Highway 78 to Glamis. The dunes are packed on weekends
with an energetic crowd of off-roaders. Hikers may prefer to visit during weekdays.
Before your trip, tank up on gas and check weather conditions at 760-352-3360.*

## DVD ITINERARY: IMPERIAL SAND DUNES

Stargate, Scenes 10–13

*The Flight of the Phoenix* (1965), Scenes 5–17, 24–29, and 32–34

*Return of the Jedi*, Scenes 11–12

# MOVIE MOUNTAINS

This is the highest point in all our land . . .
Looming above the wilderness with the
strange silence of eternity.

—*Theatrical trailer for* High Sierra *(1941),
filmed at the Eastern Sierra's Mt. Whitney*

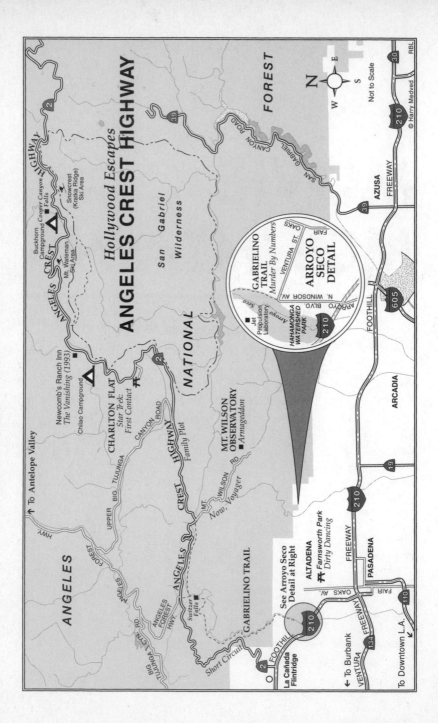

*Hollywood Escapes*
# ANGELES CREST HIGHWAY

ANGELES NATIONAL FOREST

San Gabriel Wilderness

ANGELES CREST HIGHWAY

**ARROYO SECO DETAIL**

GABRIELINO TRAIL
*Murder By Numbers*

Jet Propulsion Laboratory

HAHAMONGA WATERSHED PARK

N. WINDSOR AV.

VENTURA ST.

FAIR OAKS

ARROYO SECO BLVD

Arroyo Seco

210

N
W — E
S
Not to Scale

© Harry Medved

30

RBL

210

FREEWAY

AZUSA

39

FOOTHILL

605

ARCADIA

19

210

Buckhorn Campground
Cooper Canyon Falls
Snowcrest (Kratka Ridge) Ski Area
Mt. Waterman Ski Area

Newcomb's Ranch Inn
*The Vanishing* (1993)
Chilao Campground

CHARLTON FLAT
*Star Trek: First Contact*

Family Plot

CANYON ROAD

MT. WILSON OBSERVATORY
*Armageddon*

MT. WILSON RD.

*Now, Voyager*

ANGELES CREST HIGHWAY

UPPER BIG TUJUNGA

← To Antelope Valley

FOREST

BIG TUJUNGA CYN. RD.

ANGELES FOREST HWY

ANGELES

Switzer Falls

GABRIELINO TRAIL

*Short Circuit*

See Arroyo Seco Detail at Right

210

FOOTHILL

ALTADENA
Farnsworth Park
*Dirty Dancing*

210 FREEWAY

PASADENA

FAIR OAKS AV.

2

La Cañada Flintridge

VENTURA FREEWAY

134

110

← To Burbank

To Downtown L.A.

SAN GABRIEL CANYON ROAD

39

# 31

# ANGELES CREST HIGHWAY
## Born to Be Wild

*I gotta get off this road!*

—*Bruce Dern, maneuvering an out-of-control vehicle on the
Angeles Crest in Alfred Hitchcock's* Family Plot *(1976)*

**MAJOR ROLES:** *The Animal, Family Plot, Star Trek: First Contact*

### BEHIND THE SCENERY

Naturalist, explorer, and Sierra Club founder John Muir trudged through the Angeles National Forest region in the 1870s, long before the existence of marked trails or a highway. "[This is where] Mother Nature is most ruggedly, thornily savage," he declared. "Not even in the Sierra have I ever made the acquaintance of mountains more rigidly inaccessible." Still rugged and thorny, the forest is more accessible these days thanks to the introduction of the Angeles Crest Highway (Highway 2), a twisting mountaintop road that took over ten years to complete.

The highway starts as an offshoot from the Foothill Freeway in La Cañada Flintridge, a timeless neighborhood seen in movies like *House of Sand and Fog, Win a Date with Tad Hamilton!*, and *Old School* (Will Ferrell streaks Montrose's main street, Honolulu Avenue). Angeles Crest immediately leads to higher ground, skirting the top of the San Gabriel Mountains for some fifty miles and ending in the snow-play town of Wrightwood.

## THE ANGELES: L.A.'S BIG BACKYARD

When L.A. enjoys a rare clear day, new Angelenos are stunned to discover the snowcapped San Gabriel Mountains looming over the downtown skyline. Little do they know, hidden in those hills is the **Angeles National Forest**, a vast wilderness that has become, in the words of historian John W. Robinson, "a king-sized backyard playground for Los Angeles County."

Designated as California's first national forest by President Benjamin Harrison in 1892, these hillsides were once dotted with colorful upscale trail resorts during L.A.'s "Great Hiking Era" (1895–1938). Fires and flash floods eventually ravaged the forest's rustic lodges and camps. And with the introduction of the busy Angeles Crest Highway in the 1930s, any sense of the woods' exclusivity vanished.

Today the Angeles is the most heavily used national forest in the country, hosting an astonishing 30 million visitors each year. Each weekend the vast forest is frequented by hikers, mountain bikers, and motorcyclists who enjoy its curving roads.

You'll find plenty of roadside turnouts for taking in the views. Use them, especially if a car or motorbike wishes to pass you. You'll enjoy your ride a lot more.

And don't forget: even at higher elevations the Angeles National Forest can get hot and dry in the summertime. Travelers should anticipate the heat and bring plenty of water.

## THE DRIVE

*This drive takes the traveler only half the distance to Wrightwood, concluding at Buckhorn Campground. CAUTION: Make sure your gas tank is full before you begin this drive, as you won't find any chances to refuel along the way. Each listing indicates mileage from the 210 Freeway's La Cañada Flintridge exit.*

## ANGELES CREST TURNOUT (2.7 miles)

At the Angeles Crest's first turnout, with a clear-day view of downtown L.A., you'll get a sense of why movie crews shoot "getting out of town" driving sequences here. This is where Ally Sheedy, Steve Guttenberg, and robot "Number 5" head for Montana in *Short Circuit*.

## SWITZER FALLS (9.8 miles)

The Switzer Falls Picnic Area is an insanely popular destination on weekend afternoons. Your best bet is to arrive early in the morning and hike a mile downstream to **Commodore Switzer Trail Camp**. Located on this site many years ago was a rustic resort called "Switzer-land" (get it?) that, according to historian John Robinson, hosted celebrities such as Clark Gable, Joan Crawford, Shirley Temple, and Mary Pickford. From here you can peer down at the majestic Switzer Falls.

## MT. WILSON ROAD (14 miles, look for the turn-off at Red Box Station)

On a clear and cool day, a trip up Mt. Wilson Road is worth a detour, as it's only five miles to the observatory. This section of Angeles Crest is where Peggy Cummins and John Dall escape from the law in the 1949 film noir *Gun Crazy*, according to Donald Nicholson of the Mt. Wilson Observatory Association.

Winding Mt. Wilson Road also provides locations for *Now, Voyager* (as the site of Bette Davis and Paul Henreid's fateful taxi cab accident in South America), Wolfgang Petersen's *Shattered* (where Tom Berenger and Greta Scacchi's car careens off a cliff in the film's opening), and *Delirious* (TV soap writer John Candy prevents soap star Emma Samms from falling off a cliff at nearby Eaton Saddle).

Built in 1904 at an altitude of over 5,700 feet, the historic **Mt. Wilson Observatory** allows visitors daily. The observatory's film credits include *K-PAX*, plus the opening sequences of 1998's killer asteroid movies *Armageddon* and *Deep Impact*. *Mt. Wilson Observatory (closed in the winter): 626-440-1136; Mt. Wilson Institute: www.mtwilson.edu; 626-793-3100.*

## FOREST PRIMEVAL: AN ANGELES CREST LEGEND— BIGFOOT OR BIG HOAX?

Fall 1967. One fine afternoon rodeo rider Roger Patterson and out-doorsman Robert Gimlin are horseback riding in the Northern California woods when they meet a most unusual forest dweller.

Or so the story goes.

The two men allegedly came upon a hulking Bigfoot monster sipping water from the creek. Fast-thinking Patterson grabbed his 16mm camera and caught the Sasquatch on film. The minute-long footage includes the now-famous shot of the escaping Bigfoot turning toward the camera. After it was broadcast on a David L. Wolper documentary, the clip became more controversial than anyone could have imagined.

About thirty years later an article in *Strange Magazine* claimed the infamous footage was a Hollywood-hatched hoax. According to wide-ranging allegations, Bigfoot was actually an unidentified stuntman in an ape suit designed by *Planet of the Apes* makeup wizard John Chambers. Another claim contends that the footage's Northern California woods were actually a section of the Angeles Crest.

An entire cottage industry has grown up around the Bigfoot myth, mostly in the Northwest, and the legend has yet to be officially debunked. As Bigfoot enthusiast and special makeup effects expert Brian Penikas told CNI News, "I want that film to be as real as the next guy."

## Top Billing: CHARLTON FLAT (23.3 miles)

"Charlton Flat is the Angeles Crest's backlot," says movie ranger Annitta Keck of this frequently filmed and heavily wooded picnic area. At the end of the Charlton Flat road, there's a mile-long trail leading to the **Vetter Mountain Lookout,** a fire observation tower used for spotting enemy aircraft in World War II. The lookout is now a site for spectacular clear-day views.

Frequently, Charlton Flat is the setting for locales outside of the San Gabriel Mountains, including:

*North by Northwest* According to MGM daily production reports, a second-unit team shot scenes at Charlton Flat on December 11, 1958, possibly for establishing shots of the woods below the Vandamm (James Mason) house.

*The Young Lions* The paths of American soldiers Montgomery Clift, Dean Martin, and conflicted German soldier Marlon Brando converge in the European woods (Charlton Flat) in the film's denouement.

*Star Trek: First Contact* Jonathan Frakes, LeVar Burton, and other crew members go back in time to this forest monument to make sure that reluctant hero James Cromwell realizes his destiny as the inventor of the warp drive.

*Paulie* In DreamWorks' wise-cracking parrot saga, Charlton Flat is the setting for a rural trailer park. It's here that the title avian comforts dying artist Gena Rowlands and learns how to soar above the woods.

*The Animal* An angry mob of villagers stalk *human*-imal Rob Schneider at Charlton Flat. Among the pursuers: sharpshooter John C. McGinley, girlfriend Colleen Haskell, police chief Ed Asner, tiki-torch-wielding Norm MacDonald, and Adam Sandler. Location manager Molly Allen recalls that

# A HITCHCOCKIAN HIGHWAY

Alfred Hitchcock had a history of placing his characters in jeopardy while driving on winding roads: reckless Cary Grant and terrorized Joan Fontaine in *Suspicion*, a coercively inebriated Grant behind the wheel in *North by Northwest*, or panic-stricken Bruce Dern and Barbara Harris careening down a mountain road in a runaway auto in the director's final picture, *Family Plot*.

For *Family Plot*, assistant director Howard Kazanjian recalls that the Master of Suspense preferred the controlled environment of the studio. "He would have been happy to shoot the entire chase scene on the stage," says Kazanjian, "if he could have gotten away with it."

"Hitch first thought we should film it in Griffith Park," remembers Hitchcock's frequent collaborator and production designer Henry Bumstead. "I had to convince him that the roads in Griffith Park weren't high enough for a mountain chase, and that we had to do it on the Crest if it was going to look threatening." In fact, the crew ended up using the section of the Angeles Crest between Mt. Wilson Road and Charlton Flat.

The seventy-seven-year-old master directed the chase scene from the comfort of his air-conditioned limousine on the Angeles Crest Highway. "He very seldom came out of his car," recalls Bruce Dern. "Occasionally he'd roll down the window an inch and say, 'That was very good.' During lunch breaks, he invited me into the car for tea and would regale me with great stories from the old days."

Despite the area's warm climate, "coat and tie" was Hitchcock's requisite dress code for Bumstead, Kazanjian, and cinematographer Leonard South when working on the hot mountain road. "It was a little unusual to dress up for on-location work in the seventies," recalls Kazanjian "especially with the dust, the wind, and the heat. But we did it happily, out of respect for Mr. Hitchcock's professionalism."

the crew had to clear the area of bears every morning before shooting could begin. Schneider's extended car-crash sequence was shot nearby on San Gabriel Canyon Road. (*As Charlton Flat is subject to closure, call the Angeles ranger for accessibility; 818-899-1900.*)

## NEWCOMB'S RANCH INN CAFÉ (27 miles)
This 1939 mountain roadhouse appears three and a half miles after Charlton Flat, just past the Chilao Visitors Center. It's the only open-year-round cafe between La Cañada Flintridge and Wrightwood, so if you're hungry you'd better stop here. The inn, known for its fish and chips and spicy chili, is host to all sorts of colorful locals (and a parking lot full of motorcycles) on weekends.

## PAUL MAZURSKY: NAKED IN THE SAN GABRIELS

When asked how he got permission to film his 1969 sexual revolution satire *Bob & Carol & Ted & Alice* at the famous Esalen center on Northern California's Big Sur coast, director Paul Mazursky has a short answer: he didn't.

Mazursky and wife were allowed to attend group therapy sessions and to do casual research at Esalen, but when it was revealed he was planning a comedy about wife-swapping rituals, filming permission was denied. Instead, Mazursky's location scouts found a now-forgotten private reservoir in the San Gabriels that he converted into a retreat center.

The film's infamous opening shows Natalie Wood and Robert Culp in a sports car zipping through the Angeles National Forest on their way to "The Institute." The center is first presented on-screen with nude cast members sunbathing to the tune of Handel's "Hallelujah Chorus."

It turns out this scene wasn't Mazursky's first encounter with the San Gabriels. In 1953, when he was an aspiring twenty-two-year-old off-Broadway actor from Brooklyn, Mazursky traveled to California to make his movie debut as a soldier in a low-budget war movie shot at a San Gabriel Mountains boy scout camp. Entitled *Fear and Desire*, the movie also marked the directorial debut of a twenty-five-year-old filmmaker named ... *Stanley Kubrick*.

In George Sluizer's remake of his French-Dutch thriller *The Vanishing*, Kiefer Sutherland meets waitress Nancy Travis at Newcomb's while searching for his missing girlfriend Sandra Bullock. *626-440-1001.*

## BUCKHORN CAMPGROUND AND COOPER CANYON
### FALLS *(34 miles, just past the Mt. Waterman Ski Area)*
A hidden 6,500-foot-high campground surrounded by Jeffrey and sugar pine, cedar and oak trees, Buckhorn is one the shadiest parts of the forest and your best choice for hiking and/or camping overnight. Follow the Burkhart Trail into **Cooper Canyon** and the small but beautiful Cooper Canyon Falls.

An ominous encounter takes place at Buckhorn Campground in the disaster movie *Dante's Peak*. A bubbling hot springs set was built under these pines for the movie's sequence in which a pair of nude bathers gets boiled alive by lava-heated water. *Campground info: 818-899-1900.*

## HOW TO GET TO THE ANGELES CREST HIGHWAY

*From the 210 Foothill Freeway, take the La Cañada Flintridge exit and follow the signs to the Angeles Crest (Highway 2).*

## DVD ITINERARY: ANGELES CREST HIGHWAY

*Family Plot*, Angeles Crest Highway, Scene 12

*Star Trek: First Contact*, Charlton Flat, Scene 19

*Now, Voyager*, Mt. Wilson Road, Scene 15

# HITCHCOCK'S DANGEROUS OUTDOORS

Though the Master of Suspense preferred his films to be shot on studio soundstages, he occasionally braved California's Great Outdoors for picturesque settings and dangerous pursuits.

### Big Basin Redwoods State Park: VERTIGO
Kim Novak and James Stewart recall the past in a timeless redwood forest. The movie's forest locale, Big Basin's Redwood Trail, was close to Hitchcock's vacation home in the Santa Cruz Mountains.

### Bodega Bay: THE BIRDS
The Northern California town of Bodega Bay has changed significantly since its starring role in the 1963 thriller. The Tides restaurant has been completely remodeled. The Potter School, scene of the famous attack on the children, is now a private residence in the nearby town of Bodega. But Bodega's curving Bay Hill Road, which Tippi Hedren takes to the village, still makes for a scenic drive.

### Corcoran Road, Wasco: NORTH BY NORTHWEST
The lonely Midwest bus stop where Cary Grant has a deadly encounter with a cropduster is located north of Bakersfield (see page 300).

### Gorman Post Road: PSYCHO
Janet Leigh is awakened by a policeman here on her way to the Bates Motel.

### Highway 395: SABOTEUR
Falsely accused Robert Cummings, eluding authorities in Los Angeles, flees along this Sierra-adjacent highway as he tracks the film's wartime spies.

## Central Coast: VERTIGO, REBECCA, SUSPICION

The crashing waves and precipitous Central California coastline make an ominous backdrop for doomed lovers, including *Vertigo*'s Novak and Stewart (Cypress Point), *Rebecca*'s Joan Fontaine and Laurence Olivier (Point Lobos) and *Suspicion*'s Fontaine and Cary Grant (Hurricane Point).

## San Francisco's Fort Point: VERTIGO

This location is an old army fort directly under the Golden Gate Bridge. This is where James Stewart rescues Kim Novak from her suicidal plunge into San Francisco Bay.

## San Gabriel Mountains: FAMILY PLOT

These mountains provide the deadly highway (Angeles Crest) and cemetery (in the foothill town of Sierra Madre) for Hitchcock's last picture.

Marc Wanamaker/Bison Archives

*Hitch*ing a ride: Bruce Dern and Barbara Harris on the run.

# 32

# ARROYO SECO'S GABRIELINO TRAIL
## Mysterious Woods

One of the joys of L.A. life is discovering junglelike forests not far from downtown. . . .

—*Deborah J. Page, location manager for* Human Nature *(2001)*

**MAJOR ROLES:** *Murder by Numbers, Human Nature*

### BEHIND THE SCENERY

Much of Old Los Angeles was built along a tributary of the L.A. River, known as the Arroyo Seco, translated as "dry creek" in Spanish. Indeed, it's an appropriate designation for this often-dusty riverbed. As it winds through Pasadena, South Pasadena, and Highland Park, the Arroyo Seco is flanked by several horseback-riding trails, bike paths, and dog-walking areas.

Like other urban wilds, the area is not without a history of development. As *Variety* reported, the Arroyo Seco canyon's "ridges are dotted with baronial estates," one of which is in fact the stately Wayne Manor as seen in the 1960s *Batman* TV series.

One notable man-made landmark is the graceful 1913 Colorado Street Bridge. Once known as "Suicide Bridge," the span (renovated in 1993 with a high protective barrier) is where many a despondent Angeleno said goodbye to L.A. In the uncut version of Charlie Chaplin's 1921 classic *The Kid*, Edna Purviance makes a life-changing decision here. The bridge is also the

point of departure for a magical school bus taking superhero kids to Disney's
*Sky High*.

And another striking arroyo-facing landmark, the Gamble House, served as
the Craftsman home of mad scientist Christopher Lloyd in *Back to the Future*.

Recently, a small band of local volunteers known as "the Arroyo Brigade"
has reconstructed many pathways and staircases lost to neglect and erosion
over the decades. Their accomplishments have upgraded the condition of the
Lower Arroyo Seco between the Colorado Street Bridge and the South
Pasadena city line. (Updates on these new urban walks are available on the
Arroyo Seco Foundation's Web site, *www.arroyoseco.org*.)

The prettiest section of the arroyo lies in the headwaters north of
Pasadena and in the Angeles National Forest. The Gabrielino National
Recreation Trail, named after the Gabrielino Indians who foraged here, leads
to a lush glen near Teddy's Outpost Picnic Area. This is the location of Elijah
Wood's treehouse in Rob Reiner's *North*.

Other appearances include:

*Murder by Numbers*    High school killers Ryan Gosling and Michael Pitt
dispose of their victim here. Detectives Sandra Bullock and Ben Chaplin discover the body across the creek under the vine-shrouded trees. Producer
Richard Crystal notes, "There's something hauntingly beautiful and yet eerie
about the Arroyo Seco. It has a real sense of mystery about it."

*Human Nature*    Backpacking anthropologists Patricia Arquette and Tim
Robbins discover wildman Rhys Ifans living among the trees in the Michel
Gondry/Charlie Kaufman comedy. In this garden paradise, Arquette succumbs
to her "natural savage" urges, strips naked, and joins the ape-man in the woods
above Pasadena. "I never thought L.A. could be so primal," admits producer
and native New Yorker Anthony Bregman. "This area turned out to be the
perfect setting for our nature versus nurture story."

## WHERE TO HIKE

### Top Billing: TEDDY'S OUTPOST PICNIC AREA

It's a 1.5-mile hike to this sycamore-laden canyon. Begin at the Windsor
Avenue parking lot. You'll see two branches of the Gabrielino National
Recreation Trail; take the paved road on the right. You'll pass Pasadena
Water Department markers. The first mile is hot and without shade. You'll
cross a scenic wooden bridge, rock-hop over stream crossings and pass by
forest residences. Follow the signs to the picnic area. *Hiking info: 818-899-
1900.*

## DETOUR: FARNSWORTH PARK, ALTADENA

East of the arroyo in the San Gabriel foothills you'll find this pleasant picnic setting, complete with barbecue pits, ball fields, and playground. Farnsworth Park's main filming spot, the **Davies Memorial Building**, is a rustic 1934 clubhouse constructed with river rocks hauled by mules from the Arroyo Seco. Ask the staff to show you the Davies stage and dance floor that they claim double for the interior of *Dirty Dancing's* 1960s Catskills lodge. The park's 1938 amphitheater is the location of the band camp in *American Pie 2* and *American Pie Presents Band Camp*.

*HOW TO GET TO FARNSWORTH PARK From the 210 Freeway, take the Lake Avenue exit and head north. The Davies Memorial Building is located at 568 East Mt. Curve Ave. (at its intersection with Lake Ave.). Info: 800-267-2757.*

## HOW TO GET TO ARROYO SECO'S GABRIELINO TRAIL

*From the 210 Freeway, take the Arroyo Boulevard/Windsor Ave. exit. Head to the hills on Arroyo, which becomes Windsor. Just before Windsor's intersection with Ventura Street, look for the dirt parking area on your left.*

## DVD ITINERARY: ARROYO SECO

*Human Nature*, Scenes 11, 22–23

*Murder by Numbers*, Scenes 3 and 6

Harry Medved

The Arroyo Seco is
lovely, dark, and deep.

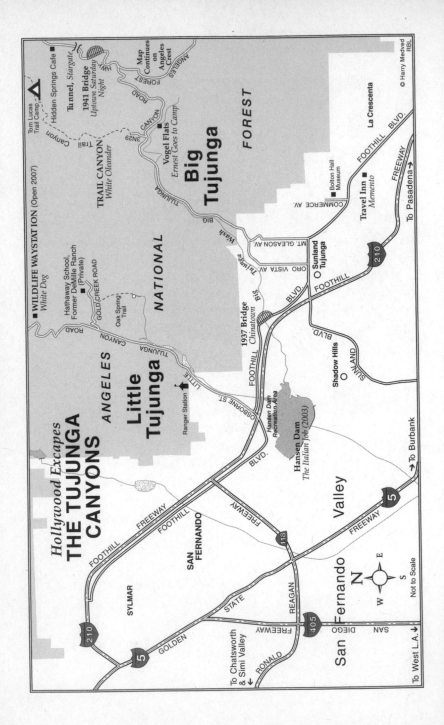

*Hollywood Excapes*
**THE TUJUNGA CANYONS**

**WILDLIFE WAYSTATION** (Open 2007)
*White Dog*

Tom Lucas
Trail Camp

Hidden Springs Cafe

Tunnel, *Stargate*

**1941 Bridge**
*Uptown Saturday Night*

Map
Continues
on
Angeles
Crest

Hathaway School,
Former DeMille Ranch
(Private)

**TRAIL CANYON**
*White Oleander*

**Vogel Flats**
*Ernest Goes to Camp*

**Big
Tujunga**

**ANGELES**

**NATIONAL**

**FOREST**

**Little
Tujunga**

Ranger Station

Oak Spring
Trail

GOLD CREEK ROAD

TUJUNGA CANYON ROAD

LITTLE TUJUNGA CANYON ROAD

BIG TUJUNGA CANYON ROAD

Big Tujunga Wash

La Crescenta

FOOTHILL BLVD.

Bolton Hall
Museum

COMMERCE AV.

**Travel Inn**
*Memento*

To Pasadena →

MT. GLEASON AV.

ORO VISTA AV.

Sunland
Tujunga

FOOTHILL BLVD.

SUNLAND BLVD.

**1937 Bridge**
*Chinatown*

FOOTHILL

OSBORNE ST.

**Shadow Hills**

Hansen Dam
Recreation Area

**Hansen Dam**
*The Italian Job (2003)*

→ To Burbank

FOOTHILL BLVD.

**SAN
FERNANDO**

FOOTHILL FREEWAY

FREEWAY

118

REAGAN

STATE

GOLDEN STATE FREEWAY

RONALD REAGAN FREEWAY

405

SAN DIEGO FREEWAY

**San Fernando
Valley**

**SYLMAR**

210

5

5

210

To Chatsworth
& Simi Valley ↓

To West L.A. ↓

**N**
W E
S
Not to Scale

© Harry Medved
RBL

# 33

# BIG AND LITTLE TUJUNGA
## The Hidden Canyons

If you want to get the feel of working class Southern California in the 1920s and 1930s ... the epicenter of "old wide-open Southern California" is in the Sunland-Tujunga area.

—David Gebhard and Robert Winter, in their guide Architecture in Los Angeles (1985)

**MAJOR ROLES:** The Rundown, Charlie's Angels: Full Throttle, Memento, Chinatown

### BEHIND THE SCENERY

Big Tujunga and Little Tujunga, known by locals as "the Big T" and "the Little T," are two well-ensconced mountain canyons on the western flank of the San Gabriels. Less traveled than other Angeles Forest destinations like Angeles Crest Highway or San Gabriel Canyon, the Tujungas present a colorful alternative for location managers.

During the Golden Age of Hollywood, the Tujunga Canyons were once "the preferred celebrity getaway for hunting, fishing, and horseback-riding," recalls Tujunga historian Mary Lou Pozzo. "Within a half-hour drive from Burbank the industry could find great scenery with pine trees, yuccas, and creeks at the hunting lodges hidden in the canyons above urban and suburban neighborhoods." Tujunga locations have attracted such diverse pictures as Chinatown, E.T., Down in the Valley, Terminator 2: Judgment Day, Terminator 3: Rise of the Machines, and Memento.

## LITTLE TUJUNGA AREA HIGHLIGHTS
## WHERE TO PICNIC

### HANSEN DAM RECREATION AREA

Built in 1940 to prevent flooding from Big Tujunga Wash, Hansen Dam is surrounded by a recreation complex of picnic areas, athletic fields, fishing ponds, a huge swimming pool, water slides, and a golf course. According to *Easy Rider* cinematographer Laszlo Kovacs, the film's final campfire sequence (in which Peter Fonda tells Dennis Hopper, "We blew it!") was filmed near the dam.

The Hansen Dam area has seen plenty of action on film. The dam bridge is where Cameron Diaz, Lucy Liu, and Drew Barrymore get ambushed by Mongolian bad guys in the opening action sequence of *Charlie's Angels: Full Throttle*. The dam basin is also the site of a Brazilian mining camp in *The Rundown*, starring The Rock, Seann William Scott, and Christopher Walken. In *The Italian Job* (2003), the climactic Mini Cooper chase features Charlize Theron and Mark Wahlberg tearing through the Hansen area. And *Herbie: Fully Loaded* features another classic compact car in the dam environs.

Southeast of the dam is the suburban Shadow Hills neighborhood, where Clark Gable reportedly owned one of his many ranches. According to sixty-year resident and community activist Anne Finn, Sunland Boulevard at Shadow Island Drive is where Gable and Claudette Colbert hitch a ride with the help of her raised skirt in Frank Capra's *It Happened One Night*.

*HOW TO GET TO HANSEN DAM RECREATION AREA Take the 210 Freeway, exit at Osborne, then follow signs to Hansen Dam.*

## WHERE TO HIKE

### OAK SPRING TRAIL

The Oak Spring trailhead can be found beside a creek near the historic Paradise Ranch. The ranch property was bought by famed director Cecil B. DeMille in 1916. For more than four decades the Paradise Ranch was his Hollywood hideaway, where some say he brought his mistress and entertained guests like Charlie Chaplin, Mary Pickford, Douglas Fairbanks, H. G. Wells, Gary Cooper, and Charlton Heston "down by the old DeMille stream."

According to historian John Robinson, the ranch's still-standing stone gate entrance was once part of a set for DeMille's 1927 version of *The King of Kings*. In later years, the aging director donated his beloved hillside to the Hathaway School "with the hope that it would be a paradise for children" from troubled backgrounds. A tiny memorial plaque on the school's gate thanks DeMille for his donation.

The ranch remains private property, but the Oak Spring trailhead is located only a few hundred feet away. After climbing several switchbacks, the trail leads to views of DeMille's retreat. At the one-mile mark, hikers will find a shady trail camp. For urbanized visitors, this mostly undeveloped canyon remains a hidden paradise.

HOW TO GET TO THE OAK SPRING TRAIL From the 210 Freeway, take the Osborne turnoff and make a left, following the NATIONAL FOREST signs. As Osborne turns into Little Tujunga you'll pass several horse ranches and a ranger station (purchase your parking pass here). At 3.8 miles, make a right on Gold Creek Road. Head up a curvy hill, and after half a mile you'll find the parking lot for Oak Spring. Walk up the road to the trailhead.

## WHERE TO EXPLORE
## THE WILDLIFE WAYSTATION

This sanctuary serves as a habitat for abandoned or mistreated animals on their way to new homes. Animal trainer Paul Winfield attempts to reprogram Kristy McNichol's racist, killer canine here in the controversial White Dog, directed by Sam Fuller and coscripted by Curtis Hanson. Waystation supporters include Sharon Stone, Drew Barrymore, and Dyan Cannon. Call for tours in 2007: 818-899-5201.

HOW TO GET TO THE WILDLIFE WAYSTATION Follow the signs from the Osborne off-ramp off the 210 Freeway.

## BIG TUJUNGA AREA HIGHLIGHTS
## WHERE TO HIKE AND CAMP
### Top Billing: TRAIL CANYON

Trail Canyon offers a wealth of natural treasures for the outdoors aficionado. From the parking lot, ascend the trail to a gorgeous viewpoint some six hundred feet above. If the winter rains have been strong, a spectacular fifty-foot-high waterfall will complete the scene. The nearby **Tom Lucas Trail Camp,** named after a barefoot wanderer who killed grizzly bears that once roamed the Big Tujunga, is the perfect overnight spot for campers seeking idyllic seclusion.

Incidentally, before you get to the Trail Canyon turnoff on Big Tujunga Canyon Road, you'll pass a site used by Tom Cruise for his 1993 directorial debut on the Showtime anthology series Fallen Angels. In the episode titled "The Frightening Frammis" (based on a story by crime novelist Jim Thompson), Peter Gallagher hitches a ride from shrewish Isabella Rossellini and hen-pecked husband John Reilly along this desolate byway.

Big Tujunga Canyon is also the location of the trailer park where Alison Lohman lives with her new foster mom, a Bible-thumping ex-stripper played by Robin Wright Penn, in White Oleander.

HOW TO GET TO TRAIL CANYON From the 210 Freeway, take the Sunland Blvd. exit. Follow Sunland north as it turns into Foothill Blvd. In a few *blocks you'll see a* NATIONAL FOREST *sign at Oro Vista. Make a left.*

You'll pass through a residential area as Oro Vista becomes Big Tujunga Canyon. In 5 miles, look for the unsigned dirt road on the left (road 3N29) that will take you to the Trail Canyon trailhead. (If you reach Vogel Flats, home of Ernest Goes to Camp, you've gone too far.) Hiking info: 818-899-1900.

## WHERE TO EAT

### HIDDEN SPRINGS CAFÉ

Located ten miles up the road from Trail Canyon, this red farmhouse features a tiny café with a 1950s circular counter. The family-owned Hidden Springs Café has been in business since 1971 and, despite fires and floods, it's still going strong. One of Charles Bronson's last movies, *Messenger of Death*, was shot here. Nearby are the Hidden Springs Picnic Grounds and the scenic Fall Creek Trail. *23155 Angeles Forest Highway, past the intersection of Big Tujunga and the Angeles Forest Highway. Open for breakfast, lunch, and early dinner. Call ahead for hours and directions: 626-792-9663.*

On the road to the cafe, you'll first cross a 1941 **Arch Bridge** seen in two Sidney Poitier–directed comedies starring Bill Cosby: *Uptown Saturday Night*

Big Tujunga's Trail
Canyon Falls.

Michele B. Medved

## A MEMORABLY FORGETTABLE PLACE: THE TRAVEL INN

A lower-budget version of a Motel 6, this complex at Foothill and Commerce is not likely to be anyone's first lodging choice. Fans of director/cowriter Christopher Nolan's *Memento*, however, may want take a peek at the premises.

The 1963 Travel Inn was renamed "the Discount Inn" for the film, in which it plays the hideout for memory-impaired Guy Pearce. Scenes with Joe Pantoliano were filmed in the lobby and parking lot.

"It's a memorably forgettable motel," says location manager Russ Fega. "The Travel Inn has a timeless anonymity and an unremarkable 1960s motel look that could be Anywhere, USA."

and *Ghost Dad*. Then you'll pass through the **Big Tujunga Tunnel,** featured as the entryway that leads James Spader and Kurt Russell to the *Stargate*.

## ON THE ROAD: BIG TUJUNGA WASH AND THE *CHINATOWN* BRIDGE

As depicted in *Chinatown*, the Big Tujunga Wash is usually a bone-dry L.A. river tributary. But in 1938 a flash flood here caused major headaches for the San Fernando Valley *and* Hollywood. According to *America's Suburb* author Kevin Roderick, too many celebrities residing in the valley found themselves unable to travel because of the inundated roads. Consequently, the Academy Awards ceremony had to be postponed for a week.

The arid Big Tujunga Wash is where *Chinatown*'s Jack Nicholson learns from a boy on a horse about the inexplicable appearance of water in the area. The original 1937 streetlamps were a factor in choosing this bridge and dry creek bed for the period location, according to *Chinatown* production manager C. O. "Doc" Erickson.

*HOW TO GET TO THE BIG TUJUNGA WASH AND CHINA-TOWN BRIDGE From the 210 Freeway, take the Sunland Boulevard exit north and head west on Foothill Boulevard. You'll see the bridge between Wentworth Street and Foothill Place. Parking on the bridge is not allowed. Inquire about parking at the nearby Angeles National Golf Club (818-352-7139).*

## "KEEP WATCHING THE CANYONS!":
## THE TUJUNGA ALIENS

Big Tujunga Canyon was the location for several major reports of UFO activity that made national headlines. In 1950, two pilots reported a lighted object in their airspace over the Tujunga Canyon area. They later tried to cover up the story. On March 22, 1953, Big Tujunga Canyon cabin mates Sarah Shaw and Jan Whitley were allegedly abducted by aliens "dressed in one-piece black body stockings."

Elements of these Tujunga sightings are oddly similar to events in Ed Wood's immortal *Plan 9 from Outer Space* (1959) which depicts aliens (wearing what appear to be satin pajamas and leggings) landing in the nearby town of San Fernando.

Coincidence? Some think not. "The mysterious and compelling Tujunga Canyons produce a favorable setting for multiple, almost contagious UFO phenomena," claim Ann Druffel and D. Scott Rogo in their 1980 book *The Tujunga Canyon Contacts*. The two authors tracked sightings of UFOs in the western flank of the San Gabriel Mountains as far back as 1949.

The San Gabriels again hosted an alien encounter near the home of Dee Wallace, Henry Thomas, Drew Barrymore, and Robert McNaughton in Steven Spielberg's *E.T. The Extra-Terrestrial*. Tujunga's Seven Hills neighborhood provided E.T.'s home on earth (although the actual forest scenes were shot in Northern California).

"They were looking for a vision of suburbia with a hint of the forest looming nearby," remembers Michael J. Burmeister, who was a production associate on *E.T.* The location manager for the film, Richard Vane, found the perfect home. "After reading the script, Richard scouted for a middle-class tract home at the end of a cul-de-sac, with mountains rising above the houses so you could imagine a left-behind E.T. scurrying down the hillside to this home.

"I don't think anyone involved in the production has any idea that there was a legendary 'Tujunga UFO milieu' or that E.T.s had supposedly been spotted in these hills some thirty years before." For his 2005 *War of the Worlds* remake, Spielberg returned to the San Gabriels to shoot tense nighttime sequences with Tom Cruise and Dakota Fanning.

## HOW TO GET TO THE TUJUNGAS

*From the 405, take the 118 East to the 210 West. Exit at Osborne (for Little Tujunga) or Sunland Boulevard North (for Big Tujunga) and follow signs to the National Forest.*

## DVD ITINERARY: BIG AND LITTLE TUJUNGA

*White Oleander*, Scene 7

*Stargate*, Scene 5

*Chinatown*, Scenes 2 and 5

*Memento's* unforgettable motel.

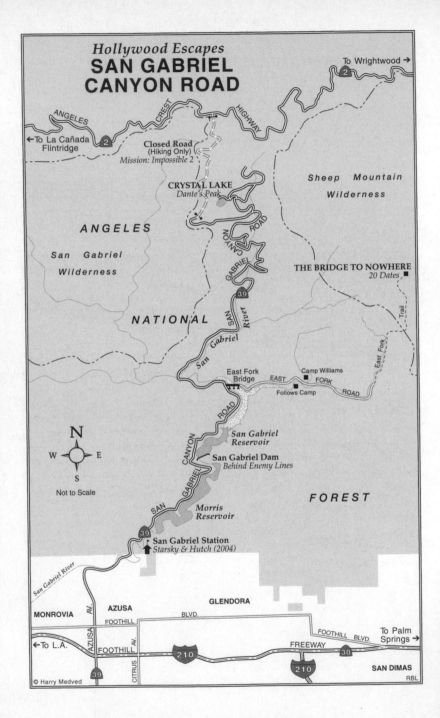

Hollywood Escapes
**SAN GABRIEL CANYON ROAD**

To Wrightwood →

ANGELES
CREST
HIGHWAY
← To La Cañada Flintridge

Closed Road
(Hiking Only)
*Mission: Impossible 2*

**CRYSTAL LAKE**
*Dante's Peak*

**Sheep** *Mountain*
*Wilderness*

ANGELES

*San Gabriel*
*Wilderness*

SAN
GABRIEL
CANYON
ROAD

**THE BRIDGE TO NOWHERE**
*20 Dates*

NATIONAL

*San Gabriel River*

East Fork Trail

East Fork
Bridge
EAST FORK ROAD
Camp Williams
Follows Camp

SAN GABRIEL CANYON ROAD

**San Gabriel Reservoir**

**San Gabriel Dam**
*Behind Enemy Lines*

**FOREST**

*Morris Reservoir*

N
W · E
S

Not to Scale

**San Gabriel Station**
*Starsky & Hutch (2004)*

*San Gabriel River*

MONROVIA

AZUSA
**GLENDORA**

FOOTHILL BLVD.

AZUSA AV.

FOOTHILL BLVD.
To Palm Springs →

← To L.A.
FOOTHILL AV.
CITRUS
FREEWAY
210
30

© Harry Medved
39

210
**SAN DIMAS**

RBL

# 34

# SAN GABRIEL CANYON ROAD Cliffhangers

> Highway 39 has the twists and turns—and hidden hideaways—
> needed for an effective suspense thriller.
>
> —*Alasdair Boyd, location manager for* The Glass House *(2001)*

**MAJOR ROLES:** *Mission: Impossible 2, Behind Enemy Lines*

## BEHIND THE SCENERY

Also known as Highway 39, the San Gabriel Canyon Road is the most popular drive in the Angeles National Forest. In fact, the road can get so congested on hot summer weekends that the Forest Service has been known to close the route when the crowds reach gridlock on the Fourth of July holiday weekend. During the week, however, there's a beautiful tranquility to be found within the scenic San Gabriel Canyon, as its twenty-five miles of memorable curves lead from the foothill town of Azusa to Crystal Lake at the top of the mountains.

Gold was discovered in the mountains near Follows Camp (along the East Fork of the San Gabriel River) in the 1850s. Hollywood discovered Follows Camp as a scenic location in the late 1910s, according to San Gabriel Mountain historian John Robinson. One memorable silent comedy shot here is the 1918 two-reeler *Moonshine*, in which actor/director Roscoe "Fatty" Arbuckle and Buster Keaton hang from the "perilous peaks of the Virginia hills."

These days Hollywood comes here for intense action scenes that call for equally dramatic roads and terrain. John Woo directed the sexy Spanish mountain chase with Tom Cruise and Thandie Newton in *Mission: Impossible 2* along these curves. As an homage to the Cary Grant/Grace Kelly Monte Carlo escapade in Hitchcock's *To Catch a Thief*, Woo says in his DVD commentary that he wanted to dramatize the Cruise/Newton courtship with an autoerotic pursuit instead of nonkinetic verbal repartee. The sunrise chase heats up as the two screeching convertibles slam and bump into each other, then climaxes with Cruise rescuing Newton as she and her car dangle from a one-hundred-foot cliff. According to rangers, Cruise was ferried daily to this mountainous location via helicopter, while the crew camped out overnight at Crystal Lake.

The All-American foothill towns of Monrovia (*Beethoven, Grosse Pointe Blank*) and Sierra Madre ("Santa Mira" in the original *Invasion of the Body Snatchers*) also see a lot of production in the shadow of the San Gabriels.

## THE DRIVE

*Starting in the town of Azusa, this tour along the scenic San Gabriel Canyon byway provides many opportunities for hiking, fishing, location spotting, and picnicking. Set your odometer to zero at the San Gabriel Canyon Entry Station. Mileage counts are approximate distances from here. All travelers will need a National Forest Service Adventure Pass to visit any of the following landmarks.*

## SAN GABRIEL CANYON ENTRY STATION

This information kiosk and forest gateway (staffed during weekends) marks the beginning of your drive. It's near the long-gone Canyon Inn, site of the biker cantina in *Starsky & Hutch*, where undercover cops Ben Stiller and Owen Wilson don *Easy Rider*–style costumes. Other films partially shot at the inn include *The Mexican* with Brad Pitt and *Hostage* with Bruce Willis.

## SAN GABRIEL DAM VIEWPOINT *(5 miles)*

Although you can't actually set foot on the 1939 dam, you can easily see the reservoir from this turnout. Previous to his *Starsky & Hutch* location shoot, Owen Wilson was on the dam for *Behind Enemy Lines*, dodging bullets from an enemy sniper and sliding down the dam's face. The reservoir also figures in the climax of Justin Lin's *The Fast and the Furious: Tokyo Drift*.

## EAST FORK BRIDGE *(9 miles)*

Located halfway up the canyon, this is the metal and concrete bridge where Owen Wilson meets up with cola-drinking, American-loving foreigners in *Behind Enemy Lines*. The 1949 bridge crosses the San Gabriel River (which is stocked with rainbow trout during the fishing season), seen in *Pushing Tin* with Billy Bob Thornton and John Cusack. Just above the bridge, a section of San

Gabriel Canyon Road was the location for the climactic confrontation in *The Glass House* between Leelee Sobieski and villainous foster father Stellan Skarsgard.

## CRYSTAL LAKE *(24 miles)*

Despite a name that's familiar to horror fans, this small body of water is not the summer camp location used in the *Friday the 13th* movie series. It does, however, appear briefly in Roger Donaldson's volcano movie *Dante's Peak*. Crystal Lake is where scientist Pierce Brosnan tests the acidity of the area's water. Several hiking trails originate from this area. The **Deer Flats Group Camp** (*626-335-1251*) is a mile away.

## DETOUR: EAST FORK ROAD AND THE BRIDGE TO NOWHERE

The East Fork Road out of San Gabriel Canyon takes you past **Follows Camp**, a former prospecting area from the late 1800s. In recent times it has been a commercial campground and RV park that periodically offers a tourist-oriented gold mining experience (*Mining info: 626-910-1388*).

One mile up the East Fork Road you'll find the **Camp Williams Cafe** (*626-910-1126*), a log cabin-style diner used for TV commercial shoots.

Dedicated outdoors people will want to continue to the end of the road, past the fire station, to the trailhead for the East Fork Trail in the Sheep Mountain Wilderness. From here, a 4.5-mile hike leads to a local landmark

This mysterious 1936 bridge is an out-of-place landmark along a hiking trail.

Harry Medved

known as the **Bridge to Nowhere**. A 1936 Works Progress Administration project built for a road that was never finished, this fascinating, out-of-place architectural span over a deep gorge is now privately owned. With ten river crossings en route to the bridge, bring appropriate gear because you're certain to get wet. On the big screen, the bridge was the site of one of Myles Berkowitz' *20 Dates* in the actor/director's 1998 reality-based romantic comedy. As seen in the film, bungee jumping is offered every weekend by reservation only (www.bungeeamerica.com; 310-322-8892).

*HOW TO GET TO THE TRAILHEAD FOR THE BRIDGE TO NOWHERE From Azusa, take San Gabriel Canyon Road 10 miles up the mountain to the East Fork Bridge. Cross the bridge and take East Fork Road 8 miles to its end, where you'll find the East Fork trailhead. From here the bridge is approximately 4.5 miles. Hiking info: 626-335-1251.*

## MOVIE GARDENS OF THE SAN GABRIELS

When a script calls for a bit of greenery on the grounds of a country estate, filmmakers find their flora at these gardens nestled beneath the San Gabriel Mountains. The following three gardens are busy with crews throughout the year. While they make pleasant strolling destinations during the cooler months, be aware that summer temperatures at these largely shade-free garden spots can soar.

### DESCANSO GARDENS

This 160-acre wonderland includes an extensive California live oak forest, streams, koi ponds, bird sanctuaries, and four hundred varieties of camellias.

Production designer Alex McDowell's *Minority Report* greenhouse features in a scene with Tom Cruise and Lois Smith at Descanso's Fern Canyon. Other Descanso appearances include the funeral site attended by Ben Affleck and Jennifer Garner in *Daredevil*, the private retreat where Reese Witherspoon interviews Raquel Welch in *Legally Blonde*, and the exotic jungle locale for *Congo* with Laura Linney. *1418 Descanso Drive, near the intersection of the 210 and 2 Freeways in La Cañada Flintridge; www.descansogardens.org; 818-949-4200.*

### THE HUNTINGTON

Railroad magnate Henry Huntington began developing his San Marino estate and gardens in 1903, with sweeping lawns and statuary. Today the grounds also house a world-renowned library of rare manuscripts and an impressive art galleries featuring Gainsborough's *Blue Boy*. In *Indecent Proposal* the Huntington estate plays Robert Redford's palatial home.

It's also a frequent location for movie weddings, as in *The Wedding*

*Singer* (where Adam Sandler's bride is a no-show), *The Wedding Planner* (Jennifer Lopez and Matthew McConaughey survey the statuary), *Wedding Crashers* (tearful Will Ferrell and sexy twins see off the film's heroes), *My Best Friend's Wedding* (Julia Roberts attends the reception), and the Coen Bros.' *Intolerable Cruelty* (Catherine Zeta-Jones weds Billy Bob Thornton).

The Huntington's Japanese Gardens are often used for the Far East, as in *Midway* (scenes with Toshiro Mifune), *Beverly Hills Ninja* (Chris Farley's training camp), and *Anger Management* (where Adam Sandler and Jack Nicholson visit monk John C. Reilly). In Rob Marshall's film of *Memoirs of a Geisha*, the Huntington plays the baron's estate visited by Ziyi Zhang and Ken Watanabe. The Rose Garden Tea Room, outside of which Reese Witherspoon and Luke Wilson get married in *Legally Blonde 2*, offers a traditional English tea served with a basket of scones and finger sandwiches. Reservations are required. *1151 Oxford Road in San Marino; enter on South Allen Ave. at Orlando Rd.; www.huntington.org; 626-405-2100.*

## THE ARBORETUM

In addition to Griffith Park and Franklin Canyon, the Los Angeles County Arboretum has always been one of the city's most frequently filmed outdoor locations, especially its swampy **Baldwin Lake**. A common misconception is that *The African Queen* "leech attack" sequence was shot here. (According to film historian Rudy Behlmer, Bogart and Hepburn filmed their scenes overseas.) However, aquatic bloodsuckers *did* prowl these waters when *Attack of the Giant Leeches* used the Arboretum's Baldwin Lake as a filming location.

Other exotic Arboretum scenes appear in *Teenage Caveman* (a prehistoric forest with Robert Vaughn), *Cobra Woman* (a Pacific island ruled by Maria Montez), *Anaconda* (a Brazilian rain forest explored by Jennifer Lopez and Ice Cube), Preston Sturges' *The Lady Eve* (Henry Fonda's Amazon jungle), *The Waterboy* (Kathy Bates' bayou home) and *Joe Dirt* (Rosanna Arquette's Florida alligator farm). In Alfred Hitchcock's *Notorious*, the grounds provide a Rio riding track where Cary Grant and Ingrid Bergman bait Claude Rains.

Constructed in 1885 by former property owner Lucky Baldwin as a honeymoon gift for his fourth wife, the Arboretum's **Queen Anne Cottage** is open for tours twice a year: on Mother's Day and around Christmas time. The Victorian-style cottage is a familiar landmark that appears as Henry Daniell's island mansion in *Wake of the Red Witch* and as a temple where Japanese soldiers hide out in the Errol Flynn war drama *Objective Burma*. In John Schlesinger's *Marathon Man*, the area plays the South American lair from which Nazi-in-hiding Laurence Olivier emerges. But the home is perhaps best known as the locale where Tattoo (Herve Villechaize) cries "Da Plane! Da Plane!" to his boss Mr. Roarke (Ricardo Montalban) on TV's *Fantasy Island*. In 2004 the cottage was dressed to play "Focker Isle," Barbra Streisand and

Dustin Hoffman's Florida homestead in *Meet the Fockers*. *Just south of the 210/Foothill Freeway at 301 North Baldwin Avenue, across from the Santa Anita Racetrack; Arboretum info: 626-821-3222.*

## HOW TO GET TO SAN GABRIEL CANYON ROAD

*From the 210 Freeway in Azusa, exit on Azusa Avenue (Highway 39) and head north into the hills.*

## DVD ITINERARY: SAN GABRIEL CANYON

*Mission: Impossible 2*, Scene 4

*Behind Enemy Lines*, Scenes 12 and 19

*Pushing Tin*, Scene 26

The Arboretum's Queen Anne Cottage plays Florida's Focker Isle in *Meet the Fockers*.

# 35

# IDYLLWILD
# Climb Every Mountain

Idyllwild? Where's that?

Oh, you'll love it . . . it's where they have the summer music festival. Way up in the mountains.

*—Albert Brooks taking girlfriend Kathryn Harrold on a romantic Idyllwild getaway in* Modern Romance *(1981)*

**MAJOR ROLES:** *Kid Galahad* (1963), *The Wild Angels, The Wrecking Crew*

## BEHIND THE SCENERY

"Where's Idyllwild?" is a familiar question asked by Southern California new-comers. Though it's nearly as close to L.A. as Big Bear or Lake Arrowhead, this five-thousand-foot-high village remains a largely undiscovered vacation hideaway for many Angelenos. How it manages to stay under the radar is a mystery, since each summer the San Jacinto Mountains are alive with the sound of music thanks to Idyllwild's classical and jazz festivals and the Idyll-wild Arts Academy (where generations of kids have learned about music from composer Roy Harris and *The Music Man's* composer/lyricist Meredith Wilson).

The former sheepherding and lumberjack homestead was a location for a number of classic silent films. Some locals believe that the snowy mountain scenes in Cecil B. DeMille's 1914 *The Squaw Man* were shot here. According to Idyllwild historian Sheila Meyer, Erich von Stroheim's 1919 *Blind Husbands*

Richard Koszarski Archives

Erich von Stroheim's *Blind Husbands* (1919), shot
in the San Jacinto Mountains.

filmed its Alpine mountain-climbing sequences in the Tahquitz Peak region
above the town.

During Hollywood's Golden Age, Idyllwild was a favorite destination
for reclusive celebrities seeking privacy, peace, and pines near Palm
Springs. Novelist and screenwriter Raymond Chandler owned a cabin here,
as did actors Charles Laughton and Elsa Lanchester, Lucille Ball, and Mar-
jorie Main (best known as "Ma Kettle" in a popular series of country-
bumpkin movies).

The nearby Garner Valley was host to a number of movies in the
1940s, including Canadian Mountie adventures and B Westerns. In the
1960s, the Valley served as a magnificent backdrop for the Elvis Presley musical *Kid Galahad*, the Dean Martin/Sharon Tate spy spoof, *The Wrecking
Crew*, and the Walter Matthau comedy-drama *Kotch*, directed by Jack Lemmon.

In the 1966 biker epic *The Wild Angels*, a pre–*Easy Rider* Peter Fonda and
his motorcycle gang descend upon Idyllwild. During the funeral of gang mem-

ber "The Loser" (Bruce Dern), the Angels trash the town church, much to the chagrin of the mountain community. "The church set was a fake," recalls crew member and future production designer Polly Platt, "but the on-camera looks of disgust from the locals were absolutely *real*. Since we had many real-life members of Hell's Angels in the cast, the good people of Idyllwild couldn't wait for our film to get out of town."

## WHERE TO HIKE

### ERNIE MAXWELL SCENIC TRAIL

Named for the town's outdoors-loving newspaper publisher, the Ernie Maxwell Scenic Trail is an easy three-mile round-trip stroll through ponderosa pines and cedar trees. It's a beautiful place during autumn to check out the fall colors, and the trail affords stunning views of Lily Rock, a granite knob rising above a dense pine forest. Lily Rock can be seen above the fight ring where Elvis Presley trains with a young Charles Bronson in *Kid Galahad*.

*The Ernie Maxwell Scenic Trail and Humber Park's Devil's Slide Trail can be found at the very top of Fern Valley Road. Hiking info: 951-659-2117, ext. 5.*

## WHERE TO EAT

### RED KETTLE

This cafe is a local breakfast-and-lunch hangout and is known for its huge pancakes, omelettes, and homemade soups and sandwiches. According to the Red Kettle's manager, actor Van Johnson used to hang out here in the 1950s. *54220 South Circle Drive; 951-659-4063.*

### CAFÉ AROMA

This earthy bistro offers pleasant outdoor seating under the pine trees and serves pasta, pizzas, and salads. The breakfast menu includes gourmet coffee, tea, and scones. Café Aroma regularly hosts concerts and art openings. Check out the memorabilia-laden Herb Jeffries Room, where the veteran jazz singer and star of *The Bronze Buckaroo* has been known to hold court during concert season. *54750 North Circle Drive; 951-659-5212.*

## WHERE TO STAY

### KNOTTY PINE CABINS

This hideaway is the surprise destination where neurotic Albert Brooks tries to patch up things with Kathryn Harrold in *Modern Romance*. The film's final sequence (in which the insecure Brooks accuses Harrold of infidelity) was shot, ironically, at "Security Lodge," one of Knotty Pine's eight units. A

1920s log cabin that sleeps up to six people, "Security" is a bargain at $150 per night. Light sleepers beware: since the property is a block away from Highway 243, you may hear the steady flow of traffic. *54340 Pine Crest; 951-659-2933.*

## SILVER PINES LODGE

Where else can you stay overnight in a former movie theater complex? This hideaway once housed the Rustic Theater, a first-run movie house in the 1940s. The low-ceilinged screening room is now a charming fireplace lounge, resembling Hollywood's version of a vintage hunting lodge. (Idyllwild's movie house has since relocated to North Circle Drive, where it adjoins a video store that stocks Idyllwild-lensed movies.)

Prior to its incarnation as a theater, Silver Pines was a rowdy tavern where General George S. Patton was a frequent visitor. You can stay in the main lodge or in one of a dozen cabins facing Strawberry Creek. The *Wild Angels* funeral procession (with Peter Fonda, Nancy Sinatra, and Diane Ladd) passes this rustic resort, which was known at the time as Hillbilly Lodge. *25955 Cedar Street; 951-659-4335.*

## ON THE ROAD: PALMS TO PINES SCENIC BYWAY (74)

Twisting Highway 74 has been christened "Palms to Pines" because of the arboreal diversity on view as the route winds its way from arid Palm Canyon below to the forests of Idyllwild in the San Jacinto Mountains above.

In *It's a Mad, Mad, Mad, Mad World*, Palms to Pines is the highway where Jimmy Durante sails off the road in his getaway car. As he reveals the location of a secret cache to passing motorists Milton Berle, Buddy Hackett, Mickey Rooney, Jonathan Winters, and Sid Caesar, Durante kicks the bucket (literally!) and sets the story in motion. After this scene was filmed, Palm Springs Historical Society director Sally McManus recalls that Durante's prop car was left behind as a memento on a figure-eight bend in the highway. "That old wreck was a local landmark for years," recalls McManus, "but eventually they had to remove it as it, was getting to be an eyesore."

Other films shot along the highway include *The Wild Angels* (where Bruce Dern meets his end) and *The Satan Bug* (where George Maharis has a rendezvous with villain Richard Basehart).

Information on the highway's scenic overlooks can be obtained from the visitors center, located on Highway 74, four miles west of Palm Desert. *Open Monday-Friday, 9 a.m.–4 p.m.; 760-862-9984.*

John W. Robinson Archives

Highway 74 ascends from the valley to the mountains.

## HOW TO GET TO IDYLLWILD

*FROM LOS ANGELES: Take the I-10 East to Banning. Take Highway 243 South and follow the road into the hills. FROM PALM SPRINGS: Follow Highway 111 South to the town of Palm Desert. Head west to the hills on Highway 74 (Palms to Pines Highway).*

## DVD ITINERARY: IDYLLWILD

*Blind Husbands*, Scenes 10–11

*The Wild Angels*, Scenes 5 and 15–16

*Kid Galahad* (1963), Scenes 1 and 3–4

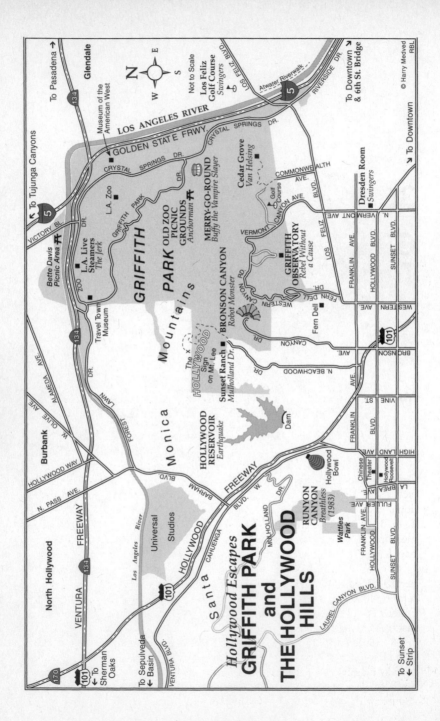

Hollywood Escapes
# GRIFFITH PARK
## and
# THE HOLLYWOOD HILLS

N
E
W
S

Not to Scale

© Harry Medved
RBL

**Glendale**

To Pasadena →

134

Museum of the American West

LOS ANGELES RIVER

Los Feliz Golf Course
*Swingers*

LOS FELIZ BLVD.

Atwater Riverwalk

5

RIVERSIDE DR.

To Downtown & 6th St. Bridge ↗

To Downtown →

GOLDEN STATE FRWY.

CRYSTAL SPRINGS DR.

CRYSTAL SPRINGS DR.

CRYSTAL SPRINGS DR.

To Tujunga Canyons ←

Bette Davis Picnic Area

5

VICTORY BL.

L.A. Zoo

L.A. Live Steamers
*The Jerk*

ZOO DR.

GRIFFITH DR.

GRIFFITH
PARK

**GRIFFITH**

**PARK**

OLD ZOO PICNIC GROUNDS
*Anchorman*

MERRY-GO-ROUND
*Buffy the Vampire Slayer*

Cedar Grove
*Van Helsing*

COMMONWEALTH AVE.

Golf Course

CANYON DR.

VERMONT AVE.

GRIFFITH OBSERVATORY
*Rebel Without a Cause*

LOS FELIZ

FRANKLIN AVE.

Dresden Room
*Swingers*

VERMONT AVE.

HOLLYWOOD BLVD.

SUNSET BLVD.

Travel Town Museum

134

FOREST LAWN DR.

M o n i c a

M o u n t a i n s

The X
HOLLYWOOD
Sign on Mt. Lee

BRONSON CANYON
*Robot Monster*

Sunset Ranch
*Mulholland Dr.*

FERN DELL DR.

Fern Dell

WESTERN CANYON RD.

WESTERN AVE.

BRONSON AVE.

N. BEACHWOOD AVE.

CANYON DR.

101

**Burbank**

ALAMEDA AVE.

W. OLIVE AVE.

HOLLYWOOD WAY

N. PASS AVE.

BARHAM BLVD.

S a n t a

Los Angeles River

Universal Studios

HOLLYWOOD FREEWAY

HOLLYWOOD RESERVOIR
*Earthquake*

Dam

MULHOLLAND DR.

RUNYON CANYON
*Breathless* (1983)

Wattles Park

Hollywood Bowl

Chinese Theater

Hollywood Roosevelt

LA BREA AVE.

HIGHLAND AVE.

**North Hollywood**

VENTURA FREEWAY

134

170

101

To Sherman Oaks

VENTURA BLVD.

To Sepulveda Basin

101

HOLLYWOOD BLVD.

CAHUENGA BLVD. W.

FULLER AVE.

FRANKLIN AVE.

HOLLYWOOD BLVD.

SUNSET BLVD.

LAUREL CANYON BLVD.

To Sunset Strip

# 36

# GRIFFITH PARK
# The Urban Wilderness

*You know what's remarkable? It's how much England looks in no way like Southern California.*

—Mike Myers on a chaparral-lined Griffith Park road in Austin
Powers: The Spy Who Shagged Me (1999)

**MAJOR ROLES:** *Rebel Without a Cause, The Rocketeer, Dragnet, Bowfinger*

## BEHIND THE SCENERY

Griffith Park was a gift to the burgeoning City of Angels from real estate benefactor and Welsh mining magnate Colonel Griffith Jenkins Griffith. Griffith donated 3,015 acres of his property to L.A. in 1896, stipulating that "it must be made a place of recreation and rest for the masses, a resort for the rank and file, for the plain people. I consider it my obligation to make Los Angeles a happier, cleaner and finer city."

Griffith Park's variety, size, and proximity to the city center make it the perfect backlot, with palm trees, creeks, valleys, and mountaintops. Its rugged terrain has appeared in war pictures like King Vidor's *The Big Parade* and Sam Fuller's *The Steel Helmet*. Robert Altman's M*A*S*H used the park for the climactic football game sequence.

Griffith Park's roads—including Western Canyon Road, Mount Hollywood Road, Crystal Springs Drive, and the private Vista Del Valle—are often used by filmmakers who need winding mountain lanes. In *Austin Powers: The Spy Who Shagged Me*, henchman Will Ferrell falls from a cliff in a roadside encounter with Mike Myers and Heather Graham.

The roads also provide a backdrop for tense sequences in David Lynch's *Mulholland Dr.* (for the titular byway) and *Lost Highway* (where Robert Loggia suffers an unforgettable case of road rage).

In Robert Zemeckis' *Who Framed Roger Rabbit?*, the tunnel at Vermont Canyon provided Bob Hoskins' entrance to Toontown. The director returned in 1989 for *Back to the Future II*'s tunnel chase involving Michael J. Fox, Thomas F. Wilson, and Christopher Lloyd. The field south of the tunnel was the location for the Sherwood, Ohio, high school jocks' cow-tipping high jinks in *Heathers*, according to production designer Jon Hutman.

With its historical movie locations and recreational opportunities, Griffith Park remains an ideal destination for both film crews and outdoors lovers looking to stay close to L.A.

## WHERE TO EXPLORE

### FERN DELL PARK
Fern Dell is a lush little park with a year-round natural spring winding through palm trees, sycamores, and hundreds of exotic ferns. Close to Los Feliz Boulevard, this former site of a Gabrielino Indian village has been featured as an overgrown setting since the silent days (including *Young Rajah* with Rudolph Valentino). On weekdays, Fern Dell is the perfect spot for a meditative afternoon idyll.

*HOW TO GET TO FERN DELL PARK From Los Feliz Boulevard, take Fern Dell Drive north to the corner of Black Oak Drive.*

### THE OBSERVATORY
The Griffith Observatory's timeless retro-futuristic architecture has served filmmakers from the late 1930s to the present day. Most famously, it was the site of an observatory show and high school knife fight with James Dean, Natalie Wood, Dennis Hopper, Corey Allen, and Sal Mineo in *Rebel Without a Cause* (1955). In 1984, cyborg Arnold Schwarzenegger is knifed here by three thugs (including Bill Paxton) in James Cameron's *The Terminator*. Other observatory appearances include:

*Dragnet*    Tom Hanks rescues Dan Aykroyd and Alexandra Paul from the clutches of bad guy Christopher Plummer.

*Devil in a Blue Dress*    Denzel Washington returns Jennifer Beals to ex-boyfriend/politician Terry Kinney for a late-night rendezvous here.

Disney's *The Rocketeer*    Hero Billy Campbell tries to rescue hostage Jennifer Connelly in the climactic shoot-out.

*Bowfinger*    Steve Martin, Heather Graham, and Christine Baranski capture reluctant star Eddie Murphy on film for a grade-Z sci-fi flick called *Chubby Rain*.

The trail to the observatory.

*Charlie's Angels: Full Throttle*  Cameron Diaz, Lucy Liu, and Drew Barrymore square off with seductive villain Demi Moore.

Additional sci-fi productions films shot at the observatory include *War of the Colossal Beast*, *The Man from Planet X*, *Phantom from Space*, and *The Phantom Empire* serial.

*Observatory info and hours: 323-664-1191.*

## WHERE TO HIKE

### FROM FERN DELL TO THE OBSERVATORY

A forty-five-minute uphill trek to the observatory starts beside the stream at Fern Dell. After crossing the stream several times, you'll walk under a small stone bridge and enter the city park at the Fern Dell Picnic Grounds. Continue past the bathrooms and stay to the right of the creek. Veer uphill to the right. As you make your ascent, the observatory's dome rises from the tree line like an Art Deco monolith.

There's an overlook at the top of the hill with astonishing views of the Spanish colonial homes in the Hollywood Hills, the Hollywood sign, L.A.'s downtown skyline, Century City, and the Pacific Ocean. This overlook is the rendezvous for observatory-based scientist Gabriel Byrne and government agent Daniel Benzali in Wim Wenders's *The End of Violence*.

## Top Billing: CEDAR GROVE

Cedar Grove is the Hollywood Hills miniforest that appears frequently as a backup location for big-budget reshoots, low-budget features, TV movies, and commercials.

Cedar Grove appears briefly in Tony Scott's *The Last Boy Scout* (in a shoot-out with Bruce Willis, Damon Wayans, and the bad guys), Penelope Spheeris' comedy *Black Sheep* (where David Spade and Chris Farley hang out in a Washington State cabin), *The Cable Guy* (site of Jim Carrey's cabin), and *Van Helsing* (a Carpathian Mountains location with Kate Beckinsale, Will Kemp, and Hugh Jackman). In *The Green Mile*, this is where Tom Hanks, Jeffrey DeMunn, Barry Pepper, and David Morse prepare inmate Michael Clarke Duncan for his visit with terminally ill Patricia Clarkson. "It was so friggin' cold in Tennessee," explains *Green Mile* director Frank Darabont, "that I moved the end of the scene to Cedar Grove so I wouldn't have to try to cut a scene together with my actors' teeth chattering." Peaceful and serene, Cedar Grove is an ideal area for picnicking and quiet contemplation . . . that is, when film crews aren't present.

*HOW TO GET TO CEDAR GROVE From Los Feliz Blvd. take Commonwealth Avenue to its end. Walk uphill past the locked T-bar gate on your left. Look for a road on the right with another T-bar gate. Walk up that road for 15 minutes. Look for a big green water tank on your left. To your right across the road is Cedar Grove.*

## WHERE TO EAT

## THE DRESDEN ROOM

Located near the southern entrance to Griffith Park, this Hollywood landmark serves old-fashioned, all-American cuisine and has been owned and operated by the same family since the 1950s. Its timeless interiors make it an ideal location for period movies like *Bugsy*, *The Two Jakes*, *That Thing You Do!*, and *Anchorman*. At night, the joint jumps to the incomparable sounds of Marty and Elayne, the two real-life lounge singers featured in *Swingers*, with Vince Vaughn and Jon Favreau.

The restaurant also doubles for a Chicago night club in *What Women Want*, with Mel Gibson and Helen Hunt. "For years, the Dresden was an unfashionable dive, a remnant of Hollywood days gone by," points out *What Women Want* production designer and L.A. native Jon Hutman. "But because of its great period décor, the Dresden made a great location and the movies shot there have helped popularize the place. Now everything old is new again and the Hollywood crowd has returned." *1760 North Vermont Avenue; 323-665-4294.*

## HOW TO GET TO GRIFFITH PARK

*The park is located west of the I-5 and south of the 134 Freeway.*

## LITTLE FEET IN CEDAR GROVE

*Director Frank Darabont recalls an unforgettable Cedar Grove moment:*

"I was taking a walk with a friend and we happened upon the usual retinue of parked trucks and milling crew at lunch at Cedar Grove. Coming toward us was a midget smoking a cigar and wearing the lower half of what appeared to be a gorilla suit. We asked what they were shooting, and the guy replied, *Little Bigfoot!* He, I assumed, was the title character. Ah, movies. Gotta love 'em! Nothing but glamour!"

Scott Dewees

Griffith Park's miniforest has hosted stars such as Tom Hanks, Kate Beckinsale, and Bruce Willis.

## DVD ITINERARY: GRIFFITH OBSERVATORY

*Rebel Without a Cause*, Scenes 8–11 and 30–35

*Charlie's Angels: Full Throttle*, Scenes 20, 22

*Devil in a Blue Dress*, Scene 27

# 37

# GRIFFITH PARK'S OLD ZOO AND MERRY-GO-ROUND
## Animal Attractions

A tree is a tree, a rock is a rock. Shoot it in Griffith Park!

—*1920s studio boss Abe Stern, admonishing his moviemaking minions who wanted to leave Hollywood to shoot an outdoor picture*

**MAJOR ROLES:** *Eraser, Buffy the Vampire Slayer, Anchorman*

### BEHIND THE SCENERY

Not far from Bronson Caves and the observatory, Griffith Park's eastern end has an entirely different feel. If you use a little imagination, the area's landmarks— the merry-go-round, old zoo, and clubhouse—will help you envision a tranquil scene from L.A.'s simpler era. And though the always busy freeways abutting this section are a jarring reminder of the present, Hollywood still shoots this side of the park to re-create another time, another place.

### WHERE TO EXPLORE

#### Top Billing: OLD ZOO PICNIC GROUNDS

The site of the old L.A. Zoo (1912–1965) features forgotten grottos, walls, and enclosures dating back to the 1930s. The ghostly cages (where you can picnic and barbecue) and trails to abandoned monkey houses "make for weird, *Island of Dr. Moreau*–like day hiking," says *CityBeat*'s Idan Ivri.

This nostalgic setting has been used to re-create old zoos for films like *Human Nature* (in home movie flashbacks with Robert Forster and Mary Kay Place) and *Anchorman* (where Will Ferrell, Christina Applegate, and Steve Carell encounter a hibernating bear). For a terrific mid-1970s look at the area, see Jonathan Demme's *Crazy Mama*, in which Cloris Leachman, Stuart Whitman, and gang engage in a shoot-out/pursuit with the cops (including Corman cast regular Dick Miller and director John Milius) in and around the zoo cages. In the early fifties the zoo was briefly featured in *The Star*, with Bette Davis and Sterling Hayden.

In *Eraser*, Arnold Schwarzenegger and Vanessa Williams elude James Caan and villains in a New York zoo re-created at the picnic grounds. "That whole complex is a fun bit of L.A. history," says *Eraser* director Chuck Russell. "The Old Zoo's barred cages supplied a nice retro touch. More importantly, the area's grassy field was big enough for us to land a helicopter, fire weapons and crash vehicles through our prop gates, activities we weren't allowed to do in New York."

A few miles from the zoo is where a mechanical octopus attacked Bela Lugosi in Ed Wood's 1955 *Bride of the Monster*. "It was in March and it was colder than a son of a bitch," recalled Wood in an unpublished manuscript found by his biographer Rudolph Grey. "We got over there and they didn't have a lake . . . so we dammed up the little river that runs through Griffith Park . . . I told the prop man to bang a hole in the dam and the water rushed out of there like a tidal wave. It completely flooded the golf course."

The crew's Griffith Park production experience was partially re-created in nearby Fern Dell Canyon for Tim Burton's 1994 biopic *Ed Wood*, starring Johnny Depp as the hapless director and Martin Landau (in his Oscar-winning performance) as Wood's down-on-his-luck star, Bela Lugosi.

## GRIFFITH PARK MERRY-GO-ROUND

Half a mile from the Old Zoo picnic grounds you'll find this fanciful 1926 carousel, the oldest in Los Angeles and home to sixty-eight hand-crafted horses. According to Griffith Park historian Mike Eberts, "Walt Disney brought his young daughters to the carousel and this is one of the places where he began to dream up the idea that would lead to Disneyland." Inspiration of a different sort came in the early seventies, when local hippies and free-love advocates gathered at the carousel for many infamous "love-ins." Today one of its highlights is the Stinson Military Band Organ which, according to travel writer Kathie Weir, "will send chills up and down your spine."

Indeed, the carousel makes the perfect setting for a spooky after-dark encounter between Paul Reubens and his first victim in the original *Buffy the Vampire Slayer* feature. Production designer Lawrence Miller recalled that "this merry-go-round seems like it landed out of nowhere in the middle of Griffith Park. It's surrounded by lots of cedar trees and at night there's a sense of danger that worked for us." The carousel also appears briefly in *Beautiful*,

Sally Field's feature directorial debut starring Minnie Driver. Trivia note: the carousel is where James Dean got his first professional acting job in a 1950 Pepsi TV commercial. *Carousel info: 323-665-3051.*

## OTHER NEARBY ATTRACTIONS

### MUSEUM OF THE AMERICAN WEST

This collection, founded by cowboy star/museum founder Gene Autry, celebrates the history and myths of the American West. Its famous collection of Western props and costumes include the Lone Ranger mask and scarf worn by Clayton Moore. The museum's Wells Fargo Theater periodically screens classic Westerns. *4700 Zoo Drive; www.museumoftheamericanwest.org; 323-667-2000.*

### LOS ANGELES LIVE STEAMERS

A favorite destination for kids since 1946, this miniature railroad appears in *The Jerk* as the babysitting spot where Steve Martin meets Bernadette Peters. It's also the home of the old **Walt Disney Barn,** open on the third Sunday of each month. Nearby is the **Travel Town Museum,** a collection of trains, antique locomotives, and steam engines that visitors are welcome to climb aboard. *Live Steamers is free to the public, but only open Sundays 11 a.m.–3 p.m., www.lals.org; 323-662-8030. Travel Town Museum: 5200 Zoo Drive; 323-662-5874.*

## WHERE TO EAT

### GRIFFITH PARK CLUBHOUSE

This 1927 Spanish Colonial landmark overlooks the Wilson/Harding Golf Course, which appears in the Eddie Murphy comedy *Daddy Day Care*, with Jeff Garlin and Kevin Nealon. *323-661-7212.*

## PRE-TRIP READING

*Griffith Park: A Centennial History* by Mike Eberts. A lively and informative cultural history of the park, filled with fun facts and photos. *Published by the Historical Society of Southern California, 200 East Avenue 43, L.A., CA 90031; 323-222-0546.*

## HOW TO GET TO THE OLD ZOO & MERRY-GO-ROUND

*Both attractions are located in the Park Center (between the current Los Angeles Zoo on the north and Los Feliz on the south). Griffith Park Visitors Information: www.laparks.org, 323-913-4688.*

Harry Medved

The Old Zoo, a climactic locale for *Anchorman*'s Will Ferrell.

## DVD ITINERARY: OLD ZOO & MERRY-GO-ROUND

*The Jerk*, L.A. Live Steamers, Scene 9

*Crazy Mama*, Old Zoo, Scenes 18–19

*Anchorman*, Old Zoo, Scenes 18–19

# 38

# BRONSON CANYON
## Aliens and Outlaws

> Bronson Canyon is as important to sci-fi history as Monument Valley is to John Ford Westerns.
>
> —Fantasy film historian Forrest J. Ackerman

**MAJOR ROLES:** *Batman* (TV series and 1966 feature), *Invasion of the Body Snatchers* (1956)

### BEHIND THE SCENERY

Griffith Park's Bronson Canyon was once a quarry where rocks were gathered to pave the streets of Hollywood and the San Pedro Breakwater. The canyon is best known for its Bronson Caves, three passages drilled through the base of a rugged mountain.

Bronson proved to be a valuable outdoor destination when many studios were located just down the street, near Hollywood Boulevard. When *I Am a Fugitive from a Chain Gang*'s hard labor scenes (starring Paul Muni) shot in the Bronson quarry on August 8, 1932, the production report noted that the crew left Warner Bros. Sunset lot at 7:30 a.m. and arrived on location at 7:40 a.m. Few outdoor locations can claim they're only *ten* minutes away from the studio.

Cult movie fans today will feel a sense of déjà vu upon seeing Bronson Caves, as they're instantly recognizable from many low-budget sci-fi epics, including Golden Turkey Award nominees *Robot Monster*, *They Saved Hitler's Brain*, and *The Phantom Empire*, a 1935 Gene Autry sci-fi/Western serial in which the caves are portals to the underground kingdom of Murania.

Other not-so-recognizable Bronson appearances include *Julius Caesar* (for a battle sequence where Marlon Brando leads an ambush with hundreds of extras), *The Adventures of Mark Twain* and *Ride the High Country* (as snowy High Sierra mining camps), and *The Scorpion King* (the Michael Clarke Duncan vs. The Rock fight). Often the biggest challenge for set decorators at Bronson Canyon is to find a way to obscure the view of the nearby Hollywood sign.

The rugged terrain around the caves suited hundreds of TV and movie Westerns including *Carson City*, *Massacre Canyon*, and *Thunder Pass*. Although John Ford's seminal *The Searchers* was predominantly filmed in Utah's Monument Valley, the climactic confrontation between Indian hostage Natalie Wood and tracker John Wayne takes place at Bronson. Shot from inside the cave so that the walls create a natural frame, Wayne takes Wood in his arms and says "Let's go home!" while walking off into the Hollywood Hills.

The cave had its greatest moment on television as the beloved Bat Cave from the *Batman* series (and subsequent 1966 feature film) starring Adam West and Burt Ward. "Though more of a tunnel than a cave, it hasn't changed a bit," says *Westways* writer and landmark historian Chris Epting. "Visitors can still imagine the Batmobile roaring out of its depths."

Bronson's environs are also the setting for the climactic earthquake in Robert Altman's *Short Cuts*. This is where Chris Penn and Robert Downey Jr. pursue a pair of young females. To prove he's a savvy Hollywood player, Downey's character boasts that the *Batman* TV show was shot nearby and even offers a tour of the Bat Cave.

## WHERE TO EAT

### THE 101 COFFEE SHOP

Located on the first floor of the Best Western Hollywood Hills Hotel, this café's best-known appearance is in the cult L.A. comedy *Swingers*. It's in a 101 booth that Vince Vaughn and Jon Favreau discuss dating strategies. *Open 7 a.m.–3 a.m. every day; 6145 Franklin Avenue, between Argyle and Gower; 323-467-1175.*

## IT CAME FROM CALIFORNIA: THE BRONSON CAVES

Many a creature made the Bronson Caves its lair in the 1950s and '60s: an intergalactic gorilla wearing a deep-sea diving helmet in the infamous *Robot Monster*, a sinister cerebrum in *The Brain from Planet Arous*, an oversize arachnid in *Earth vs. the Spider*, killer carrots in *Invasion of the Star Creatures*, and a prehistoric giant in *Eegah!*. Low-budget movie maven Roger Corman was here with a demonic Venusian cucumber in *It Conquered the World* and the alien-controlled crustaceans in *Attack of the Crab Monsters*. Other Corman fantasy features partially shot at Bronson include *Teenage Caveman*, *Day the World Ended*, and *The Viking Women and the Sea Serpent*.

Wade Williams Archives

*Robot Monster*'s Bronson
Canyon lair.

In one classic case, it was the *humans* that hid here from the aliens. In the original *Invasion of the Body Snatchers*, Bronson Caves provide shelter for Kevin McCarthy and Dana Wynter as they flee the pod people. It's inside this tunnel that Wynter falls asleep and succumbs to alien forces.

Other sci-fi and fantasy films shot in Bronson Canyon include *Sleeper* (Woody Allen and Diane Keaton discover a two-hundred-year-old Volkswagen in the cave), *Dreamscape, Teenagers from Outer Space, I Married a Monster from Outer Space, Equinox, The Sword and the Sorcerer, The Cyclops, Octaman, King Dinosaur, Monster from Green Hell, Night of the Blood Beast, Invisible Invaders*, the alternate ending of Sam Raimi's *Army of Darkness* (viewable on various DVD editions), and Larry Blamire's horror spoof *The Lost Skeleton of Cadavra*.

## HOW TO GET TO BRONSON CANYON CAVES

*From Hollywood Blvd, take Bronson Avenue north. At Canyon Drive, make a left. Drive past the stone gates, playground, and picnic area and you'll find parking near the road's end.*

*To walk to the caves, look for the gated fire road (signed "49") on the right side of the street. Follow the dirt path as it bends left to the caves.*

## DVD ITINERARY: BRONSON CANYON

*Invasion of the Body Snatchers* (1956), Scenes 22–23

*The Searchers*, Scene 43

*The Lost Skeleton of Cadavra*, Scene 9

## 39

# THE HOLLYWOOD SIGN TRAIL
## Icon See for Miles

> To any moviegoer, in any country on this planet, this landmark represents all the dreams, glamour, and history of the film industry.
>
> —Hollywood historian Marc Wanamaker

**MAJOR ROLES:** *Hollywood Boulevard* (1976), *The Day of the Locust*, *The Day After Tomorrow*

### BEHIND THE SCENERY

Originally the Hollywood*land* sign, this world-famous landmark was erected in 1923 as a promotion for a Hollywood Hills real estate development backed by comedy king Mack Sennett and *Los Angeles Times* publisher Harry Chandler. By the mid-1940s the sign atop Mt. Lee fell into disrepair, after the development company went bankrupt. The Hollywood Chamber of Commerce saved it from demolition in 1949, and during the restoration they removed the last four letters. Over the years the sign has become L.A.'s most prominent movie-related icon.

The fifty-foot-high sign is often glimpsed in establishing shots of past, present, and future Los Angeles. In fact, sci-fi and fantasy filmmakers have found it easy to annihilate the sign via special visual effects: in John Carpenter's *Escape from L.A.* and the Sylvester Stallone/Wesley Snipes action epic *Demolition Man* the unfortunate landmark is consumed by fires.

Lara Mars

Tinseltown's most iconic landmark.

## THE HIKE TO A VIEW OF THE HOLLYWOOD SIGN

If you're a hiker, the three-mile round-trip along the **Hollyridge Trail** to Mt. Lee is the best way to see the Hollywood sign. As the landmark is completely fenced off to the public and violators are subject to arrest, be aware that you won't be able to walk among the letters. On a clear day, however, you'll be rewarded with stunning L.A. and San Fernando Valley views.

Park at the end of Beachwood Drive and follow the Hollyridge Trail signs as you head uphill on a dirt path. At the top of the hill, make a left. You will pass a SUNSET RANCH sign and continue uphill. Soon you will make a sharp left at the hairpin turn and you will arrive at a paved service road.

### The Best Photo Op
For those who want a picture-postcard view of the Hollywood sign, make a left on the paved road and take a ten-minute downhill walk to the perfect vantage point of the sign. Struggling newcomer Naomi Watts poses here in *Ellie Parker*. To continue the hike to Mt. Lee, backtrack on the paved road, passing the dirt trail. Stay to the left on the paved road and continue uphill to Mt. Lee.

### Ascending Mt. Lee
The road to the top of this dusty 1,680-foot-high mountain is a moderately strenuous workout, but it's worth the hike. As of this writing, an unmarked rock-scramble trail to the very top of Mt. Lee offers unobstructed views.

Marc Wanamaker/Bison Archives

The Body Snatchers invade
Beachwood Canyon.

## WHERE TO EAT

### THE VILLAGE COFFEE SHOP

Located at the intersection of Beachwood and Belden Drives, this homey neighborhood eatery is located on a corner where Kevin McCarthy and Dana Wynter flee the *Invasion of the Body Snatchers*. Beachwood Market next door is a great place to pick up sandwiches for the trail and can be spotted in the evacuation scene of another 1956 sci-fi chiller, Roger Corman's *It Conquered the World*, with Peter Graves, Beverly Garland, and Lee Van Cleef. *Call ahead for hours. 2695 N. Beachwood Drive; 323-467-5398.*

## HOW TO RIDE TO THE SIGN

### THE HOLLYWOOD STABLES SUNSET RANCH

You can rent a horse and ride to a view of the sign from Sunset Ranch. This riding facility prides itself as the "Home of the Famous Dinner Ride," a three-hour journey through Griffith Park with a meal break in Burbank. David Lynch's *Mulholland Dr.* used the stables as the mysterious meeting place for film director Justin Theroux and the enigmatic "cowboy." *3400 N. Beachwood Drive, 323-469-5450; www.sunsetranchhollywood.com.*

## LETTERS OF RECOMMENDATION: THE HOLLYWOOD SIGN ON FILM

**H** In 1932, down-on-her-luck actress Peg Entwistle climbed atop this letter and jumped to her death, a tragic Hollywood tale retold in John Schlesinger's *Day of the Locust.* As Karen Black and William Atherton people watch at the site, a tour guide recalls the Entwistle saga at "this mammoth monument to the mecca of broken dreams."

**O** In Disney's remake of *Mighty Joe Young,* the oversize, lost-in-L.A. simian leaps through this letter while looking for his object of affection, Charlize Theron.

**L** Lightning strikes the middle letters of the sign, behind which lurks Dr. Evil and his Hollywood lair in the third Austin Powers movie, *Goldmember.* From this secret hideaway, henchman Robert Wagner unveils the newly formed "Hollywood Talent Agency," a ruthless industry conglomerate.

**Y** This letter crushes villainess Mary Woronov in *Hollywood Boulevard,* the irreverent salute to low-budget filmmaking from directors Joe Dante and Allan Arkush.

**WOOD** And in the disaster pic *The Day After Tomorrow,* these four letters are obliterated by killer tornados.

Two period movies offer fanciful explanations for how "Hollywoodland" became the abbreviated "Hollywood" sign. In the Steven Spielberg comedy *1941,* wacky fighter pilot John Belushi strafes the "L-A-N-D" while trying to shoot down a supposed enemy aircraft flown by Tim Matheson and Nancy Allen. In Disney's *The Rocketeer,* Nazi-sympathizing swashbuckler Timothy Dalton is blasted into oblivion and takes the extraneous letters with him.

The sign in its earlier, longer days.

## HOW TO GET TO THE HOLLYWOOD SIGN

*From Hollywood Boulevard and Highland Ave., take Highland north to Franklin and head east on Franklin to N. Beachwood Drive. Take Beachwood 2 miles north to its end. Park at the intersection of Beachwood and Hollyridge Drive.*

## DVD ITINERARY: HOLLYWOOD SIGN

*Hollywood Boulevard* (1976), Scene 24

*Mighty Joe Young*, Scene 14

*The Day After Tomorrow*, Scene 10

Harry Medved

The view from behind the sign.

**40**

# RUNYON CANYON AND THE HOLLYWOOD HILLS
## In Like Flynn

> No matter where I start out for, I always end up right back here in Hollywood.
>
> —Joel McCrea in Sullivan's Travels (1942)

**MAJOR ROLES:** *Breathless (1983), It's My Party*

### BEHIND THE SCENERY

Once an outdoorsman's paradise in the early twentieth century, the Hollywood Hills underwent a major change in the 1910s and 1920s when the wilderness area was subdivided to make way for upscale homes.

In a 1931 article in *The Topics of the Town* magazine, local resident and actor Joel McCrea bemoaned that in his beloved Nichols Canyon "paved roads are going in, trees cut down, banks cleared. I resent the civilizing of Nature, the unnecessary destruction of trees and shrubs." Further development was inevitable, but thanks to a 1984 purchase by the City of Los Angeles, one wild patch remains: Runyon Canyon.

Originally called "No Man's Canyon," the rugged property was once owned by coal magnate Carman Runyon, who used it as a hunting and riding retreat. Irish tenor John McCormack, who had come to Hollywood to star in *Song O' My Heart*, bought the estate in 1929. Supermarket heir Huntington Hartford built a hillside development called "The Pines" at the foot of the canyon in 1942. According to historian Marc Wanamaker, Errol Flynn was friends with Hartford and caroused with buddies at the estate's pool house. (Flynn, notorious for his wild parties, also had a home at the top of the canyon at Torreyson Place.)

You can still see ruins of the home, pool house, and tennis courts near the grassy lawn. In the 1983 remake of *Breathless*, the estate ruins provide a hideout for lovestruck fugitives Richard Gere and Valerie Kaprisky.

*Grease* director Randal Kleiser shot part of his drama *It's My Party* at the ranch house and corral (also seen in *Scream 3* and *Hollywood Homicide*) at the top of the canyon. Kleiser was stunned by the emerging popularity of the canyon as a social scene. "In the eighties, I might have seen five people all day long. Now you can see five people in ten seconds. It's become L.A.'s favorite place for dog walking." As Paul Brownfield writes in the *Los Angeles Times*, "It's where young Hollywood goes to hike."

## WHERE TO HIKE

### THE TRAIL TO CLOUD'S REST

Start at the end of Fuller Street, where you will find the park entrance behind a set of stone gates. This is the old "Pines" estate, in front of which Richard Gere has his final confrontation with the police in the remake of *Breathless*.

After passing through the gates, check the map at the kiosk. Follow the trail as it winds uphill for a steep three-mile loop (it's all downhill on the way back). On the way up, you'll pass two lookouts, Inspiration Point and Cloud's Rest, where you'll enjoy clear-day views of downtown L.A., Hollywood, and Century City. This is where Jennifer Jason Leigh and Alan Cumming have a marital spat in their directorial effort *The Anniversary Party* and where Pell James and Steven Strait admire the view in *Undiscovered*.

Near the top of the hill you'll intersect a fire road. If you make a left, heading downhill, you'll return to the trailhead.

## WHERE TO EAT

### YAMASHIRO RESTAURANT

This exotic home was built by Oriental antique importers the Bernheimer Brothers in the 1910s. It became "the Club of Hollywood 400" in the 1920s, a gathering place for Hollywood actors who weren't accepted at country clubs. The Japanese-style estate opened as a restaurant in 1960 and since has become one of L.A.'s favorite spots for evening drinks and sensational views of the city.

Although used as a nightclub in *Memoirs of a Geisha* (where Ziyi Zhang makes her debut), Yamashiro is best seen as a location in the comedic "Fistful of Yen" sequence from John Landis' *Kentucky Fried Movie*. It also plays the

American officers' club in the 1957 melodrama *Sayonara*, with Marlon Brando, James Garner, and an oddly cast Ricardo Montalban as "Mr. Naka-mura." The *Sayonara* club supposedly affords a great view of Japan, but sharp-eyed viewers will notice the iconic spire of the Capitol Records building in the background. *1999 N. Sycamore Ave.; www.yamashirorestaurant.com; 323-466-5125.*

## MUSSO AND FRANK'S

A favorite watering hole for the Hollywood literary crowd since 1919, Musso's claims Raymond Chandler, F. Scott Fitzgerald, William Faulkner, and Ernest Hemingway as bygone regulars. *Ed Wood, Ocean's Eleven* (2001), *The Last Shot,* and *The Man Who Wasn't There* feature brief scenes here. *6667 Holly-wood Blvd. 323-467-7788.*

## WHERE TO STAY

## HOLLYWOOD ROOSEVELT HOTEL

This is the home of the first Academy Awards ceremony in 1929. The hotel's 1920s lobby and 1950s pool areas have been a filming location for the Dean Martin/Jerry Lewis comedy *Hollywood or Bust* and Steven Spielberg's *Catch Me If You Can,* where Leonardo DiCaprio eludes Tom Hanks by the Tropicana pool. In Cameron Crowe's autobiographical *Almost Famous,* the lobby is where Patrick Fugit receives an embarrassing message from his mother while on the road with rocker Billy Crudup's band Stillwater. *7000 Hollywood Blvd.; www.hollywoodroosevelt.com; 323-466-7000 or 800-950-7667.*

## DETOUR: WATTLES PARK AND MANSION

Surrounded by a dozen stately palm trees, Wattles Park is a fine retreat for a picnic. In Lucky McKee's unsettling *May,* Angela Bettis and Jeremy Sisto have an unusual lunch date under the palms. The main entrance to Wattles Park is on the west side of the property at 1858 North Curson Avenue, just north of Hollywood Boulevard. Look for the tall gates near the corner of N. Curson Avenue and Curson Terrace.

Adjacent to Wattles Park, the 1907 **Wattles Mansion** is now the offices of Hollywood Heritage, a local architectural preservation group. The mansion serves as the sanitarium at the conclusion of *Rain Man,* in which director Barry Levinson, playing a doctor, confers with Dustin Hoffman and Tom Cruise. It also appears as an old-age home in *Troop Beverly Hills* and as the Westside mansion where gardener Jacob Vargas first lays eyes on future wife Jennifer Lopez in *My Family/Mi Familia.*

## THE HOLLYWOOD BOWL: THE HILLS ARE ALIVE

One night we walked up into the hills behind the
Hollywood Bowl. . . . I could relax and let go a little.

—*Fred MacMurray*, Double Indemnity

As Charles Moore enthuses in his guide *Los Angeles: The City Observed*,
this world-famous concert venue is tucked away in "a mysteriously en-
closed valley where time seems to have stopped." Indeed, the country's largest natural amphitheatre still has the same hushed aura as
when superstar Norman Maine (played by Fredric March) had his unforgettable drunken outburst here in David O. Selznick's 1937 production of *A Star Is Born*. Other scenes featured at the Bowl include
*Anchors Aweigh* (with Frank Sinatra and Gene Kelly); *Champagne for
Caesar* (with Ronald Colman and Vincent Price); *Hollywood or Bust*
(with Dean Martin and Jerry Lewis); *Olly, Olly, Oxen Free* (with
Katharine Hepburn); *Xanadu* (starring Olivia Newton-John and Gene
Kelly), and *Beaches* (starring Bette Midler).

The Bowl is rife with Hollywood arcana. Near the top escalator
lies an historical marker donated by actor Tyrone Power. It memorializes Hollywood's first outdoor community performance, a 1916 theatre production of Shakespeare's *Julius Caesar* in Beachwood Canyon.
Starring Tyrone Power Sr., Theodore Roberts, and William Farnum, the
production helped pave the way for the Bowl concept in the early
1920s. The sleek 1940 entrance fountain and statue entitled "Muse of
Music" was fashioned by Oscar sculptor George Stanley. Hidden ter-
races with picnic tables make the Bowl a great spot for an outdoor
date (recommended spot: picnic area #7). *Hollywood Bowl info: www.hol-
lywood bowl.org; 323-850-2000.*

On the other side of busy Highland Avenue, across the street from
the Bowl, Hollywood Heritage has relocated the old barn where Cecil
B. DeMille shot *The Squaw Man* (1914), the first major feature filmed in
Hollywood. Today it's the **Hollywood Heritage Museum**, home of
memorabilia from the industry's early days and site of frequent screenings of The Silent Society. *2100 N. Highland Ave. at Odin Street, open
Saturday and Sunday 11 a.m.– 4 p.m.; www.hollywoodheritage.org; 323-874-
2276.*

Harry Medved

Runyon is one of the Hollywood Hills' last vestiges of wilderness.

*The mansion can be viewed by appointment only. 1824 N. Curson Avenue; 323-874-4005.*

## HOW TO GET TO RUNYON CANYON

*To reach the entrance of Runyon Canyon, take Hollywood Boulevard to Fuller (between Fairfax and La Brea). Go north on Fuller, past Franklin. You'll find the park entrance at the end of Fuller. On weekends, parking spots on Fuller are rare, so you may need to park on side streets. www.runyon-canyon.org; 323-666-5046.*

## DVD ITINERARY: RUNYON CANYON

*Breathless* (1983), Runyon Canyon, Scenes 27–28 and 30–31

*Anchors Aweigh*, Hollywood Bowl, Scenes 30–31

*Sayonara*, Yamashiro Restaurant, Scenes 2 and 8

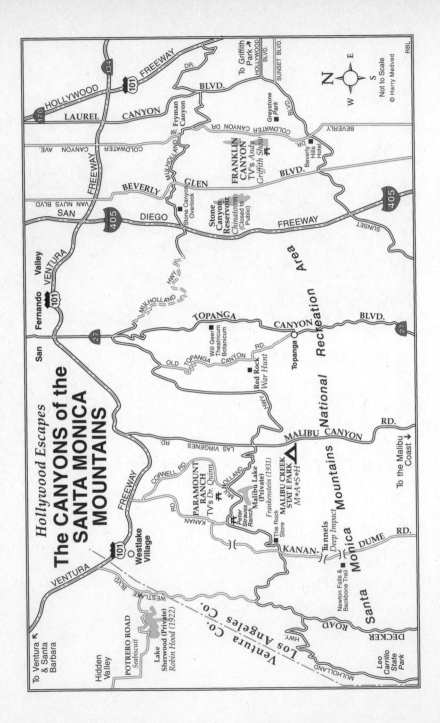

*Hollywood Escapes*

# The CANYONS of the SANTA MONICA MOUNTAINS

Not to Scale
© Harry Medved

# 41

# THE CANYONS OF THE SANTA MONICA MOUNTAINS
## Wild at Heart

> A man may enjoy a lifetime in these hills yet never discover the half of their nooks and dingles . . . these hills are waiting for human invasion.
>
> —*Author John Russell McCarthy,* These Waiting Hills: The Santa Monicas *(1924)*

**MAJOR ROLES:** *Easy Rider, Panic in Year Zero!*

### BEHIND THE SCENERY

This vast range, stretching from the Hollywood Bowl to the Ventura county line, has always attracted filmmakers as a place not only to work but to live. As a result of decades of widespread development in these hills and the fear of suburban saturation, the Santa Monica Mountains National Recreation Area was established in 1978. This recreation area is an official unit of the National Park Service, and covers a good portion of the land west of the 405 Freeway.

For the traveler it helps to put the mountains in perspective by examining them canyon road by canyon road, moving west to east. These well-traveled corridors are not necessarily destinations unto themselves but may serve as points of departure for off-the-beaten-path adventures.

## THE "WILD" CANYONS
## (WEST OF THE 405 FREEWAY)
### DECKER CANYON

Of the following canyons, this is the wildest and least traveled, mainly because Decker Canyon Road (Highway 23) frequently dips, turns, and loops around like a roller-coaster track. The user-unfriendly nature of the narrow and treacherous road keeps the area rustic to this day. The road provides W. C. Fields' first glimpses of California in *It's a Gift*.

On the valley side of the mountain, Decker Canyon Road becomes Westlake Boulevard, at its intersection with rustic **Carlisle Canyon Road.** Carlisle plays an oak-strewn Northern California byway in the Coen Brothers' black-and-white noir homage, *The Man Who Wasn't There*. As Billy Bob Thornton and piano student Scarlett Johansson speed down the road, she makes an unforgettably forward proposition that almost costs them their lives.

### WHERE TO HIKE IN DECKER CANYON
## NICHOLAS FLAT

Officially part of Leo Carrillo State Park, Nicholas Flat's highlight is a scenic, catfish-inhabited duck pond surrounded by boggy cattails and dramatic rocks overlooking the Pacific Ocean.

*HOW TO GET TO NICHOLAS FLAT From PCH, head approximately 2.5 miles up curving Decker Canyon Road to the easy-to-miss Decker School Road (if you hit Decker School Lane, you've missed the turn-off). Continue on Decker School Rd. for 1.5 miles. You'll find the trailhead at road's end.*

### KANAN-DUME CANYON

With the widest roads in the Santa Monica Mountain canyons, Kanan-Dume is often chosen by filmmakers for its three tunnels and open stretches of four-lane mountain highway. In *Charlie's Angels: Full Throttle*, a high-speed action sequence takes place here along Kanan-Dume Road with Lucy Liu and Robert Patrick. Kanan's Tunnel #1 is where bicycling Warren Beatty has a fateful accident before finding himself in the hereafter in *Heaven Can Wait*. Tunnel #1 is also the scene of the entrance to the Ark Cave where Elijah Wood bids farewell to his parents in *Deep Impact*.

### WHERE TO EAT NEAR KANAN-DUME
## THE ROCK STORE

Ed and Vern Savko's biker bar has seen its share of celebrities come and go, including bike enthusiast Jay Leno and the late David Janssen, a local resident who Ed and Vern claim shot episodes of TV's *The Fugitive* here.

The Rock Store, named after the river rocks used to build the 1925 café, is used frequently by commercial and feature film companies as a country gas station outfitted with 1920s pumps. The Rock Store appears in the 1962 end-of-the-world thriller *Panic in Year Zero!* as Ray Milland tries to buy gas at the then-unthinkable price of three dollars a gallon. In the cult monster movie *Schlock!*, it's the store where the titular simian steals bananas. In *Cobra*, it's a roadside stop where Brigitte Nielsen finds out more about cop Sylvester Stallone from his partner Reni Santoni. In Albert Brooks' *Mother*, it's a gas stop somewhere between L.A. and Northern California (Brooks tells the owner he's not going to Big Sur, but to "Big Mama"). And in the female gross-out comedy *The Sweetest Thing*, Cameron Diaz and Christina Applegate make an emergency stop to use the Rock Store's men's room—and encounter a rude, *Porky's*-style surprise. *30354 Mulholland Highway, west of Kanan-Dume; 818-889-1311.*

## MALIBU CANYON

Site of the murder scene in *The Postman Always Rings Twice*, Malibu Canyon Road is described by John Garfield in that 1946 classic as "the worst piece of road in Los Angeles County." Today this much-improved thoroughfare offers a scenic drive to Malibu Creek State Park *(see page 263).*

## WHERE TO EAT IN MALIBU CANYON

## SADDLE PEAK LODGE

Housed in a former bordello on Piuma Road just east of Malibu Canyon, this intimate restaurant has a roaring fireplace and caters primarily to meat eaters; you'll find elk, buffalo, boar, and other wild game items on the menu. Saddle Peak appears as a roadside diner in the 1954 crime thriller *The Fast and the Furious* and in *Panic in Year Zero! Open for dinner and Sunday brunch. Closed Mondays and Tuesdays; 419 Cold Canyon Road (at Piuma); 818-222-3888.*

## MALIBU CANYON DETOUR: PIUMA ROAD

According to *L.A. On Foot* author David Clark, twisty Piuma Road was frequently used for movie stunt sequences because "the locale was perfect for scenes of flaming jeeps careening off mountain roads . . . At times it drops almost straight down on both sides."

On Piuma Road, three miles east of Malibu Canyon Road, you'll find a Santa Monica Mountains Conservancy roadside overlook that offers expansive views of Saddle Peak to the northeast and Paramount Ranch and Malibu Creek State Park to the west.

From the picnic tables at this overlook, you can see the spectacular set-

Marc Wanamaker/Bison Archives

*Easy Rider's* Peter Fonda surveys the Santa Monica Mountains.

ting for the 1941 MGM adventure *They Met in Bombay,* where Clark Gable and Rosalind Russell dodge enemy gunfire. According to *Easy Rider* stars Peter Fonda and Robert Walker Jr., the Piuma Road area is also the main location for the film's Taos commune sequence.

## TOPANGA CANYON

In the Shoshone Indian language, *topanga* means the "above place." That's an appropriate designation for this mountaintop hideaway beloved by head-trippers, recluses, outcasts, and nature lovers. In 1952, "This Land Is Your Land" balladeer Woody Guthrie moved to Topanga to live in the hills with his struggling (due to the blacklist) friend and labor activist, Will Geer (later famous as "Grandpa" on TV's *The Waltons*). "Woody's Shack," an old tool shed-turned-bedroom, remains on the Geer property and has been preserved as a landmark.

As with all of the canyons in the Santa Monica Mountains, Topanga has seen its share of natural disasters. In 1961, a major conflagration tore through Topanga and transformed it into "the perfect setting for a war-torn landscape," says producer Terry Sanders. Terry and his brother, director Denis Sanders, decided to shoot their 1962 movie *War Hunt* in Topanga with three relatively unknown stars: Robert Redford, Sydney Pollack, and Tom Skerritt. The sec-

# MALIBU CANYON'S SPIRITUAL NATURE

There are three garden spots in Malibu Canyon that were once filming locations and privately owned by spiritual institutions.

### Serra Retreat (*Franciscan*)

A Spanish Colonial complex originally designed as the hilltop mansion for Malibu's first family, the Rindges, it's now a private hideaway for spiritual groups. Serra played the Puerto Rican convent seen in the 1960s TV series *The Flying Nun*, starring Sally Field; *www.serraretreat.com*

### The Malibu Temple (*Hindu*)

Just east of Malibu Creek State Park is this Hindu shrine that was a setting for the martial arts comedy *Beverly Hills Ninja*, with Chris Farley and Nicollette Sheridan; *www.malibuhindutemple.com*.

### Soka University (*Buddhist-inspired*)

The former ranch of razor blade pioneer King Gillette was purchased in the 1930s by MGM director Clarence Brown, the man behind *The Yearling*, *National Velvet*, and the Irene Dunne soaper *The White Cliffs of Dover* (which Brown shot here). Located across the road from Malibu Creek State Park, it has been the home of Buddhist-inspired Soka University. (In 2005 it was sold to the Santa Monica Mountains Conservancy.) The eucalyptus tree—lined driveway can be seen as the finish line for the Tour de France bicycle race in Tim Burton's *Pee-wee's Big Adventure*; *www.soka.edu*.

ond unit assistant on the picture was twenty-three-year-old future director Francis Ford Coppola, whose daily duties included driving Redford through Topanga's twisting roads to the location.

## WHERE TO HIKE IN TOPANGA

## RED ROCK CANYON

For a sense of nostalgic mystery, get off the main drag of Topanga Canyon Road and head onto *Old* Topanga Canyon Road. A few miles past the Inn of the Seventh Ray restaurant, you'll find Red Rock Canyon. The canyon's fantastically shaped rocks were a big hit with stoners and old Hollywood, according to David Clark's 1972 guide *L.A. On Foot*. "The group Taj Mahal lives on Red Rock," Clark reported, "as did Buffalo Springfield and Cream. The first house on the road was built by Cecil B. DeMille. The old dilapidated mansion at the end was the home of movie actress Pola Negri."

*HOW TO GET TO RED ROCK CANYON From Topanga Canyon Road, head west on Old Topanga Canyon Road 1.7 miles to Red Rock Road. Continue .8 miles to the park entrance, where limited parking is available.*

## WHERE TO EAT IN TOPANGA CANYON

### INN OF THE SEVENTH RAY
Here is arguably the most romantic (and priciest) organic foods restaurant in Los Angeles. Formerly the 1930s mountain retreat for evangelist Aimee Semple McPherson, the creekside inn has become a popular destination for Valentine's Day, Sunday brunch, and rustic weddings. While waiting to be seated, peruse the gift shop's hiking guides, crystals, and incense. *Reservations required. 128 Old Topanga Canyon Road; 310-455-1311.*

### COUNTRY NATURAL FOODS
Those looking for organic food for the trail should visit this village market, a location for the Bruce Willis actioner *Hostage*. *415 Topanga Canyon Road at Fernwood Pacific Dr.; 310-455-3434.*

## THE "SUBURBAN" CANYONS
## (EAST OF THE 405 FREEWAY)

*More developed than their seaside counterparts, these commuter canyons (often traffic-heavy during the week) are largely outside National Park Service jurisdiction, yet visitors can still find occasional pockets of wilderness and movie history.*

### BEVERLY GLEN
Known to locals simply as "the Glen," Beverly Glen Boulevard once featured a bordello and speakeasy halfway up the canyon, near Scenario Lane.

The upper Beverly Glen canyon area can be seen in two cult favorites. In the 1966 Ann-Margret vehicle *The Swinger*, the motorcycle-riding star leads the police on a chase near the intersection of Beverly Glen Boulevard and Mulholland Drive. Another motorcycle chase ensues just west of Beverly Glen, near Nicada Drive and Raybet Road, in 1972's *The Thing with Two Heads*. This sensitive look at race relations stars Ray Milland as a white bigot whose head is grafted onto Rosey Grier's body.

## THEATER IN TOPANGA:
## THE WILL GEER THEATRICUM BOTANICUM

This rustic amphitheater offers summertime performances of Shakespeare as well as contemporary plays and folk music. The theater was founded by character actor Will Geer, who built it behind the garden on his personal property. Started as a lark for out-of-work actors, the venue eventually drew enthusiastic crowds. Favorites include A Midsummer Night's Dream and As You Like It performed under the sycamores. Bring a picnic lunch; www.theatricumbotanicum.com.

## LAUREL CANYON

This rustic hollow was well known in the 1970s as a meeting place for rock legends like David Crosby, Neil Young, Jim Morrison, Glenn Frey and Joni Mitchell, who immortalized the community in her song "Ladies of the Canyon."

The music scene is celebrated in a Lisa Cholodenko's *Laurel Canyon*, starring Frances McDormand, Kate Beckinsale, and Christian Bale. The film features a number of Laurel Canyon landmarks like the Canyon Country Store, views from Lookout Mountain and the Laurel-adjacent hotel, Chateau Marmont.

Although its music connections are well known, Laurel also holds a place in the annals of movie trivia. Gary Cooper shared a hideaway with "Mexican Spitfire" Lupe Velez in the canyon, and silent star Ramon Novarro was murdered here. Legendary magician and movie star (*Terror Island*) Harry Houdini was rumored to live halfway up the canyon; the ruins of his supposed home are a frequent mecca each Halloween. According to author Paul Young in *L.A. Exposed*, a secret government-run movie studio was located at the top of Lookout Mountain until 1997.

John Landis' *Schlock!* features a banana-hungry simian whose "cave" lair was actually a cleverly photographed rocky hillside on Laurel Canyon Boulevard. Landis recalls the Laurel Canyon filming of his first feature: "It was easier than finding a real cave. We just shot at night and lit the place *like* a cave. Don't tell anyone, but there's empty sky just above the frame line!"

# THE STONE CANYON OVERLOOK: DARK VIEWS OF L.A.

Located on the south side of Mulholland Drive and two blocks west of Beverly Glen Blvd., the Stone Canyon Overlook provides clear-day views of Catalina and the San Gabriel Mountains. This turnout also features displays on the local wildlife and terrain. Movie fans will note that this vantage point looks down on locations significant in the on- and off-screen life of exiled director Roman Polanski:

**Mulholland Drive**, the famed mountain route on which the overlook sits, was named after Department of Water and Power engineer William Mulholland. Screenwriter Robert Towne used Mulholland as an inspiration for water tycoon Noah Cross, the *Chinatown* character played by John Huston.

Closed to the public but clearly visible from the overlook, **Stone Canyon Reservoir** is the *Chinatown* reservoir where Darrell Zwerling's body is recovered by the police, according to producer Robert Evans. It's also where Polanski, in an unsettling cameo appearance ("Hold it there, kitty cat!"), slices Jack Nicholson's nose.

In 1969, the director and his wife Sharon Tate lived in **Benedict Canyon**, just a few blocks from the overlook. While Polanski was in Europe in August of that year, their home (since demolished) was a site of the multiple murders committed by Charles Manson's "family." Pregnant Sharon Tate was among the five victims of the notorious crime that sent waves of fear and paranoia throughout the L.A. and the Hollywood community. Polanski would one day return to these hills as a famous houseguest of area resident Jack Nicholson.

# STAR PARKS: FOLLOWING ACTORS' FOOTSTEPS

*The following parks are situated on land that was named after or donated by some of Hollywood's best-known performers. Everyone comes out a winner: the public has access to these previously off-limits spaces and the actors are commemorated for something more than their screen or TV credits.*

## Dixie Canyon (Warren Beatty)

Located on the Sherman Oaks side of Mulholland Highway, this parcel was donated by Beatty in the 1990s. The actor/producer, who shot the final sequence in *Shampoo* (with Julie Christie) on a Mulholland hilltop, still maintains an office in the area. Today this compact hillside landscape is home to a perennial stream and is a nice place for a walk or jog under the oak trees. *Located at the end of Dixie Canyon Place, near the intersection Dixie Canyon Avenue and Ventura Boulevard.*

## Dan Blocker Beach

Originally known as Corral State Beach, the half-mile stretch of sand was bought for two million dollars in the 1960s by cast members from TV's *Bonanza*, including Lorne Greene, Michael Landon, and Dan Blocker ("Hoss Cartwright"). When the Texas-born Blocker (a long-time Malibu resident) died in 1972, Greene and Landon donated the land to the state in his memory. (Down the coast, near Pepperdine University, you'll find the Michael Landon Community Center at Malibu Bluffs Park.) *North of Malibu Canyon Road on Pacific Coast Highway, between Puerco Canyon and Corral Canyon.*

## Bette Davis Picnic Area

North of Griffith Park (near the intersection of the 101, 134, and 5 freeways), this welcome bit of green space alongside the L.A. River is a popular bird-watching spot Davis, a frequent contributor to the nearby Equestrian Center, lived with her family close to this picnic area in the 1930s while working for Warner Bros. in nearby Burbank. *Corner of Victory Blvd. and Riverside Drive in Glendale.*

### William S. Hart Park

Located north of the San Fernando Valley, the Newhall area was untamed when silent Western actor Hart chose this land to build his twenty-two-room hacienda/mansion ranch in 1925. Hart wanted to thank his audience for making him a star (he made his first film at the ripe old age of forty-nine and went on to headline sixty more "authentic Westerns") and thus left his property to the County of Los Angeles. The grounds include a museum, large picnic areas and a small menagerie of goats, pigs, and buffalo donated by Disney Studios. Hart's former West Hollywood home is also a park. *24151 N. San Fernando Road, just a half mile from the Antelope Valley Highway (14); 661-259-0855*

### Joel McCrea Wildlife Preserve

Located in Camarillo's Santa Rosa Valley north of Thousand Oaks, this old ranch was purchased by the likeable leading man in 1933 for a mere twelve dollars an acre. McCrea and family have given parcels to the YMCA and a local school (where he coached the softball team). This 220-acre open space includes a deep canyon that offers a water source for local wildlife. Public access is limited. *Call Conejo Recreation & Parks 805-495-6471 for info, location and reservations.*

### Will Rogers State Historic Park

One of America's top movie stars and humorists of his time, Oklahoma-born Rogers built his thirty-one-room ranch house in the Pacific Palisades. The small visitors center shows a short film about Rogers' life and work, which ended tragically in a plane crash in 1935. The property, deeded to the state by Rogers' family, includes a polo field (where Gable, Tracy, and Disney once played) and trails to the performer's favorite **Inspiration Point**, an overlook that offers views of the Pacific and the surrounding hillside. Film appearances include *Cutter's Way, The Story of Us, Star Trek IV: The Voyage Home,* and the remake of *The Parent Trap. 1501 Will Rogers State Park Road, off Sunset Boulevard; 310-454-8212.*

### Reagan Ranch

Before acquiring their famed Western White House ranch near Santa Barbara, Ronald and Nancy Reagan owned and lived at this Santa Monica Mountains property from 1951 to 1967. A chase scene from *It's a Mad, Mad, Mad, Mad World* was filmed just outside of the Reagans' property at the ranch crossroads of Cornell Road and Mulholland Highway. The Reagan barn and garage are still standing and used by the California State Parks system.

### Peter Strauss Ranch

While working on the mid-1970s TV miniseries *Rich Man, Poor Man* near this old Santa Monica Mountains hot spot called Lake Enchanto, actor Peter Strauss was so impressed with the historic lot that he decided to purchase it in 1976. He lived there until 1985, and two years later sold the land to the Santa Monica Mountains Conservancy. Legend has it that some of the Manson gang used to hang out here in the

Actors get top billing in their parks.

1960s, but today the most dangerous residents are a gang of aggressive peacocks that roam the property and may interrupt your picnic. A half-mile, oak-strewn trail switchbacks up the hill above the ranch house and ends near a playground and eucalyptus grove. Weddings and concerts often take place in the large grassy area. *30000 Mulholland Highway, Agoura, across from The Old Place restaurant; event reservations: 805-370-2308.*

### Ramirez Canyon Park (Streisand Center)

Barbra Streisand purchased this 22.5 acre estate in 1974 and lived here for almost twenty years before donating the grounds to the Santa Monica Mountains Conservancy. Open to the public by reservation only, the Streisand property (now the conservancy's headquarters) can be viewed on a ninety-minute docent-led garden tour that includes tea and scones. *Located on 5750 Ramirez Canyon Road, near the Paradise Cove-Point Dume area of Malibu; Tour reservations required: 310-589-2850.*

## WHERE TO WALK IN LAUREL CANYON

### FRYMAN CANYON

According to Occidental College location expert Jerry Schneider, Fryman (also known as Wilacre Park, named after cowboy actor Will Acres) was once a movie ranch in the 1930s. Located north of Mulholland in Studio City, the canyon's steep trails will take you to clear-day views of the San Fernando Valley as seen in *2 Days in the Valley* with Teri Hatcher.

## WHERE TO EAT IN LAUREL CANYON

### PACÉ RESTAURANT

The canyon's only café serves great Italian food. This former tavern was a reputed hangout for cowboy star Tom Mix. The upper floor of this complex is the 1928 **Canyon Country Store**, seen in 2002's *Laurel Canyon*. The store serves as a hippie haven in director Clint Eastwood's 1973 May-December romance *Breezy*, starring William Holden and Kay Lenz. The market can also be seen in the opening sequence of John Carpenter's *The Fog*.

# HOW TO GET TO THE SANTA MONICA MOUNTAINS NATIONAL RECREATION AREA

*For park info, visit www.nps.gov/samo, or call 805-370-2301. For info on a bus connecting the parks, visit www.parklinkshuttle.com or call 888-734-2323.*

## DVD ITINERARY: THE CANYONS OF THE SANTA MONICAS

*Pee-wee's Big Adventure*, Soka University, Scene 2

*Heaven Can Wait* (1978), Kanan-Dume, Scenes 1–2

*Easy Rider*, Piuma Road, Scenes 11–14

The Rock Store (seen here in the 1950s) plays a pit-stop for Cameron Diaz, Albert Brooks, and Sylvester Stallone.

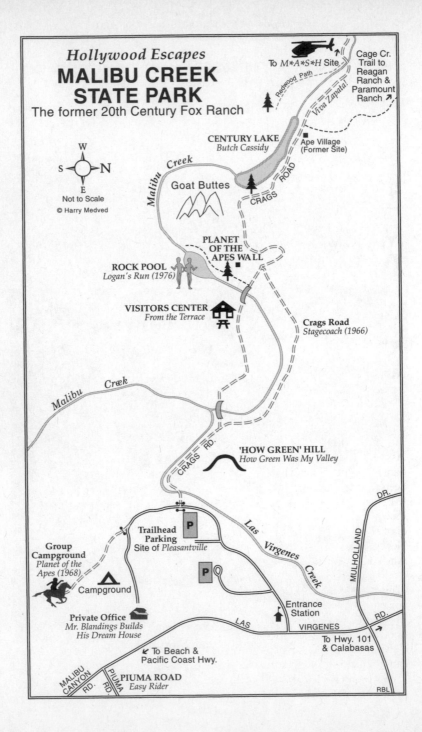

## Hollywood Escapes
# MALIBU CREEK
# STATE PARK
### The former 20th Century Fox Ranch

To *M*A*S*H* Site

Cage Cr. Trail to Reagan Ranch & Paramount Ranch

Redwood Path

Viva Zapata!

**CENTURY LAKE**
*Butch Cassidy*

Ape Village (Former Site)

**Goat Buttes**

CRAGS ROAD

W
N
S
E

Not to Scale
© Harry Medved

**PLANET OF THE APES WALL**

**ROCK POOL**
*Logan's Run (1976)*

**VISITORS CENTER**
*From the Terrace*

**Crags Road**
*Stagecoach (1966)*

*Malibu Creek*

CRAGS RD.

**'HOW GREEN' HILL**
*How Green Was My Valley*

Las Virgenes Creek

MULHOLLAND DR.

**Trailhead Parking**
Site of *Pleasantville*

P

P

CRAGS RD.

**Group Campground**
*Planet of the Apes (1968)*

Campground

**Private Office**
*Mr. Blandings Builds His Dream House*

Entrance Station

LAS VIRGENES

RD.

To Hwy. 101 & Calabasas

← To Beach & Pacific Coast Hwy.

MALIBU CANYON RD.

PIUMA RD.

**PIUMA ROAD**
*Easy Rider*

RBL

# 42

# MALIBU CREEK STATE PARK
## Twentieth-Century Walks

*Green it was and possessed of the plenty of the earth . . .*

—Opening narration in John Ford's How Green
Was My Valley (1941)

**MAJOR ROLES:** *Planet of the Apes (1968), How Green Was My Valley, M\*A\*S\*H, Viva Zapata!*

### BEHIND THE SCENERY

As the former Twentieth Century Fox Ranch, Malibu Creek State Park in the Santa Monica Mountains has enjoyed a geographically diverse film career. Its deep canyons, open plains, and mountain peaks have enabled it to play Korea (*M\*A\*S\*H*), a futuristic version of planet earth (*Planet of the Apes*), Polynesia (*South Pacific*), China (*Love Is a Many-Splendored Thing, The Sand Pebbles*), India (*The Rains of Ranchipur*), Africa (*Tarzan Escapes*), Mexico (*Viva Zapata!*), New England (*Mr. Blandings Builds His Dream House*), and a mythical, Middle American small town (*Pleasantville*).

This Malibu Creek ranchland originally belonged to the Crags Country Club, "one of the exclusive social organizations of the country with the wildest and most picturesque surroundings," according to the *Los Angeles Times* in 1910. The club dammed the creek, created a lake, built a main lodge, and planted redwood trees. According to Santa Monica Mountains historian Brian Rooney, the club started renting out the property as early as 1927 for the MGM men-in-kilts battle-romance *Annie Laurie*, starring Lillian Gish.

For John Ford's *How Green Was My Valley*, production designers Nathan Juran and Richard Day built a tremendous Welsh coal mining village. (The film later won the 1941 Best Picture Oscar, beating *Citizen Kane*.) Scenes shot here include Maureen O'Hara's wedding, and a beautiful mountaintop sequence where Walter Pidgeon tries to rehabilitate disabled youngster Roddy McDowall.

Twentieth Century Fox, the studio behind *Valley*, was so impressed with the Malibu Creek property that they bought it in 1946. Later known as "Century Ranch" and "the Fox Ranch," the land was used extensively for the *Planet of The Apes* movies and short-lived TV series.

The ranch is perhaps most famous for the opening scene in Robert Altman's 1970 feature film M*A*S*H, in which surgical unit helicopters swoop over the park's craggy peaks. Some of this footage was reused in the credits sequence for the long-running television series. Fox sold its ranch to the state in 1974 and the park opened to the public in 1976.

## WHERE TO HIKE

### CRAGS ROAD TO M*A*S*H SITE

Pick up a detailed map at the main gate before embarking on your adventure, since the network of intersecting trails can be confusing. You'll want to explore **Crags Road**, which passes by sites of several landmark films.

The remains of the M*A*S*H compound at Malibu Creek.

As you enter the parking area, immediately to your right is *How Green Was My Valley*'s grassy hill. Park in the second lot. This is where the sets once stood for the town in *Pleasantville* (starring Reese Witherspoon and Tobey Maguire), and the ranch in *Love Me Tender* (starring Elvis Presley in his movie debut).

Look for the BACKCOUNTRY TRAILS sign. Follow the trail across the shady culvert and begin your hike on Crags Road. You'll reach a fork, but stay to your right on the high road. The land on the other side of the culvert was used for farmhouses and barns in *Desire Under the Elms* (with Sophia Loren and Anthony Perkins) and the 1964 comedy *What a Way to Go!* (starring Shirley MacLaine and Dean Martin). The nearby field with the eucalyptus trees helped provide scenery for the Humphrey Bogart/Gene Tierney drama *The Left Hand of God*.

As this leafy lane follows the bank of Malibu Creek, you'll be walking under a canopy of sheltering oak trees. Crags Road appears in a number of films where coaches thunder past, including Gordon Douglas' 1966 *Stagecoach* remake (starring Ann-Margret and Red Buttons) and the ridiculously high-concept *Snow White and the Three Stooges*.

On your right you'll notice an old cement shed once used to store explosives for special effects sequences. Make a left at the fork in the road and cross the bridge to the **Visitors Center** (open on weekend afternoons only), which displays photos of movies shot at Malibu Creek. A former home for the Fox Ranch groundskeeper, the Visitors Center appears as Ina Balin's East Coast country home visited by Paul Newman in *From the Terrace*. In the 2004 TV movie *Helter Skelter*, it serves as the home of Sharon Tate and Roman Polanski. Outside the center you'll find picnic tables facing the creek.

Retrace your steps over the bridge. You'll see a small sign for the Rock Pool. Follow this trail upstream, passing by pine trees and picnic tables. On your right you'll see the pock-marked cliff face that rock climbers have dubbed the **Planet of the Apes Wall**. Atop the cliff face is the foundation and stairs of the old Crags Country Club lodge. This is where Charlton Heston, Linda Harrison, and other humans are caged in the first *Apes* movie. The wall itself is visible in the last *Apes* movie, *Battle for the Planet of the Apes*, where Claude Akins tries to take control of the simian forum. Bit player and burgeoning director John Landis makes a cameo here as a human who is rounded up by the apes. (His one line of dialogue? "Hey!")

Past the Apes Wall, you'll find the historic **Rock Pool**, with volcanic goat buttes rising above the water. Fugitive Elvis Presley hides at the pool in *Wild in the Country*. The pool is also where the ape children and human children come together to learn from the Lawgiver (John Huston) in the final scene of *Battle for the Planet of the Apes*.

The exotic-looking Rock Pool has doubled as a South Seas locale in two different Hawaii-lensed films: the musical *South Pacific* and the action drama

*Windtalkers*. In the 1958 big-screen adaptation of the Rodgers and Hammerstein play, this is where Rossano Brazzi and John Kerr dodge gunfire from enemy planes. In John Woo's war epic, Native American Adam Beach fights racist Noah Emmerich in the Rock Pool until they are stopped by Nicolas Cage.

From the Rock Pool, retrace your steps to the main trail, Crags Road. Make a left and head uphill and over a crest. As you head downhill take the short spur on your left to the hidden-from-view seven-acre **Century Lake**. This is the site where Redford and Newman's stunt doubles leap into a river when trapped in *Butch Cassidy and the Sundance Kid*, in a sequence that also incorporates footage shot in Utah and Colorado. It's also where James Coburn's stunt double jumps into the water from an exploding volcanic island in *In Like Flint*.

Return to Crags Road. Just uphill from the lake is the former site of production designer William Creber's imaginative **Ape Village,** used in many of the *Apes* movies and the TV series. The set stood here for many years, but unfortunately for film buffs, it was dismantled when the state bought the land.

Stay to the left and follow the creek bed. You'll be following the path of Mexican revolutionary leader Emiliano Zapata, as played by Marlon Brando in his Oscar-nominated performance in Elia Kazan's 1952 *Viva Zapata!* It's along this section of Crags Road that Brando is marched off to prison by *federales* and later rescued by hundreds of peasants emerging from Malibu Creek's hillsides.

To reach the M*A*S*H site, continue over a little bridge and veer to the right along the rock-lined creek bed. (The trail now becomes an indistinct and rocky path with uneven footing; do not attempt walking here after a heavy rain.) About a mile after Century Lake, you'll eventually arrive at the old M*A*S*H site, used for the feature film and TV series. Here you'll find the helicopter landing pad where Sally Kellerman (as "Hot Lips") arrives at the camp and where Elliott Gould and Donald Sutherland practice their golf swing in the 1970 film. A fire that swept the park in 1982 destroyed most of the compound's tents and props, but a charred ambulance and jeep still remain. The fire was written into the Alan Alda–directed "Goodbye, Farewell, and Amen," the last episode of the TV series. The M*A*S*H site is your turnaround point.

## WHERE TO STAY

### MALIBU CREEK CAMPGROUND

There is more film history to be found at this campground complex. The group campground section is the grassy savannah where apes on horseback hunt humans in the original *Planet of the Apes*. And behind individual Campsite #37 you'll find the two-story colonial house where Cary Grant carries Myrna Loy over the threshold in *Mr. Blandings Builds His Dream House*. The rural area is supposed to represent the sylvan charm of the film's Connecticut. (Today it's a

## NAKED IN THE SANTA MONICAS:
## FANTASY FILM SKINNY-DIPPING IN THE ROCK POOL

Name one other park in Los Angeles County where Tanya Roberts and Charlton Heston appeared naked (on film, that is). Ever since 1937 the Rock Pool has been a locus for male and female nudity in fantastic settings.

*Lost Horizon*   In the 1937 Frank Capra classic, Shangri-La's free-spirited muse Jane Wyatt takes a dip in the pool, according to historian Kendall Miller. From the rocks a flirtatious Ronald Colman and a friendly squirrel eavesdrop on her frolicking.

*Planet of the Apes*   This is the spot where Charlton Heston and fellow astronauts find the first sign of a thriving ecosystem on what initially appeared to be a desolate planet. When their clothes are stolen, the unsuspecting bathers discover that they're not alone. For this scene, a waterfall was created by placing firehoses above the rocks.

*Logan's Run*   This is where Michael York and Jenny Agutter—having escaped the domed city of the future—take a dip in one of their first experiences in the great "outside."

*The Beastmaster*   *Charlie's Angels* and future *That '70s Show* cast member Tanya Roberts bares herself on the rocks, only to find the title hero's (Marc Singer) pet ferrets stealing her towel. On the film's DVD commentary, producer/cowriter Paul Pepperman recalls that Ms. Roberts was not very happy during this scene; it was shot in the wintertime when the water was freezing.

private office housing the state parks' Angeles District Headquarters.) *www.reserveamerica.com; 818-880-0367.*

## HOW TO GET TO MALIBU CREEK STATE PARK

FROM THE BEACH: *From PCH take Malibu Canyon Road 6 miles to the park entrance.* FROM THE VALLEY: *From the Ventura Freeway (101) take Las Virgenes Road 3 miles south to the park entrance.*

## DVD ITINERARY: MALIBU CREEK STATE PARK

*Planet of the Apes* (1968), Scenes 7–9

M\*A\*S\*H (1970), Scenes 1, 9, and 25

*How Green Was My Valley*, Scenes 2–3 and 6

Harry Medved

Malibu Creek's Rock Pool
is a popular spot
for getting naked
in the movies.

# 43

# PARAMOUNT RANCH
## Adventure on the Mountain

This thing of working outdoors was forced on me.... There wasn't any room at the studio, so I had to go out to the Paramount Ranch.

—*Henry Hathaway, who directed Zane Grey Westerns here*

**MAJOR ROLES:** *Bwana Devil, The Virginian, The Love Bug*

### BEHIND THE SCENERY

Befitting a studio whose corporate logo is a mountain peak, Paramount Pictures bought a 2,700-acre portion of the hilly Rancho Las Virgenes for use as a movie property in 1927. Whenever Paramount needed an extensive outdoor set, more

National Park Service/Paramount Ranch

The Western Town, seen on TV's *Dr. Quinn.*

often than not the crews headed out to this location just a little northwest of Malibu Creek State Park (the old Fox Ranch), on the other side of Mulholland Highway. The many Westerns shot here include Victor Fleming's *The Virginian* (1929), in which young Gary Cooper strides down the old frontier town's wooden walkways in his first starring role.

Cooper returned to the ranch for the 1938 Samuel Goldwyn production of *The Adventures of Marco Polo*, a strange bit of miscasting where he played the suave Venetian globetrotter. The film's Chinese fortress location is known as **Marco Polo Hill**, which appeared a year later as a Foreign Legion outpost for another Gary Cooper adventure, *Beau Geste*. Decades later, Marco Polo Hill served as the setting for "Slaghoople Manor" in *The Flintstones in Viva Rock Vegas*.

Perhaps the ranch's most notable credit is Preston Sturges' *Sullivan's Travels*, where Joel McCrea is forced to work on a chain gang. According to Paramount daily production reports, the prison camp sequence was shot over two days, using fifty extras and several bloodhounds.

The ranch has been a prime location for action-filled family films like the TV-to-big-screen *Munster, Go Home!* and Walt Disney's *The Love Bug* (starring Dean Jones and a beloved Volkswagen named Herbie).

In 1980 the National Park Service purchased the ranch and continued to make it available to productions. In the 1990s, CBS Television used Paramount Ranch as the site for the series *Dr. Quinn, Medicine Woman*, completely rebuilding the ranch's Western town at a cost of $600,000. The town was also a site for the offbeat HBO series *Carnivale*.

## GUIDED PARK TOURS

*Although there are several well-maintained trails traversing Paramount Ranch, film buffs may be interested in ranger-led tours. Check www.nps.gov/paramountranch or call 805-370-2301 and ask for their free activities calendar.*

### "FROM COLORADO TO KOREA"

This six-mile tour connects the faux Colorado town of TV's *Dr. Quinn* at Paramount Ranch to the former Korean War location for M*A*S*H in Malibu Creek State Park.

### "AROUND THE WORLD IN 180 MINUTES"

Created by Park Ranger Mike Malone, this tour takes you through park locations that have played exotic locales as diverse as the Pacific Islands (*So Proudly We Hail, Ebb Tide*), Transylvania (*Van Helsing's* fiery windmill), and even New Jersey (*Reds'* barn meeting attended by Warren Beatty).

## LOCAL MOVIE CELEBRATION
# PARAMOUNT RANCH'S "SILENTS UNDER THE STARS"

This summer series of silent films at the Paramount Ranch is one of L.A.'s many *Cinema Paradiso*–like viewing experiences. Bring food and a blanket for a preshow picnic dinner on the grassy lawn under the eucalyptus trees. Presented by the Silent Society of Hollywood Heritage. *805-370-2301.*

## PRETRIP READING

*Three Magical Miles: An Appreciation of the Past and Present of Malibou Lake & Vicinity* by Brian Rooney. This beautifully illustrated and impeccably researched piece of history examines a three-mile radius around Malibou Lake in the Santa Monica Mountains. *Published by the Cornell Preservation Organization. P.O. Box 1875, Agoura Hills, CA 91376-1875; 310-280-0200.*

# THE *DEVIL* MADE ME DO IT:
# FROM SUMMER CAMPER TO LOCATION PRO

*Location manager Ned Shapiro (Wayne's World, Indecent Proposal, The Man Who Wasn't There) recalls how an early experience in the Santa Monica Mountains led to a life engaged in location work.*

"In the summer of 1952 I was an eight-year-old on my way to summer camp at Calamigos Ranch in the Santa Monica Mountains above Malibu. Though we were only a few minutes from town, our bus passed what appeared to be a wild African setting, complete with thatched huts, railroad tracks, and a train, plunked down in the middle of nowhere.

"I remember wondering how this jungle got there and why. I was thrilled when I found out it was all a set for the first 3-D movie, *Bwana Devil.*

"From then on I wanted to find out everything I could about California and the movies. Indeed, this first glimpse at film production made a lasting impression that may have planted the seed for my future career in locations."

## LOST AND FOUND: CORNELL'S THE OLD PLACE

At one time the Santa Monica Mountains had its own little rustic town. Named Cornell, this community near Paramount Ranch existed from the early 1900s till the 1950s. During its heyday in the 1940s, Cornell's Seminole Hot Springs resort attracted many Hollywood luminaries. Although Cornell is long gone, its spirit lives on, thanks to the Cornell Preservation Organization and a few old structures like The Rock Store (see *page 250*), the Peter Strauss Ranch buildings, and the Old Place.

**The Old Place** is Cornell's former 1930s general store and post office. Now it's a refurbished but creaky Western-style building with an oak bar and wooden booths. Managed by septuagenarians Tom and Barbara Runyon, the bill of fare is limited to stew, steak, or clams, and there's only one menu item offered per night. Despite the limited dining choices, many visitors come by simply to soak up the atmosphere.

Some of the stars who have partied around the antique piano include Al Pacino, Goldie Hawn, Jackson Browne, Bob Dylan, and Steve McQueen, who Tom claimed as a close friend.

One local resident recalls that actors Strother Martin and Jason Robards often got hammered at the Old Place. On the night of December 8, 1972, Robards got behind the wheel after one too many at the Old Place and drove his car off a cliff on Encinal Canyon Road. Luckily, a worried Runyon had been following Robards in his own car and apparently saved the actor from choking to death on his knocked-out teeth. Robards, of course, went on to many more accolades and Oscar nominations, but on this night the honors went to Tom Runyon for his foresight and quick thinking.

The Old Place is best showcased in Don Siegel's *Telefon,* in which the roadhouse plays the Texas diner/bar where Russian agent Charles Bronson and American ally Lee Remick put an end to the wave of sabotage masterminded by mad KGB agent Donald Pleasance. The bar can also be seen in Hampton Fancher's 1999 indie *The Minus Man*, with Owen Wilson and Sheryl Crow.

Nearby **Malibou Lake** is a private community with its own share of cinematic history. The man-made lake is best known for its appearance in the original *Frankenstein,* in which it played the bucolic backdrop where Frankenstein's monster (Boris Karloff) befriends a young village girl as she tosses flowers into the water. In this famous scene (later satirized in Mel Brooks' *Young Frankenstein*) the simple-minded creature throws the girl into the lake when she runs out of petals. Decades later, a fog-enshrouded Malibou Lake cabin appears in *The Ring,* with Naomi Watts and Jane Alexander.

Other Malibou Lake scenes include Adenoid Hynkel's capture in Charles Chaplin's *The Great Dictator,* a romantic reunion for Diane Lane and John Cusack in *Must Love Dogs,* and a summer camp sequence with Bruce Willis and Michelle Pfeiffer in Rob Reiner's *The Story of Us.* The lake's private clubhouse was used as a Catskills resort in Billy Crystal's *Mr. Saturday Night,* and as an Arkansas country club in the climactic shootout in Jonathan Demme's *Crazy Mama.*

*HOW TO GET TO THE OLD PLACE: Located on Mulholland Drive, directly across from Peter Strauss Ranch and in between Kanan-Dume and Malibu Canyon. Call ahead for hours, as The Old Place is often closed. 818-706-9001.*

## HOW TO GET TO PARAMOUNT RANCH

FROM THE BEACH: *From PCH head up Malibu Canyon Road into the mountains. Several hundred yards past the entrance to Malibu Creek State Park make a left on Mulholland Drive. Continue 3 miles to Cornell Road, and turn right. Look for the entrance to Paramount Ranch on your left.* FROM THE VALLEY: *Take Highway 101 to the Kanan Road exit. Head south on Kanan. In .3 miles make a left onto Cornell Road. In 2 miles you'll see the entrance to Paramount Ranch on your right.*

## DVD ITINERARY: PARAMOUNT RANCH

*Sullivan's Travels,* Paramount Ranch, Scene 19

*The Love Bug,* Paramount Ranch, Scene 14

*Must Love Dogs,* Malibou Lake, Scene 23

# 44

# SHOWDOWN WITH DEVELOPMENT
## The Movie Ranches of the Santa Susanas and Simi Hills

> In another ten years we're going to have to go away from Southern California altogether for Westerns. . . . sometimes you can't use a spot anyway on account of the smog. . . . you can't blame the ranch owners for selling out.
>
> —*Location manager Pierre "Frenchie" Valin to Kevin Thomas in the Los Angeles Times, September 12, 1967*

### BEHIND THE SCENERY

Much of the San Fernando and Conejo valleys in the 1930s was endless farmland and orange groves. For filmmakers there was also plenty of wild terrain to be found on private movie ranches. But in the post–World War II years, says *America's Suburb* author Kevin Roderick, "suburban sprawl gobbled up many of the valley's classic film locations. Most Western towns or movie ranches were subdivided for homes, and the battle with development continues to this day." A few of these movie ranches have won the showdown with developers . . . for now.

*For directions, visit www.lamountains.com and search for the specific park info.*

### THE GARDEN OF THE GODS AT IVERSON RANCH

Unfortunately, there's not much left to see at the old Iverson Movie Ranch, a hot spot for action features and serials from 1912 to the 1960s. Alas, housing developments now surround and mar the landscape made famous by film and TV.

The good news is that the Santa Monica Mountains Conservancy has preserved a small patch of the ranch, with the main destination being a collection of boulders known as the Garden of the Gods. There's no marked trail here, but visitors can rock-scramble up to an impressive view of the valley below.

Among the rocks in the Garden of the Gods is the **Lone Ranger Rock**, from which "Hi-Yo Silver" was heard in the 1950s TV series, starring Clayton Moore. The same jagged rock, which looks like a detached stone head from Easter Island, appears in the background of John Ford's *Stagecoach,* near the cantina. It can also be seen in several Buster Keaton comedies, including the caveman sequences in *Three Ages.* And it was the backdrop for the Black Hills capture of Crazy Horse (Anthony Quinn) in *They Died With Their Boots On.*

If you listen quietly, you can hear the train going through the **Santa Susana Pass Tunnel**. Dozens of movie railroad scenes have been shot here, including the brutal train robbery opening of *White Heat* and the amusingly Freudian final shot of Hitchcock's *North by Northwest.*

## SANTA SUSANA PASS STATE HISTORICAL PARK

Cowboy star Roy Rogers used to own most of the property near Santa Susana Pass Road, an old stagecoach route. This included Trigger Street, a road he named after his horse. Kevin Spacey and Val Kilmer are among the actors who grew up in the neighborhood; Spacey even named his production company TriggerStreet. "We dreamed of building a movie theater there," he says. "It's where I first dreamed of pursuing a career in the cinema."

Although much of this area is developed, a state park has preserved the hills around the historic Santa Susana Pass Road. Nearby **Stoney Point**, a popular rock-climbing mecca on the other side of Topanga Canyon Blvd., is a precarious ledge for Buster Keaton in *Sherlock Jr.*, according to *Star Wars* sound designer and Iverson Ranch superfan Ben Burtt. The point can also be seen in the 1978 low-budget sci-fi thriller *Clonus.*

Located on the south side of Santa Susana Pass Road and just down the street from Iverson was another ranch, known as the Spahn Ranch. Once owned by cowboy star William S. Hart, it was known as a ranch that provided horses for Westerns. But it also served as the main outdoor location for the immortal *The Creeping Terror*, in which a ridiculous carpetlike monster from outer space hunts human prey. In 1969, Spahn Ranch became infamous as the main Manson Family hideaway. Today the property is owned by the Church at Rocky Peak.

The eastern end of the Santa Susanas features two community parks where films have been shot. **Porter Ridge Park** is where Henry Thomas and Robert MacNaughton ditch their stolen van and help *E.T.* escape. Granada

Hills' **Bee Canyon Park** can be seen in the "Age of Aquarius" finale to *The 40-Year-Old Virgin*, starring Steve Carell and Catherine Keener.

## UPPER LAS VIRGENES CANYON (AHMANSON RANCH)

In a major win for outdoors enthusiasts, Washington Mutual Bank, the former owner of the Ahmanson Ranch, decided in 2003 to sell its property for parkland rather than develop it for homes. It was fortunate for movie location buffs too, as Ahmanson includes the former Lasky Mesa (named after Paramount cofounder Jesse Lasky), whose wide-open spaces set the scene for many classic movies, including *Gone With the Wind* (the cotton fields), *The Grapes of Wrath* (Muley's homestead), *Duel in the Sun* (site of the horsemen's revolt), and *They Died with Their Boots On* (Custer's Last Stand).

## CORRIGANVILLE PARK

Before Universal Studios Tours, there was Simi Valley's Corriganville, one of the few active filming locations open for tourists. Once owned by Ray "Crash" Corrigan—B Western cowboy star, stuntman, and erstwhile man in a gorilla suit—Corriganville was a popular site for cowboy stunt shows in the 1950s. The property was eventually sold to Bob Hope and it became Hopetown. The park features its own Sherwood Forest, but don't be

Corriganville's *Fort Apache* set became a tourist destination
in the 1950s.

## SLOW-MOTION DEATH IN THOUSAND OAKS: THE END OF *BONNIE AND CLYDE*

Directed by Arthur Penn and produced by Warren Beatty, the 1967 landmark film *Bonnie and Clyde* was shot to great effect in locations all over Texas in colorful hamlets like Venus and Red Oak. Many of these were the actual towns where the real-life Bonnie and Clyde robbed banks.

But one filming location that has never been revealed is the actual site of the famous slow-motion finale. The scene was shot not in the Lone Star State, but much closer to Hollywood, just outside of the San Fernando Valley in the community of Thousand Oaks.

The Warner Bros. daily production report called for fifty pigeons (to fly from the bushes) and "heavy explosives/squibs" on the "Albertson Ranch, Simi Road" location. Today the area is a quiet residential suburb.

deceived: Corriganville was merely a location for a forgotten 1950 Robin Hood spin-off called *Rogues of Sherwood Forest*, *not* the Errol Flynn classic.

Perhaps the most distinguished film shot on the property was John Ford's *Fort Apache*, in which John Wayne, Ward Bond, John Agar, and Shirley Temple have scenes in front of the old fort set (burned down in the 1980s) and the knobby rocks above. They also ride their horses over the Corriganville hills (and arrive some seven hundred miles away in Ford's beloved Monument Valley in Utah!). Less distinguished yet more horrific Corriganville appearances include *Jesse James Meets Frankenstein's Daughter*, *Billy the Kid vs. Dracula*, and *The Incredible Two-Headed Transplant*.

# 45

# WILDWOOD PARK
# Wuthering Hikes

There are few places in Southern California with such beautiful rolling hills, mystery mesas, and rocky outcroppings.

—Vincent McEveety, director of the James Stewart/Henry Fonda Western Firecreek (1968)

**MAJOR ROLES:** Wuthering Heights (1939), Flaming Star, Spartacus, The Man Who Shot Liberty Valance

### BEHIND THE SCENERY

Thousand Oaks' Wildwood Park is one small section of a Conejo Valley land grant bought by the Janss family in 1910. Ten thousand acres were called the Janss Conejo Ranch and the vast grasslands were used for raising cattle, sheep, and thoroughbred horses. In 1966, the family donated part of their holdings to the city of Thousand Oaks to create a protected wilderness area of fields, creeks, and mesas.

The land was a natural backlot with its wide plains and jagged mountain saddle called Mountclef Ridge. The horse training sequences in the 1939 Bette Davis melodrama *Dark Victory* were filmed here with Humphrey Bogart, Geraldine Fitzgerald, and Ronald Reagan.

The ranch's open spaces play the Scottish highlands in *Lassie Come Home*, starring Roddy McDowall and Donald Crisp. The terrain also doubles as the site of the flag-raising at Iwo Jima in the Tony Curtis war drama *The Outsider*, according to the film's director Delbert Mann.

Westerns shot on the ranch include Walt Disney's *Westward Ho the Wagons!*, Arthur Penn's *The Left Handed Gun* (with Paul Newman), and John

Ford's *Cheyenne Autumn*. Ford was also here to film the classic scene in which John Wayne teaches Jimmy Stewart how to shoot in *The Man Who Shot Liberty Valance*. Stewart returned to Wildwood when the ranch played the title Western towns in *Welcome to Hard Times* and *Firecreek*. Wildwood was also popular with TV Westerns such as *Gunsmoke*, *Rawhide*, *The Rifleman*, *Wagon Train*, *The Big Valley*, and *Bonanza*.

Now a real estate developer, Larry Janss spent his childhood playing on Wildwood's movie sets. He recalls an affable Elvis Presley shooting one of his best pictures here: director Don Siegel's Western *Flaming Star*.

Janss also remembers the location as the site for the Vesuvius slave camp in Stanley Kubrick's *Spartacus*. "I remember they brought in a whole army of dummies from Hollywood to hurl off Mountclef Ridge," recalls Janss. "They left one of them behind, up in the rocks. Since I was ten years old, this was very exciting news to me. I've been looking for that missing dummy ever since."

## WHERE TO HIKE

### THE SANTA ROSA TRAIL TO MOUNTCLEF RIDGE

From the parking lot, take the Mesa Trail to the signed Santa Rosa Trail. The trail briefly winds along a housing development, but continues straight up to the top of volcanic Mountclef Ridge for an enthralling view. On a clear day you'll see the Conejo Valley and the western edge of the Santa Monica Mountains to the south. To the north you'll see the remaining farms of Santa Rosa Valley, home of *Chinatown*'s orange groves.

Mountclef posed as Peniston Crag on the moors of England for director William Wyler's 1939 classic *Wuthering Heights*. The film features star-crossed lovers Laurence Olivier and Merle Oberon anxiously scaling the hillside to their secret meetings in these magnificent "castle rocks." The stars' close-ups, however, were filmed on a studio soundstage.

Harry Medved

This way to Mountclef Ridge, seen in *Wuthering Heights*.

## ACTOR DENNIS WEAVER ON WILDWOOD

"I worked at the Janss Conejo Ranch for many years on *Gunsmoke*. With its rolling terrain, long vistas, and open spaces you really got the feeling you were in the Old West.

"And I'll never forget Mountclef Ridge. As the sun went down you lost your light in the valley and we'd grab our equipment and run up the ridge to get our close-ups. We rushed to the top of that mountain so many times that we nicknamed it 'Panic Peak.'"

## Top Billing: PARADISE FALLS

It's hard to believe there's a seventy-foot-high waterfall so close to suburbia, but you'll find one at the bottom of Wildwood Canyon. From the parking lot, follow the signed Moonridge Trail as it descends into the canyon. Head toward the oversized teepee landmark and follow the signs to Paradise Falls. You'll find several tables adjacent to the falls and Wildwood Creek, with additional great picnic spots (with tables and barbecue pits) farther downstream.

## DETOUR: CAMARILLO'S SANTA ROSA VALLEY

In the 1930s, this area was packed with citrus groves as far as the eye could see, thus providing a good location for a tense scene in *Chinatown*. As detective Jack Nicholson investigates mysterious land acquisitions in the valley, he drives to a private orange grove and gets into a fight with field worker Jesse Vint and family. In real life, the area was home to retired Western actors like Joel McCrea and Walter Brennan. (Vint even recalls an on-set visit from Brennan.)

Today's visitors can still get a sense of that era by heading to these groves just off the Santa Rosa Valley Road, north of Wildwood. Or for a hands-on Conejo Valley farm experience, visit **Underwood Family Farms** in nearby Moorpark (*www.underwoodfamilyfarms.com; 805-529-3692*).

## DETOUR: HIDDEN VALLEY

Tucked away in a corner of the Santa Monica Mountains on Potrero Road, this private Thousand Oaks flatland was the site of a handful of B Westerns in the forties, including *My Pal Trigger*. Residents have included Sophia Loren, Eve Arden, and Richard Widmark.

Hollywood has showcased Hidden Valley's bucolic countryside and estate in a variety of films, including *Seabiscuit* (Chris Cooper trains the future prizewinner at Jeff Bridges' Ridgewood Ranch), *The Hand* (Michael Caine loses his appendage in a horrible country road accident), *Hollywood or Bust* (a

Brian Rooney

Hidden Valley's Potrero Road is Hollywood's country lane.

Martin and Lewis roadtrip), *Hot Shots!* (motorcycle-riding Charlie Sheen and equestrian Valeria Golino outdo each other's stunts), *Monster-in-Law* (Jane Fonda embarrasses Jennifer Lopez at a reception), and *American Dreamz* (Hugh Grant and Mandy Moore take a ride through the Ohio countryside).

According to a November 12, 1958 Warner Bros. daily production report, part of Cary Grant's nighttime drunk-driving sequence in *North by Northwest* was shot here. And Elvis Presley made no less than two appearances singing on Potrero Road, in *Roustabout* and *Spinout*.

## HOW TO GET TO WILDWOOD PARK

*Take the 101 Ventura Freeway East to the Lynn Road exit. Turn right and go 2.5 miles north to Avenida de Los Arboles. Make a left and follow the road to the park. Park info: 805-495-6471.*

## DVD ITINERARY: WILDWOOD PARK

*Wuthering Heights* (1939), Scenes 5, 7, and 9

*Spartacus [The Criterion Collection]*, Scene 20

*The Man Who Shot Liberty Valance*, Scene 8

# 46

# OJAI AND THE HERITAGE VALLEY
## The Towns That Time Forgot

Only ninety minutes from L.A., these communities have always managed to retain a Norman Rockwell–like small-town charm.

—*Patricia L. Fry, author of* The Ojai Valley *(1999)*

**MAJOR ROLES**: *Pat and Mike, The Two Jakes, La Bamba, Happy, Texas, A Star Is Born (1954)*

### BEHIND THE SCENERY

When Hollywood needs Small Town U.S.A., it often comes to Ojai and its neighboring Ventura County towns that offer a number of well-preserved streets that look as if they're straight out of a fifties TV series. It's no surprise that *Leave It to Beaver*, the 1997 feature version of the classic TV show, re-created suburban Ohio in Santa Paula. And TV's all-American robotic couple, *The Six Million Dollar Man* and *The Bionic Woman*, hailed from Ojai.

Ojai (pronounced *OH-high*) means "Moon" in the Chumash Native American language. The close-to-L.A. town is famous for its daily "pink moment," as the sky takes on a rosy hue when the sunset reflects on the Topa Topa Mountains. Hollywood celebrities who've called Ojai home include Larry Hagman, Jennifer Tilly, and Ted Danson and Mary Steenburgen. Local culture includes Krishnamurti's sanctuary, Beatrice Wood's pottery studio, the local music festival (at beautiful Libbey Bowl), the Shakespeare festival, and the Ojai Film Festival.

*Pat and Mike*'s Spencer Tracy and Katharine Hepburn
filmed at the Ojai Valley Inn.

Marc Wanamaker/Bison Archives

## WHERE TO HIKE

### Top Billing: SANTA PAULA CANYON

These colorful hills above the town of Santa Paula are home to a gorgeous hiking trail and swimming hole. You'll find the canyon on Highway 150, 5.8 miles north of Santa Paula on the way to Ojai. Park near Thomas Aquinas College at Sulphur Springs, where you can still see some oil seepage by the side of the road. The area's inescapable aroma of rotten eggs is due to the sulfur deposits. Walk past the campus of Aquinas College, Ferndale Ranch, and two oil rigs. Then take the trail into the Los Padres National Forest that follows Santa Paula Creek and leads to "The Punchbowl," a large pool of water fed by a seasonal waterfall. The **Santa Paula Canyon Trail Camp** contains six sites that are available for overnight stays. The early 1910s adventure *The Ghost of Sulphur Mountain* was shot nearby. *For more info, contact the Los Padres National Forest Ranger at 805-646-4348.*

## SHANGRI-LITTLE: OJAI'S *LOST HORIZON* CAMEO

For more than fifty years, the Ojai Chamber of Commerce has proudly proclaimed its picturesque village to be the site of Shangri-La in Frank Capra's *Lost Horizon*. According to local legend, the town's Dennison Grade lookout provides Ronald Colman's first glimpse of the movie's utopian destination.

But in the grand tradition of Hollywood hype, Ojai Valley is glimpsed in the movie for all of *four seconds*, in the form of an overhead view of the Valley of the Blue Moon. Contrary to legend, Ronald Colman never filmed any of his scenes near this spot. And, according to production chronicler Rudy Behlmer and Capra historian Kendall Miller, even director Capra didn't come to Ojai for the shot.

## WHERE TO EAT

### THE RANCH HOUSE

One of the pioneers of California cuisine, this romantic restaurant is set in a beautiful garden by a stream. Celebrity diners have included Paul Newman, Tom Ewell, and John Lennon and Yoko Ono. *Corner of South Lomita Avenue and Tico Road; 805-646-2360.*

### RUBEN'S BURRITOS and RAINBOW BRIDGE NATURAL FOODS

Down the street from the Ojai post office is **Ruben's Burritos** (805-646-6111), a tiny Mexican takeout spot that is a favorite among locals. For those who prefer health food to go, nearby **Rainbow Bridge Natural Foods** (805-646-4017) offers fresh deli sandwiches and wraps every day. You can picnic in **Libbey Park**, the town's central meeting place since the 1910s.

## WHERE TO STAY

### OJAI VALLEY INN AND SPA

With its sensational grounds framed by the Topa Topa Mountains, this 1923 Spanish-style luxury resort is the most scenic place to stay in town. Its guest list of stars included inn investor Loretta Young, Ronald and Nancy Reagan, and Judy Garland. The inn's signature clubhouse, Neff Lounge (named after celebrity architect Wallace Neff), can be seen in the George Cukor comedy

*Pat and Mike*, with Katharine Hepburn and Spencer Tracy. On the inn's green, Hepburn competes with real-life golf pro Babe Didrikson Zaharias. In the *Chinatown* sequel *The Two Jakes*, Jack Nicholson and Harvey Keitel also compete in a game of golf in front of the Neff Lounge.

It was in Ojai two decades earlier that Nicholson and collaborators Bob Rafelson, Bert Schneider, and the pop group the Monkees came up with the story for the cult film *Head*. According to legend, the group spent three days in a drug-induced haze hashing out their rambling story ideas into a tape recorder. Although the Monkees received no screenplay credit, Monkee Michael Nesmith allegedly still has the secret Ojai tapes to prove their contribution. *www.ojairesort.com; 800-422-6524.*

## MATILIJA CANYON RANCH

Owned by movie and television director Richard A. Colla (*Battlestar Galactica*, the Burt Reynolds/Raquel Welch action-comedy *Fuzz*), this isolated property includes a hundred-year-old farmhouse, cottages, and guest barns available for rent with a three-night minimum. It's a little bit of paradise, so be prepared to pay a premium price for your stay. *www.thedenthouse.com*

## THE LAVENDER INN

This quaint bed-and-breakfast was once Ojai's schoolhouse, dating back to 1874. The Romantic Suite is the nicest of the seven rooms. A short walk four blocks down the road is the must-see **Bart's Books**, an outdoor bookstore and Ojai landmark. *210 East Matilija Street; www.lavenderinn.com; 805-646-6635.*

## ON THE ROAD:
## THE HERITAGE VALLEY

Ojai-bound travelers may want to take scenic **Highway 126**, passing by the Ventura County towns of Piru, Fillmore, and Santa Paula. Collectively these citrus towns call themselves "the Heritage Valley," as all of them are surrounded by rolling hills, historic groves of oranges, lemons, and avocadoes, and feature decades-old architecture and colorful main streets. After completing your Heritage Valley tour in Santa Paula, the bucolic Highway 150 will take you over the hills and into Ojai.

### *PIRU*

Colorful Piru has a tiny main drag, "Center Street," which serves as the secret wedding getaway for stars James Mason and Judy Garland in George Cukor's *A Star Is Born*, according to the film's production designer Gene Allen. The town's Old Telegraph Road **Trestle Bridge** is the site of a train crash in *I Love*

*Trouble* (with Julia Roberts and Nick Nolte) and a plane crash in *Hero* (with Dustin Hoffman and Geena Davis). It's also a murder site in *The Cell* visited by Vince Vaughn and James Gammon. And **Piru Creek** plays the Colombian river where Vin Diesel gets busted for drugs in *XXX*, according to location manager Bob Craft.

Piru's **Heritage Valley Inn** at 691 North Main Street (805-521-0700), can be seen as a Southern stopover in the Robert Townsend musical *The Five Heartbeats* and as a boarding house in *Happy, Texas*. This picturesque plantation-style villa dates back to 1888. According to the hotel register it was where Mary Pickford and director D. W. Griffith stayed when they shot the California saga *Ramona* at nearby Rancho Camulos in 1910.

## FILLMORE

This Midwestern town is recognized for its vintage main street (which appears in *In the Mood*), ninety-nine-seat Towne Theater, and its nearby **Sespe Condor Sanctuary**. The orange groves around town were used to create 1910 Hollywood for Richard Attenborough's *Chaplin* biopic with Robert Downey Jr. They can also be seen in the opening of *La Bamba*.

Its classic railroad appears in the Jake Gyllenhaal comedy *Bubble Boy*, *Almost an Angel*, *City Slickers II*, *Nixon*, *Of Mice and Men* (1992), and *Seabiscuit*. Youngsters may want to ride the **Fillmore and Western Railway's Movie Trains** (*www.movietrains.com*) or check out the local fish hatchery.

## SANTA PAULA

Santa Paula is best known for its 1890 **California Oil Museum** (805-933-0076), which plays a Midwest general store where *Joe Dirt*'s David Spade takes his supposed meteor for a closer examination. In real life, the museum chronicles the 1867 discovery of oil in the local hills and screens 1960s Union 76 commercials featuring Marilyn Monroe and Buster Keaton.

Hollywood discovered Santa Paula soon after the oil companies did. The American Film Manufacturing Company ("Flying A") set up studios here in the 1910s. The town's "Main Street USA" look has served movies like *Leave It to Beaver* and *Welcome Home, Roxy Carmichael*, with Winona Ryder and Jeff Daniels. For Brian De Palma's *Carrie*, Santa Paula provided production designer Jack Fisk with a suitably creepy Victorian home for Sissy Spacek and Piper Laurie.

## HOW TO GET TO OJAI

*Take I-5 North past Six Flags Magic Mountain in Valencia. Exit at Highway 126 West. Head west 11 miles and you'll find your first Heritage Valley town of Piru. (Along 126 you'll also find turnoffs for Fillmore and Santa Paula.) To get to Ojai, take the Highway 150 off-ramp in Santa Paula. Follow the road through town and over the hills.*

## DVD ITINERARY: OJAI AND THE HERITAGE VALLEY

*Pat and Mike*, Ojai Valley Inn, Scenes 3–4 and 8–11

*The Two Jakes*, Ojai Valley Inn, Scene 10

*Bubble Boy*, Fillmore and Western Railway, Scenes 8–9

Harry Medved

The Fillmore movie trains appear in *Seabiscuit, Of Mice and Men* (1992) and *Bubble Boy.*

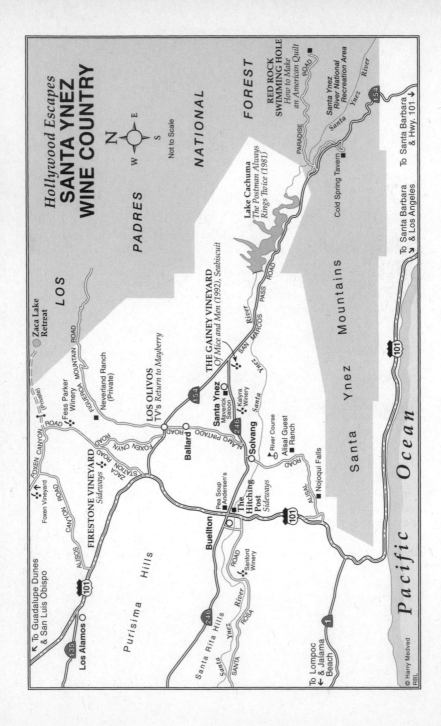

*Hollywood Escapes*
# SANTA YNEZ
# WINE COUNTRY

N
W · E
S

Not to Scale

**LOS PADRES NATIONAL FOREST**

Zaca Lake Retreat

Neverland Ranch (Private)

Fess Parker Winery

FIGUEROA MOUNTAIN ROAD

Foxen Vineyard

FOXEN CANYON ROAD

ALISOS CANYON ROAD

STATION ROAD

ZACA STATION ROAD

**FIRESTONE VINEYARD** *Sideways*

**LOS OLIVOS** *TV's Return to Mayberry*

154

FOXEN CNYN ROAD

**Ballard**

ALAMO PINTADO ROAD

**THE GAINEY VINEYARD** *Of Mice and Men (1992), Seabiscuit*

Santa Ynez River

SAN MARCOS PASS ROAD

**Lake Cachuma** *The Postman Always Rings Twice (1981)*

**RED ROCK SWIMMING HOLE** *How to Make an American Quilt*

PARADISE ROAD

**Santa Ynez River National Recreation Area**

Santa Ynez River

154

Cold Spring Tavern

To Santa Barbara & Hwy. 101

**Santa Ynez**
Maverick Saloon

Kalyra Winery

**Solvang**

River Course

Alisal Guest Ranch

ALISAL ROAD

Nojoqui Falls

2:46

**Santa Ynez Mountains**

*Pacific Ocean*

To Santa Barbara & Los Angeles

101

To Guadalupe Dunes & San Luis Obispo

135

**Los Alamos**

**Buellton**

Pea Soup Andersen's

**The Hitching Post** *Sideways*

101

Sanford Winery

SANTA ROSA ROAD

Santa Ynez River

2:46

Santa Rita Hills

**Purisima Hills**

101

To Lompoc & Jalama Beach

1

© Harry Medved
RBL

# 47

# SANTA YNEZ WINE COUNTRY
## Hollywood and Wine

Not as storied as Napa-Sonoma or Paso Robles, Santa Ynez Valley is California's most-filmed wine country.

—*Ronnie Mellen, Santa Barbara Location Services*

**MAJOR ROLES:** *Sideways, Seabiscuit, The Postman Always Rings Twice (1981)*

### BEHIND THE SCENERY

The kitschy Danish village of Solvang may be the area's most popular stop for tour buses, but the Santa Ynez Valley provides an abundance of less visited and more scenic alternatives.

The Santa Ynez wine country north of Santa Barbara encompasses oak-strewn rolling hills, timeless villages, quiet country roads, and breathtaking hiking trails. Winemaking has been a Santa Ynez Valley tradition since the early 1900s. The prohibition of the 1920s put an end to the practice until its resurgence in the sixties. Today there are over seventy wineries in the valley, celebrated in the Rex Pickett novel and Alexander Payne movie *Sideways*.

The valley has also been home to celebrities like Noah Wyle, Matt LeBlanc, Bo Derek, Cheryl Ladd, John Cleese, and Michael Jackson, whose legal problems brought worldwide attention to his Neverland Ranch nestled in the hills above Los Olivos.

# WHERE TO EXPLORE

## THE WINERIES

### THE GAINEY VINEYARD

Sitting on 1,800 acres of land, this 1984 winery is the site of a Wild West show with Chris Cooper in *Seabiscuit*. The property's century-old barn is where actor/director Gary Sinise shot his 1992 adaptation of John Steinbeck's *Of Mice and Men* (starring John Malkovich and Sherilyn Fenn). To see the barn, you must make an appointment with event coordinator Diane Connors, who supervises its rental for weddings and parties. Picnic supplies are available at the tasting room. *3950 East Highway 246; 805-688-0558.*

### FIRESTONE VINEYARD

One of the largest of the local wineries, Firestone's tasting room (located on a hillside affording a remarkable view of the vineyards below) twice served as a location for the television series *Falcon Crest*. Established in 1972, Firestone is the oldest family-owned-and-operated winery in Santa Barbara County. The vineyard's Barrel Room and extensive landscapes can be seen in *Sideways*. *www.firestonewine.com; 805-688-3940.*

### FESS PARKER WINERY

TV's former Davy Crockett owns a good deal of Santa Barbara County real estate, including this vineyard and Fess Parker's Wine Country Inn in Los Olivos, where his *Daniel Boone* costar Ed Ames occasionally plays piano. Fess is often seen at the winery welcoming guests (yes, the gift shop is stocked with Davy Crockett memorabilia). It's seen in *Sideways* as the touristy winery where Paul Giamatti chugs wine, making a scene by dousing himself with a wine spit bucket.

## THE TOWNS

### SANTA YNEZ

This is a Western-style town best represented by the **Longhorn Coffee Shop** (*805-688-5912*). The Longhorn is often used for commercials and music videos, including Shania Twain's "Whose Bed Have Your Boots Been Under?"

### BALLARD

This tiny town's 1883 little red school house and the Ballard Country Church are still in use today. The church is briefly glimpsed as the spot where Jack

Harry Medved

The expansive Firestone Vineyard, seen in *Sideways*.

Nicholson and Jessica Lange get hitched before their fateful accident in *The Postman Always Rings Twice*.

### Top Billing: LOS OLIVOS
This old-fashioned village is the center of wine country. Los Olivos stood in for America's favorite North Carolina town in the 1986 TV movie *Return to Mayberry*, reuniting Andy Griffith, Ron Howard, Don Knotts, and George "Goober" Lindsey.

### LOS ALAMOS
Despite over fifty antique merchants within its borders, this Western town on the outskirts of the Santa Ynez Valley looks like a movie set. Los Alamos' Price Ranch was used for *Seabiscuit*'s first track sequence, where young Red (Michael Angarano) works as an apprentice.

## WHERE TO EAT

## BROTHERS RESTAURANT AT MATTEI'S TAVERN
One of the oldest continuously operating restaurants in the state, Mattei's is a former stagecoach and railway stop in Los Olivos that dates back to 1886. Run by

brothers Matt and Jeff Nicols, the tavern is a fine dining establishment and is known for its old-fashioned "slow food" like prime rib, rack of lamb, and classic crème brulée. Diners over the years have included Mary Pickford, John Barrymore, Bing Crosby, Clark Gable, and Ronald Reagan, when he was state governor. *Open for dinner and Sunday brunch. 805-688-4820.*

## LOS OLIVOS CAFÉ
A less pricey alternative to Mattei's, this stylish cafe specializes in California/ Mediterranean cuisine and gourmet pizzas. **The Wine Merchant**, a gourmet wine shop stocking over three hundred labels, adjoins the café. It's the scene of the double date in *Sideways* with Paul Giamatti, Virginia Madsen, Thomas Haden Church, and Sandra Oh. *www.losolivoscafe.com; 805-688-7265.*

# WHERE TO STAY
## UNION HOTEL AND VICTORIAN MANSION
Los Alamos' fantasy hotel is a collection of buildings dating back to the 1880s. Its exteriors combine cowboy retro with Victorian romance, while the interiors include movie-related rooms such as the "Fifties Drive-In" and the "*Ben Hur* Chariot Room." The Union Hotel has appeared in two memorable music videos: Jon Bon Jovi's "Bang a Drum" and Paul McCartney and Michael Jackson's "Say Say Say" (their shaving sequence was shot in Room 12). *362 Bell Street; www.unionhotelvictmansion.com; 805-344-2744.*

## ZACA LAKE RETREAT
A nominal membership fee is required for an overnight stay at this rustic getaway and yoga retreat near Los Olivos. The dock at secluded Zaca Lake is a great nighttime spot for stargazing. A forgotten thriller entitled *The Zaca Lake Mystery* was shot here in 1915. The resort was the Crystal Lake location for *Friday the 13th: The Final Chapter. www.zacalakeretreat.com; 805-688-5699.*

## ALISAL GUEST RANCH AND RESORT
A working ranch with upscale accommodations, the exclusive Alisal Ranch is a dream getaway near Solvang that protects ten thousand acres of pristine wilderness in the Santa Ynez Valley. Filming is rarely allowed here, though one exception was made for Alisal neighbor Jimmy Stewart. One of his last feature film appearances, in *The Magic of Lassie,* was shot at the ranch in 1978.

Over the years the Alisal has hosted celebrities from Doris Day and Clark Gable (who married his fourth wife, socialite Lady Sylvia Ashley, in the Alisal library in 1949) to more recent guests like Oprah Winfrey, Barbra Streisand, and James Brolin.

If you're here off-season, a boat ride on private Alisal Lake, horseback riding, and a lavish breakfast and dinner are all included with the price of your stay. Although it's an expensive escape, the cost of your stay pays for the upkeep and preservation of this private wilderness. *1054 Alisal Road; www.alisal.com; 805-688-6411.*

Another way to see this countryside is **Alisal Road**, a peaceful lane that winds through the hills from Solvang to Gaviota Pass. The main destination along the road is magical **Nojoqui Falls**, once Alisal property and now part of a county park. The falls display a seventy-foot cascade in season.

## CACHUMA LAKE RECREATION AREA

This fisherman's paradise with over four hundred campsites appears briefly in Bob Rafelson's remake of *The Postman Always Rings Twice*. The film's Twin Oaks set was erected near the Rancho San Marcos Golf Course. *www.cachuma.com; 805-686-5054.*

## ON THE ROAD: SAN MARCOS PASS

*The best route from Santa Barbara to the Santa Ynez wine country is the San Marcos Pass Road, also known as Highway 154. High in the hills above the city you'll find several gems worth exploring.*

## COLD SPRING TAVERN RESTAURANT

This 1886 stagecoach stop offers grilled venison, wild boar tenderloin, and charbroiled elk steak. The tavern also features a bar and gift shop located beside the creek. The nearby Cold Spring Arch Bridge can be seen briefly in Andrew Davis' *Steal Big, Steal Little* and dozens of commercials.

*HOW TO GET TO COLD SPRING TAVERN From the 101 in Santa Barbara, head up into the hills on Highway 154 (San Marcos Pass) for 14 miles. Look for Stagecoach Road on your left and follow the winding road five minutes to the tavern. Open seven days a week for breakfast, lunch, and dinner. Call ahead for road conditions and dinner reservations. 5995 Stagecoach Road; www.coldspringtavern.com; 805-967-0066.*

## DETOUR: PARADISE ROAD, SANTA YNEZ RIVER NATIONAL RECREATION AREA

*NOTE: Visitors to this part of the Los Padres National Forest will need an Adventure Pass, which can be picked up at the Paradise General Store, the ranger station (closed Sundays) or area campgrounds.*

The aptly named ten-mile-long Paradise Road takes you deep into the wilderness via a twenty-five-minute drive. As the country lane frequently

# GETTING *SIDEWAYS* IN SANTA YNEZ VALLEY

Ever since Paul Giamatti and Thomas Haden Church explored the scenery of Santa Ynez Wine Country's backroads in the award-winning comedy *Sideways*, the film's fans have had an irresistible urge to follow their path. To satisfy the demand of movie tourists, the Santa Barbara County Film Commission helped put together a map of sixteen tourist-friendly locations from the film. Bike tours are also available (consult *www.filmsantabarbara.com*). Among the favorite stops:

**Sanford Winery:** The roadhouse winery where Giamatti teaches Church the subtleties of wine appreciation (*www.sanfordwinery.com;* 805-688-3300).

**Days Inn:** Giamatti and Church's spartan Windmill Inn lodgings (*www.daysinn-solvang.com*); *805-688-8448*).

**The Hitching Post:** The restaurant where Virginia Madsen waits tables (*www.hitchingpostwines.com; 805-688-0676*).

**Kalyra Winery:** The tasting room where Giamatti and Church meet flirtatious wine-pourer Sandra Oh (*www.kalyrawinery.com;* 805-693-8864).

**Firestone Vineyard:** A scenic hillside where Giamatti freaks out over news about his ex, and the barrel room to which the couples escape (*www.firestonewine.com; 805-688-3940*).

**Los Olivos Café:** Scene of the double-date where Giamatti refuses to drink Merlot (*www.losolivoscafe.com; 888-946-3748*).

**River Course at the Alisal:** The green where Giamatti and Church terrorize fellow golfers (*www.rivercourse.com; 805-688-6042*).

**Fess Parker Winery:** The Frass Canyon winery where Giamatti goes ballistic (*www.fessparker.com; 800-841-1104*).

**A.J. Spurs:** The Wild West–themed restaurant where Church picks up a waitress/fan. "This place is a trip," says Giamatti on the film's DVD commentary (*www.ajspurs.com; 805-686-1655*).

crosses the Santa Ynez River, your car may get pretty wet. Call the Los Prietos Ranger Station for road conditions (805-967-3481).

Along Paradise Road you'll see Fremont campground, site of the hot air balloon finale with Andy Garcia and Rachel Ticotin in *Steal Big, Steal Little*. Across from the campground is the private ranch that location manager Mike Neale picked for the evacuation scene in *Star Trek: Insurrection*. And nearby is the dirt road (5N15) in *Seabiscuit* where Jeff Bridges' son takes a tragic drive.

At five miles you'll reach a fork in the road at Lower Oso Campground. Stay to the right on Santa Ynez River Road (5N18). At the end of the road you'll reach Red Rock Campground. Park and look for the trailhead near the restrooms on the left.

A twenty-minute walk from the parking area leads to the **Red Rock Swimming Hole**. There's no signage for this popular spot along the Santa Ynez River, but you'll know you've arrived when you see the telltale crimson rocks. In *How to Make an American Quilt*, this is the secluded hiding place where Samantha Mathis and Loren Dean share a seductive swim. Though you're sure to enjoy this idyllic pool, don't even think about emulating Mathis' graceful plunge: diving here is strictly prohibited and extremely dangerous.

## HOW TO GET TO THE SANTA YNEZ WINE COUNTRY

*Take the 101 North to Highway 154 (San Marcos Pass Road), through the hills, past Lake Cachuma to the town of Los Olivos, heart of the wine country.*

## DVD ITINERARY: SANTA YNEZ WINE COUNTRY

*Of Mice and Men*, Scenes 6–7 and 9

*Seabiscuit*, Scenes 2 and 4–6

*Sideways*, Scenes 5–12, 20–21, and 24

# 48

# SOUTHERN SAN JOAQUIN VALLEY HIGHWAYS
## Farm from Heaven

From Arkansas to Texas, the San Joaquin is the perfect Hollywood stand-in for the heart of rural America.

—*Michael Neale, location manager for* Thelma & Louise *(1991)*

**MAJOR ROLES:** *Joy Ride, The Cell, North by Northwest, The Grapes of Wrath, Five Easy Pieces*

### BEHIND THE SCENERY

A lone individual stands in the middle of a Midwest road, a blip on the bare horizon. He's New York City ad exec Roger Thornhill, played by Cary Grant in Alfred Hitchcock's 1959 classic *North by Northwest*. The cinematic landscape that dwarfs this desperate character lies a few hours north of L.A., near Bakersfield, in the Southern San Joaquin Valley. Although this valley abuts the High Sierras, filmmakers come here when they want to re-create everything from the Midwest plains to the southern farmbelt.

### ALONG THE WEEDPATCH HIGHWAY (HIGHWAY 184)

*The Weedpatch Highway branches off Highway 99 and Interstate 5. If you're en route to the Western Sierras, it's a faster alternate route.*

Harry Medved

"Cary's Indiana": Grant's *North by Northwest* rural scenes were filmed near Bakersfield.

## Top Billing: ARVIN'S WEEDPATCH CAMP

When Tom Joad (Henry Fonda) and family pull into "Wheat Patch," the government-run migrant camp in John Ford's 1941 classic *The Grapes of Wrath*, the rejection-weary "Okies" have actually entered a Hollywood replica of the real-life shanty town known as Weedpatch.

Although it can be found on a street called Sunset Boulevard, Weedpatch is a long way from Hollywood. Located south of Bakersfield on the outskirts of the town of Arvin, this federal camp was an inspiration for John Steinbeck's 1939 Depression-era novel of Oklahoma farmers leaving behind the wind, dust, and drought on their "great journey in search of peace, security, and another home."

Today the remaining Weedpatch structures include a 1935 community hall, library, and the post office. Currently listed on the National Register of Historic Places, the Weedpatch Camp can be found just east of the original Weedpatch Market, which dates back to 1919. Hollywood returned to the area in 1976 for another Oscar-nominated Dust Bowl–era drama, *Bound for Glory*, starring David Carradine as "This Land Is Your Land" balladeer Woody Guthrie.

## ALONG HIGHWAYS 99 AND 46

*Branching off Interstate 5 near Bakersfield, Highway 99 cuts through the Central California farmlands. Highway 46 intersects 99 near Wasco.*

## RICHMAR FARMS

Iowa has its *Field of Dreams;* California has its diabolical counterpart, a cinematic field of nightmares. This private parcel is part of a 45,000-acre farm of corn, wheat, and alfalfa that the owner has rented to Hollywood for use in heart-pounding sequences set in the heartland.

Peter Weir's unforgettable opening sequence in *Fearless* features Jeff

Bridges and Oscar nominee Rosie Perez emerging from a devastating plane crash in the middle of the Richmar cornfield. "Some folks driving by the set were convinced it was real and reported a plane crash to 911," recalls Kern County Film Liaison Dave Hook.

For *The X Files* movie the farm doubles as a mysterious Texas cornfield, through which Gillian Anderson and David Duchovny are chased by helicopters. Location manager Michael J. Burmeister remembers the tall stalks "projecting a scary, claustrophobic image at night."

The farm also appears in John Dahl's homicidal highway thriller *Joy Ride*, starring Steve Zahn, Paul Walker, and Leelee Sobieski. Tearing through the stalks, the film's psychopathic truck driver terrorizes the trio in a climactic burst of road rage.

The Richmar Farm can best be seen from nearby **Beryl's Café** (*at the corner of Union and Bear Mountain Highway*), an old-fashioned country inn from the 1920s that appears briefly in *Fearless* and specializes in home-baked meals. The owner proudly displays a framed copy of a local traffic citation that was issued to James Dean just before his untimely death farther north in San Luis Obispo County.

## WASCO

The agricultural communities near the towns of Bakersfield and Wasco have long been used by Hollywood as a fertile breeding ground for fear, dating back to Alfred Hitchcock's *Psycho*. After antiheroine Janet Leigh flees Phoenix with stolen cash, she drives into Bakersfield, and then takes Highway 99 to her fateful stay at the Bates Motel.

The self-proclaimed "Rose Capital of the Nation," Wasco is the town north of Bakersfield used by actor Bill Paxton for his feature directorial debut, the psychological thriller *Frailty*. It is at a dilapidated barn (*at Hanawalt and Leonard Avenues, north of Highway 46*) where murderous mechanic Paxton receives his first sign from God in the form of a shiny axe.

Another cinematic predator kept his victims twenty minutes away from here, closer to Interstate 5. *The Cell*'s Vincent D'Onofrio held his prey near Blackwell's Corner (*on Brown Material Road, south of Highway 46*). The water pumping station and the shed from the Jennifer Lopez thriller are still standing.

## CORCORAN ROAD

Hitchcock chose a lonely stretch of barren farmland along Corcoran Road for one of the most famous suspense sequences in cinema history. In *North by Northwest*, Cary Grant is pursued into a cornfield by a machine-gun-equipped, crop-dusting plane.

Longtime associate and actor Norman Lloyd remembers, "Hitchcock loved driving through California, from his Bel-Air home to his home in Santa

Cruz. On the way, he'd see the crop dusters hovering over the farms. He thought someday he'd use them in a picture."

Corcoran Road looks pretty much the same today. You won't see any corn stalks here, however, as they were live props transplanted by students from Wasco High School.

A few miles up the road is the **Kern National Wildlife Refuge**, a marshy sanctuary for wintering waterfowl established in 1960 . . . just three years before Hitchcock would direct *The Birds*. *661-725-2767*.

*HOW TO GET TO CORCORAN ROAD Off Highway 99, three miles north of Highway 46, due west of Wasco.*

## COLONEL ALLENSWORTH STATE HISTORIC PARK

The site of a forgotten chapter in California history, Allensworth Park lies twenty miles north of Wasco on Highway 43. Built in 1908 by former Kentucky slave-turned-Civil War army chaplain Allen Allensworth, it is the state's only town that was founded, financed, and governed by African Americans. Home to hundreds of families during its most prosperous years, by the 1930s the farm town was in dire straits, due in part to the Great Depression. Some historians, however, speculate the area's envious white power structure led to Allensworth's economic downfall by way of a deliberately engineered water shortage and redirection of the utopian community's much needed Santa Fe Railroad traffic.

Stories of African American townships similar to Allensworth are told in 1990s films such as Mario Van Peebles' *Posse* (starring Peebles and Blair Underwood) and John Singleton's *Rosewood* (with Ving Rhames and Don Cheadle). Today more than a dozen restored and re-created buildings remain at Allensworth. A thirty-minute documentary on the colony can be seen at the visitors center (reservations suggested). *www.parks.ca.gov.; Visitors Center: 661-849-3433*.

## ALONG INTERSTATE 5

*One of the busiest freeways in the state, I-5 is the most traveled route from Southern to Northern California.*

## GORMAN

Right along Interstate 5 and the foothills above the San Joaquin Valley is the tiny town of Gorman, a frequent refuge for movie characters on the run. It's the site of the truck-stop motel (the Econo Lodge; *661-248-6411*) where traumatized Geena Davis and Susan Sarandon as *Thelma & Louise* stop to gather their wits. As they resume their escape and discuss fleeing to Mexico, they drive down the steep "Grapevine" portion of the highway (so named for vegetation that once choked the nearby Grapevine Hills) into the San Joaquin Valley.

## THE PRODUCTION DESIGNER & THE CROP DUSTER

When Hitchcock told production designer Robert Boyle he needed a flat, desolate landscape for *North by Northwest's* famous crop-dusting sequence, Boyle knew just what the Master of Suspense was looking for. "Hitch, I grew up in the flattest place on earth: the San Joaquin Valley," Boyle recalls telling his boss. "It was perfect because you had nothing but horizon as far as the eye could see." A native of San Joaquin's town of Tulare, Boyle was happy to bring Hollywood to his homeland.

Another San Joaquin local was instrumental in creating this memorable scene: pilot Robert Coe. Working for the Wasco Crop Dusting Company, Coe was hired by the production to fly his N3N biplane in the scene for three hundred dollars.

Coe remembers both Hitchcock and Cary Grant on location in Wasco, though he never actually "buzzed" the actor. "That was all special effects, done in a studio," he claims. Coe remembers that Cary Grant would happily pose for photos with area locals for a mere 25 cents. Coe adds with a wink, "He said the money was going to his favorite charity."

Wasco crop duster
Robert Coe still lives
in town.

Gorman is also known for its striking springtime wildflower displays in the hills along Gorman Post Road. This road is where Janet Leigh is approached by a cop in Hitchcock's *Psycho*. Anne Heche plays the confused on-the-lam heroine in the 1998 version, shot along the same route.

A few miles north of Gorman is the Frazier Park exit for the Mt. Piños Recreation Area in Los Padres National Forest, a great snowplay destination and a partial location for such diverse films as *City of Angels*, *Deep Impact*, *Van Helsing*, and *The Astounding She-Monster*. A worthy detour for sandwiches and espresso is Frazier Park's Coffee Cantina, 3 miles off the I-5 Freeway (661-245-3166).

## TAFT

Less than thirty minutes off Interstate 5, Taft is a small town on State Route 119 known for its antique stores and nearby oil wells. Taft prospered when the "world's largest gusher" blew here in 1910. Taft's historic drilling rigs have served many cinematic sagas, including *Boom Town*, *Five Easy Pieces*, and *Bound for Glory*.

Several blocks of the original Center Street remain intact. The Robin Williams/Kurt Russell sports comedy *The Best of Times* details the real-life high school football rivalry between Taft and Bakersfield. The story by Ron Shelton partially concerns the revitalization of Taft, which Russell's on-screen wife calls "a hellhole." A key scene features Williams and Russell discussing renovation plans in front of the old Fox Theater.

---

## DETOUR: SPIELBERG'S WORLD WAR II PLATEAU— CARRIZO PLAIN NATIONAL MONUMENT

Located some fifty miles west of Bakersfield, the Carrizo Plain is the detour to end all detours. Here, north of the Los Padres National Forest, serious off-roaders may explore the largest remaining remnant of the San Joaquin Valley habitat. This monumentally barren terrain is home to birds of prey, Native American petroglyphs, and wildflowers in season.

According to the *San Luis Obispo New Times*, Steven Spielberg's *Empire of the Sun* crew built a pagoda and a series of arches here for his World War II saga starring Christian Bale and John Malkovich. In 2001 the wild land was declared a national monument.

Visitors to the monument are advised to gas up their vehicles and have a meal at **The Buckhorn** (*661-766-2591*) as this is the last stop for services and facilities. This rural country bar/motel/café complex is located in New Guyana along Highway 146.

*CAUTION: Carrizo Plain is hot throughout the year—as there's no shade on the land—so only experienced travelers should think about attempting this detour. Summertime, needless to say, is not the season to visit.*

North of Taft, near the town of **Derby Acres** and alongside the Westside Highway (Highway 33), Geena Davis and Susan Sarandon as *Thelma & Louise* first encounter hitchhiking hustler (and soon to be major star) Brad Pitt. They later elude the police on a side road by the oil wells.

## *FIVE EASY PIECES* OFF-RAMP

Heading north on Interstate 5, sharp-eyed viewers may recognize the Highway 43 Shafter-Wasco off-ramp from an iconic scene in 1970s American cinema: this is the site of the bumper-to-bumper traffic jam in *Five Easy Pieces*, in which frustrated oil rig worker and former classical musician Jack Nicholson climbs onto a flatbed truck and discovers a piano. He then gives an impromptu performance as the truck takes the exit and drives away.

## HOW TO GET TO THE SOUTHERN SAN JOAQUIN VALLEY HIGHWAYS

*Take I-5 North toward Bakersfield, where you'll find many of these highways. Check directions at www.ohwy.com/ca.*

## DVD ITINERARY: SOUTHERN SAN JOAQUIN VALLEY HIGHWAYS

*North by Northwest*, Scenes 23–26

*Thelma & Louise*, Scenes 10–13

*Joy Ride*, Scenes 22–23

# 49

# MOUNTAIN HOME STATE FOREST
## Redwood Hideaway

> The Big Tree is nature's forest masterpiece . . . [it] has a strange air of other days about it . . . the auld lang syne of trees.
>
> —*Naturalist and Sierra Club founder John Muir*

**MAJOR ROLE:** *Hulk*

### BEHIND THE SCENERY

When Angelenos head for the Sierras, their destination is most likely Mammoth Lakes, Yosemite, or Lake Tahoe. Little do they know, some of the most unexplored reaches of the Sierra Nevada Mountains are closer to home, a mere four-hour drive from L.A. One of the most majestic places to see the Giant Sequoias is Mountain Home State Forest, a hidden gem located at an elevation of more than six thousand feet.

When *Hulk* director Ang Lee asked location manager Laura Sode-Matteson in 2002 for a site that had never been captured on film, she had a tall order to fill. But Sode-Matteson, a part-time resident of the nearby mountain town of Camp Nelson, remembered the unspoiled woods of Mountain Home State Forest and had always thought they'd make a great location for the right movie.

The only access to Mountain Home is a twisting loop route a full hour from the tiny town of Springville, northeast of Bakersfield. The road is steep and narrow, but adventurous explorers will be rewarded with a redwood paradise.

## WHERE TO EXPLORE

### Top Billing: LOWER POND, BALCH PARK

If you're heading up to Mountain Home on Balch Park Road, this clearing is your first opportunity to really enjoy the wilderness. The Lower Pond is an idyllic picnic spot, fishing hole, and campground. Drop by the small museum (only open on weekends), then explore the meandering nature trail that takes you to the **Lady Alice Tree** (billed as the tallest tree in the world in the early 1900s) and the **Hollow Sequoia Log**, a fallen, carved-out giant. A farmer once stored his crops in here and used the interior as a shelter. Visitors can walk atop and through the tree. *559-539-3896.*

### HEDRICK POND

The *Hulk* crew built a prefabricated cabin at this small fishing pond, a striking movie location thanks to the real-life twin redwoods towering over the water. To heighten the rustic feel of scientist Jennifer Connelly's Hedrick Pond hideaway, the set was augmented with prop trees, stumps, and rocks. Scenes of the monstrous dog mutations engaged in a fearsome battle with hulking Eric Bana were shot in the campground nearby.

Three miles away you'll find the **Hercules Tree** (between Frasier Mill and Hidden Falls), where in 1897 a hermit carved a cabinlike room out of the tree's interior.

## WHERE TO EAT

### SPRINGVILLE INN'S STAGECOACH BAR AND GRILL

If you're heading to Mountain Home from Porterville, Springville is your last chance for gas and supplies. This dusty foothill town served as a location in Cliff Robertson's 1972 rodeo/drifter movie *J.W. Coop*, with Geraldine Page.

The remodeled Springville Inn, built in 1911, offers country-casual accommodations. The Stagecoach Bar and Grill's menu includes pasta, fish, steaks, and salads. Dinner is served Wednesday through Sunday. Reservations required. *35634 Highway 190; 800-484-3466.*

L. B. Jeffreys

A View with a Room:
the Hercules Tree's unusual
living quarters.

## WHERE TO STAY

### BALCH PARK CAMPGROUND

This popular campground is shaded by giant Sequoias, and features a museum, running water, and picnic tables. The 71 tent sites are available on a first-come, first-served basis. *Campground info: 559-539-3896.*

### PORTERVILLE BEST WESTERN INN

With Mountain Home State Forest a good ninety minutes away, this is the best stopover for those too tired to complete the trip. This Porterville motel's lobby has a "celebrity wall" covered with autographs from visiting actors like Larry Hagman, Paul Rodriguez, Bo Hopkins, and Katharine Ross. *350 West Montgomery; 559-781-7411.*

## HOW TO SEE THE SEQUOIAS ON HORSEBACK

### BALCH PARK PACK STATION

One-hour, half-day and full-day guided tours are offered, with longer trips available for groups. *www.balchpark.com; 559-539-2227.*

## ON THE ROAD: TRAIL OF 100 GIANTS

The Trail of 100 Giants is located south of Mountain Home State Forest, making it an even closer-to-L.A. option for outdoors people who need a big tree fix. This easy half-mile loop trail is paved for both strollers and wheelchairs, offering an ideal family outing. President Bill Clinton dedicated the Giant Sequoia Monument here in the 1990s. Across the Great Western Divide Highway, you'll find a scenic picnic area near the **Redwood Meadow Campground**.

*HOW TO GET TO THE TRAIL OF 100 GIANTS From Bakersfield, take Highway 65 North to the Ducor exit. Head east toward California Hot Springs. Continue uphill toward Parker Pass. At the top of the hill, turn left (north) onto the Western Divide Highway. In 2 miles you'll find the parking area at Redwood Meadow Campground.*

## HOW TO GET TO MOUNTAIN HOME STATE FOREST

*Take I-5 North toward Bakersfield. Take the 99 North to Highway 190 East, passing through Porterville, Lake Success, and Springville. One mile past Springville, turn left onto Balch Park Road. In three miles, turn right onto Bear Creek Road and follow it to Balch Park and Mountain Home. Park info: 559-539-2607.*

## DVD ITINERARY: MOUNTAIN HOME STATE FOREST

*Hulk*, Hedrick Pond, Scenes 6 and 16

# 50

# SEQUOIA NATIONAL PARK
## Land of the Giants

Fresh air! Scent of pine!

—*Raul Julia at Sequoia Lake, in* Addams Family Values *(1993)*

**MAJOR ROLES:** *Sequoia, The Big Trail, Hulk*

### BEHIND THE SCENERY

Established as California's first national park in 1890, Sequoia is home to the oldest and largest living things on the planet, making it one of the state's great cinematic locations. When major roads opened in the 1920s, the film industry started to take advantage of the area's breathtaking scenery.

One local booster was character actor/director Paul Hurst, Scarlett's Yankee deserter attacker in *Gone With the Wind*. Hurst ran his own production company and was one of the first filmmakers to work in the Sequoias. In 1925, he shot *The Gold Hunters* in Tokopah Valley, a spectacular setting with a waterfall and five lakes, which stood in for the Canadian Rockies. Hurst returned to the park as an actor in the 1934 MGM wildlife drama *Sequoia*, in which he plays an evil hunter who is head-butted off a precipitous cliff by a vengeful deer.

Director Raoul Walsh (*High Sierra*) filmed in Sequoia National Park at least twice. In 1930, he featured the big trees in *The Big Trail*, a sprawling epic that showcased both 70mm widescreen photography and John Wayne's first major leading role. In 1932, Walsh returned for his Western melodrama *Wild Girl*, starring Joan Bennett, Ralph Bellamy, and Charles Farrell.

## WHERE TO EXPLORE

### Top Billing: GIANT FOREST

The most popular area of Sequoia National Park is also the gateway for a variety of great hiking destinations. One of the best bets is **Tharp's Log**, where pioneer Hale Tharp built a cabin inside a fallen Giant Sequoia in the 1860s. The redwoods here are also seen at the climax of *The Big Trail*, where twenty-three-year-old John Wayne and Marguerite Churchill reunite at Huckleberry Meadow. Nearby attractions include the Auto Log, the Tunnel Log, and the General Sherman, the biggest tree in the world.

### PEAR LAKE

In the climax of *The Hulk*, the mutated forms of Eric Bana and Nick Nolte battle it out in the dark, craggy environs of this beautiful body of water. During post-production, the crew departed from Giant Forest and rode mules for 6.5 miles along the Lake Trail to get to Pear Lake, where they captured footage for the film's CGI–filled showdown. "It was a great ride to a spectacular location," recalls *Hulk* location manager Laura Sode-Matteson. *For directions to Giant Forest or Pear Lake, visit www.nps.gov/seki.*

## WHERE TO EAT

### THE GATEWAY RESTAURANT AND LODGE

Located just before the southern entrance to Sequoia National Park near the town of Three Rivers, this rustic motel/restaurant offers continental cuisine with a view of the Kaweah River. *www.gateway-sequoia.com; 559-561-4133.*

## WHERE TO STAY

### WUKSACHI LODGE

These modern park accommodations offer clean rooms, Internet access, and a large wood-beamed dining room with a picture window of the forest. "The main lodge appears freshly sprung from Alfred Hitchcock's *North by Northwest* [Mt. Rushmore dining room sequence]" says *Los Angeles Magazine*. *Located at the intersection of Highways 180 and 198; 888-252-5757.*

The High Sierras Trail will take you to Bearpaw Meadow.

## BEARPAW MEADOW HIGH SIERRA CAMP

The only way to get to this eight-thousand-foot-high backcountry paradise is by hiking eleven miles along the High Sierra Trail (from the Giant Forest's Crescent Meadow). All you need to bring is a change of clothes, because hot showers, lemonade, delicious meals, and down comforters are all provided at this tent-cabin hotel. *Reservations are required and hard to come by. 559-253-2199; or visit www.rescentre.com/bearpaw.htm.*

## MONTECITO-SEQUOIA LODGE

Located between Kings Canyon and Sequoia, this family-friendly camp on a private lake has 36 lodge rooms and 13 rustic cabins, with buffet-style meals included. *www.mslodge.com; 800-227-9900.*

### DETOUR: MINERAL KING

In 1965, the National Forest Service entertained the idea of developing the remote Mineral King wilderness area south of Giant Forest. Two different

Hollywood personalities submitted competing proposals. One plan was submitted by Beverly Hills businessman Robert Brandt, fourth husband of actress Janet Leigh. The other contender was Walt Disney, who had visited Mineral King Valley and envisioned it as a future ski resort/amusement park.

The $35 million Disney plan was chosen. It proposed a new thousand-cars-per-hour superhighway, a monorail and gondola system, and two hotels as part of "a completely self-contained village nestled in an alpine setting" (*Disney News*, 1965). The Sierra Club sued to block the development in 1969 and succeeded. Mineral King was annexed to Sequoia National Park in 1978.

Thankfully, it's still possible to see the wilderness area that was once threatened by development. An invigorating four-mile hike will take you to **White Chief Meadows**, where you can explore a quiet lake. On Mineral King Road, **The Silver City Resort** (*559-561-3223*) is one of the Sierra's more secluded places to stay. Its roadside cafe and bakery look like something out of David Lynch's TV series *Twin Peaks* . . . and they serve great pie too.

*HOW TO GET TO MINERAL KING Take Highway 198 East through the town of Three Rivers and follow the narrow and winding 23-mile Mineral King Road to its end. Not recommended for trailers or RVs, this road has 698 curves! Mineral King Ranger info: 559-565-3768.*

## DETOUR: SEQUOIA LAKE

In Barry Sonnenfeld's *Addams Family Values*, Sequoia Lake (located just outside the national park) plays "Camp Chippewa," an Adirondack summer camp where Christina Ricci tries to subvert the Thanksgiving Day play staged by camp directors Peter MacNicol and Christine Baranski. The camp areas are privately owned by the YMCA, but the public is welcome to hike to the lake (although fishing and swimming are not allowed) via a spur trail off Sunset Trail from Kings Canyon's Visitor Center. *Visitor's Center info: 559-565-4307.*

## HOW TO GET TO SEQUOIA NATIONAL PARK

*Take I-5 North to Highway 99 North into Bakersfield. Continue on 99 North to Visalia and take Highway 198 East, past the town of Three Rivers, into the mountains. Look for signs to the park.*

Marc Wanamaker/Bison Archives

Raoul Walsh's *Wild Girl*, on location in the redwoods.

## DVD ITINERARY: SEQUOIA NATIONAL PARK

*The Big Trail*, Scene 35

*Hulk*, Scene 28

*Addams Family Values*, Scenes 5 and 9–12

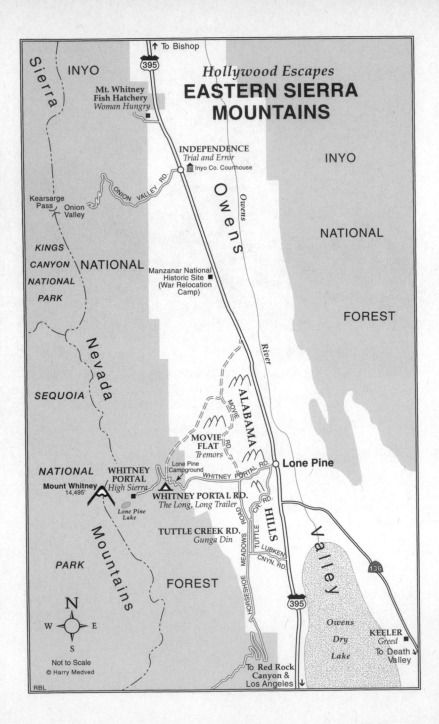

Hollywood Escapes
**EASTERN SIERRA**
**MOUNTAINS**

To Bishop
395

INYO

INYO

Mt. Whitney
Fish Hatchery
*Woman Hungry*

**INDEPENDENCE**
*Trial and Error*
🏛 Inyo Co. Courthouse

Kearsarge
Pass
Onion
Valley

ONION VALLEY RD.

Owens

Owens

River

**KINGS
CANYON
NATIONAL
PARK**

NATIONAL

NATIONAL

Manzanar National
Historic Site
(War Relocation
Camp)

FOREST

Nevada

ALABAMA

MOVIE RD.

**SEQUOIA**

**MOVIE
FLAT**
*Tremors*

HILLS

Lone Pine
Campground

**Lone Pine**

**NATIONAL**
Mount Whitney
14,495'

**WHITNEY
PORTAL**
*High Sierra*

WHITNEY PORTAL RD.

**WHITNEY PORTA L RD.**
*The Long, Long Trailer*

Lone Pine
Lake

**TUTTLE CREEK RD.**
*Gunga Din*

TUTTLE CR. RD.

LUBKEN
CNYN. RD

HORSESHOE MEADOWS ROAD

**PARK**

**FOREST**

Valley

136

N
W E
S

Owens
Dry
Lake

**KEELER**
*Greed*
To Death
Valley

395

Not to Scale
© Harry Medved

To Red Rock
Canyon &
Los Angeles

RBL

# 51

# THE ALABAMA HILLS AND MT. WHITNEY
## Where the West Was Filmed

You can't make a bad shot in Lone Pine. It's the greatest
Western location in the world.

—*Director Budd Boetticher on the Alabama Hills landscape (as
quoted by Turner Classic Movies historian Robert Osborne)*

**MAJOR ROLES:** *High Sierra, Joe Kidd, Tremors, Brigham Young,
Seven Men from Now*

### BEHIND THE SCENERY

Just outside the high desert town of Lone Pine towers majestic Mt. Whitney,
California's highest peak. The jagged Sierra Nevada range also looms above the
famed Alabama Hills. These rounded granite outcroppings sprawling below the
mountain were named in 1863 by Southern sympathizers during Civil War to
celebrate the victories of the Confederate cruiser, the *Alabama*.

Hollywood discovered the Alabama Hills area in the 1920s as a unique
backdrop for movies. They've been a versatile location ever since, spanning
the genre spectrum in over three hundred films, from Westerns (*The Gunfighter, Yellow Sky, Maverick*), to comedies (*The Great Race, The New Age*),
film noir (Ida Lupino's *The Hitch-Hiker*), colonial action pictures (*The Charge
of the Light Brigade, Kim, Gunga Din, King of the Khyber Rifles*), monster movies
(*Tremors*), and military dramas (Ridley Scott's *G.I. Jane*). In Scott's *Gladiator*,
Lone Pine Peak and Mount Whitney provide a brief but stunning backdrop
for Russell Crowe as he rides home. Top stunt coordinator and Alabama Hills

veteran Loren Janes comments, "The 'Alabams' are among the most versatile players in Hollywood. They've got everything you need."

A number of actors and filmmakers have had great affection for this area and the nearby town of Lone Pine and have returned time and again. John Wayne worked here on *North to Alaska*, *Tycoon*, and many B Westerns. Barbara Stanwyck, who starred here in *The Violent Men*, requested that her ashes be spread across the Alabama Hills. Director Budd Boetticher shot four of his Randolph Scott Westerns here, including *Seven Men from Now* and *Ride Lonesome*.

## WHERE TO EXPLORE

### MUSEUM OF LONE PINE FILM HISTORY

Stocked with rare photos, exhibits, and memorabilia of the films shot in the area, this movie museum features movie props such as the car from *High Sierra* and the graboid worms from *Tremors*. Before venturing into the Alabamas, you can pick up a Movie Location Map and Alabama Hills Driving Tour Map here. *www.lonepinefilmhistorymuseum.org* 760-876-9909.

### MOVIE ROAD

The Movie Road area is a circuitous network of graded dirt roads, usually safe for even passenger sedans. Don't forget the movie map from the museum to help identify the landmarks along the way.

From the town of Lone Pine, head west on Whitney Portal Road toward the mountains. In 2.7 miles, you'll see a marble marker (which Roy Rogers dedicated in 1990) at Whitney Portal's intersection with Movie Road. (If you reach Horseshoe Meadows Road, you've gone too far.) In the Movie Road area, you'll find such B Western locales as Gene Autry Rock, Hoppy Rocks, and Lone Ranger Canyon (named by the late Lone Pine film historian Dave Holland), as well as recognizable backgrounds for bigger-budget action films such as *How the West Was Won* (where Cheyenne Indians chase covered wagons carrying pioneers Debbie Reynolds, Robert Preston, and Thelma Ritter), *The Lives of a Bengal Lancer* (starring Gary Cooper and Franchot Tone) and John Sturges' *Joe Kidd* (where Clint Eastwood and Robert Duvall pursue John Saxon's gang hiding in the rocks).

Other titles shot in the area include *Tremors* (Kevin Bacon, Fred Ward, and Finn Carter flee giant worms and pole-vault from rock to rock), and Sturges' *Bad Day at Black Rock* (Ernest Borgnine sadistically tailgates mysterious one-armed stranger Spencer Tracy).

### Top Billing: TUTTLE CREEK ROAD

A paved alternative to the Movie Road experience, this narrow road winds its way through the twisted rocks, and offers a close and dramatic look at the Alabama Hills from your car. As you approach Horseshoe Meadows Road, you'll be near the Temple of Kali location for *Gunga Din* (starring Cary Grant and Douglas Fairbanks Jr.). Cowboy star William "Hopalong Cassidy" Boyd often stayed in a railroad-tie cabin along Tuttle Creek while making his B Westerns here in the 1930s.

## WHERE TO EAT

### THE RANCH HOUSE CAFÉ, OLANCHA

This popular country eatery (on Highway 395 on the way to Lone Pine) features home-style American cooking. Bear, elk, and moose heads adorn the walls, so vegans be forewarned. *760-764-2363.*

### TOTEM CAFÉ

This Lone Pine coffee shop is open for breakfast, lunch, and dinner, but the real attraction is the **Indian Trading Post** next door, where stars as diverse as Lee Marvin, Steve McQueen, Errol Flynn, Jack Palance, John Travolta, Gary Cooper, Virginia Grey, and Iron Eyes Cody have signed their autographs on the wooden walls. *Located in the center of Lone Pine at the stoplight on Highway 395 and Whitney Portal Road. 760-876-1120.*

## WHERE TO STAY

### DOW VILLA MOTEL

This lodge was built in 1924 to house the Hollywood talent already flocking to Lone Pine as a movie location. John Wayne stayed here while filming his 1930s B Westerns.

In 1953, Ernest Borgnine stayed at the Dow during the shooting of *Bad Day at Black Rock*. It was here that screenwriter Paddy Chayefsky and director Delbert Mann auditioned him for the title role of *Marty*. Film buffs will enjoy the Dow's historic wing of 1930s-era motel rooms. *310 S. Main Street; 760-876-5521.*

### LONE PINE CAMPGROUND

This pleasant, tree-lined camping spot sits at the base of the mountains on Whitney Portal Road. According to Lone Pine historian Dave Holland, the campground area is featured in a brief *How the West Was Won* scene in which George Peppard visits buffalo hunter Henry Fonda at his creekside cabin. *For info, call the Inyo National Forest Ranger at 800-280-2267.*

### ON THE ROAD: LITTLE LAKE AND FOSSIL FALLS

According to Twentieth Century Fox records, a small town set for the James Mason adventure *Journey to the Center of Earth* was built at the edge of Little

Lake. The lake, often dry, is not a destination in itself as you can easily see it from the road without stopping.

However, proceed north on Highway 395 and two miles past Little Lake you'll find a more interesting turnoff: the Bureau of Land Management property, **Fossil Falls**. Follow the signs to the Fossil Falls trailhead; from there it's a half-mile walk to a volcanic area featuring two dry waterfalls with an otherworldly look suitable for a sci-fi epic.

## DETOUR: WHITNEY PORTAL

Whitney Portal Road consists of twelve twisting miles that take you straight up into the Sierras, from the hot Alabama Hills to the cooler pine forest at the base of Mt. Whitney. Here at Whitney Portal you'll find a fishing pond, rushing creek, and waterfall (in season).

Whitney Portal Road has played several memorable roles on screen. This is the challenging route taken by newlywed RV owners Lucille Ball and Desi Arnaz in Vincente Minnelli's *The Long, Long Trailer*. In this 1954 MGM comedy, Whitney Portal Road's steep incline is as exaggerated as Lucy's trademark mugging when she sees the Owens Valley floor thousands of feet below. Dean Jagger as *Brigham Young* is more appreciative of the same view of the Owens Valley, posing as Utah's valley of the Great Salt Lake.

In a far more dramatic ascent, Humphrey Bogart leads Lone Pine police on a high-speed, high-elevation chase in Raoul Walsh's classic 1941 film noir *High Sierra*. Warner Bros. publicity department claimed that "the fourteen-mile pursuit sequence called for fifteen motorcycles and eight motorcars . . . on a road with seventy-seven bends and hairpin turns." Fourteen years later,

*Gunga Din* re-created colonial India in the Alabama Hills, below Mt. Whitney.

Marc Wanamaker/Bison Archives

this four-minute chase was re-created with Jack Palance in the Bogart role in the *High Sierra* remake, *I Died a Thousand Times*.

At the end of the road is the 8,631-foot-high trailhead to Mt. Whitney, where Bogart tries to elude the police in the mountain crags.

Bogart's rock-scramble may look rough on screen, but it's nothing compared to the actual twenty-two-mile round-trip hike to the top of Mt. Whitney. This breathtaking yet grueling trek is *not* a journey anyone should attempt in a single day, as you'll need a day or two just to adjust to the higher elevations. A wilderness permit, bear canister, several prepackaged meals, toilet paper, water purifier, and plenty of stamina are required. Inquire at the **Whitney Portal Store and Cafe** (*www.whitneyportalstore.com*; 760-876-0300) for supplies. A hiking permit must be obtained from the ranger station in Lone Pine.

Mt. Whitney's serrated crest has appeared on film many times, including *Gunga Din, The Great Race,* and *Joe Kidd*. A spectacular aerial shot of Whitney's peak opens *How the West Was Won*, giving prospective hikers a semblance of the sensational view from the hightest mountain in the contiguous United States.

Explorers seeking a far more pleasant hike will enjoy the six-mile round-trip from Whitney Portal to **Lone Pine Lake,** an outing that offers a comparable taste of the High Sierra country experience. *For more info, call the Mt. Whitney Ranger Station at 760-876-6200.*

## LOCAL MOVIE CELEBRATION
### LONE PINE FILM FESTIVAL
Held every October on the weekend closest to Columbus Day, this is a terrific annual get-together for heroes, villains, and fans of the cinema's Wild, Wild West. Past guests have included Gregory Peck, Douglas Fairbanks, Jr., and Ernest Borgnine. Highlights include tours of Alabama Hills movie locations and movies shot in Lone Pine. *www.lonepinefilmfestival.org.*; 760-876-9103.

### PRE-TRIP READING

The late historian Dave Holland's *On Location In Lone Pine* is an indispensable and comprehensive movie tour of the area with maps to the locations. *Order from: Holland House, 19932 Avenue of the Oaks, Santa Clarita, CA 91321;* 661-299-6664.

### HOW TO GET TO THE ALABAMA HILLS

*Take I-5 North to Highway 14 North to Highway 395 North. Continue on Highway 395 to Lone Pine. Turn left at Whitney Portal Road. Lone Pine Chamber: www.lonepinechamber.org; 877-253-8981.*

## SURVEY SAYS: HOW MT. WHITNEY
## SHRUNK FIVE FEET IN FIFTEEN YEARS

You're looking at the pride of the Sierras, brother—Mt. Whitney. The highest peak in the United States. 14,501 feet above sea level.

> —Gas station attendant Spencer Charters to Humphrey Bogart in John Huston's screenplay for High Sierra, written in 1940

You're looking at the High Sierras, mister. Mt. Whitney's in there. Try to find her. She's the tallest peak in the United States, 14,496 feet above sea level.

> —Gas station attendant Dub Taylor to Jack Palance in the High Sierra remake, I Died a Thousand Times (1955)

Californians have always been proud of their sawtoothed peak, Mt. Whitney, the highest peak in the contiguous United States. Over the years, however, Whitney's true elevation has been a point of contention.

In 1926, the National Park Service estimated the mountain's elevation as 14,501 feet, but years later Whitney was resurveyed at 14,496 feet. When Warner Bros. decide to remake High Sierra as I Died a Thousand Times, the filmmakers revised the script to reflect the recalculation. As of this writing, in fact, the elevation has decreased yet again to 14,495 feet.

Indeed, Whitney could be renamed "the Incredible Shrinking Mountain."

## DVD ITINERARY: ALABAMA HILLS AND MT. WHITNEY

How the West Was Won, Scene 16

Tremors, Scenes 16–17, 32–37

Gladiator, Scene 8

Brigham Young, Scene 22

Joe Kidd, Scenes 6–12

# 52

# INDEPENDENCE
## Born of the Fourth of July

It was an inspiring scene ... in the background the snow-capped Sierra, in the foreground the little lake with the trout flashing in the sun.

—The Inyo Independent *newspaper, describing a 1930 film shoot at Independence's Mt. Whitney Fish Hatchery*

**MAJOR ROLES:** *Farewell to Manzanar (TV), Trial and Error*

### BEHIND THE SCENERY

As befits its name, Independence was proudly founded on the Fourth of July, 1859 as a U.S. Army fort. Over the years, however, this peaceful Owens Valley town witnessed at least two dark episodes in California history.

In 1862, after bloody skirmishes with U.S. troops, nearly one thousand Native Americans were taken from their homes in this area and forced to march hundreds of miles south. In 1942, amid wartime hysteria resulting from Japan's attack on Pearl Harbor, the U.S. government relocated thousands of Japanese Americans (mostly from California and Washington) to the Manzanar internment camp just outside of Independence.

Today the town of Independence does not see much controversy and serves as a friendly and fascinating stopover for travelers en route to Mammoth and Yosemite. As the center of Inyo County, Independence now promotes itself as a gateway to the Eastern Sierras, with glacial 10,000-foot-high Onion Valley only thirteen miles away.

## WHERE TO EXPLORE

## MANZANAR NATIONAL HISTORIC SITE

There's not much left of this former detention center that was once "home" to ten thousand U.S. citizens of Japanese descent during World War II. The tar paper barracks, orphanage, and Bank of America branch are all gone. The stone guardhouses, gymnasium/social hall, and camp cemetery with its white Buddhist monument are among the last visible reminders of a grim chapter in local history. The National Park Service has renovated the high·school auditorium and turned it into a visitors center.

Key sequences were shot here for the 1976 television movie *Farewell to Manzanar*, starring Yuki Shimoda, Nobu McCarthy, and Pat Morita. (Hollywood also depicted the internment camp experience in John Hancock's *Baby Blue Marine*, Alan Parker's *Come See the Paradise*, and Scott Hicks' *Snow Falling on Cedars*.) And the classic *Bad Day at Black Rock*, John Sturges' look at simmering racism in a dusty World War II–era desert town, was filmed in the Independence and Lone Pine areas.

In a lighter vein, Richard Donner's *Maverick* used the area for a sequence in which Mel Gibson encounters a group of frontier widows, including Donner's former "Lois Lane," Margot Kidder. *On Highway 395, 5 miles south of Independence and 12 miles north of Lone Pine; 760-878-2194.*

### Top Billing: EASTERN CALIFORNIA MUSEUM

Robert Towne's script for *Chinatown* was loosely based on the real-life California water scandals of the early part of the twentieth century. Stories abound

Harry Medved

Manzanar War Relocation Camp is now a national historic site.

regarding L.A. power brokers who secretly bought farmland here to access the Owens River water supply. The entire history is recounted in the museum's exhibits, in part with framed newspaper headlines bearing slogans such as STEAL MY HORSE, RUN OFF WITH MY WIFE, BUT DAMN YOU, DON'T TOUCH MY WATER! Other displays include remnants from the Manzanar War Relocation Camp, and local Native American artifacts. *Closed Tuesdays–Wednesdays; 155 N. Grant Street; 760-878-0258.*

## WHERE TO EAT

### STILL LIFE CAFÉ

With fine-art photography gracing the walls, this is a surprisingly fashionable Mediterranean cuisine restaurant in downtown Independence. Across the street is the garage where Will Patton tracks down retired car thief Nicolas Cage for one last job in the 2000 remake of *Gone in Sixty Seconds*. *www. stilllifecafe.com; 760-878-2555.*

## WHERE TO STAY

### THE WINNEDUMAH

This vintage boardinghouse was built in 1926 by the owners of Lone Pine's Dow Villa as overflow lodging for cast and crews shooting in the Alabama Hills. Guests included Western stars Gary Cooper, George "Gabby" Hayes, and Iron Eyes Cody. Across the street is the **Inyo County Courthouse**, where Charles Manson was once arraigned. The courthouse also served as a location for Jonathan Lynn's small-town comedy *Trial and Error*, starring Jeff Daniels, Michael Richards, and Charlize Theron. *211 N. Edwards Street; 760-878-2040.*

## ON THE ROAD: MT. WHITNEY STATE FISH HATCHERY

The hatchery is a pleasant stop for a shady picnic by a 1917 Tudor building and trout pond. According to Inyo Film Commissioner Chris Langley, the Fish Hatchery was a location for a 1931 Western entitled *Woman Hungry*, starring Sidney Blackmer and Lila Lee. *From Independence, go north on Highway 395 for 2.3 miles and turn left at Fish Hatchery Road; 760-878-2272.*

## HOW TO GET TO INDEPENDENCE

*Take I-5 North to Highway 14 North to Highway 395 North. Independence is located on Highway 395, between the towns of Lone Pine and Big Pine; www.independence-ca.com.*

## DVD ITINERARY: INDEPENDENCE

*Maverick*, Scenes 19–20

*Trial and Error* (1997), Scenes 15 and 17

*Gone in Sixty Seconds* (2000), Scene 3

Chris Langley/Inyo Film Commission

Downtown Independence is featured in movies with Jeff Daniels,
Charlize Theron, and Nicolas Cage.

# 53

## YOSEMITE NATIONAL PARK
## Splendor in the Granite

Everyone knows I love Lucy, but can you imagine having her around on a camping trip? Yet the beautiful scenery around Yosemite makes it a wonderful place for a second honeymoon ...

—*Desi Arnaz in the theatrical trailer for* Forever, Darling

**MAJOR ROLES:** *The Last of the Mohicans (1920), Maverick, Star Trek V: The Final Frontier, Forever, Darling*

### BEHIND THE SCENERY

Long before Hollywood's arrival, park landmarks like Half-Dome, El Capitan, and Yosemite Falls were world-famous icons of natural history thanks to widely published landscape photographs and paintings. And ever since the silent era, when movies such as the sprawling 1920 adventure *The Last of the Mohicans* was filmed in Yosemite Valley, dozens of filmmakers have come to capture on film the park's jaw-dropping California grandeur.

Yet, in spite of Yosemite's endless visual splendor, a number of filmmakers who've come here have not progressed beyond the location scouting stage. Clint Eastwood's *The Eiger Sanction*, Stanley Kubrick's *The Shining*, and even Anthony Minghella's *Cold Mountain* all reportedly came to the park for inspiration but ultimately commenced principal photography in other states or countries.

You may want to avoid the park during its crowded summer season, especially on the Memorial Day, Fourth of July, and Labor Day holidays. If you can only make it for a summer weekend, explore the popular valley waterfalls during the early morning (before 9 a.m.) or evening hours (after 6 p.m.). Throughout the midday, visit the less popular areas outside of the valley.

## WHERE TO EXPLORE

*Consult park maps for directions to the following destinations:*

### TUNNEL VIEW

If you're approaching the park from the west, you'll marvel at the first panoramic view of Yosemite Valley as you emerge from the Wawona Tunnel. From this turnout, as seen in Desi and Lucy's *The Long, Long Trailer*, you can see the famed Half-Dome, Cathedral Rocks, Sentinel Rock, Bridalveil Fall, Cloud's Rest, and El Capitan.

This sweeping viewpoint also serves as a vacation location for Captain Kirk, Spock, and Bones in the opening sequence of William Shatner's directorial film debut, *Star Trek V: The Final Frontier*. Though Shatner appears to be scaling the 3,500-foot-high El Capitan, in reality he's climbing a fake rockwall that was erected at the Tunnel View parking lot and cleverly positioned to block the real monolith from camera view.

### Top Billing: GLACIER POINT

A great sixteen-mile drive from the valley floor ascends thousands of feet to Glacier Point, the park's most spectacular viewing area. On the way you'll pass **Washburn Point**, the location where Mel Gibson (disguised as a Native American) swindles tourist Paul Smith in *Maverick*. The view of Half-Dome from here is breathtaking.

Glacier Point provides an equally stunning vista in two vintage MGM films: *Thrill of a Romance*, a Technicolor musical with Van Johnson and Esther Williams, and Clarence Brown's melodrama *A Free Soul*, featuring Norma Shearer and Lionel Barrymore in a performance that earned him a Best Actor Oscar. You can see El Capitan, Yosemite Falls, Half-Dome, Nevada Falls, and Vernal Falls from here. To escape the crowds, walk the trails to Taft Point and Sentinel Dome.

### YOSEMITE FALLS

With a height of almost twenty-five hundred feet, the most popular destination in the park is also one of the tallest waterfalls in North America. The falls are seen briefly in both of Lucy and Desi's Yosemite excursions, *The Long, Long*

*Trailer* and *Forever, Darling*. Although you can view the cascade from the parking lot, it's worth taking an extra fifteen-minute stroll on the paved walkway to get an up-close and personal view of Lower Yosemite Falls.

## BRIDALVEIL FALL
Also on view in *The Long, Long Trailer*, this popular destination is a favorite spot for marriage proposals, as the 620-foot-tall plunge does indeed resemble a wedding veil. A short, .25-mile stroll from the parking lot will take you to the base of the fall. Be prepared to get wet from Bridalveil's misty spray.

## LEIDIG MEADOW AND SENTINEL FALLS
Just west of Yosemite Lodge is Leidig Meadow, a picnic spot best visited in the spring, when the grass is a dazzling green. The park's majestic Merced River winds its way through this tranquil idyll and visitors are rewarded with views of Sentinel Rock and Sentinel Falls, the third tallest waterfall in California.

This pastoral area has been used in three different films: It's the camping spot visited by guardian angel James Mason in *Forever, Darling*. In *Maverick*, this is the site of Graham Greene's Native American village where Mel Gibson grabs some rest and relaxation. In Joe Dante's *Small Soldiers* it's where teenager Gregory Smith bids a final farewell to the Gorgonites as they sail toward El Capitan in search of their homeland.

## THE TUOLOMNE RIVER
Riding the Tuolomne is an adrenaline-pumping experience featuring eighteen miles of white water coursing through a steep-walled canyon in Stanislaus Na-

Marc Wanamaker/Bison Archives

Yosemite provides
a change of scenery for
*The Caine Mutiny.*

tional Forest (due west of Yosemite National Park). Because the Tuolomne is designated a Wild and Scenic River and features Class IV and Class V rapids, it is recommended for rafting experts only (or beginners when the water is low).

According to production manager Robert L. Brown, the Lumsden Falls portion of the Tuolomne River is where rafting doubles for Harrison Ford, Kate Capshaw, and child actor Ke Huy Quan ride the current in *Indiana Jones and the Temple of Doom*. And according to river guide veteran Chris Condon, the Lumsden "put-in" area appears in 1943's *For Whom the Bell Tolls* with Gary Cooper. *Zephyr Whitewater Expeditions: 800-431-3636; Sierra Mac: 800-457-2580.*

## WHERE TO EAT AND STAY

### THE AHWAHNEE

Set in a pristine meadow, the upscale Ahwahnee was completed in 1927 by Gilbert Stanley Underwood in a blend of California Craftsman, Art Deco, and Native American styles. Visitors not accustomed to classic National Park lodges will be awestruck by the dining room's cathedral-like, thirty-four-foot-high ceilings. The hotel's Honeymoon Table (jacket required) offers a staggering picture window view of Yosemite Falls. The rooms are on the pricey side, but even if you're not a guest at the Ahwahnee, it's worth a visit just to marvel at the hotel's lobby.

According to the hotel staff, the art department for Stanley Kubrick's *The Shining* used the Ahwahnee as an inspiration for the film's haunted Overlook Hotel. Kubrick did use the Timberline Lodge (interestingly, another Underwood design) at Mt. Hood, Oregon, for brief shots of the hotel's exterior.

The Ahwahnee did appear, however, in a film most moviegoers wouldn't associate with Yosemite: the seagoing drama *The Caine Mutiny*, directed by Edward Dmytryk. In a subplot, Navy man Robert Francis gets shore leave and takes his sweetheart May Wynn to the Ahwahnee. Among the sights they see are Yosemite Falls and Glacier Point's glowing "Firefall" a once-beloved Yosemite summertime attraction. *www.yosemitepark.com; 209-372-1407.*

### WAWONA HOTEL

This Victorian hotel dates back to the 1870s. In the evenings, a piano player plays nostalgic tunes that transport listeners to a more genteel era. In the World War II suspense thriller *36 Hours*, the Wawona Hotel plays an imitation U.S. military hospital built in the Bavarian woods. The complex is used to dupe American soldier James Garner into believing the war is over. Eva Marie Saint and Rod Taylor pose as Garner's nurse and doctor, and the three leads are frequently shown strolling the Wawona grounds.

Nearby the Wawona is the popular **Mariposa Grove of Giant Sequoias**, home to more than six hundred big trees including the three-hundred-ton

Bass Lake, as seen in 1952's *Hiawatha*.

"Grizzly Giant," the "Three Graces," the "Bachelor," and the famous Wawona Tunnel Tree. Mariposa Grove was a location for the 1929 Rin Tin Tin movie *Tiger Rose*. *Located on Highway 41, near the park's south entrance; 209-375-6556.*

## DETOUR: THE GREAT OUTDOORS AT BASS LAKE

An hour away from Yosemite is scenic Bass Lake, an aquatic recreation area where many outdoors enthusiasts choose to spend the day as they approach the National Park from the west. You won't find Yosemite's awesome granite here, but you will encounter a popular mountain lake surrounded by an endless pine forest.

Maverick director Sam Peckinpah spent his childhood summers on a family ranch near Bass Lake in the 1930s. In fact, a creek, meadow, and a mountain bear the Peckinpah name.

In the movies, Bass Lake often doubled for a woodsy Minnesota or East Coast getaway. In the Technicolor film noir *Leave Her to Heaven*, Bass Lake is the Maine retreat where author Cornel Wilde escapes to write his novel. A memorably dark sequence involves Wilde's scheming wife, played by Gene

Tierney, as she idly sits in a rowboat and watches her young brother-in-law drown. Other Bass Lake films include *Hiawatha* and *Meatballs IV*.

In the John Hughes–scripted comedy *The Great Outdoors*, vacationing family man John Candy gets a surprise visit from city dwelling friends Dan Aykroyd and Annette Bening (in her movie debut). The film was shot at **The Pines** resort complex on Bass Lake, which doubles as Wisconsin's North Woods. The Pines' fashionable restaurant, **Ducey's on the Lake** (559-642-3200) serves as the film's rustic Paul Bunyan eatery.

More remote and less forested accommodations can be found a few miles from Bass Lake at North Fork's **Bonnie B Ranch**, where a snowy New England mansion set was built for Gore Verbinski's *Mouse Hunt*.

*HOW TO GET TO BASS LAKE Take I-5 North to Highway 99 North through Bakersfield. Continue on 99 to the town of Fresno. Take Highway 41 North to the town of Oakhurst. Follow the signs to Bass Lake. Area info: www.basslakechamber.com; 559-642-3676.*

## HOW TO GET TO YOSEMITE NATIONAL PARK

*Take I-5 North to Highway 99 North through Bakersfield. Continue on 99 to the city of Fresno. Take Highway 41 North (past Oakhurst/Bass Lake) into the mountains. Follow the signs to Yosemite National Park. www.nps.gov/yose; 209-372-0200.*

## DVD ITINERARY: YOSEMITE NATIONAL PARK

*The Caine Mutiny*, The Ahwahnee, Scene 7

*Star Trek V: The Final Frontier*, Yosemite Valley, Scenes 1–2

*The Great Outdoors*, Bass Lake, Scene 5

*Leave Her to Heaven*, Bass Lake, Scenes 2 and 11

# MOVIE LAKES AND RIVERS

For God's sake, this is beautiful country here!
Take a good look!

> —John Candy to Dan Aykroyd in The Great
> Outdoors (1988), shot at Bass Lake in
> the High Sierras

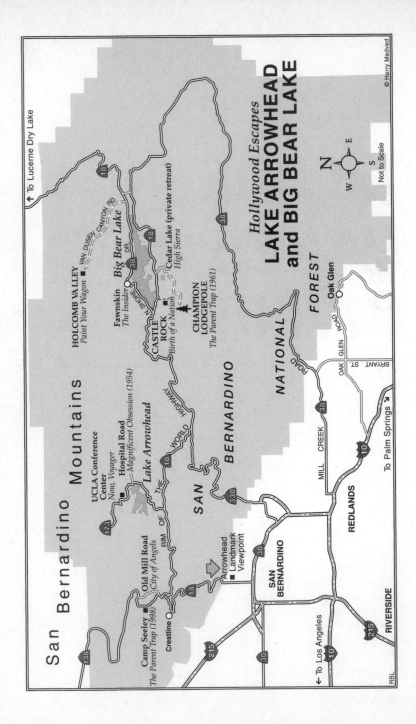

Hollywood Escapes
**LAKE ARROWHEAD and BIG BEAR LAKE**

© Harry Medved

N
W E
S
Not to Scale

San Bernardino Mountains

← To Lucerne Dry Lake

**HOLCOMB VALLEY**
*Paint Your Wagon* ■

Big Bear Lake

VAN DUSEN CANYON RD.

**Fawnskin** ○
*The Insider*

Cedar Lake (private retreat)
*High Sierra*

CASTLE
ROCK ■
*Birth of a Nation*

**CHAMPION
LODGEPOLE**
*The Parent Trap (1961)*

**UCLA Conference
Center**
*Now, Voyager*

**Hospital Road**
*Magnificent Obsession (1954)*

Lake Arrowhead

**Old Mill Road**
*City of Angels*

**Camp Seeley** ■
*The Parent Trap (1998)*

Crestline ○

Arrowhead
■ Landmark
Viewpoint

SAN BERNARDINO

NATIONAL FOREST

Oak Glen ○

OAK GLEN ROAD

BRYANT ST.

MILL CREEK

REDLANDS

→ To Palm Springs

SAN
BERNARDINO

RIVERSIDE

← To Los Angeles

RBL

# 54

# LAKE ARROWHEAD
## Hollywood's Magnificent Obsession

*Suddenly below me was a small oval lake deep in trees and rocks and wild grass, like a drop of dew caught in a curled leaf.*

—*Raymond Chandler in his novel* The Lady in the Lake *(1943)*

**MAJOR ROLES:** *Sunrise (1954), Magnificent Obsession (1954), Now, Voyager*

### BEHIND THE SCENERY

The river valley that is now Lake Arrowhead was dammed in the 1890s to provide water for the orange groves of San Bernardino below. Decades later, the reservoir was sold to a consortium of L.A. businessmen as a recreational lake.

"After the lake was developed, Hollywood moved in," says historian and Arrowhead resident Lee Cozad, author of *Those Magnificent Mountain Movies.* "The studios found Arrowhead to be a magnificent location. Actors and moviemakers bought property while they were here filming because they found a sense of seclusion in the mountains only ninety miles from L.A."

F. W. Murnau built an elaborate set and streetcar track on the western edge of the lake for his lyrical *Sunrise,* considered one of the greatest films of all time. In fact, so many movies utilized this western islet of Arrowhead that it was dubbed "Movie Point."

Among the reclusive personalities who have owned property in the area are Charlie Chaplin and Bugsy Siegel. Other Hollywood transplants have included Doris Day, Liberace, Frankie Avalon, and Heather Locklear.

Over the years Arrowhead has doubled for different European locales including Bavaria (*Heidi*, with Shirley Temple), Switzerland (*Three Smart Girls*, *Stolen Holiday*, and Laurel and Hardy's *Swiss Miss*) and Scandinavia (*I'll Take Sweden* with Bob Hope and Frankie Avalon).

Although it's usually portrayed as a bucolic destination, Lake Arrowhead also has its grim side on film; its tranquil waters seem to exert a dangerous effect on couples, sparking in the men a murderous urge to drown their women. George O'Brien and Janet Gaynor in *Sunrise*, and Phillips Holmes and Sylvia Sidney in Josef von Sternberg's *An American Tragedy* fall victim to what seems to be Arrowhead's deadly influence. And the titular disembodied extension of cartoonist Michael Caine's twisted psyche claims several victims among the Arrowhead environs in Oliver Stone's *The Hand*.

On a lighter note, Bugs Bunny kidnaps Michael Jordan at the fifteenth hole of the Lake Arrowhead Country Club golf course in *Space Jam*, much to the astonishment of Bill Murray, Wayne Knight, and Larry Bird.

## HOW TO SEE THE LAKE

### THE ARROWHEAD QUEEN

Since most of the lake is off-limits to the public, the best way to see those private pockets where moviemakers once shot scenes is to catch a ride on the restored paddlewheel boat, the Arrowhead Queen. During the fifty-minute guided tour, you'll see such historical points of interest as Lone Pine Island (where Shirley Temple and Gary Cooper play in *Now and Forever*), Totem Pole Point (site of an Alaskan fishing village in *Spawn of the North*, with Henry Fonda) and Point Hamiltair/Movie Point (the lake crossing location in *The Yearling*, with Gregory Peck and Claude Jarman Jr.). Other films shot at the point include Murnau's *Sunrise*, Victor Fleming's silent comedy *Mantrap*, and Clarence Brown's *Of Human Hearts*, with James Stewart. *Purchase tickets at Leroy's retail store/beach shop in the village; call 909-336-6992 for departure times.*

## WHERE TO HIKE

### NORTH SHORE TRAIL

One of the few trails close to the perimeter of Lake Arrowhead, the North Shore Trailhead is located just behind the Mountains Community Hospital. This hike through the woods (scarred by fire in 2003) begins at the far right of **North Shore Campground**, following trail 3W12. Parking is available at the campground located on Hospital Road, where a bewildered Rock Hudson collapses in front of Jane Wyman's car in *Magnificent Obsession*. *For guided group hikes in the Arrowhead area, visit www.mountaintophiking.com.*

## WHERE TO EAT

### Top Billing: DEL LAGO'S

This European-style coffeehouse, bookstore, and Internet café is located in Arrowhead Village, a pleasant lakeside shopping mecca located on Arrowhead's only publicly accessible side. Diners can enjoy croissants, soup and sandwiches, and gourmet coffee in front of a magnificent picture-window view of the lake. This is the area where Jack Lemmon and Peter Falk try to torpedo Tony Curtis's speedboat in *The Great Race*. Open 7 days a week, with live entertainment on Saturday nights. *28200 Highway 189; 909-336-6884.*

## WHERE TO STAY

### BRACKEN FERN MANOR

Originally known as Club Arrowhead of the Pines, Benjamin "Bugsy" Siegel's 1.3-million-dollar gambling casino, brothel, and speakeasy resort was instantly popular with Hollywood upon its 1929 opening. Aspiring starlets reportedly came to the mountains to meet industry bigwigs, who used an underground tunnel to get to the girls' rooms. These quarters now make up the bed-and-breakfast inn called the Bracken Fern Manor. One of this location's advantages, Siegel felt, was its seclusion on a quiet, wooded side street. Be advised there are no lakeside views from here, but you will find peace and tranquility. *www.brackenfernmanor.com; 909-337-8557.*

### LAKE ARROWHEAD RESORT & SPA

Those looking for a more traditional, family-friendly lakeside hotel with its own little beach should seek out this former Hilton Hotel. *www.laresort.com; 800-800-6792.*

Bracken Fern Manor

The Manor was once a Hollywood haunt and bordello run by gangster Bugsy Siegel.

## WHERE TO HOLD A RETREAT

## UCLA CONFERENCE CENTER

Located on Arrowhead's exclusive North Shore, this French Norman–style center was built in 1921 as the North Shore Tavern, erected to house workers during construction of Arrowhead Village.

On-screen, this is the sanitarium where Bette Davis recuperates under the care of psychiatrist Claude Rains in *Now, Voyager*. The tennis courts and grounds look the same as they did in the 1942 film, in which Davis plays tennis with troubled teenager Bonita Granville.

In a more recent blink-and-you'll-miss-it cameo, the conference grounds plays the snowbound Camp David, an escape for president Michael Douglas and love interest Annette Bening in Rob Reiner's *The American President*.

The UCLA Conference Center is available for educational or religious retreats only from September–June. In the summer months the grounds become *Camp Bruin*, a retreat for the university's alumni. *850 Willow Creek Road; 909-337-2478.*

## DETOUR: SEELEY CREEK TRAIL, CRESTLINE

Half an hour from Lake Arrowhead is the mountain hamlet of Crestline, home to a spectacular trail to Seeley Creek and a series of curving, undeveloped roads that make for pleasant scenic drives.

Perhaps the most cinematic stretch is Crestline's **Old Mill Road**, part of which was the site of the tragic conclusion of *City of Angels* with Meg Ryan and Nicolas Cage. (Two other locations were also used for the crash sequence involving the cycling Ryan and a logging truck: the Lake Tahoe environs and Cuddy Valley Road in Kern County's Mt. Pinos area.)

The **Seeley Creek Trail** is an easy two-mile round-trip hike among Jeffrey pines, incense cedars, and black oak. The key destination along the Seeley Creek Trail is **Heart Rock**, a natural bowl with a twenty-five-foot waterfall. According to hiking guide author John Robinson, "for an introduction to the San Bernardinos, you can do no better than this magnificent forest stroll."

You can find the trailhead just outside of Crestline at **Camp Seeley**, originally a lumber mill owned by Mormon brothers and purchased by L.A. County in 1914. In Disney's 1998 *Parent Trap* remake, this camp doubles for Maine's Camp Walden, where preteen Lindsay Lohan (in a dual role) meets up with her long-lost identical twin.

*HOW TO GET TO THE SEELEY CREEK TRAIL From Crestline, follow Highway 138 to the Camp Seeley entrance road and make a left. Make another left at the Camp Seeley gate and follow the paved road to the parking area. You'll see a sign for trail #4W07.*

The Deanna Durbin musical *Three Smart Girls*,
on location at Lake Arrowhead.

*Marc Wanamaker/Bison Archives*

## PRE-TRIP READING

*Those Magnificent Mountain Movies* by W. Lee Cozad, Rim of the World Historical Society. This coffee-table book is a treasure trove of historical lore and amazing photos from films shot at both Lake Arrowhead and Big Bear Lake. *www.rimoftheworldhistory.com.*

## HOW TO GET TO LAKE ARROWHEAD

*Take I-10 East, then take the 215 Freeway north for 6 miles. Bear right on the 30 Freeway marked* MOUNTAIN RESORTS. *Exit at Highway 18, making a left at Waterman Avenue and proceed north for 22 winding miles to the Lake Arrowhead turn-off.*

## DVD ITINERARY: LAKE ARROWHEAD

*The Great Race*, Lake Arrowhead, Scene 5

*The Yearling*, Movie Point, Scenes 27

*Now, Voyager*, UCLA Conference Center, Scene 33

# 55

# BIG BEAR LAKE
# Trail of the Awesome Pines

*How clear it is! ... We're on top of the world!*

—Ann Harding to Gary Cooper atop Big Bear's Castle Rock in
Henry Hathaway's Peter Ibbetson (1935)

**MAJOR ROLES:** *The Birth of a Nation, The Trail of the Lonesome
Pine, The Parent Trap (1961), The Opposite of Sex*

## BEHIND THE SCENERY

Located in Big Bear Valley—so named for the majestic predators that once roamed this region—this reservoir is separated from Lake Arrowhead, its sister body of water, by a forty-five-minute drive along the San Bernardino Mountains Rim of the World Highway.

Mormons settled the town of San Bernardino in 1851 and milled lumber from the mountains around Big Bear to build their homes. In 1883, Redlands farmers needed water and so Big Bear Valley was dammed, forming the then-largest man-made lake in the world and submerging over nine thousand trees in the process. Despite the development, the terrain here is still known for its magnificent pines and towering, jumbled rocks.

Hollywood arrived in the 1910s. Cecil B. DeMille shot his Canadian-based *The Call of the North* around the lake in 1914. Many other silent films (including the classic *The Birth of a Nation*) followed. "A local old-timer told me that so many motion picture companies were shooting up here in the 1920s that they were practically tripping over one another," says area historian Lee Cozad. Movie sets were built and left intact, as it would only be a matter of months before they were reused by other productions.

Because of its numerous summer camps and wintertime snow play areas, Big Bear holds a natural allure for children. Indeed, a number of kid-oriented flicks have been shot here, including the original version of *The Parent Trap*, the St. Bernard saga *Beethoven's 3rd*, and the Eddie Murphy *Doctor Dolittle* movies.

Most Angelenos head to Big Bear for family summer vacations or for the wintertime powder at its Snow Summit and Big Bear Mountain ski resorts. (Summer days can get surprisingly hot and winter weekends see the arrival of tens of thousands of visitors.) Outdoors enthusiasts may prefer to explore Big Bear during the cooler, quieter spring and autumn seasons.

## HOW TO SEE THE LAKE

### THE *BIG BEAR QUEEN*

A ninety-minute summertime cruise on the *Big Bear Queen* offers a nice overview of local history. The lake has been a film location from silent movies to Paul Thomas Anderson's *Magnolia*, in which a scubadiver is accidentally scooped out of the water by a fire-fighting aquaplane. On the tour you may see *WarGames'* two-story log cabin that serves as scientist John Wood's hideaway sought by high school students Matthew Broderick and Ally Sheedy. The same lakeside retreat plays a Canadian hideout for a pregnant Christina Ricci at the conclusion of *The Opposite of Sex*. *Reservations required. www.bigbearmarina.com; 909-866-3218.*

## WHERE TO HIKE

### CASTLE ROCK TRAIL

A breathtaking mile-long and relatively steep hike takes you to the Castle Rock overlook, a 100-foot-high jagged outcropping of granite boulders with 360-degree views of the lake. On film, this is the spot for a notorious scene of racist melodrama in D. W. Griffith's 1915 *The Birth of a Nation*. According to mountain historian Lee Cozad, it's where Little Sister, played by Mae Marsh, runs from the clutches of Walter Long (in blackface). Rather than submit to his advances she jumps from Castle Rock to her death below. Five years later, Castle Rock saw a fight between Wallace Beery and Alan Roscoe in *The Last of the Mohicans*.

In *The Trail of the Lonesome Pine*, Appalachian mountain girl Sylvia Sidney scampers among the rocks here as she espies wandering minstrel Fuzzy Knight. In Disney's original version of *The Parent Trap*, the trail to Castle Rock is where identical twins (both played by Hayley Mills) slyly embarrass Joanna Barnes in front of their dad Brian Keith.

*HOW TO GET TO THE CASTLE ROCK TRAIL On State Highway 18, the hard-to-spot trailhead is one mile east of Big Bear Dam. Look for the green, BIG BEAR LAKE city limits sign and park here. You'll find the signed trailhead nearby. Because parking is limited, get here early in the day.*

## CHAMPION LODGEPOLE PINE TRAIL

A 45-minute stroll though a high mountain forest and grassland takes hikers to this 450-year-old giant pine tree (or tamarack), the largest of its kind in the world. On the trail you'll encounter white fir, bracken ferns, wild columbine, mistletoe, Jeffrey pine, and lichens. Adjacent to the lodgepole is a spectacular meadow that's full of wildflowers in the spring. It's also near the location of Camp Inch in the original *The Parent Trap*. In *Dr. Dolittle 2*, this is where Eddie Murphy speeds up the ursine courtship of the bear couple voiced by Steve Zahn and Lisa Kudrow.

*HOW TO GET TO THE CHAMPION LODGEPOLE PINE TRAIL On state Highway 18, head three miles past the dam and turn right on Tulip Lane, and right again on Mill Creek Road. Follow Mill Creek (as it turns into dirt road #2N10 for four miles. Turn right on #2N11 and follow it for a mile to the trailhead. Recommended for high-clearance vehicles. Call Big Bear Discovery Center for road conditions: 909-866-3437.*

## WHERE TO EXPLORE

### HOLCOMB VALLEY

A series of hard-to-find dirt roads takes you to this former mining area north of Big Bear Lake. If you're weary of the development and traffic on Big Bear Lake Boulevard, Holcomb is the area where you'll find the wide open spaces you'd expect from these mountains.

Holcomb Valley's inaccessibility makes it a perfect location for Westerns, including many episodes of TV's *Bonanza*. According to location manager Mike Neale, Christopher Guest's little-seen Lewis and Clark satire *Almost Heroes* (cowritten by *Right Stuff* author Tom Wolfe) used this area for a fight scene between Chris Farley and Matthew Perry and French bad guys Kevin Dunn and Eugene Levy. Holcomb's wide open spaces can be glimpsed in the musical *Paint Your Wagon*; during the "There's a Coach Comin' In" number, a drunken Lee Marvin shanghais a stagecoach full of ladies of the evening and rushes them to eager and anxious miners. Holcomb Valley's real-life highlights include Hangman's Tree, Ross' Grave, and the Lucky Baldwin Mine.

*CAUTION: If you set out for Holcomb Valley, be prepared for a slow and bumpy ride along dirt roads that may require 4WD or high suspension. If you want to follow the entire fifteen-mile loop, it can take up to three hours.*

*HOW TO GET TO HOLCOMB VALLEY There are several dirt road op-*

*tions to Holcomb Valley. Pick up a map and self-guided auto tour at the Big Bear Discovery Center (909-866-3437).*

## WHERE TO EAT

### THE CAPTAIN'S ANCHORAGE

Opened in 1947 by gravel-voiced character actor Andy Devine (*Stagecoach*), this steak-and-seafood restaurant was originally a roadhouse and gambling parlor called The Sportsman's Tavern. Today the place still has plenty of character with its he-man menu ("the Andy Devine Cut" is a 22-ounce hunk of New York steak), huge stone fireplace, and pine walls featuring photos of Ricardo Montalban, Esther Williams, and other stars who have visited Big Bear. *42148 Moonridge Way; 909-866-3997.*

### NORTH SHORE CAFÉ

This rustic 1940s café serves French provincial food plus house specialties like breakfast burritos and onion rings. Located in the peaceful North Shore town of Fawnskin, the cafe appears as a Montana diner in Michael Mann's *The Insider*. It's at the middle window table where news producer Al Pacino confronts Wanda De Jesus and Paul Perri, Federal agents posing as geologists. *39226 North Shore Drive; 909-866-5879.*

## WHERE TO STAY

*Many Big Bear lodgings are located along busy Big Bear Boulevard and offer little seclusion. A few suggested places far from the madding crowd:*

### KNICKERBOCKER MANSION COUNTRY INN

A log cabin mansion built in 1920 for Big Bear's first dam keeper is now a bed-and-breakfast inn with extensive pine and cedar paneling throughout the main house. Although the mansion doesn't afford views of the lake, its vertical log design is impressive. *869 Knickerbocker Road; www.knickerbockermansion.com; 909-878-9190.*

### SERRANO CAMPGROUND

Located within walking distance to the lake, this popular sixty-acre summer destination has a highly desirable asset for campers: hot showers. The Pacific Crest Trail and a paved wheelchair path are nearby. Nearby is the location where Adam Sandler pulls Winona Ryder from an icy pond in *Mr. Deeds*. *Reservations are a must. www.reserveamerica.com; 877-444-6777.*

## WINDY POINT INN

Located in the quieter North Shore town of Fawnskin, this five-room bed-and-breakfast features panoramic views and a small boat dock. *Act of Violence*, Fred Zinnemann's classic 1949 noir with Robert Ryan and Van Heflin, was shot at nearby Boulder Bay. *39015 North Shore Dr.; www.windypointinn.com; 909-866-2746.*

## IT CAME FROM CALIFORNIA: BIG BEAR

If a filmmaker needs his big monster to lurk behind big rocks or big trees, where better to film than a forested location with the name of Big Bear? Because it provides thick woods where a creature can effectively hide. Big Bear has a tradition of hosting a number of low-budget productions in the horror and fantasy genre.

B-movie master Richard Cunha headed to the hills to avoid the attention of Hollywood unions when he shot his killer conquistador picture *Giant from the Unknown* in the Big Bear town of Fawnskin. The finale of the film shows the Diablo Giant (played by heavyweight boxer Buddy Baer) tumbling over a dam at Cedar Lake. Similarly, Columbia Pictures' 1956 *The Werewolf* concludes with the local townspeople surrounding the lycanthropic lead on the bridge of Big Bear Dam. *Sabretooth*, a 2002 Big Bear creature feature, resurrects a prehistoric tiger that roams the woods.

Several low-budget bigfoot comedies were shot in Big Bear Village, including *Little Bigfoot* and *They Call Him Sasquatch*, starring Neal McDonough and Garry Marshall.

Perhaps the most malevolent denizen of Big Bear is the titular fiend from the popular direct-to-video "chiller" *Jack Frost* (1997). The film's serial killer is reincarnated as a snowman and terrorizes Big Bear's North Shore town of Fawnskin. In the most memorable scene, the incredible melting snowman shares a sinister bath with future *American Pie* star Shannon Elizabeth.

## WHERE TO HOLD A RETREAT

## CEDAR LAKE CAMP AND CONFERENCE CENTER

Originally known as Bartlett's Lake, this resort covered 3.5 acres when it opened in 1929. The man-made pond at Cedar Lake is one of those familiar cinematic bodies of water that appears in several outdoor adventures, including *The Royal Mounted Patrol, Trail of the Yukon,* and *Call of the Klondike*. A mill set was built here for *The Trail of the Lonesome Pine* and has been reused in such pictures as *The Shepherd of the Hills* (with John Wayne), and *High Sierra*, where it plays Shaw's Camp, the destination where Humphrey Bogart has a rendezvous with Arthur Kennedy, caretaker Willie Best, and Ida Lupino.

In *Kissin' Cousins*, returning air force serviceman Elvis Presley cavorts by the mill's waterwheel with Smokey Mountain babes Pamela Austin and Yvonne Craig

Marc Wanamaker/Bison Archives

Humphrey Bogart
and Ida Lupino at
Cedar Lake in *High
Sierra*.

(TV's "Batgirl") and croons "One Boy, Two Little Girls." In *North to Alaska*, John Wayne participates in a tree-climbing contest and picnic by the lake.

Cedar Lake appears in two different 1970s boxing movies as a mountain get-away: *The Great White Hope*, with James Earl Jones and Jane Alexander, and *The Main Event*, with Barbra Streisand and Ryan O'Neal. Cedar Lake is now home to a private Christian retreat center. *Scheduling Info: 909-866-5714.*

## HOW TO GET TO BIG BEAR

*Take I-10 East to Redlands. Take the Highway 30 exit (*RUNNING SPRINGS*) and continue 3 miles to Highway 330. Take the* MOUNTAIN RESORTS/BIG BEAR LAKE *exit. Follow the signs to Big Bear, 27.5 miles into the mountains.*

## DVD ITINERARY: BIG BEAR LAKE

*The Parent Trap* (1961), Scenes 2, 4 and 21–22

*Dr. Dolittle 2*, Scenes 11 and 16–17

*Paint Your Wagon*, Scene 9

*The Birth of a Nation*, Scene 28

## THEY WENT "HATHAWAY":
## CAPTURING THE COLOR OF CALIFORNIA

"Nobody does tough outdoor action better than Henry Hathaway," states Turner Classic Movies host and film historian Robert Osborne. Directors like John Ford, Howard Hawks, William Wellman, Henry King, Raoul Walsh, Anthony Mann, King Vidor, and Sam Peckinpah created memorable cinematic images of the West, but none of them came close to matching California native Hathaway's flair for capturing the Golden State's visual splendor.

His Westerns, war movies and action-adventure pictures—starring the likes of John Wayne, Gary Cooper, Randolph Scott, and Steve McQueen—play like picturesque showcases for the state's geographical diversity.

Hathaway earned a footnote in film history for bringing to life the first three-strip Technicolor feature shot outdoors. It was for the 1936 family feud saga set in the Blue Ridge Mountains called *The Trail of the Lonesome Pine*, starring Fred MacMurray, Henry Fonda, and Sylvia Sidney. The film was shot at Big Bear's Cedar Lake and marked the first of the director's many visits to the area. Years later, Hathaway would make the most of another motion picture breakthrough when he used the three-panel Cinerama widescreen format for his segments of the epic *How the West Was Won*.

"He clearly enjoyed working in the outdoors and exploring new scenery," recalled the late Big Bear historian Tom Core, who helped build the mill set for Hathaway's *Trail*. "This was a guy who seemed to thrive in the mountain air." Among Hathaway's favorite locations:

- **Alabama Hills and Mt. Whitney**
  *The Thundering Herd, The Lives of a Bengal Lancer, Rawhide, How the West Was Won, From Hell to Texas, North to Alaska, Brigham Young*

- **Anza-Borrego Desert State Park**
  *The Desert Fox*

- **Big Bear**
  *The Trail of the Lonesome Pine, The Shepherd of the Hills, Brigham Young, Peter Ibbetson, To the Last Man, North to Alaska*

- **Convict Lake**
  *How the West Was Won, Nevada Smith*

- **Hot Creek**
  *North to Alaska, Nevada Smith, True Grit*

- **Lake Arrowhead**
  *Now and Forever (1934), Spawn of the North*

- **Red Rock Canyon**
  *Wild Horse Mesa, Heritage of the Desert*

To learn more about the director, read *Henry Hathaway: A Director's Guild of America Oral History*, edited and annotated by Rudy Behlmer, with interviews conducted by Polly Platt. Scarecrow Press, 2001.

Marc Wanamaker/Bison Archives

California's great outdoors director Henry Hathaway with *True Grit*'s Kim Darby.

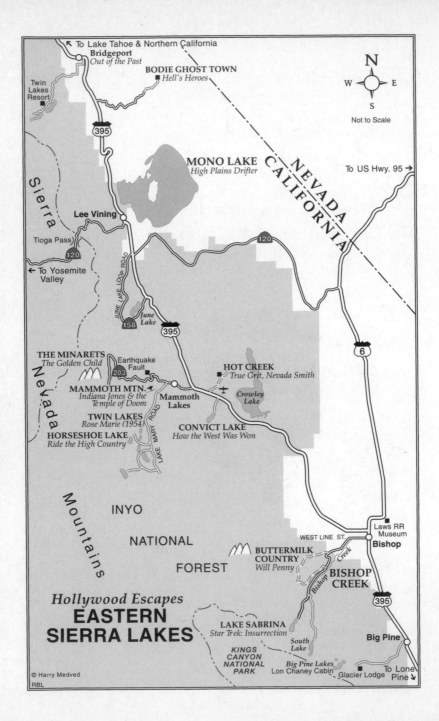

To Lake Tahoe & Northern California →

**Bridgeport**
*Out of the Past*

**BODIE GHOST TOWN**
■ *Hell's Heroes*

Twin Lakes Resort

395

N
W   E
S

*Not to Scale*

**MONO LAKE**
*High Plains Drifter*

NEVADA
CALIFORNIA

To US Hwy. 95 →

Sierra

**Lee Vining**

Tioga Pass

120

← To Yosemite Valley

120

JUNE LAKE LOOP ROAD

*June Lake*

158

395

6

**THE MINARETS**
*The Golden Child*

Earthquake Fault

203

**HOT CREEK**
■ *True Grit, Nevada Smith*

**MAMMOTH MTN.**
*Indiana Jones & the Temple of Doom*

**Mammoth Lakes**

*Crowley Lake*

**TWIN LAKES**
*Rose Marie (1954)*

**CONVICT LAKE**
*How the West Was Won*

**HORSESHOE LAKE**
*Ride the High Country*

LAKE MARY ROAD

Nevada

**INYO**

**NATIONAL**

**FOREST**

Mountains

Laws RR Museum

WEST LINE ST.

**Bishop**

**BUTTERMILK COUNTRY**
*Will Penny*

Bishop Creek

**BISHOP CREEK**

395

*Hollywood Escapes*
**EASTERN SIERRA LAKES**

**LAKE SABRINA**
*Star Trek: Insurrection*

South Lake

**KINGS CANYON NATIONAL PARK**

*Big Pine Lakes*
Lon Chaney Cabin

Glacier Lodge

**Big Pine**

To Lone Pine ↓

© Harry Medved

RBL

# 56

# BISHOP CREEK AND LAKE SABRINA
## Inyo Dreams

> With its jagged peaks and unearthly blue waters, Lake Sabrina is a perfectly fantastic alien landscape.
>
> —*Michael Neale, location manager for* Star Trek: Insurrection *(1998)*

**MAJOR ROLES:** *Star Trek: Insurrection, Will Penny, Nevada Smith*

### BEHIND THE SCENERY

Many tourists know the town of Bishop as a quick stopover on the way to Yosemite; especially popular is the Schats Bakery with its famed Sheepherder Bread. Fans of 1970s biopics may recognize Bishop as the home of tragically disabled skier Jill Kinmont, as the town played itself in *The Other Side of the Mountain Part 2*. But outdoor enthusiasts know Bishop as a point of departure for Bishop Creek, home to some of the best trout fishing in the Sierras and many national forest designations including the Ansel Adams Wilderness, John Muir Wilderness, and Inyo National Forest.

In the 1960s and 1970s, Inyo National Forest often received a prominent on-screen credit on such films as *Ride the High Country, How the West Was Won,* and *High Plains Drifter*.

Many of the most breathtaking parts of the Inyo Forest are located in the Bishop Creek vicinity. In their sheer beauty and tranquility, these trails and hideaways easily rank among the finest locations in the Eastern Sierras.

## WHERE TO HIKE

### Top Billing: LAKE SABRINA

This sensational and easily accessible destination will please hikers and fishermen alike. The dramatic peaks above sparkling blue Sabrina serve as the Ba'ku refuge in *Star Trek: Insurrection*. According to location manager Michael Neale, the cast and crew were helicoptered to the mountaintop location. Hikers will want to use Sabrina as a trailhead for a 6.2-mile round-trip to Blue Lake.

*HOW TO GET TO LAKE SABRINA From Highway 395 in Bishop, head west on Highway 168/Line Street. Follow the road as it leaves town and climbs toward the Sierras. Drive 18.8 miles to the Sabrina Basin Trail. You'll find boat rentals and a snack bar at the lake. If you need to rent fishing equipment, stop at Bishop Creek Lodge along the way.*

## WHERE TO EXPLORE

### BUTTERMILK COUNTRY WILDLIFE AREA

A graded dirt road in Bishop Creek Canyon leads to a cluster of strange-looking boulders made famous by Ansel Adams' photographs. The name "Buttermilk Country" refers to a 1870s dairy that used to operate here. Today the Buttermilk rocks are a popular spot for bouldering. It's among these huge stones that Henry Fonda is caught in a shoot-out in *The Return of Frank James*. Years later, Bruce Dern and Donald Pleasence ambush and torture Charlton Heston here in Tom Gries' elegiac 1968 Western, *Will Penny*. Despite its brutal cinematic heritage, Buttermilk is a beautiful springtime destination for wildflower viewing.

*HOW TO GET TO BUTTERMILK COUNTRY From Highway 395 in Bishop, head west on Highway 168/Line Street. At 7.3 miles, look for Buttermilk Road on your right. It crosses a cattle guard and turns into a dirtroad after leaving the highway. Stay on the maintained gravel road. At 3.5 miles you'll reach another cattle guard and get your first look at the Buttermilk's Peabody Boulders. Park here, because after this point the road becomes extremely rough.*

## WHERE TO EAT

### BISHOP CREEK LODGE

This roadside diner, cabin complex, and general store on Highway 168 is a good place to stock up on supplies, rent fishing gear, and get a quick bite on the way to the lakes. *2100 South Lake Road; 760-873-4484.*

## WHERE TO STAY

### PARCHERS RESORT

Parchers is a collection of small cabins tucked away among the lodgepole pines and aspens of the High Sierras. Twenty-five minutes from the town of

Bishop (on Highway 168), these accommodations are the most scenic in Bishop Creek Canyon. Breathtaking Lake Sabrina and South Lake are nearby. A country café is located on the property. *Near the end of South Lake Road; www.parchessresort.net; 760-873-4177.*

## DETOUR:
## LON CHANEY'S PHANTOM HIDEAWAY

Lon Chaney Sr. was best known as the star of such classic silent horror films as *The Phantom of the Opera, The Hunchback of Notre Dame,* and *The Unholy Three.* But when not behind the mask, he enjoyed escaping to the Sierras for the summer. In the late 1920s, Chaney built a river rock cabin for his fishing expeditions in Big Pine Lakes. It became such an essential part of his life that the rustic home was re-created on the Universal backlot for the 1957 biopic *Man of a Thousand Faces,* starring James Cagney as Chaney.

　　Chaney's real-life stone cabin still stands today, now used for storage by the forest service. "The Chaney Cabin is a fascinating bit of Hollywood history and one of the most intriguing structures in the High Sierras," says travel writer Matthew Jaffe of *Sunset Magazine.* "For Chaney to build a cabin all the way up here, you get the sense that he really wanted to get as far from Hollywood as possible."

Richard Koszarski Archives

Director
Erich von Stroheim
scouting locations
near Big Pine Lakes.

To reach the Chaney Cabin, you'll need to hike along a steep trail starting at the Big Pine Lakes Trailhead at 7,750 feet. At 3 miles, you'll find Chaney's home along the creek.

Though you can't stay overnight at the Chaney Cabin, you *can* stay overnight at **Glacier Lodge** (760-938-2837), right near the trailhead, which figured prominently in the life of another silent screen legend, martinet director Erich von Stroheim. He shot scenes (with Fay Wray) at the lodge and in Big Pine Lakes for his Viennese spectacle *The Wedding March,* according to the *Big Pine Progress-Citizen* newspaper in 1926. The footage, however, ended up in the movie's long-lost sequel, *The Honeymoon.*

*HOW TO GET TO THE BIG PINE LAKES TRAILHEAD Take Highway 395 to the town of Big Pine. From the traffic light in the center of town look for the signs for Big Pine Creek and turn onto Crocker Street. Continue west as Crocker becomes Glacier Lodge Road. You'll reach road's end and Big Pine trailhead in 10.6 miles. For more info, call Inyo National Forest at 760-873-2500.*

## HOW TO GET TO BISHOP CREEK AND LAKE SABRINA

*Take Highway 395 to Bishop. Make a left at Highway 168 and follow the road for 17 miles to Lake Sabrina.*

## DVD ITINERARY: BISHOP CREEK AND LAKE SABRINA

*Star Trek: Insurrection*, Lake Sabrina, Scene 18

*Will Penny*, Buttermilk Country, Scene 7

# 57

# MAMMOTH LAKES
# Ride the High Country

In all the stirring legends of the frontier West, there is none as exciting as the reckless saga of the men who pushed the last outposts of civilization across the Sierra Nevadas . . .

—*Theatrical trailer for Sam Peckinpah's* Ride the High Country *(1962)*

**MAJOR ROLES:** *Indiana Jones and the Temple of Doom, Ride the High Country, True Grit*

## BEHIND THE SCENERY

The Mammoth Lakes region is a good five-and-a-half-hour drive from L.A. production companies and tourists can certainly find mountains closer to Hollywood, so why head to Mammoth? Easy. There's nothing quite as awe-inspiring as this high mountain region in the Eastern Sierras, where you'll find over 100 lakes surrounded by craggy ridges, endless pine forests, and a world-class ski resort.

Hollywood came to ski Mammoth Mountain in the 1940s, with Claudette Colbert, Tyrone Power, and Henry Fonda as frequent guests. Moviemakers who came to Mammoth cast the mountain as a closer-to-home stand-in for Tibet, Nepal, Switzerland, Austria, Alaska, New England, and the Rockies.

In the 1960s, Mammoth became a popular location for six-shooting dramas, as Paramount Pictures filmed major sequences from three classic westerns here: *Nevada Smith, Will Penny,* and *True Grit.*

Productions continue to shoot among the snowy mountains and lakes, including commercials and features like the Ben Affleck comedy *Surviving Christmas*. Today Mammoth's high-end complex, the Village, continues to bring the Hollywood crowd to the slopes.

## WHERE TO EXPLORE

### MAMMOTH MOUNTAIN

Twenty-five hundred miles of skiing and snowboarding trails twist and turn within the Mammoth Mountain Ski Area. In the summertime, when the area becomes the Mammoth Adventure Center, mountain bikers can take the gondola to the top and use the trails to cycle down the mountain. Films with snowy sequences shot in the ski area include *Return to Peyton Place, Caprice, The Other Side of the Mountain, Perfect*, and *Indiana Jones and the Temple of Doom*, in which Harrison Ford, Kate Capshaw, and youngster Ke Huy Quan take a wild ride down the mountain in an inflatable life raft. *www.mammothmountain.com;* 800-*MAMMOTH.*

Harry Medved

Horseshoe Lake, seen in Sam Peckinpah's *Ride the High Country*.

## EARTHQUAKE FAULT
This unusual geological phenomenon will appeal to kids of all ages and can be found on the road to Mammoth Mountain Ski Area. The earth is literally split asunder here, creating an impressive sixty-foot-deep gorge where the two sides would fit together like a jigsaw puzzle if closed. Troop leader Shelley Long leads her girls across a log precariously spanning the fault in *Troop Beverly Hills*.

## HORSESHOE LAKE
Just past the Twin Falls Picnic Area is this lake with a wide beach seen in Sam Peckinpah's *Ride the High Country*. It appears in the opening credits and in scenes with Randolph Scott, Joel McCrea, Ronald Starr, and young Mariette Hartley. In the 1954 *Rose Marie* remake, Horseshoe is the setting for a Native American teepee village. The lake features a campground, picnic areas, and hiking and biking trails.

### Top Billing: HOT CREEK
A popular natural spa for Mammoth visitors, Hot Creek produces steam formed by a bubbling underground hot spring that reacts with the creek's ice-cold waters. In the 1960s, three classics were shot here by outdoor adventure director Henry Hathaway. In *North to Alaska*, John Wayne brings French showgirl Capucine to a cabin by the creek's warm waters. Hot Creek is where *Nevada Smith*, played by Steve McQueen, meets mentor Brian Keith and where he later engages in a climactic shoot-out with bad guy Karl Malden. "It was hot as hell down there," remembers Loren Janes, McQueen's stunt double, "but Henry really loved that place." For *True Grit*, Hathaway brought John Wayne back to Hot Creek and directed a performance that would earn the Duke his Academy Award. This time around, Wayne, Glen Campbell, and Kim Darby encounter bad guys Jeremy Slate, Dennis Hopper, and Robert Duvall along Hot Creek's banks.

Hikers, skiers, and filmmakers cautiously enjoy Hot Creek's waters.

Greg Tucker

*HOW TO GET TO HOT CREEK Three miles east of Highway 395 via Long Valley Airport Road, Hot Creek is a twenty-minute drive from Mammoth Lakes, next to the Mammoth-Yosemite airport. Open sunrise to sunset.*

## WHERE TO PICNIC

### TWIN FALLS PICNIC AREA

From the picnic area at the top of Twin Falls you'll get a sweeping view of **Twin Lakes** in the magnificent valley below. This is where Robert Young declares his love to Joan Crawford in Dorothy Arzner's *The Bride Wore Red*. Joel McCrea and Randolph Scott walk their horses here in *Ride the High Country*. Canadian Mountie Howard Keel meets Indian girl Ann Blyth at Twin Falls and later at the picnic area in *Rose Marie*. And on the other side of the highway is **Lake Mamie,** briefly seen in *The Long, Long Trailer*, with Lucille Ball and Desi Arnaz.

### THE MAMMOTH MUSEUM

This 1920s log cabin houses the Southern Mono Historical Society. A grassy lawn and tables along Mammoth Creek make it an ideal picnic spot. Horseback riding is available at the nearby **Sierra Meadows Ranch,** a *Nevada Smith* location surrounded by majestic green mountains. 760-934-6918.

## WHERE TO EAT

### THE RESTAURANT AT CONVICT LAKE

It's a twenty-minute drive from downtown Mammoth Lakes, but the Restaurant at Convict Lake offers some of the finest cuisine in the area. The lake itself is a scenic highlight and can be seen in *Nevada Smith* (where Brian Keith teaches Steve McQueen how to play cards) and in the opening of *How the West Was Won* (as the site of a Native American village visited by mountain man James Stewart). Because of its lower elevation in the hot Owens Valley during the summer, Convict Lake is best enjoyed during the cooler evening hours. 760-934-3803.

## WHERE TO STAY

### TAMARACK LODGE, TWIN LAKES

Although you can find plenty of chain hotels and fashionable condos in downtown Mammoth, the most scenic accommodations are in the hills along Lake Mary Road, a short drive from the city limits. Great cabin lodging can be found at **Woods Lodge** on Lake George, **Wildyrie Resort** on Lake Mamie, and **Crystal Crag Lodge** on Lake Mary. (See *www.visitmammoth.com* for details.)

Of all the cabin accommodations, **Tamarack Lodge** is the most expansive. Tamarack has its own fine-dining restaurant, general store, and main lodge building with a large stone fireplace. The lodge was built in the 1920s by Mary Foy, member of the famed show biz family depicted in the Bob Hope musical biopic *The Seven Little Foys*. Many of the family's Hollywood friends would later come to visit. From the lodge, short hikes take you to scenic Panorama Dome or to the base of Twin Falls. *Twin Lakes Road at Lake Mary Road; www.tamaracklodge.com; 800-626-6684 or 760-934-2442.*

## HOW TO GET TO MAMMOTH LAKES

*Take I-5 North to Highway 14 to the town of Mojave. Continue on 14 until its intersection with Highway 395. Take 395 North for approximately 170 miles to the Mammoth Lakes turnoff (Highway 203).*

## DVD ITINERARY: MAMMOTH LAKES

*Ride the High Country*, Horseshoe Lake, Scene 9

*How the West Was Won*, Convict Lake, Scene 3

*True Grit*, Hot Creek, Scenes 6–7

# 58

# MONO LAKE
# High Plains Drama

Mono Lake has a weird look to it, a lot of strange colors—never looks the same way twice during the day.

—*Clint Eastwood in* Film Comment Magazine, *Jan.–Feb. 1978*

**MAJOR ROLES:** *High Plains Drifter, Fair Wind to Java*

### BEHIND THE SCENERY

Over three hundred miles away from Los Angeles, the haunting environs of Mono Lake (one of the oldest lakes in the Western hemisphere) feel like another world. In fact, in his 1860s memoirs *Roughing It,* Mark Twain recalls the lake as a "lonely tenant of the loneliest spot on earth" and "one of the strangest freaks of nature in any land."

Mono Lake took on an even more bizarre look after Los Angeles started diverting the lake's fresh water sources in 1941, thus revealing more of Mono's strangely shaped, brine-covered *tufa* formations similar to the Trona Pinnacles.

In 1953, Republic Pictures deemed the area suitably exotic and created prop volcanoes on several Mono Lake islets for the Fred MacMurray/Vera Ralston adventure *Fair Wind to Java.* Today these small islands are called *Krakatoa* and *Java* in memory of the movie and, according to park ranger Janet Carle, the decaying remnants of the wooden volcanoes are still there.

By the time Clint Eastwood used Mono Lake as the prime location for *High Plains Drifter* in the early 1970s, the lake had dropped thirty feet. Since 1978, environmental groups have helped save the incredible shrinking lake. Thankfully, their efforts are ongoing.

## WHERE TO EXPLORE

### Top Billing: MONO LAKE'S SOUTH SHORE

Due to the water's high salt content (three times that of the ocean), adventurous swimmers can float Dead Sea–style in Mono Lake. Terrestrial explorers, however, may prefer to take the boardwalk trail in the **South Tufa Area**. This is where production designer Henry Bumstead built a complete Western town, including interior sets, for Clint Eastwood's eerie 1973 Western *High Plains Drifter*. Though the town is initially known as "Lago," by the film's climax Eastwood's vengeful character literally has painted the town red and renamed it "Hell." (The town was dismantled after production.) Visitors should keep in mind that summer temperatures at Mono Lake can be infernal.

Perhaps the best way to experience Mono Lake is via a naturalist-guided canoe trip highlighting Mono's natural springs, migrating birds, and crystalline waters. Tours are offered on summer weekend mornings.

*Mono Basin Scenic Area Visitors Center: 760-647-3044; Canoe Tour info and reservations: 760-647-6595.*

## BRIDGEPORT

Twenty minutes north of Mono Lake is a small but picturesque mountain town that appears to have been frozen in time, rarely seen except in old movies. In fact, Bridgeport was one of the main locales in Jacques Tourneur's classic 1947 film noir *Out of the Past*. As the film opens, it's Bridgeport that Robert Mitchum has chosen as the place to start a new life, far away from crime.

Many of the film's Main Street exteriors are still standing, including the 1880s courthouse. The adjacent building doubled as the town café. "It was a charming little place," recalls Dick Moore, who plays a mute attendant at Mitchum's gas station. "The locals were very excited when Hollywood came to town."

Bridgeport hasn't been used much by Hollywood since that time, although actor Jesse Vint remembers the town fondly from when he worked on the 1979 motorcycle action-comedy *Fast Charlie the Moonbeam Rider*, starring David Carradine. "I love this part of California for its history and remoteness," recalls Vint. "I still come here on vacation with my son to get away from it all."

*HOW TO GET TO BRIDGEPORT From Mono Lake, head 25 miles north on Highway 395. Info: Bridgeport Chamber of Commerce: 760-932-7500.*

## BODIE GHOST TOWN

A forty-five-minute drive from Mono Lake takes you to California's largest ghost town, a State Historic Park eerily preserved in a state of perpetual decay. Director William Wyler shot one of his early films here in 1930: *Hell's Heroes*, a precursor to *Three Godfathers*, stars Charles Bickford and uses Bodie as a

Greg Tucker

The bizarre *tufa* formations at Mono Lake give it an otherworldly aura.

Western town called New Jerusalem. A fire tore through Bodie after the film was completed, so Wyler's picture remains a cinematic record of the town's onetime guise. Bodie still has an old jail, church, and saloons, but there's no shade and no operating stores, so bring plenty of water and supplies for your visit.

*HOW TO GET TO BODIE From Mono Lake, head 13 miles north on Highway 395 to Highway 270. Take 270 for 10 miles until the paved road ends. Continue on the unpaved road for 3 more miles. www.bodie.com.*

## WHERE TO EAT

### TIOGA GAS MART, LEE VINING

Although a gas station isn't exactly the first place that comes to mind when you're looking for a gourmet restaurant, the Mart's "Whoa Nellie Deli" is the exception. The menu includes fish tacos, grilled salmon salad, and herb-crusted pork tenderloin. An outdoor patio and play area provide a terrific view of Mono Lake. *22 Vista Point Road, near the intersection of Highway 120 West and Highway 395; www.thesierraweb.com/tiogagasmart; 760-647-1088.*

### THE MONO INN AT MONO LAKE

This Lee Vining dining option offers California cuisine close to Mono Lake's shores. The Inn is run by Sarah Adams, granddaughter of legendary photographer Ansel Adams. The Lakeview Lounge features classic Adams photos, rustic Stickley furniture, and outstanding views of the lake. *Reservations recommended. www.monoinn.com; 760-647-6581.*

## WHERE TO STAY

### TWIN LAKES RESORT
Not to be confused with Mammoth's Twin Lakes, this popular fishing destination is located on Lower Twin Lake in Toiyabe National Forest, an hour northwest of Mono Lake. In *Out of the Past,* former criminal Robert Mitchum courts nice girl Virginia Huston at Twin Lakes. *www.lowertwinlakeresort.com; 877-932-7751.*

### THE LAKEVIEW LODGE
Those seeking lodging closer to Mono Lake may prefer this recently remodeled Lee Vining motel that features a comfy espresso bar. Most rooms, as the name suggests, offer lake vistas. *30 Main Street; www.bwlakeviewlodge.com; 760-647-6543.*

Lucas Illing

Mark Twain claimed Mono Lake's rugged location, beneath the Sierras, was "the loneliest spot on Earth."

# CLINT EASTWOOD'S OUTDOOR CALIFORNIA

Long before he became state park commissioner, Clint Eastwood was well known for his passionate stance on environmental issues and maintaining California wilderness areas. This is reflected both in his films (e.g., *Pale Rider*'s strip mining scenario) and in his private interests. (His Mission Ranch property has preserved wetlands and meadows by the Carmel River.) Not by coincidence, his production company, Malpaso, is named after a creek in the Big Sur region.

"Clint loves California's landscape," says the actor-director's longtime collaborator, Oscar-winning production designer Henry Bumstead. "He has a knack for the classic look of Western pictures." In addition to *High Plains Drifter*'s Mono Lake, a fistful of picturesque Golden State locations have played significant roles in Eastwood's work:

### Alabama Hills: JOE KIDD
These ancient rocks near the town of Lone Pine provide a rugged backdrop as Eastwood is caught in a New Mexico range war between Robert Duvall and John Saxon. Specific locations include the terrain just east of Movie Road (including iconic Gene Autry Rock) and the Sage Flats to the west of Horseshoe Meadow Road.

### Alcatraz Island: ESCAPE FROM ALCATRAZ
Several years after shooting the climax of *The Enforcer* (his third *Dirty Harry* outing) on the infamous island, Eastwood reportedly kept visiting tourists happy (and quiet) by signing autographs while he and director Don Siegel filmed this taut and tense tale based on a real-life 1962 prison break.

### Carmel River State Beach: PLAY MISTY FOR ME
Before being menaced by psychopathic Jessica Walter, Eastwood and Donna Mills question the future of their relationship as they stroll along this cypress-laden beach in the Carmel/Big Sur area. Eastwood speeds across the iconic Bixby Bridge in the opening credits.

## Columbia Historic State Park and Jamestown's
## Sierra Railroad: PALE RIDER

Columbia, a well-preserved Western town, and Jamestown's Sierra Railroad are visited by preacher Eastwood before he lays down his collar and picks up his six-shooters. Incidentally, both locations previously appeared in Fred Zinnemann's classic *High Noon,* an acknowledged Eastwood favorite.

## Feather River: THE OUTLAW JOSEY WALES

Northern California's Gold Country river stands in for a Missouri territory waterway where eagle-eyed marksman Eastwood foils his pursuers (led by John Vernon and Bill McKinney) by disabling a ferry with one high-powered rifle shot.

Marc Wanamaker/Bison Archives

*Drifter's* Eastwood (with Verna Bloom) offers a humorous tribute to his mentor at Mono Lake.

### Hat Creek: FIREFOX

A rustic cabin nestled in the Northern California wilderness provides the perfect hideaway for reclusive, combat-shaken Vietnam vet pilot Eastwood . . . until the military comes calling for a mission only he can accomplish.

### Lucerne Dry Lake: SPACE COWBOYS

In the film's black-and-white prologue, the young incarnations of Eastwood, Tommy Lee Jones, Donald Sutherland, and James Garner test jet aircraft at this classic location.

### Land's End: SUDDEN IMPACT

Vigilante Sondra Locke claims her first victim at this secluded seaside overlook with a perfect view of the Golden Gate Bridge. It's also where Eastwood later growls the immortal line, "Nobody, I mean *nobody* puts ketchup on a hotdog!"

### Yosemite National Park: THE EIGER SANCTION

Though he did not shoot in Yosemite, Eastwood trained at the park's mountaineering school to prepare for *Eiger*'s extensive rock-climbing sequences in the Alps.

## HOW TO GET TO MONO LAKE

*Take 1-5 North to Highway 14 to the town of Mojave. Continue on 14 until it joins Highway 395. At 20 miles past Mammoth Lakes, turn right on Highway 120 and follow the signs to Mono Lake's South Tufa area. www.monolake.org.*

## DVD ITINERARY: MONO LAKE

*High Plains Drifter*, Mono Lake, Scenes 1, 8, and 12–13

*Out of the Past*, Bridgeport, Scenes 1, 2, and 26–27
Lower Twin Lake, Scene 3

# 59

# THE KERN RIVER
## Untamed Water

It's too deep! . . . I can't cross here! This is like Niagara Falls!

—*Phil Silvers, trying to cross the Kern River in* It's a Mad, Mad, Mad, Mad World *(1963)*

**MAJOR ROLES**: *The Treasure of the Sierra Madre, Stagecoach, Saboteur, The Defiant Ones, Short Cuts*

## BEHIND THE SCENERY

The closest whitewater river to Los Angeles is a prime destination for fishermen, picnickers, and rafters seeking thrills along the rapids. The Kern has also long been a prime location for cinematic jeopardy. According to historian Harold Zinkin, stuntman Russell Saunders (doubling for cop-evading hero Robert Cummings) made a classic jump into the Kern for Alfred Hitchcock's suspenser *Saboteur* in 1942. The Kern is also featured in the Sidney Poitier/Tony Curtis chase drama, *The Defiant Ones,* in which the chained-together inmates try to cross the river. Stuntman Bob Hoy, who doubled for Curtis, considered his river stunt the most dangerous in his career. "The current was moving along at about six knots," Hoy told the press. "There were many outcroppings and rocks, some of them below the water . . . there was no element of control. All we could do was try to stay alive, but it all looked great on film."

Perhaps the darkest moment in Kern film history occurs in Robert Altman's *Short Cuts*. In a morbid passage, Fred Ward, Huey Lewis, and Buck Henry go fishing and discover a dead nude woman in the Kern. Realizing their trip will be ruined if they report the fatality, they keep on fishing.

Marc Wanamaker/Bison Archives

John Ford's *Stagecoach* makes a Kern River Crossing.

A lighter Kern River trip is made by comedian Phil Silvers, whose convertible sinks in the too-deep waters in *It's a Mad, Mad, Mad, Mad World*, thanks to the misguided directions of a local miner's kid. You, however, can take the dry land route that follows the river, as the winding Highway 178 parallels the Kern for many miles.

## HOW TO SEE THE RIVER

### SIERRA SOUTH PADDLE SPORTS

There are many rafting companies in Kernville offering whitewater trips along the Kern. Sierra South specializes in short and affordable Class II and III trips for beginners. Its staff has worked behind the scenes on locations for *Jurassic Park III* and *K-PAX*. *Reservations required. 11300 Kernville Road; www.sierrasouth.com; 800-457-2082.*

## WHERE TO EXPLORE

### KERN VALLEY MUSEUM

This Kernville museum is a good place to soak up local history and get your bearings. The historical society has put together an entire gallery devoted to the movies shot in the area, featuring photos of the stars and news clippings about location filming. A rusty old stagecoach, purported to be from the classic John Wayne movie of the same name, is on display in their courtyard. *Call for hours. 49 Big Blue Road, next to the post office; open Thursday–Sunday; 760-376-6683.*

## WHATEVER HAPPENED TO "OLD KERNVILLE"?

The Southern Sierra town of Kernville used to be a hotbed of B Western filming activity. An entire false-front "Movie Street" was built here in the 1920s to accommodate the demand. This set was located in a part of town known as Old Kernville, on which the likes of John Wayne, Harry Carey Sr., Hoot Gibson, William "Hopalong Cassidy" Boyd, Gene Autry, and many others traded gunfire with the bad guys. As *The New York Times* surmised, "more catsup blood was spilled there than perhaps in any other place in the country."

When the cameras weren't rolling in the 1930s and early '40s, the stars typically mingled with the Kernville locals. "We kids would play baseball with the movie team," recalled late local historian Bob Powers, author of *Kern River Country*. "Roy Rogers would pitch and Andy Devine would umpire. I never got an autograph, isn't that awful? But I did get to dance with Dale Evans one time. We thought those days would never end."

But end they did. In 1943, the United States Army decided to buy Movie Street for $1,500. According to the *Kern Valley Sun*, "The false fronts were dismantled and moved out into the (Mojave) desert where they were rebuilt and used as bombing targets. Many a sack of flour descended upon those ghosts of the past."

While Movie Street was eventually blown to smithereens, the rest of the Old Kernville neighborhood suffered an equally ignominious fate. When the Kern was dammed to create Lake Isabella in 1948, buildings like the old school house were submerged underwater. But ghostlike vestiges persist. According to *The Bakersfield Californian*, "Foundations of Old Kernville are still visible today when the lake level is low."

## KEYSVILLE ON THE KERN

Movie fans who want to see where John Ford's *Stagecoach* made a river crossing on its way to Lordsburg can head to the Keysville part of the river, just south of Lake Isabella. Keysville is a quarter of a mile below the dam, where the highway crosses the river, according to Bob Powers. "A truck helped pull the stage team across the river for this scene but it was hidden off camera," recalled Powers. "Wayne was friendly to all of us kids, and he became a town hero after that picture."

## JOHNSONDALE BRIDGE

The scenic River Trail originates below this bridge, in the same canyon where Universal shot the pteranodon chase in *Jurassic Park III*, featuring Tea Leoni, William H. Macy, and Sam Neill. According to the *Kern Valley Sun*, this is the section of the river where Tony Curtis and Sidney Poitier battle the rapids in *The Defiant Ones. Hiking info: 760-376-3781.*

## WHERE TO EAT

## EWING'S ON THE KERN

This landmark Kernville restaurant is easily identified by its vintage 1954 marquee. Tab Hunter and Natalie Wood dined and danced here and posed for publicity photos while on location for the Warner Bros. Western *The Burning Hills.* Request a table on the balcony facing the Kern. *125 Buena Vista; 760-376-2411.*

## WHERE TO STAY

## RANKIN RANCH, WALKER'S BASIN

Many "Marlboro Country" commercials were shot at this family-friendly, *City Slickers*–style resort. It has also been a working 31,000-acre cattle ranch since 1863. Nestled in Walker's Basin, a beautiful hidden valley with endless meadows, the ranch has been run by the same family for 140 years. *Box 36, Caliente, California 93518; www.rankinranch.com; 661-867-2511.*

## WHISPERING PINES LODGE

Locals claim Barbra Streisand and husband James Brolin honeymooned in Room 116 at this motel, but then innkeeper sightings of the California couple are as frequent as those of Gable (who Brolin once played) and Lombard. The riverview rooms are your best option. *13745 Sierra Way, Kernville; www.kern-valley.com/inns; 760-376-3733.*

## KERNVILLE'S TRAIL TO THE "SIERRA MADRE"

John Huston's classic *The Treasure of the Sierra Madre* was set in Mexico's Sierra *Madre* Mountains, and was partially shot in California's Sierra *Nevada* Mountains over a twenty-two day period in 1947.

To create an authentic prospector camp, Warner Bros. built a mineshaft and sluice gates below the 3,000-foot-elevation Harley Mine near the Cannell Meadow Trail. This is where Humphrey Bogart, Walter Huston, and Tim Holt discover gold in the mountains and encounter the infamous Mexican banditos who don't need any "stinkin' badges." According to *Bogart* coauthor Eric Lax on the film's DVD commentary, the Kernville area also provided locations for the gila monster and mining sequences. The Kern Valley Museum's Marge Powers recalls watching the action on the set when her father worked at nearby Camp Owen. Almost sixty years later she still walks to the mountain location for fun.

If you are interested in hiking this region, be advised that a summer visit isn't recommended, as the intense heat is as dangerous as Bogart's "gold fever." *The Cannell Trail begins at the horse corrals two miles north of Kernville on State Mountain 99. For hiking info, call the Cannell Meadow Ranger District at 760-376-3781.*

### HOW TO GET TO THE KERN RIVER

*Take I-5 North to Highway 99 to Bakersfield. Take the 178 turnoff and follow the signs to Lake Isabella/Kernville.*

### DVD ITINERARY: KERN RIVER

*The Defiant Ones,* Scene 4

*Stagecoach* (1939), Scene 15

*The Treasure of the Sierra Madre,* Scene 15

# 60

# FRANKLIN CANYON
## Beyond Beverly Hills

Hollywood's favorite lakeside forest is no farther than the
industry's favorite watering holes.

—*Diane Isaacs, Franklin Canyon's film historian/docent*

**MAJOR ROLES:** *The Manchurian Candidate (1962),
It Happened One Night*

### BEHIND THE SCENERY

Tucked away in the canyons behind the Beverly Hills Hotel is this peaceful retreat that many Angelenos may not realize exists. Yet they know it from a
memorable TV series opening in which a sheriff and his young son skip rocks
on a pond to the tune of a whistling theme song. The series? *The Andy Griffith
Show*, costarring a young Ron Howard. The location? Franklin Canyon.

Oil baron Edward Doheny, who also built Greystone Mansion in Beverly
Hills, long ago decided to preserve this ranchland as a family retreat. Thus,
while the rest of Beverly Hills has been developed, this parcel has remained
rustic since 1912.

Franklin Canyon's uniqueness stems from its two reservoirs (one of which
is open to the public today), which can easily double for lakes, ponds, or rivers
surrounded by pine trees. In fact, in a November 1976 survey reported in *The
Los Angeles Times*, Franklin won hands down as L.A.'s top exterior filming location and ranked fifth of all sites.

Hollywood started shooting movies on the property as early as the early
1930s. In 1931, Franklin Canyon appeared in the film version of Noel Cow-
ard's play *Private Lives*, as the honeymoon spot for Norma Shearer and Regi-

Harry Medved

Upper Franklin Reservoir appeared each week on TV's
*The Andy Griffith Show.*

nald Denny. For Josef von Sternberg's *Blonde Venus*, this is a secret getaway for
Cary Grant and Marlene Dietrich.

Among the other films shot here:

*It Happened One Night*   Clark Gable slings Claudette Colbert over his
shoulder and carries her through a Franklin Canyon stream. (Locals would
like to take credit for the famous hitchhiking scene too, but Sunland-Tujunga
citizens claim it as their own.)

*The Manchurian Candidate*   In the opening of John Frankenheimer's 1962
thriller, Franklin plays the dark Korean countryside where Laurence Harvey,
Frank Sinatra, and fellow soldiers get ambushed by the enemy. In a later sequence, Franklin Canyon is the setting for a flashback in which snakebite victim Harvey gets special first-aid care from the senator's daughter, Leslie Parrish.

*Stephen King's Sleepwalkers*   In Mick Garris' 1992 film, this is where cat
creature Brian Krause attacks girlfriend Madchen Amick. The movie's Homeland Cemetery was built on upper Franklin Reservoir. Horror buffs will recognize cameos by Stephen King (as the caretaker), Clive Barker, and Tobe
Hooper in a later scene at Franklin Canyon. (Other horror-fantasy films shot
at Franklin include *Octaman*, *The Sword and the Sorcerer*, and the remakes of
*The Blob* and *When a Stranger Calls*.)

*Big Momma's House*   Martin Lawrence joins Nia Long and son on a fishing trip in the Georgia woods, actually Franklin Canyon. Producer Rodney Liber remembers the studio-close lake was "secluded enough for production purposes and yet lush enough to double for a Southern pond."

In addition to serving as a location for TV shows like *Combat* (which used Franklin's culverts for its entire five-season run) and *The Beverly Hillbillies* (their Ozarks shanty seen in the opening credits), the park has been a haven for still photographers and commercial directors. 1960s album covers like Simon and Garfunkel's *Sounds of Silence* and the Rolling Stones' *Big Hits* (*High Tide and Green Grass*) were shot in the area.

## WHERE TO EXPLORE

### UPPER FRANKLIN RESERVOIR

Starting from the parking area, you can easily walk around the entire canyon lake, going from a reeds-and-cattails ecosystem to a forest of pines, cedars, and occasional redwoods. The trail partially follows the road and at times dips down into the lake embankment.

### SOOKY GOLDMAN NATURE CENTER

This informative visitors center was named after the Beverly Hills woman who helped save the park from development. In addition to exhibits on natural history and the environment, the center offers a movie map of the canyon and hosts monthly film location tours. *2600 Franklin Canyon Drive; 310-858-3834 ext. 131.*

## WHERE TO SOAK UP HOLLYWOOD HISTORY

### THE BEVERLY HILLS HOTEL

Not to be confused with the Beverly *Wilshire* Hotel (where Richard Gere and Julia Roberts stay in *Pretty Woman*), the 1912 Beverly Hills Hotel has extensive grounds for exploring and lovely gardens adjacent the bungalows. Renovated in 1949 by architect Paul Williams (a popular designer of stars' homes), the hotel over the years has become known as "the Pink Palace" for its color motif. The famed **Polo Lounge** is a favorite deal-making spot for the industry, home of the original "power breakfast," and a fabled watering hole for "the Rat Pack."

Future stars who got an early taste of the industry at the Beverly Hills Hotel include Aaron Eckhart and Bill Paxton (both worked as valet parkers, according to the *Los Angeles Times*). Future producer Robert Evans was discovered at the pool by actress Norma Shearer, who chose him to play her late husband, Irving Thalberg, in *Man of a Thousand Faces*.

On film, a hotel bungalow is where *The Bad and the Beautiful*'s Kirk Douglas (as a megalomaniacal producer) puts up novelist Dick Powell and his Southern belle wife Gloria Grahame (in an Oscar-winning performance). The hotel is also the Hollywood rendezvous for Maggie Smith and Michael Caine in Neil Simon's *California Suite* and the hangout for star Will Ferrell and his agent Jason Schartzman in *Bewitched*. *www.beverlyhillshotel.com; 9641 Sunset Blvd.; 310-276-2251.*

## DETOUR: GREYSTONE PARK

Built in 1927 on 425 acres, the Greystone Mansion was a 55-room estate built by oil tycoon Edward Doheny as a wedding present for his son Edward L. "Ned" Doheny Jr. According to biographer Margaret Leslie Davis, Doheny Jr. didn't have the chance to enjoy his dad's gift for long: he was murdered here in 1929 by longtime friend and personal assistant Hugh Plunkett. (Both Doheny Jr. and Plunkett had been implicated in the notorious "Teapot Dome" government corruption scandals of the 1920s.)

The mansion's dark past and sculpted gardens make it an appropriate location for the "Whispering Glades" cemetery in director Tony Richardson's grimly comic 1965 adaptation of Evelyn Waugh's novel *The Loved One*.

In the 1970s, Greystone became the headquarters for the burgeoning American Film Institute (AFI). Future director David Lynch lived on the premises and even shot much of *Eraserhead*, his first feature, near the Greystone Stables. The stables are also on view in *All of Me* with Steve Martin.

When the AFI departed in the eighties, the property became a city park and garden complex open to the public. The mansion has appeared as the baronial estate of several film and TV characters, including *The Big Lebowski*, *The Witches of Eastwick*, and Barnabas Collins, the resident vampire of the 1990s revival of TV's *Dark Shadows*.

These days Greystone is a popular site for lavish weddings. Its gardens are open during daylight hours, but the mansion is accessible by appointment only or during special civic events. *905 Loma Vista Drive; 310-550-4654.*

## HOW TO GET TO FRANKLIN CANYON

*At the eastern end of the Beverly Hills Hotel, take Beverly Dr. north and veer left at the TO COLDWATER sign. Veer left again when you reach the fire station. Follow Beverly (Coldwater Canyon Park will be on your right) for roughly a mile. Make a right on Franklin Canyon Dr. and follow this narrow and steep road up and over the hills to the park entrance.*

Marc Wanamaker/Bison Archives

Masters of horror Stephen King, Tobe Hooper, and director Mick Garris at Franklin Canyon for *Sleepwalkers*.

## DVD ITINERARY: FRANKLIN CANYON

*The Manchurian Candidate* (1962), Scenes 2 and 21

*It Happened One Night*, Scene 16

*Big Momma's House*, Scene 12

# 61

# HOLLYWOOD RESERVOIR
## Lake of Dreams

> [The lake] will make some forget, for a moment, that they live in a gargantuan city . . . it is also a good place to scope the athletic prowess of stars and models.
>
> —*Christine Pelisek,* LA Weekly

**MAJOR ROLES:** *Kid Galahad (1962), Earthquake*

### BEHIND THE SCENERY

A common misconception about the Hollywood Reservoir (also known as Lake Hollywood) is that *Chinatown* was shot here. It wasn't—the filming site was actually Stone Canyon Reservoir. But a central character in that film was based on the reservoir's chief engineer, L.A. water baron William Mulholland, who completed the dam in 1924.

Ever since a pathway around the Hollywood Reservoir was opened to the public in the 1970s, it's become popular as a social and recreational destination. Though the fenced-off lakeshore is inaccessible to visitors, the reservoir remains one of the few sites in L.A. where at any given moment you can hear birds chirping, frogs croaking, pinecones falling, and actors rehearsing their lines.

In *Kid Galahad*, Elvis Presley and Joan Blackman attend a Fourth of July country picnic here while Elvis regales the crowd singing "I Got Lucky." Trivia note: this wholesome musical number (despite its title) was penned by actress-songwriter Dolores Fuller, beloved by bad-film buffs for her role as Ed Wood's fiancée in *Glen or Glenda*.

Brian Rooney

A popular three-mile walk takes you around the reservoir.

In the quintessential L.A. disaster picture *Earthquake*, several ominous scenes take place at the reservoir as its structure is compromised by the killer quake's tremors and aftershocks. And in director Richard Tuggle's 1986 L.A. thriller *Out of Bounds*, the reservoir's dam crossing is a quiet rendezvous for farm boy Anthony Michael Hall and tough girl Jenny Wright as they discuss their plans to elude the police.

## THE MULHOLLAND DAM WALK

A 3.2-mile paved loop trail will take you to the reservoir's Mulholland Dam and back. When you reach the dam crossing, you'll have views of the Hollywood sign and Castillo del Lago, a colorful castle that was once home to gangster Bugsy Siegel and pop icon Madonna. According to *The New York Times'* David Handelman, Madonna often jogged this route with her bodyguard in the 1990s.

## HOW TO GET TO THE HOLLYWOOD RESERVOIR

*From the Barham Blvd. exit off the Hollywood Freeway (101), head east on Barham to Lake Hollywood Drive, and make a right. Follow the road for 0.7 miles to the lake and park on the side of the road. The walking path will be on your right. Gates close at dusk.*

## DVD ITINERARY: HOLLYWOOD RESERVOIR

*Earthquake*, Scenes 1–2, 4, 10, and 17

# 62

# THE LOS ANGELES RIVER
# Water Under the Bridge

The L.A. River? It's dry as a bone!

—*Jack Nicholson in* Chinatown *(1974)*

**MAJOR ROLES:** *Them!, Grease, Point Blank, To Live and Die in L.A.*

### BEHIND THE SCENERY

Taking advantage of this 51-mile-long river as a freshwater source, the city of Los Angeles was built near this waterway in the late 1700s. Today, much of the L.A. River is encased in concrete as a result of flood control projects over the decades. In some places it looks more like an urban stream and in others it's dry as a bone. Nevertheless, California State Parks and the County of Los Angeles

The urban L.A. River has surprising pockets of nature.

Harry Medved

are leading a multiagency "regreening" of the L.A. River, with the aim of transforming it into a scenic river parkway of walking trails, bike paths, and natural habitats.

## WHERE TO WALK: THE ATWATER RIVER WALK

The L.A. River has a number of natural areas, but this segment that abuts Griffith Park is one of the best pathways for dog walking, bicycling, or urban strolling.

Park on the south side of Los Feliz Blvd. near Glenfeliz Blvd. Follow the grassy area toward the river. If the Atwater Riverwalk gate is locked, look for an entry along the fence to your left, approximately a hundred yards from the gate. Head south along the riverwalk and follow it to the Sunnynook Footbridge for a great midstream view of the river. Return the way you came, keeping an eye out for the many bird species that gather here.

Cyclists can ride the L.A. River Bikeway for five miles from Victory Blvd. to Fletcher Drive.

## WHERE TO EAT

### EATZ CAFE
A former World War II–era Quonset hut, Eatz offers traditional diner food (including its famous milk shakes) with outdoor dining views of the Los Feliz Municipal Golf Course. This compact course is where Ron Livingston and Jon Favreau hit the links in *Swingers*. *Cash only. 3207 Los Feliz Boulevard, next to the Los Feliz Municipal Golf Course; 323-661-2355.*

## THE FOURTH AND SIXTH STREET BRIDGES: SPANNING DECADES

Adjacent to the Boyle Heights railyards near downtown, the L.A. River's Fourth and Sixth Street Bridges have been much-used locations for decades. The drainage tunnel directly under the Sixth Street span make the Sixth Street overpass a visually striking locale for urban tension and excitement.

In the classic 1954 sci-fi thriller *Them!*, James Whitmore and James Arness discover the nest of giant ants in the L.A. River's vast network of storm drains beneath the bridge. In John Boorman's *Point Blank*, sniper James B. Sikking silences businessman Lloyd Bochner from the Fourth Street Bridge as Lee Marvin watches from the tunnel below. The unforgettable chase in *To Live and Die in L.A.* begins below the bridge area and continues through the riverbed as undercover treasury agents William Petersen and John Pankow desperately try to outmaneuver the armed federal agents pursuing them. An Apache helicopter hunts Nicolas Cage as he speeds along the riverbed in *Gone in 60 Seconds*. Cops

Harry Medved

The Sixth Street
Bridge's environs
have been a choice
location for
sequences with John
Travolta, Samuel L.
Jackson, Colin
Farrell, and giant
radioactive ants.

Colin Farrell and Samuel L. Jackson converge on a Lear jet that lands on the bridge in the big-screen action hit *S.W.A.T.* And in *The Core*, Hilary Swank and Bruce Greenwood land a space shuttle below the bridges.

The river environs are also the scene of drag racing sequences in the American International Pictures comedy-chiller *Ghost of Dragstrip Hollow*, Alex Cox's *Repo Man*, and *Grease*, with John Travolta and Olivia Newton-John.

## FUTURE SHOCK: SCI-FI IN THE SEPULVEDA BASIN

The section of the L.A. River that cuts through the Sepulveda Basin Wildlife Reserve is where the river exists in a surprisingly natural state. Here in the San Fernando Valley you can find the memorable locations of two modern sci-fi action favorites.

Upstream from the basin, the tributary stream Bull Creek becomes a narrow concrete box. This is where the menacing cyborg Robert Patrick relentlessly pursues Edward Furlong and Arnold Schwarzenegger in *Terminator 2: Judgment Day*'s memorable motorcycle/truck chase sequence.

John Carpenter's *Escape from New York* showcases the Sepulveda Dam as headquarters for the United States Police Force, where Kurt Russell is given orders for his deadly mission. Production designer Joe Alves chose the 1940s dam (clearly visible from both 405 and 101 freeways) for its "fascistic look."

## FROM EAST COAST RANTS TO WEST COAST ANTS

Instead of nesting and wreaking havoc in the Los Angeles River region, the giant ants of the classic horror film *Them!* at one time were supposed to swarm the Big Apple. But, according to the Warner Bros. research department, the plans were scuttled when New York City's transportation secretary William J. Daley reacted in "horror at our plan to have these creatures invade the New York subway system."

According to a Warner Bros. interoffice communication, the New York subway system also proved "uneconomical." Also, a look at the chase scenes in the Alfred Werker/Anthony Mann L.A. noir *He Walked By Night* convinced a Warner Bros. exec that the "storm drain tunnel system beneath the streets of Los Angeles is a very filmic neighborhood."

Warner Bros. head of research Carl Milliken Jr. alerted Daley about the change in plans for the oversized insects. "You will be relieved to know," reassured Milliken in a July 13, 1954 letter, "that the picture shows them as invading our own water draining system here in Los Angeles . . . We have left New York in peace and relative quiet."

Although future filmmakers would go there (Guillermo Del Toro's killer cockroach movie *Mimic,* for example), the Brooklyn-based Daley showed Hollywood that you don't mess with the New York City rail system.

Unless, of course, you're King Kong.

Recalls *Grease* director Randal Kleiser, "The L.A. River was the only space big enough to re-create the drag race from *Ben Hur*, with hot rods instead of chariots. And I really liked the idea of shooting on the L.A. River because it had a lot of scope for the big screen. I loved the wide open space, as well as the bleached, urban look."

Other L.A. River or bridge appearances include Larry Cohen's *It's Alive*, *The Italian Job* (2003), *Freaky Friday* (1977), *The Naked Gun*, *My Family/Mi Familia*, *Born in East L.A.*, *Blood In, Blood Out*, *The Thirteenth Floor*, *Joe Dirt*, *Terminator 3: Rise of the Machines*, *Torque*, *Cradle 2 the Grave*, *L.A. Story*, *The Mask*, and *Jackass: The Movie*.

## HOW TO GET TO THE L.A. RIVER'S
## ATWATER RIVERWALK

*Take I-5 to Los Feliz Blvd. and head east. Park near the intersection of Los Feliz and Glenfeliz Blvds.*

## DVD ITINERARY: THE LOS ANGELES RIVER

*Grease*, Scene 15

*Them!*, Scene 24

*To Live and Die in L.A.*, Scene 23

# The Best of Southern California's Cinematic Outdoors

## 25 CLASSIC SONGS FOR THE HIGHWAY

1. "Born to Be Wild," Steppenwolf
2. "Low Rider," War
3. "Truckin'," Grateful Dead
4. "On the Road Again," Willie Nelson
5. "Magic Carpet Ride," Steppenwolf
6. "Ramblin' Man," Allman Brothers Band
7. "Radar Love," Golden Earring
8. "I've Been Everywhere," Johnny Cash
9. "Phantom 309," Red Sovine
10. "Six Days on the Road," Dave Dudley
11. "The Letter," The Box Tops
12. "Hitching a Ride," Vanity Fair
13. "Sweet Hitchhiker," Creedence Clearwater Revival
14. "2-4-6-8 Motorway," Tom Robinson Band
15. "Born to Run," Bruce Springsteen
16. "Surfin' USA," The Beach Boys
17. "Road to Nowhere," Talking Heads
18. "Route 66," Bobby Troup/Nat "King" Cole
19. "Highway to Hell," AC/DC
20. "Wheels," Gram Parsons
21. "Roadhouse Blues," The Doors
22. "Two of Us," The Beatles
23. "Rubberneckin'," Elvis Presley

24. "Running on Empty," Jackson Browne
25. "Hit the Road, Jack," Ray Charles

—List provided by Jack Barth, author of *Roadside Hollywood*

## BEST MOVIE CAVES

1. Mitchell Caverns, East Mojave: *The Doors*
2. Bronson Canyon, Griffith Park: *Batman* (1966)
3. Leo Carrillo Cave, Malibu: *The Craft*
4. Blue Cavern Point, Catalina Island: *Jupiter's Darling*

## BEST MOVIE WATERFALLS

1. Twin Falls, Mammoth Lakes: *Rose Marie* (1954)
2. Bridalveil Fall, Yosemite: *Forever, Darling*
3. Yosemite Falls, Yosemite: *The Long, Long Trailer*
4. Tahquitz Falls, Palm Springs: *Lost Horizon*

## FIVE GREAT SAND DUNES

1. Stovepipe Wells, Death Valley: *Star Wars Episode IV: A New Hope*
2. Guadalupe Dunes, Central California Coast: *Hidalgo*
3. Buttercup Valley, Imperial Sand Dunes: *Jarhead*
4. Dumont Dunes, south of Death Valley: *Hulk*
5. The Great Sand Dune, the Malibu Coast: *Spartacus*

## BEST KID-FRIENDLY OUTINGS

1. Vasquez Rocks: *The Flintstones*
2. Paramount Ranch: *The Love Bug*
3. Leo Carrillo State Beach: *The Pacifier*
4. Paradise Cove: *The SpongeBob SquarePants* Movie
5. L.A. Live Steamers: *Beethoven's 3rd*

## BEST MOVIE LOCATIONS FOR ROMANCE

1. Mountclef Ridge, Wildwood Park: *Wuthering Heights*
2. Portuguese Point, Palos Verdes: *The Ghost and Mrs. Muir*
3. Leo Carrillo State Beach: *50 First Dates*

4. Las Brisas, Laguna Beach: *Now, Voyager*
5. Palisades Park, Santa Monica: *The Truth About Cats & Dogs*

## FIVE GREAT PLACES FOR WHEELCHAIRS AND STROLLERS

1. Palisades Park, Santa Monica
2. Heisler Park, Laguna Beach
3. The Arboretum, Arcadia
4. The Huntington, San Marino
5. Hollywood Reservoir

## FIVE GREAT MOVIE RESORTS

1. Hotel del Coronado: *Some Like It Hot*
2. Ojai Valley Inn: *Pat and Mike*
3. Furnace Creek Inn: *Winter Kills*
4. Two Bunch Palms: *The Player*
5. The Ahwahnee: *The Caine Mutiny*

## MOVIE GHOST TOWNS

1. Bodie: *Hell's Heroes*
2. Ballarat: *Easy Rider*
3. Keeler: *Saboteur*
4. Randsburg: *Faster, Pussycat! Kill! Kill!*

## TEN MEMORABLE L.A. FILM NOIRS

1. *L.A. Confidential*
2. *Chinatown*
3. *Double Indemnity*
4. *Kiss Me Deadly*
5. *He Walked by Night*
6. *Heat* (1995)
7. *The Long Goodbye*
8. *The Killer Is Loose*
9. *Criss Cross*
10. *Pitfall*

## FIVE MOVIES SHOT AT L.A.'S 1893 BRADBURY BUILDING

1. *Blade Runner*
2. *D.O.A. (1950)*
3. *The Indestructible Man*
4. *Wolf*
5. *Marlowe*

## FIVE MOVIES ABOUT APOCALYPTIC L.A.

1. *Miracle Mile*
2. *Panic in Year Zero!*
3. *The War of the Worlds (1953)*
4. *Escape from L.A.*
5. *The Omega Man*

## TEN UNIQUE LOOKS AT L.A. LIFE

1. *The Loved One*
2. *Model Shop*
3. *Boogie Nights*
4. *Short Cuts*
5. *Mulholland Dr.*
6. *The Exiles*
7. *Better Luck Tomorrow*
8. *To Sleep with Anger*
9. *El Norte*
10. *Crash*

## TEN MOVIES ABOUT HOLLYWOOD PLAYERS

1. *The Bad and the Beautiful*
2. *Sunset Boulevard*
3. *Singin' in the Rain*
4. *The Player*
5. *Ed Wood*
6. *The Big Picture*
7. *Sullivan's Travels*
8. *The Star*
9. *Bowfinger*
10. *Get Shorty*

## TWENTY CLASSIC L.A. THEATERS ON FILM:

1. Mann's Chinese Theater: *Blazing Saddles*
2. Mayfair Music Hall: *Young Frankenstein*
3. The Wilshire: *Silent Movie*
4. Aero: *Donnie Darko*
5. Village Theater: *Tales from the Crypt Presents Demon Knight*
6. Warner Grand: *Pearl Harbor*
7. The Pantages: *Ed Wood*
8. The Mayan: *Rock 'n' Roll High School*
9. Nuart Theater: *Foul Play*
10. The Rialto: *The Player*
11. El Rey: *Night of the Comet*
12. The Wiltern: *Escape from New York*
13. The Los Angeles Theater: *Escape from L.A.*
14. The Orpheum: *That Thing You Do!*
15. Fox Venice: *Messiah of Evil*
16. Vista: *True Romance*
17. The Tower: *Mulholland Dr.*
18. The Raymond: *This Is Spinal Tap*
19. Criterion: *Pee-wee's Big Adventure*
20. Million Dollar: *Blade Runner*

For more info on L.A.'s Classic buildings, visit *www.laconservancy.org*.

## WHERE ELVIS SWIVELED ON SCREEN IN SOUTHERN CALIFORNIA

1. Idyllwild: *Kid Galahad*
2. Big Bear's Cedar Lake: *Kissin' Cousins*
3. Hollywood Reservoir: *Kid Galahad*
4. Malibu Creek State Park: *Love Me Tender*
5. Wildwood Park: *Flaming Star*
6. Potrero Road: *Roustabout*
7. Mulholland Drive: *Spinout*
8. UCLA: *Wild in the Country*
9. San Pedro: *Easy Come, Easy Go*
10. Leo Carrillo State Beach: *Live a Little, Love a Little*

## CALIFORNIA'S FOREIGN LEGION OF DESERT-MAD DIRECTORS

1. Austria's Erich von Stroheim: *Greed*
2. Italy's Michelangelo Antonioni: *Zabriskie Point*
3. Germany's Percy Adlon: *Bagdad Café*
4. Japan's Takeshi Kitano: *Brother*
5. France's Serge Bourguignon: *The Reward*
6. Russia's Andrei Konchalovsky: *Homer and Eddie*
7. Uruguay's Leonardo Ricagni: *29 Palms* (2002)
8. France's Bruno Dumont: *Twentynine Palms* (2003)

## IT'S A MAD, MAD, MAD, MAD STATE

Fifteen California communities in Stanley Kramer's 1963 comedy *It's a Mad, Mad, Mad, Mad World* receive a humorous apology in the opening titles for their on-screen abuse:

1. Agoura
2. Kernville
3. Long Beach
4. Malibu
5. Oxnard
6. Palm Desert
7. Palm Springs
8. Palos Verdes Estates
9. San Pedro
10. Santa Ana
11. Santa Barbara
12. Santa Monica
13. Twentynine Palms
14. Universal City
15. Yucca Valley

## THE *TRUE ROMANCE* "YOU'RE SO COOL" HONEYMOON TOUR

1. Vista Theater, Hollywood
2. Rae's Restaurant, Santa Monica
3. The Safari Inn, Burbank
4. Six Flags Magic Mountain, Valencia
5. El Matador State Beach, Malibu

## TEN GREAT *CHINATOWN* LOCATIONS

1. Echo Lake, Echo Park
2. Avalon, Catalina Island
3. Palos Verdes Riding Club, Palos Verdes
4. Walker's Café, San Pedro
5. City Hall, Downtown L.A.
6. Archer School for Girls, Brentwood
7. Chinatown, Downtown L.A.
8. Santa Rosa Valley orange groves, Camarillo
9. Big Tujunga Wash, Sunland Tujunga
10. Stone Canyon Reservoir, Bel Air

## THE KOREAN WAR IN THE SANTA MONICA MOUNTAINS

1. Griffith Park: *The Steel Helmet*
2. Topanga Canyon: *War Hunt*
3. Franklin Canyon: *The Manchurian Candidate* (1962)
4. Malibu Creek State Park: *M\*A\*S\*H*

# Cautionary Tail-Lights: Southern California Road Thrillers

The American road picture winds its way through most every genre: comedies, dramas, romances, musicals, and Westerns take unfolded on our country's highways, byways, and big trails.

But there's a dangerous side to movie motoring in the United States. Crime stories (*Badlands*), horror tales (*The Texas Chain Saw Massacre*), and science fiction thrillers (*Damnation Alley*) often show us a nation whose blind curves and wrong turns lead to dark alleys and dead ends, places best visited only on the silver screen.

At the risk of encouraging readers to stay home and curl up with a good book (or DVD), here's a selection of memorable white-line nightmares set in or partially filmed around Southern California:

### Identity (2003)
During a brutal downpour, a cross section of humanity (including ex-cop John Cusack, actress Rebecca DeMornay, and call girl Amanda Peet) converges at a seedy desert motel. One unsettling coincidence is that they all share the same birthday. Another is that they're all potential victims of a never-seen killer. This haunting whodunit will keep you guessing until the very end of the road.

### Panic in Year Zero! (1962)
Actor/director Ray Milland plays a desperate father who'll do anything to keep his family alive after an atomic bomb obliterates L.A. Alas, sharing the roads with this truly *post*nuclear family are murderers, deviants, and thieves. An effectively grim yet ultimately hopeful apocalyptic adventure.

### Joy Ride (2001)

Leelee Sobieski, Paul Walker, and Steve Zahn come down with a deadly case of the CB-jeebees when they play a humiliating prank on an unidentifiable highway traveler (voiced by *The Silence of the Lambs'* Ted Levine). Definitely no good buddy, this mobile bad guy retaliates by methodically steering a truly devious course of vengeance.

### The Devil Thumbs a Ride (1947)

In an unforgettable role some forty-five years before *Reservoir Dogs*, Lawrence Tierney plays an armed and very dangerous robber who makes life hell for affable traveling salesman Ted North. Their night of dark deeds and murder begins in San Diego; Tierney comes to a no-good end near Newport Beach. A notorious favorite among noir fans.

### Breakdown (1997)

When their SUV dies on a lonely desert road, husband Kurt Russell lets wife Kathleen Quinlan catch a ride to a nearby diner with good Samaritan trucker J.T. Walsh. Bad move. So begins a terrifying tale of missing persons, mounting paranoia, and nail-biting highway havoc.

### Hot Rods to Hell (1967)

Father figure Dana Andrews puts his family's life on the double yellow line when he stands up to a gang of road-hogging juvenile delinquents who rev roughshod over anyone in their way. Until now, that is. John Milius' Showtime movie *Motorcycle Gang* (with Jake Busey and Carla Gugino) and *The Road Killers* (starring Christopher Lambert) travel similarly rough terrain.

### Duel (1971)

Dennis Weaver stars as the average Joe commuter who can't fathom why he's being stalked by an unstoppable semi with an extreme case of road rage. The unseen trucker's motivation? Unnervingly—and brilliantly—writer Richard Matheson and young director Steven Spielberg never explain.

### The Sadist (1963)

Arch Hall Jr. will sear his way into your nightmares with his portrayal of a cold-blooded delinquent who, with his equally demented sex-kitten girlfriend, torments a trio of schoolteachers stranded at an abandoned gas station. Photographed for maximum impact by Vilmos Zsigmond. *Watch out for those rattlesnakes!*

### The Hills Have Eyes (1977)

A prototypical American family becomes stranded in a harsh desert landscape and Mom, Dad, and the kids find themselves facing off with their mutant, cannibalistic counterparts. In the DVD documentary *Looking Back on The Hills Have Eyes*, director Wes Craven says movies like this are "about getting off the main road, off the beaten track and in essence leaving civilization." Once you've survived these hills, you'll agree.

### Kalifornia (1993)

Researching the nation's most infamous murderers, writer David Duchovny and photographer Michelle Forbes unwisely share the interstate drive with simmering killer Brad Pitt and clueless girlfriend Juliette Lewis. It's only a matter of miles before Duchovny and Forbes realize they've gotten *way* too close to their work. . . .

### Detour (1945)

En route to L.A. to meet his fiancée, down-on-his-luck Tom Neal thumbs a ride from a kindly stranger who suddenly and inexplicably dies. Neal makes his first mistake by continuing the trip in the dead man's car. His second? Picking up ferocious femme fatale Ann Savage. Director Edgar G. Ulmer's fatalistic cult classic begins grimly and spirals inexorably downward.

### The Hitch-Hiker (1953)

Actress/director Ida Lupino helmed this tense tale of vacationing friends (Frank Lovejoy and Edmond O'Brien) whose south-of-the-border fishing trip hits a snag when they're taken hostage by the creepy title villain (William Talman) . . . who sleeps *with one eye open!*

### The Hitcher (1986)

Even though his mother has told him "never to do this," nice guy driver C. Thomas Howell offers a ride to clearly demented Rutger Hauer. Enough said. (*See Hitcher Desert Tour* on page 146.)

### Hitch-Hike (1977)

There's something terribly shocking about this highway odyssey of greed, betrayal, and murder. No, it's not the depravity that married couple Franco Nero and Corinne Clery and deranged passenger David Hess inflict on each other. The kicker is this: although set along on the roads between Las Vegas, Barstow, and L.A., director Pasquale Festa Campanile's suspenser was lensed entirely in the mountains of the Gran Sasso, near the city of L'Aquila . . . *in Italy!* Indeed, there's no geography like cinematic geography.

# Index

# About the Authors

Native Southern Californian **Harry Medved** is a top PR chief who has directed public relations for the Screen Actors Guild, Yahoo! Movies, Warner Bros. Online, and Fandango. He previously co-authored four movie books, including *The Fifty Worst Films of All Time* and *The Golden Turkey Awards*.

Los Angeles native **Bruce Akiyama** has worked in motion picture advertising and has written for the TV series *Curious George*, *Maya & Miguel*, and *Arthur*, the latter for which he received a Daytime Emmy and a Peabody Award.